D0721899

Selected Plays of
Edward Albee

Selected Plays of

Edward Albee

○ ○ ○ ○ ○ ○ ○ ○ ○

Introduction by

Edward Albee

Nelson Doubleday, Inc.
Garden City, New York

Contents

Contents

Introduction

Many playwrights—I among them—enjoy seeing our work in print as much as we do on stage. Despite the energy and presence of a stage production, the only perfect performance is that on the page with the play neither altered nor disproved. Plays—good ones, at any rate—are literature, and the pervasive notion that a play comes to full life only on stage speaks either of an inability to realize a production through reading or a flawed play.

There is, as well, a kind of "proof of existence" that print gives. I remember being thirteen and in the presence of my first published poem —in a school literary magazine—and I remember studying the quality of the paper and the setting of the ink in it with both awe and sense of reality unaccompanying the typed page I had submitted to the magazine.

So, there is an illusion, at least, of permanence to print, and while, given a preference, I would prefer an endlessly running perfect production of a play of mine over publication, plays *do* close—vanish, often; forever, one feels—and books do not. They may go out of print, but that is not quite the same thing.

I was delighted, then, with the prospect of this volume—a collection of eight of my twenty four plays, printed in order of composition, and—oh, wonder!—chosen by the author—*me!* (How too often one sees plays of one's own selected for anthology by doubtless well-meaning others for no reason beyond the fame of the work. Fame equals excellence? I take it to be so, if we are to judge innumerable tedious collections.)

So here was a chance of having some of my forgotten, ignored or dismissed plays sit in print beside their better known fellows, perhaps letting each shed new light on the other.

Naturally, some of the plays published here are very well known—I doubt the volume would have gotten off the ground were I not the author of some well known plays—but there is not a play here which I am not very proud of and which I do not consider to be a very good play. (Oh, really? Who the hell does he think he is? Well, he considers himself to be a rather intelligent, gifted creative artist with a comprehensive knowledge of dramatic literature and the sad awareness that excellence has shockingly little to do with either critical reception or public acceptance. *That's* who he thinks he is.)

I am aware of a danger, though, in being encouraged to tinker with the contents of this volume: it is simply that authors behave like most parents, are proud of all their children, are grateful that a number of them are out earning their own living—may even support their parent in his old age, yet maintain a special, possibly perverse affection for the diffident, the misunderstood and the complex.

Have I, then, included plays here which I admire *because* they are unpopular, misunderstood, too complex for easy assimilation? I don't think so, but I can never be sure.

I have excluded from this collection any of the four adaptations I accomplished between 1963 and 1983, in spite of my affection for them, simply because they *are* adaptations—my work on others' work. What we are supposed to have here is pure Albee (or impure, if you like) and while the adaptations tell the interested a lot about my craft they do not really belong.

Of the four, the one I am most distressed about is my putting to the stage of Nabokov's LOLITA. The other three—the adaptation of Carson McCullers' THE BALLAD OF THE SAD CAFE, of James Purdy's novel MALCOLM, and a translation from English to American (a translation of idiom, environment and psychology) of Giles Cooper's play EVERYTHING IN THE GARDEN—were quite on the mark. THE BALLAD OF THE SAD CAFE ran on Broadway for six months and pleased McCullers even before it opened to generally enthusiastic press; MALCOLM continues to please James Purdy in spite of its persistently hostile reception (in the U.S., that is) during its infrequent revivals. EVERYTHING IN THE GARDEN ran on Broadway for a comfortable stretch and, through the fortune of a film sale, returned a profit to its investors.

My adaptation of Nabokov's LOLITA, on the other hand, has never been seen in the U.S. The production of it which was briefly (happily!) presented on Broadway was such a corruption of Nabokov's and my intention that I become enraged whenever I think of it. A combination of disrespect for Nabokov's and my text, directorial vulgarity, salacious shortchanging of the production *by* the production, and a lax and insensitive turn by a leading performer whose aim, I could swear, was the undermining of the venture, resulted in a disgusting misrepresentation of a faithful adaptation of a book I cherish. The critics determined—by what method I lack even the foggiest notion—the fault to be solely mine. One day the play will be properly presented, and Nabokov (at least) will get his due.

Well, here are eight plays, beginning with THE ZOO STORY, the first play I wrote as an adult, which had to have its world premiere in Europe, to THE MAN WHO HAD THREE ARMS, my last but two, greatly admired by my fellow playwrights and greatly loathed by the tastemakers who were—oddly enough—its subject. If you enjoy reading them anywhere near as much as I have enjoyed writing them, then we will be even.

Edward Albee
Montauk, N.Y.
August, 1987

THE
ZOO STORY
A Play in One Scene (1958)

For William Flanagan

FIRST PERFORMANCE: September 28, 1959.
Berlin, Germany.

Schiller Theater Werkstatt.

FIRST AMERICAN PERFORMANCE: January 14, 1960.
New York City.

The Provincetown Playhouse.

The Players:

PETER: A man in his early forties, neither fat nor gaunt, neither handsome nor homely. He wears tweeds, smokes a pipe, carries horn-rimmed glasses. Although he is moving into middle age, his dress and his manner would suggest a man younger.

JERRY: A man in his late thirties, not poorly dressed, but carelessly. What was once a trim and lightly muscled body has begun to go to fat; and while he is no longer handsome, it is evident that he once was. His fall from physical grace should not suggest debauchery; he has, to come closest to it, a great weariness.

The Scene:

It is Central Park; a Sunday afternoon in summer; the present. There are two park benches, one toward either side of the stage; they both face the audience. Behind them: foliage, trees, sky. At the beginning, Peter is seated on one of the benches.

As the curtain rises, PETER *is seated on the bench stage-right. He is reading a book. He stops reading, cleans his glasses, goes back to reading.* JERRY *enters.*

JERRY. I've been to the zoo. (PETER *doesn't notice)* I said, I've been to the zoo. MISTER, I'VE BEEN TO THE ZOO!

PETER. Hm? . . . What? . . . I'm sorry, were you talking to me?

JERRY. I went to the zoo, and then I walked until I came here. Have I been walking north?

PETER *(Puzzled)*. North? Why . . . I . . . I think so. Let me see.

JERRY *(Pointing past the audience)*. Is that Fifth Avenue?

PETER. Why yes; yes, it is.

JERRY. And what is that cross street there; that one, to the right?

PETER. That? Oh, that's Seventy-fourth Street.

JERRY. And the zoo is around Sixty-fifth Street; so, I've been walking north.

PETER *(Anxious to get back to his reading)*. Yes; it would seem so.

JERRY. Good old north.

PETER *(Lightly, by reflex)*. Ha, ha.

JERRY *(After a slight pause)*. But not due north.

PETER. I . . . well, no, not due north; but, we . . . call it north. It's northerly.

JERRY *(Watches as* PETER, *anxious to dismiss him, prepares his pipe)*. Well, boy; *you're* not going to get lung cancer, are you?

PETER *(Looks up, a little annoyed, then smiles)*. No, sir. Not from this.

JERRY. No, sir. What you'll probably get is cancer of the mouth, and then you'll have to wear one of those things Freud wore after they took one whole side of his jaw away. What do they call those things?

PETER *(Uncomfortable)*. A prosthesis?

JERRY. The very thing! A prosthesis. You're an educated man, aren't you? Are you a doctor?

5

PETER. Oh, no; no. I read about it somewhere; *Time* magazine, I think. *(He turns to his book)*

JERRY. Well, *Time* magazine isn't for blockheads.

PETER. No, I suppose not.

JERRY *(After a pause)*. Boy, I'm glad that's Fifth Avenue there.

PETER *(Vaguely)*. Yes.

JERRY. I don't like the west side of the park much.

PETER. Oh? *(Then, slightly wary, but interested)* Why?

JERRY *(Offhand)*. I don't know.

PETER. Oh. *(He returns to his book)*

JERRY *(He stands for a few seconds, looking at PETER, who finally looks up again, puzzled)*. Do you mind if we talk?

PETER *(Obviously minding)*. Why . . . no, no.

JERRY. Yes you do; you do.

PETER *(Puts his book down, his pipe out and away, smiling)*. No, really; I don't mind.

JERRY. Yes you do.

PETER *(Finally decided)*. No; I don't mind at all, really.

JERRY. It's . . . it's a nice day.

PETER *(Stares unnecessarily at the sky)*. Yes. Yes, it is; lovely.

JERRY. I've been to the zoo.

PETER. Yes, I think you said so . . . didn't you?

JERRY. You'll read about it in the papers tomorrow, if you don't see it on your TV tonight. You have TV, haven't you?

PETER. Why yes, we have two; one for the children.

JERRY. You're married!

PETER *(With pleased emphasis)*. Why, certainly.

JERRY. It isn't a law, for God's sake.

PETER. No . . . no, of course not.

JERRY. And you have a wife.

PETER *(Bewildered by the seeming lack of communication)*. Yes!

JERRY. And you have children.

PETER. Yes; two.

JERRY. Boys?

PETER. No, girls . . . both girls.

JERRY. But you wanted boys.

PETER. Well . . . naturally, every man wants a son, but . . .

JERRY *(Lightly mocking)*. But that's the way the cookie crumbles?

6

PETER *(Annoyed)*. I wasn't going to say that.

JERRY. And you're not going to have any more kids, are you?

PETER *(A bit distantly)*. No. No more. *(Then back, and irksome)* Why did you say that? How would you know about that?

JERRY. The way you cross your legs, perhaps; something in the voice. Or maybe I'm just guessing. Is it your wife?

PETER *(Furious)*. That's none of your business! *(A silence)* Do you understand? (JERRY *nods*. PETER *is quiet now)* Well, you're right. We'll have no more children.

JERRY *(Softly)*. That *is* the way the cookie crumbles.

PETER *(Forgiving)*. Yes . . . I guess so.

JERRY. Well, now; what else?

PETER. What were you saying about the zoo . . . that I'd read about it, or see . . . ?

JERRY. I'll tell you about it, soon. Do you mind if I ask you questions?

PETER. Oh, not really.

JERRY. I'll tell you why I do it; I don't talk to many people—except to say like: give me a beer, or where's the john, or what time does the feature go on, or keep your hands to yourself, buddy. You know—things like that.

PETER. I must say I don't . . .

JERRY. But every once in a while I like to talk to somebody, really *talk;* like to get to know somebody, know all about him.

PETER *(Lightly laughing, still a little uncomfortable)*. And am I the guinea pig for today?

JERRY. On a sun-drenched Sunday afternoon like this? Who better than a nice married man with two daughters and . . . uh . . . a dog? (PETER *shakes his head)* No? Two dogs. (PETER *shakes his head again)* Hm. No dogs? (PETER *shakes his head, sadly)* Oh, that's a shame. But you look like an animal man. CATS? (PETER *nods his head, ruefully)* Cats! But, that can't be your idea. No, sir. Your wife and daughters? (PETER *nods his head)* Is there anything else I should know?

PETER *(He has to clear his throat)*. There are . . . there are two parakeets. One . . . uh . . . one for each of my daughters.

JERRY. Birds.

PETER. My daughters keep them in a cage in their bedroom.

JERRY. Do they carry disease? The birds.

PETER. I don't believe so.

7

JERRY. That's too bad. If they did you could set them loose in the house and the cats could eat them and die, maybe. (PETER *looks blank for a moment, then laughs*) And what else? What do you do to support your enormous household?

PETER. I . . . uh . . . I have an executive position with a . . . a small publishing house. We . . . uh . . . we publish textbooks.

JERRY. That sounds nice; very nice. What do you make?

PETER *(Still cheerful)*. Now look here!

JERRY. Oh, come on.

PETER. Well, I make around eighteen thousand a year, but I don't carry more than forty dollars at any one time . . . in case you're a . . . a holdup man . . . ha, ha, ha.

JERRY *(Ignoring the above)*. Where do you live? (PETER *is reluctant*) Oh, look; I'm not going to rob you, and I'm not going to kidnap your parakeets, your cats, or your daughters.

PETER *(Too loud)*. I live between Lexington and Third Avenue, on Seventy-fourth Street.

JERRY. That wasn't so hard, was it?

PETER. I didn't mean to seem . . . ah . . . it's that you don't really carry on a conversation; you just ask questions. And I'm . . . I'm normally . . . . uh . . . reticent. Why do you just stand there?

JERRY. I'll start walking around in a little while, and eventually I'll sit down. *(Recalling)* Wait until you see the expression on his face.

PETER. What? Whose face? Look here; is this something about the zoo?

JERRY *(Distantly)*. The what?

PETER. The zoo; the zoo. Something about the zoo.

JERRY. The zoo?

PETER. You've mentioned it several times.

JERRY *(Still distant, but returning abruptly)*. The zoo? Oh, yes; the zoo. I was there before I came here. I told you that. Say, what's the dividing line between upper-middle-middle-class and lower-upper-middle-class?

PETER. My dear fellow, I . . .

JERRY. Don't my dear fellow me.

PETER *(Unhappily)*. Was I patronizing? I believe I was; I'm sorry. But, you see, your question about the classes bewildered me.

JERRY. And when you're bewildered you become patronizing?

PETER. I . . . I don't express myself too well, sometimes. *(He attempts a joke on himself)* I'm in publishing, not writing.

JERRY *(Amused, but not at the humor).* So be it. The truth *is I* was being patronizing.

PETER. Oh, now; you needn't say that.

(It is at this point that Jerry may begin to move about the stage with slowly increasing determination and authority, but pacing himself, so that the long speech about the dog comes at the high point of the arc)

JERRY. All right. Who are your favorite writers? Baudelaire and J. P. Marquand?

PETER *(Wary).* Well, I like a great many writers; I have a considerable . . . catholicity of taste, if I may say so. Those two men are fine, each in his way. *(Warming up)* Baudelaire, of course . . . uh . . . is by far the finer of the two, but Marquand has a place . . . in our . . . uh . . . national . . .

JERRY. Skip it.

PETER. I . . . sorry.

JERRY. Do you know what I did before I went to the zoo today? I walked all the way up Fifth Avenue from Washington Square; all the way.

PETER. Oh; you live in the Village! *(This seems to enlighten* PETER*)*

JERRY. No, I don't. I took the subway down to the Village so I could walk all the way up Fifth Avenue to the zoo. It's one of those things a person has to do; sometimes a person has to go a very long distance out of his way to come back a short distance correctly.

PETER *(Almost pouting).* Oh, I thought you lived in the Village.

JERRY. What were you trying to do? Make sense out of things? Bring order? The old pigeonhole bit? Well, that's easy; I'll tell you. I live in a four-story brownstone roominghouse on the upper West Side between Columbus Avenue and Central Park West. I live on the top floor; rear; west. It's a laughably small room, and one of my walls is made of beaverboard; this beaverboard separates my room from another laughably small room, so I assume that the two rooms were once one room, a small room, but not necessarily laughable. The room beyond my beaverboard wall is occupied by a colored queen who always keeps his door open; well, not always, but *always* when he's plucking his eyebrows, which he does with Buddhist concentration. This colored queen has rotten teeth, which is rare, and he has a Japanese kimono, which is also pretty rare; and he wears this kimono to and from the john in the hall, which is pretty frequent. I mean, he goes to the john a lot. He never bothers me, and he never brings anyone up to his room. All he

9

does is pluck his eyebrows, wear his kimono and go to the john. Now, the two front rooms on my floor are a little larger, I guess; but they're pretty small, too. There's a Puerto Rican family in one of them, a husband, a wife, and some kids; I don't know how many. These people entertain a lot. And in the other front room, there's somebody living there, but I don't know who it is. I've never seen who it is. Never. Never ever.

PETER *(Embarrassed)*. Why . . . why do you live there?

JERRY *(From a distance again)*. I don't know.

PETER. It doesn't sound like a very nice place . . . where you live.

JERRY. Well, no; it isn't an apartment in the East Seventies. But, then again, I don't have one wife, two daughters, two cats and two parakeets. What I do have, I have toilet articles, a few clothes, a hot plate that I'm not supposed to have, a can opener, one that works with a key, you know; a knife, two forks, and two spoons, one small, one large; three plates, a cup, a saucer, a drinking glass, two picture frames, both empty, eight or nine books, a pack of pornographic playing cards, regular deck, an old Western Union typewriter that prints nothing but capital letters, and a small strongbox without a lock which has in it . . . what? Rocks! Some rocks . . . sea-rounded rocks I picked up on the beach when I was a kid. Under which . . . weighed down . . . are some letters . . . please letters . . . please why don't you do this, and please when will you do that letters. And when letters, too. When will you write? When will you come? When? These letters are from more recent years.

PETER *(Stares glumly at his shoes, then)*. About those two empty picture frames . . . ?

JERRY. I don't see why they need any explanation at all. Isn't it clear? I don't have pictures of anyone to put in them.

PETER. Your parents . . . perhaps . . . a girl friend . . .

JERRY. You're a very sweet man, and you're possessed of a truly enviable innocence. But good old Mom and good old Pop are dead . . . you know? . . . I'm broken up about it, too . . . I mean really. BUT. That particular vaudeville act is playing the cloud circuit now, so I don't see how I can look at them, all neat and framed. Besides, or, rather, to be pointed about it, good old Mom walked out on good old Pop when I was ten and a half years old; she embarked on an adulterous turn of our southern states . . . a journey of a year's duration . . . and her most constant companion . . . among others, among many others . . .

was a Mr. Barleycorn. At least, that's what good old Pop told me after he went down . . . came back . . . brought her body north. We'd received the news between Christmas and New Year's, you see, that good old Mom had parted with the ghost in some dump in Alabama. And, without the ghost . . . she was less welcome. I mean, what was she? A stiff . . . a northern stiff. At any rate, good old Pop celebrated the New Year for an even two weeks and then slapped into the front of a somewhat moving city omnibus, which sort of cleaned things out family-wise. Well no; then there was Mom's sister, who was given neither to sin nor the consolations of the bottle. I moved in on her, and my memory of her is slight excepting I remember still that she did all things dourly: sleeping, eating, working, praying. She dropped dead on the stairs to her apartment, my apartment then, too, on the afternoon of my high school graduation. A terribly middle-European joke, if you ask me.

PETER. Oh, my; oh, my.

JERRY. Oh, your what? But that was a long time ago, and I have no feeling about any of it that I care to admit to myself. Perhaps you can see, though, why good old Mom and good old Pop are frameless. What's your name? Your first name?

PETER. I'm Peter.

JERRY. I'd forgotten to ask you. I'm Jerry.

PETER *(With a slight, nervous laugh)*. Hello, Jerry.

JERRY *(Nods his hello)*. And let's see now; what's the point of having a girl's picture, especially in two frames? I have two picture frames, you remember. I never see the pretty little ladies more than once, and most of them wouldn't be caught in the same room with a camera. It's odd, and I wonder if it's sad.

PETER. The girls?

JERRY. No. I wonder if it's sad that I never see the little ladies more than once. I've never been able to have sex with, or, how is it put? . . . make love to anybody more than once. Once; that's it. . . . Oh, wait; for a week and a half, when I was fifteen . . . and I hang my head in shame that puberty was late . . . I was a h-o-m-o-s-e-x-u-a-l. I mean, I was queer . . . *(Very fast)* . . . queer, queer, queer . . . with bells ringing, banners snapping in the wind. And for those eleven days, I met at least twice a day with the park superintendent's son . . . a Greek boy, whose birthday was the same as mine, except he was a year older. I think I was very much in love . . . maybe just with sex. But that was the jazz of a very special hotel, wasn't it? And now; oh, do I love the little ladies; really, I love them. For about an hour.

PETER. Well, it seems perfectly simple to me. . . .

JERRY *(Angry)*. Look! Are you going to tell me to get married and have parakeets?

PETER *(Angry himself)*. Forget the parakeets! And stay single if you want to. It's no business of mine. I didn't start this conversation in the . . .

JERRY. All right, all right. I'm sorry. All right? You're not angry?

PETER *(Laughing)*. No, I'm not angry.

JERRY *(Relieved)*. Good. *(Now back to his previous tone)* Interesting that you asked me about the picture frames. I would have thought that you would have asked me about the pornographic playing cards.

PETER *(With a knowing smile)*. Oh, I've seen those cards.

JERRY. That's not the point. *(Laughs)* I suppose when you were a kid you and your pals passed them around, or you had a pack of your own.

PETER. Well, I guess a lot of us did.

JERRY. And you threw them away just before you got married.

PETER. Oh, now; look here. I didn't *need* anything like that when I got older.

JERRY. No?

PETER *(Embarrassed)*. I'd rather not talk about these things.

JERRY. So? Don't. Besides, I wasn't trying to plumb your post-adolescent sexual life and hard times; what I wanted to get at is the value difference between pornographic playing cards when you're a kid, and pornographic playing cards when you're older. It's that when you're a kid you use the cards as a substitute for a real experience, and when you're older you use real experience as a substitute for the fantasy. But I imagine you'd rather hear about what happened at the zoo.

PETER *(Enthusiastic)*. Oh, yes; the zoo. *(Then, awkward)* That is . . . if you. . . .

JERRY. Let me tell you about why I went . . . well, let me tell you some things. I've told you about the fourth floor of the roominghouse where I live. I think the rooms are better as you go down, floor by floor. I guess they are; I don't know. I don't know any of the people on the third and second floors. Oh, wait! I do know that there's a lady living on the third floor, in the front. I know because she cries all the time. Whenever I go out or come back in, whenever I pass her door, I always hear her crying, muffled, but . . . very determined. Very determined indeed. But the one I'm getting to, and all about the dog, is the landlady. I don't like to use words that are too harsh in describing people. I don't like to. But the landlady is a fat, ugly, mean, stupid, unwashed, misanthropic, cheap, drunken bag of garbage. And you may have noticed that I very seldom use profanity, so I can't describe her as well as I might.

PETER. You describe her . . . vividly.

JERRY. Well, thanks. Anyway, she has a dog, and I will tell you about the dog, and she and her dog are the gatekeepers of my dwelling. The woman is bad enough; she leans around in the entrance hall, spying to see that I don't bring in things or people, and when she's had her mid-afternoon pint of lemon-flavored gin she always stops me in the hall, and grabs ahold of my coat or my arm, and she presses her disgusting body up against me to keep me in a corner so she can talk to me. The smell of her body and her breath . . . you can't imagine it . . . and somewhere, somewhere in the back of that pea-sized brain of hers, an organ developed just enough to let her eat, drink, and emit, she has some foul parody of sexual desire. And I, Peter, I am the object of her sweaty lust.

PETER. That's disgusting. That's . . . horrible.

JERRY. But I have found a way to keep her off. When she talks to me, when she presses herself to my body and mumbles about her room and how I should come there, I merely say: but, Love; wasn't yesterday enough for you, and the day before? Then she puzzles, she makes slits of her tiny eyes, she sways a little, and then, Peter . . . and it is at this moment that I think I might be doing some good in that tormented house . . . a simple-minded smile begins to form on her unthinkable face, and she giggles and groans as she thinks about yesterday and the day before; as she believes and relives what never happened. Then, she motions to that black monster of a dog she has, and she goes back to her room. And I am safe until our next meeting.

PETER. It's so . . . unthinkable. I find it hard to believe that people such as that really *are*.

JERRY. *(Lightly mocking)*. It's for reading about, isn't it?

PETER *(Seriously)*. Yes.

JERRY. And fact is better left to fiction. You're right, Peter. Well, what I have been meaning to tell you about is the dog; I shall, now.

PETER *(Nervously)*. Oh, yes; the dog.

13

JERRY. Don't go. You're not thinking of going, are you?

PETER. Well . . . no, I don't think so.

JERRY *(As if to a child)*. Because after I tell you about the dog, do you know what then? Then . . . then I'll tell you about what happened at the zoo.

PETER *(Laughing faintly)*. You're . . . you're full of stories, aren't you?

JERRY. You don't *have* to listen. Nobody is holding you here; remember that. Keep that in your mind.

PETER *(Irritably)*. I know that.

JERRY. You do? Good.

(The following long speech, it seems to me, should be done with a great deal of action, to achieve a hypnotic effect on PETER, and on the audience, too. Some specific actions have been suggested, but the director and the actor playing JERRY might best work it out for themselves)

ALL RIGHT. *(As if reading from a huge billboard)* THE STORY OF JERRY AND THE DOG! *(Natural again)* What I am going to tell you has something to do with how sometimes it's necessary to go a long distance out of the way in order to come back a short distance correctly; or, maybe I only think that it has something to do with that. But, it's why I went to the zoo today, and why I walked north . . . northerly, rather . . . until I came here. All right. The dog, I think I told you, is a black monster of a beast: an oversized head, tiny, tiny ears, and eyes . . . bloodshot, infected, maybe; and a body you can see the ribs through the skin. The dog is black, all black; all black except for the bloodshot eyes, and . . . yes . . . and an open sore on its . . . *right* forepaw; that is red, too. And, oh yes; the poor monster, and I do believe it's an old dog . . . it's certainly a misused one . . . almost always has an erection . . . of sorts. That's red, too. And . . . what else? . . . oh, yes; there's a gray-yellow-white color, too, when he bares his fangs. Like this: Grrrrrrr! Which is what he did when he saw me for the first time . . . the day I moved in. I worried about that animal the very first minute I met him. Now, animals don't take to me like Saint Francis had birds hanging off him all the time. What I mean is: animals are indifferent to me . . . like people *(He smiles slightly)* . . . most of the time. But this dog wasn't indifferent. From the very beginning he'd snarl and then go for me, to get one of my legs. Not like he was rabid, you know; he was sort of a stumbly dog, but he wasn't half-assed,

either. It was a good, stumbly run; but I always got away. He got a piece
of my trouser leg, look, you can see right here, where it's mended; he
got that the second day I lived there; but, I kicked free and got upstairs
fast, so that was that. *(Puzzles)* I still don't know to this day how the
other roomers manage it, but you know what I *think:* I think it had to
do only with me. Cozy. So. Anyway, this went on for over a week,
whenever I came in; but never when I went out. That's funny. Or, it
was funny. I could pack up and live in the street for all the dog cared.
Well, I thought about it up in my room one day, one of the times after
I'd bolted upstairs, and I made up my mind. I decided: First, I'll kill the
dog with kindness, and if that doesn't work . . . I'll just kill him. (PE-
TER *winces)* Don't react, Peter; just listen. So, the next day I went out
and bought a bag of hamburgers, medium rare, no catsup, no onion;
and on the way home I threw away all the rolls and kept just the meat.
(Action for the following, perhaps)
When I got back to the roominghouse the dog was waiting for me. I
half opened the door that led into the entrance hall, and there he was;
waiting for me. It figured. I went in, very cautiously, and I had the
hamburgers, you remember; I opened the bag, and I set the meat down
about twelve feet from where the dog was snarling at me. Like so! He
snarled; stopped snarling; sniffed; moved slowly; then faster; then faster
toward the meat. Well, when he got to it he stopped, and he looked at
me. I smiled; but tentatively, you understand. He turned his face back
to the hamburgers, smelled, sniffed some more, and then . . . RRR-
AAAAGGGGGHHHH, like that . . . he tore into them. It was as if
he had never eaten anything in his life before, except like garbage.
Which might very well have been the truth. I don't think the landlady
ever eats anything but garbage. But. He ate all the hamburgers, almost
all at once, making sounds in his throat like a woman. *Then,* when he'd
finished the meat, the hamburger, and tried to eat the paper, too, he sat
down and smiled. I think he smiled; I know cats do. It was a very
gratifying few moments. Then, BAM, he snarled and made for me
again. He didn't get me this time, either. So, I got upstairs, and I lay
down on my bed and started to think about the dog again. To be
truthful, I was offended, and I was damn mad, too. It was six perfectly
good hamburgers with not enough pork in them to make it disgusting. I
was offended. But, after a while, I decided to try it for a few more days.
If you think about it, this dog had what amounted to an antipathy

toward me; really. And, I wondered if I mightn't overcome this antipathy. So, I tried it for five more days, but it was always the same: snarl; sniff; move; faster; stare; gobble; RAAGGGHHH; smile; snarl; BAM. Well, now; by this time Columbus Avenue was strewn with hamburger rolls and I was less offended than disgusted. So, I decided to kill the dog.

(PETER *raises a hand in protest*)

Oh, don't be so alarmed, Peter; I didn't succeed. The day I tried to kill the dog I bought only one hamburger and what I thought was a murderous portion of rat poison. When I bought the hamburger I asked the man not to bother with the roll, all I wanted was the meat. I expected some reaction from him, like: we don't sell no hamburgers without rolls; or, wha' d'ya wanna do, eat it out'a ya han's? But no; he smiled benignly, wrapped up the hamburger in waxed paper, and said: A bite for ya pussy-cat? I wanted to say: No, not really; it's part of a plan to poison a dog I know. But, you can't say "a dog I know" without sounding funny; so I said, a little too loud, I'm afraid, and too formally: YES, A BITE FOR MY PUSSY-CAT. People looked up. It always happens when I try to simplify things; people look up. But that's neither hither nor thither. So. On my way back to the roominghouse, I kneaded the hamburger and the rat poison together between my hands, at that point feeling as much sadness as disgust. I opened the door to the entrance hall, and there the monster was, waiting to take the offering and then jump me. Poor bastard; he never learned that the moment he took to smile before he went for me gave me time enough to get out of range. BUT, there he was; malevolence with an erection, waiting. I put the poison patty down, moved toward the stairs and watched. The poor animal gobbled the food down as usual, smiled, which made me almost sick, and then, BAM. But, I sprinted up the stairs, as usual, and the dog didn't get me, as usual. AND IT CAME TO PASS THAT THE BEAST WAS DEATHLY ILL. I knew this because he no longer attended me, and because the landlady sobered up. She stopped me in the hall the same evening of the attempted murder and confided the information that God had struck her puppy-dog a surely fatal blow. She had forgotten her bewildered lust, and her eyes were wide open for the first time. They looked like the dog's eyes. She sniveled and implored me to pray for the animal. I wanted to say to her: Madam, I have myself to pray for, the colored queen, the Puerto Rican family, the person in the front room whom I've never seen, the woman who cries deliberately behind her closed door, and the rest of the people in all roominghouses, everywhere; besides, Madam, I don't understand how to pray. But . . . to simplify things . . . I told her I would pray. She looked up. She said that I was a liar, and that I probably wanted the dog to die. I told her, and there was so much truth here, that I didn't want the dog to die. I didn't, and not just because I'd poisoned him. I'm afraid that I must tell you I wanted the dog to live so that I could see what our new relationship might come to.

(PETER *indicates his increasing displeasure and slowly growing antagonism*)

Please understand, Peter; that sort of thing is important. You must believe me; it *is* important. We have to know the effect of our actions. *(Another deep sigh)* Well, anyway; the dog recovered. I have no idea why, unless he was a descendant of the puppy that guarded the gates of hell or some such resort. I'm not up on my mythology. *(He pronounces the word myth-o-*logy) Are you?

(PETER *sets to thinking, but* JERRY *goes on*)

At any rate, and you've missed the eight-thousand-dollar question, Peter; at any rate, the dog recovered his health and the landlady recovered her thirst, in no way altered by the bow-wow's deliverance. When I came home from a movie that was playing on Forty-second Street, a movie I'd seen, or one that was very much like one or several I'd seen, after the landlady told me puppykins was better, I was so hoping for the dog to be waiting for me. I was . . . well, how would you put it . . . enticed? . . . fascinated? . . . no, I don't think so . . . heart-shatteringly anxious, that's it; I was heart-shatteringly anxious to confront my friend again.

(PETER *reacts scoffingly*)

Yes, Peter; friend. That's the only word for it. I was heart-shatteringly et cetera to confront my doggy friend again. I came in the door and advanced, unafraid, to the center of the entrance hall. The beast was there . . . looking at me. And, you know, he looked better for his scrape with the nevermind. I stopped; I looked at him; he looked at me. I think . . . I think we stayed a long time that way . . . still, stone-statue . . . just looking at one another. I looked more into his face than he looked into mine. I mean, I can concentrate longer at looking into a dog's face than a dog can concentrate at looking into mine, or

17

into anybody else's face, for that matter. But during that twenty seconds or two hours that we looked into each other's face, we made contact. Now, here is what I had wanted to happen: I loved the dog now, and I wanted him to love me. I had tried to love, and I had tried to kill, and both had been unsuccessful by themselves. I hoped . . . and I don't really know why I expected the dog to understand anything, much less my motivations . . . I hoped that the dog would understand.

(PETER *seems to be hypnotized*)

It's just . . . it's just that . . . (JERRY *is abnormally tense, now*) . . . it's just that if you can't deal with people, you have to make a start somewhere. WITH ANIMALS! *(Much faster now, and like a conspirator)* Don't you see? A person has to have some way of dealing with SOMETHING. If not with people . . . if not with people . . . SOMETHING. With a bed, with a cockroach, with a mirror . . . no, that's too hard, that's one of the last steps. With a cockroach, with a . . . with a . . . with a carpet, a roll of toilet paper . . . no, not that, either . . . that's a mirror, too; always check bleeding. You see how hard it is to find things? With a street corner, and too many lights, all colors reflecting on the oily-wet streets . . . with a wisp of smoke, a wisp . . . of smoke . . . with . . . with pornographic playing cards, with a strongbox . . . WITHOUT A LOCK . . . with love, with vomiting, with crying, with fury because the pretty little ladies aren't pretty little ladies, with making money with your body which is an act of love and I could prove it, with howling because you're alive; with God. How about that? WITH GOD WHO IS A COLORED QUEEN WHO WEARS A KIMONO AND PLUCKS HIS EYEBROWS, WHO IS A WOMAN WHO CRIES WITH DETERMINATION BEHIND HER CLOSED DOOR . . . with God who, I'm told, turned his back on the whole thing some time ago . . . with . . . some day, with people. (JERRY *sighs the next word heavily*) People. With an idea; a concept. And where better, where ever better in this humiliating excuse for a jail, where better to communicate one single, simple-minded idea than in an entrance hall? Where? It would be A START! Where better to make a beginning . . . to understand and just possibly be understood . . . a beginning of an understanding, than with . . .

(Here JERRY *seems to fall into almost grotesque fatigue)*

. . . than with A DOG. Just that; a dog.

(Here there is a silence that might be prolonged for a moment or so; then JERRY *wearily finishes his story)*

A dog. It seemed like a perfectly sensible idea. Man is a dog's best friend, remember. So: the dog and I looked at each other. I longer than the dog. And what I saw then has been the same ever since. Whenever the dog and I see each other we both stop where we are. We regard each other with a mixture of sadness and suspicion, and then we feign indifference. We walk past each other safely; we have an understanding. It's very sad, but you'll have to admit that it is an understanding. We had made many attempts at contact, and we had failed. The dog has returned to garbage, and I to solitary but free passage. I have not returned. I mean to say, I have *gained* solitary free passage, if that much further loss can be said to be gain. I have learned that neither kindness nor cruelty by themselves, independent of each other, creates any effect beyond themselves; and I have learned that the two combined, together, at the same time, are the teaching emotion. And what is gained is loss. And what has been the result: the dog and I have attained a compromise; more of a bargain, really. We neither love nor hurt because we do not try to reach each other. And, *was* trying to feed the dog an act of love? And, perhaps, was the dog's attempt to bite me *not* an act of love? If we can so misunderstand, well then, why have we invented the word love in the first place?

(There is silence. JERRY *moves to* PETER*'s bench and sits down beside him. This is the first time* JERRY *has sat down during the play)*

The Story of Jerry and the Dog: the end.

*(*PETER *is silent)*

Well, Peter? *(*JERRY *is suddenly cheerful)* Well, Peter? Do you think I could sell that story to the *Reader's Digest* and make a couple of hundred bucks for *The Most Unforgettable Character I've Ever Met?* Huh? *(*JERRY *is animated, but* PETER *is disturbed)*

Oh, come on now, Peter; tell me what you think.

PETER *(Numb)*. I . . . I don't understand what . . . I don't think I . . . *(Now, almost tearfully)* Why did you tell me all of this?

JERRY. Why not?

PETER. I DON'T UNDERSTAND!

JERRY *(Furious, but whispering)*. That's a lie.

PETER. No. No, it's not.

19

JERRY *(Quietly).* I tried to explain it to you as I went along. I went slowly; it all has to do with . . .

PETER. I DON'T WANT TO HEAR ANY MORE. I don't understand you, or your landlady, or her dog. . . .

JERRY. *Her* dog! I thought it was my . . . No. No, you're right. It *is* her dog. *(Looks at* PETER *intently, shaking his head)* I don't know what I was thinking about; of course you don't understand. *(In a monotone, wearily)* I don't live in your block; I'm not married to two parakeets, or whatever your setup is. I am a *permanent transient,* and my home is the sickening roominghouses on the West Side of New York City, which is the greatest city in the world. Amen.

PETER. I'm . . . I'm sorry; I didn't mean to . . .

JERRY. Forget it. I suppose you don't quite know what to make of me, eh?

PETER *(A joke).* We get all kinds in publishing. *(Chuckles)*

JERRY. You're a funny man. *(He forces a laugh)* You know that? You're a very . . . a richly comic person.

PETER *(Modestly, but amused).* Oh, now, not really. *(Still chuckling)*

JERRY. Peter, do I annoy you, or confuse you?

PETER *(Lightly).* Well, I must confess that this wasn't the kind of afternoon I'd anticipated.

JERRY. You mean, I'm not the gentleman you were expecting.

PETER. I wasn't expecting anybody.

JERRY. No, I don't imagine you were. But I'm here, and I'm not leaving.

PETER *(Consulting his watch).* Well, you may not be, but I must be getting home soon.

JERRY. Oh, come on; stay a while longer.

PETER. I really should get home; you see . . .

JERRY *(Tickles* PETER's *ribs with his fingers).* Oh, come on.

PETER *(He is very ticklish; as* JERRY *continues to tickle him his voice becomes falsetto).* No, I . . . OHHHHH! Don't do that. Stop, Stop. Ohhh, no, no.

JERRY. Oh, come on.

PETER *(As* JERRY *tickles).* Oh, hee, hee, hee. I must go. I . . . hee, hee, hee. After all, stop, stop, hee, hee, hee, after all, the parakeets will be getting dinner ready soon. Hee, hee. And the cats are setting the table. Stop, stop, and, and . . . (PETER *is beside himself now)* . . . and we're having . . . hee, hee . . . uh . . . ho, ho, ho.

(JERRY *stops tickling* PETER, *but the combination of the tickling and*

20

his own mad whimsy has PETER *laughing almost hysterically. As his laughter continues, then subsides,* JERRY *watches him, with a curious fixed smile)*

JERRY. Peter?

PETER. Oh, ha, ha, ha, ha, ha, ha. What? What?

JERRY. Listen, now.

PETER. Oh, ho, ho. What . . . what is it, Jerry? Oh, my.

JERRY *(Mysteriously)*. Peter, do you want to know what happened at the zoo?

PETER. Ah, ha, ha. The what? Oh, yes; the zoo. Oh, ho, ho. Well, I had my own zoo there for a moment with . . . hee, hee, the parakeets getting dinner ready, and the . . . ha, ha, whatever it was, the . . .

JERRY *(Calmly)*. Yes, that was very funny, Peter. I wouldn't have expected it. But do you want to hear about what happened at the zoo, or not?

PETER. Yes. Yes, by all means; tell me what happened at the zoo. Oh, my. I don't know what happened to me.

JERRY. Now I'll let you in on what happened at the zoo; but first, I should tell you why I went to the zoo. I went to the zoo to find out more about the way people exist with animals, and the way animals exist with each other, and with people too. It probably wasn't a fair test, what with everyone separated by bars from everyone else, the animals for the most part from each other, and always the people from the animals. But, if it's a zoo, that's the way it is. *(He pokes* PETER *on the arm)* Move over.

PETER *(Friendly)*. I'm sorry, haven't you enough room? *(He shifts a little)*

JERRY *(Smiling slightly)*. Well, all the animals are there, and all the people are there, and it's Sunday and all the children are there. *(He pokes* PETER *again)* Move over.

PETER *(Patiently, still friendly)*. All right.

(He moves some more, and JERRY *has all the room he might need)*

JERRY. And it's a hot day, so all the stench is there, too, and all the balloon sellers, and all the ice cream sellers, and all the seals are barking, and all the birds are screaming. *(Pokes* PETER *harder)* Move over!

PETER *(Beginning to be annoyed)*. Look here, you have more than enough room! *(But he moves more, and is now fairly cramped at one end of the bench)*

JERRY. And I am there, and it's feeding time at the lions' house, and the lion keeper comes into the lion cage, one of the lion cages, to feed one of the lions. *(Punches* PETER *on the arm, hard)* MOVE OVER!

21

PETER *(Very annoyed)*. I can't move over any more, and stop hitting me. What's the matter with you?

JERRY. Do you want to hear the story? *(Punches PETER's arm again)*

PETER *(Flabbergasted)*. I'm not so sure! I certainly don't want to be punched in the arm.

JERRY *(Punches PETER's arm again)*. Like that?

PETER. Stop it! What's the matter with you?

JERRY. I'm crazy, you bastard.

PETER. That isn't funny.

JERRY. Listen to me, Peter. I want this bench. You go sit on the bench over there, and if you're good I'll tell you the rest of the story.

PETER *(Flustered)*. But . . . whatever for? What *is* the matter with you? Besides, I see no reason why I should give up this bench. I sit on this bench almost every Sunday afternoon, in good weather. It's secluded here; there's never anyone sitting here, so I have it all to myself.

JERRY *(Softly)*. Get off this bench, Peter; I want it.

PETER *(Almost whining)*. No.

JERRY. I said I want this bench, and I'm going to have it. Now get over there.

PETER. People can't have everything they want. You should know that; it's a rule; people can have some of the things they want, but they can't have everything.

JERRY *(Laughs)*. Imbecile! You're slow-witted!

PETER. Stop that!

JERRY. You're a vegetable! Go lie down on the ground.

PETER *(Intense)*. Now *you* listen to me. I've put up with you all afternoon.

JERRY. Not really.

PETER. LONG ENOUGH. I've put up with you long enough. I've listened to you because you seemed . . . well, because I thought you wanted to talk to somebody.

JERRY. You put things well; economically, and, yet . . . oh, what is the word I want to put justice to your . . . JESUS, you make me sick . . . get off here and give me my bench.

PETER. MY BENCH!

JERRY *(Pushes PETER almost, but not quite, off the bench)*. Get out of my sight.

PETER *(Regaining his position)*. God da . . . mn you. That's enough! I've had enough of you. I will not give up this bench; you can't have it, and that's that. Now, go away.

(JERRY *snorts but does not move*)

Go away, I said.

(JERRY *does not move*)

Get away from here. If you don't move on . . . you're a bum . . . that's what you are. . . . If you don't move on, I'll get a policeman here and make you go.

(JERRY *laughs, stays*)

I warn you, I'll call a policeman.

JERRY *(Softly)*. You won't find a policeman around here; they're all over on the west side of the park chasing fairies down from trees or out of the bushes. That's all they do. That's their function. So scream your head off; it won't do you any good.

PETER. POLICE! I warn you, I'll have you arrested. POLICE! *(Pause)* I said POLICE! *(Pause)* I feel ridiculous.

JERRY. You look ridiculous: a grown man screaming for the police on a bright Sunday afternoon in the park with nobody harming you. If a policeman *did* fill his quota and come sludging over this way he'd probably take you in as a nut.

PETER *(With disgust and impotence)*. Great God, I just came here to read, and now you want me to give up the bench. You're mad.

JERRY. Hey, I got news for you, as they say. I'm on your precious bench, and you're never going to have it for yourself again.

PETER *(Furious)*. Look, you; get off my bench. I don't care if it makes any sense or not. I want this bench to myself; I want you OFF IT!

JERRY *(Mocking)*. Aw . . . look who's mad.

PETER. GET OUT!

JERRY. No.

PETER. I WARN YOU!

JERRY. Do you know how ridiculous you look *now?*

PETER *(His fury and self-consciousness have possessed him)*. It doesn't matter. *(He is almost crying)* GET AWAY FROM MY BENCH!

JERRY. Why? You have everything in the world you want; you've told me about your home, and your family, and *your own* little zoo. You have everything, and now you want this bench. Are these the things men fight for? Tell me, Peter, is this bench, this iron and this wood, is this your honor? Is this the thing in the world you'd fight for? Can you think of anything more absurd?

PETER. Absurd? Look, I'm not going to talk to you about honor, or even try to explain it to you. Besides, it isn't a question of honor; but even if it were, you wouldn't understand.

JERRY *(Contemptuously)*. You don't even know what you're saying, do you? This is probably the first time in your life you've had anything more trying to face than changing your cats' toilet box. Stupid! Don't you have any idea, not even the slightest, what other people *need?*

PETER. Oh, boy, listen to you; well, you don't need this bench. That's for sure.

JERRY. Yes; yes, I do.

PETER *(Quivering)*. I've come here for years; I have hours of great pleasure, great satisfaction, right here. And that's important to a man. I'm a responsible person, and I'm a GROWNUP. This is my bench, and you have no right to take it away from me.

JERRY. Fight for it, then. Defend yourself; defend your bench.

PETER. You've *pushed* me to it. Get up and fight.

JERRY. Like a man?

PETER *(Still angry)*. Yes, like a man, if you insist on mocking me even further.

JERRY. I'll have to give you credit for one thing: you *are* a vegetable, and a slightly nearsighted one, I think . . .

PETER. THAT'S ENOUGH. . . .

JERRY. . . . but, you know, as they say on TV all the time—you know— and I mean this, Peter, you have a certain dignity; it surprises me . . .

PETER. STOP!

JERRY *(Rises lazily)*. Very well, Peter, we'll battle for the bench, but we're not evenly matched.

(He takes out and clicks open an ugly-looking knife)

PETER *(Suddenly awakening to the reality of the situation)*. You *are* mad! You're stark raving mad! YOU'RE GOING TO KILL ME!

(But before PETER *has time to think what to do,* JERRY *tosses the knife at* PETER*'s feet)*

JERRY. There you go. Pick it up. You have the knife and we'll be more evenly matched.

PETER *(Horrified)*. No!

JERRY *(Rushes over to* PETER, *grabs him by the collar;* PETER *rises; their faces almost touch).* Now you pick up that knife and you fight with me. You fight for your self-respect; you fight for that goddamned bench.

PETER *(Struggling).* No! Let . . . let go of me! He . . . Help!

JERRY *(Slaps* PETER *on each "fight").* You fight, you miserable bastard; fight for that bench; fight for your parakeets; fight for your cats, fight for your two daughters; fight for your wife; fight for your manhood, you pathetic little vegetable. *(Spits in* PETER*'s face)* You couldn't even get your wife with a male child.

PETER *(Breaks away, enraged).* It's a matter of genetics, not manhood, you . . . you monster.

(He darts down, picks up the knife and backs off a little; he is breathing heavily)

I'll give you one last chance; get out of here and leave me alone!

(He holds the knife with a firm arm, but far in front of him, not to attack, but to defend)

JERRY *(Sighs heavily).* So be it!

(With a rush he charges PETER *and impales himself on the knife. Tableau: For just a moment, complete silence.* JERRY *impaled on the knife at the end of* PETER*'s still firm arm. Then* PETER *screams, pulls away, leaving the knife in* JERRY. JERRY *is motionless, on point. Then he, too, screams, and it must be the sound of an infuriated and fatally wounded animal. With the knife in him, he stumbles back to the bench that* PETER *had vacated. He crumbles there, sitting, facing* PE-TER, *his eyes wide in agony, his mouth open)*

PETER *(Whispering).* Oh my God, oh my God, oh my God. . . .

(He repeats these words many times, very rapidly)

JERRY (JERRY *is dying; but now his expression seems to change. His features relax, and while his voice varies, sometimes wrenched with pain, for the most part he seems removed from his dying. He smiles).* Thank you, Peter. I mean that, now; thank you very much.

(PETER*'s mouth drops open. He cannot move; he is transfixed)*

Oh, Peter, I was so afraid I'd drive you away. *(He laughs as best he can)* You don't know how afraid I was you'd go away and leave me. And now I'll tell you what happened at the zoo. I think . . . I think this is what happened at the zoo . . . I think. I think that while I was at the zoo I decided that I would walk north . . . northerly, rather . . . until I found you . . . or somebody . . . and I decided that I would talk to you . . . I would tell you things . . . and things that I would tell you

25

would . . . Well, here we are. You see? Here we *are*. But . . . I don't know . . . could I have planned all this? No . . . no, I couldn't have. But I think I did. And now I've told you what you wanted to know, haven't I? And now you know all about what happened at the zoo. And now you know what you'll see in your TV, and the face I told you about . . . you remember . . . the face I told you about . . . my face, the face you see right now. Peter . . . Peter? . . . Peter . . . thank you. I came unto you *(He laughs, so faintly)* and you have comforted me. Dear Peter.

PETER *(Almost fainting).* Oh my God!

JERRY. You'd better go now. Somebody might come by, and you don't want to be here when anyone comes.

PETER *(Does not move, but begins to weep).* Oh my God, oh my God.

JERRY *(Most faintly, now; he is very near death).* You won't be coming back here any more, Peter; you've been dispossessed. You've lost your bench, but you've defended your honor. And Peter, I'll tell you something now; you're not really a vegetable; it's all right, you're an animal. You're an animal, too. But you'd better hurry now, Peter. Hurry, you'd better go . . . see?

(JERRY takes a handkerchief and with great effort and pain wipes the knife handle clean of fingerprints)

Hurry away, Peter.

(PETER begins to stagger away)

Wait . . . wait, Peter. Take your book . . . book. Right here . . . beside me . . . on your bench . . . my bench, rather. Come . . . take your book.

(PETER starts for the book, but retreats)

Hurry . . . Peter.

(PETER rushes to the bench, grabs the book, retreats)

Very good, Peter . . . very good. Now . . . hurry away.

(PETER hesitates for a moment, then flees, stage-left)

Hurry away. . . . *(His eyes are closed now)* Hurry away, your parakeets are making the dinner . . . the cats . . . are setting the table . . .

PETER *(Off stage).*

(A pitiful howl)

OH MY GOD!

JERRY *(His eyes still closed, he shakes his head and speaks; a combination of scornful mimicry and supplication).* Oh . . . my . . . God. *(He is dead)*

CURTAIN

CURTAIN

THE AMERICAN DREAM

A Play in One Scene (1959–1960)

For David Diamond

First Performance: January 24, 1961,

New York City. York Playhouse

The Players:

MOMMY
DADDY
GRANDMA
MRS. BARKER
YOUNG MAN

The Scene:

A living room. Two armchairs, one toward either side of the stage, facing each other diagonally out toward the audience. Against the rear wall, a sofa. A door, leading out from the apartment, in the rear wall, far stage-right. An archway, leading to other rooms, in the side wall, stage-left.

At the beginning, MOMMY *and* DADDY *are seated in the armchairs,* DADDY
in the armchair stage-left, MOMMY *in the other.*
Curtain up. A silence. Then:

MOMMY. I don't know what can be keeping them.

DADDY. They're late, naturally.

MOMMY. Of course, they're late; it never fails.

DADDY. That's the way things are today, and there's nothing you can do
about it.

MOMMY. You're quite right.

DADDY. When we took this apartment, they were quick enough to have
me sign the lease; they were quick enough to take my check for two
months' rent in advance . . .

MOMMY. And one month's security . . .

DADDY. . . . and one month's security. They were quick enough to check
my references; they were quick enough about all that. But now! But
now, try to get the icebox fixed, try to get the doorbell fixed, try to get
the leak in the johnny fixed! Just try it . . . they aren't so quick about
that.

MOMMY. Of course not; it never fails. People think they can get away with
anything these days . . . and, of course they can. I went to buy a new
hat yesterday.

(Pause)

I said, I went to buy a new hat yesterday.

DADDY. Oh! Yes . . . yes.

MOMMY. Pay attention.

DADDY. I *am* paying attention, Mommy.

MOMMY. Well, be sure you do.

DADDY. Oh, I am.

MOMMY. All right, Daddy; now listen.

DADDY. I'm listening, Mommy.

MOMMY. You're sure!

33

DADDY. Yes . . . yes, I'm sure, I'm all ears.

MOMMY *(Giggles at the thought; then)*. All right, now. I went to buy a new hat yesterday and I said, "I'd like a new hat, please." And so, they showed me a few hats, green ones and blue ones, and I didn't like any of them, not one bit. What did I say? What did I just say?

DADDY. You didn't like any of them, not one bit.

MOMMY. That's right; you just keep paying attention. And then they showed me one that I did like. It was a lovely little hat, and I said, "Oh, this is a lovely little hat; I'll take this hat; oh my, it's lovely. What color is it?" And they said, "Why, this is beige; isn't it a lovely little beige hat?" And I said, "Oh, it's just lovely." And so, I bought it. *(Stops, looks at* DADDY*)*

DADDY. *(To show he is paying attention)*. And so you bought it.

MOMMY. And so I bought it, and I walked out of the store with the hat right on my head, and I ran spang into the chairman of our woman's club, and she said, "Oh, my dear, isn't that a lovely little hat? Where did you get that lovely little hat? It's the loveliest little hat; I've always wanted a wheat-colored hat *myself.*" And, I said, "Why, no, my dear; this hat is beige; beige." And she laughed and said, "Why no, my dear, that's a wheat-colored hat . . . wheat. I know beige from wheat." And I said, "Well, my dear, I know beige from wheat, too." What did I say? What did I just say?

DADDY *(Tonelessly)*. Well, my dear, I know beige from wheat, too.

MOMMY. That's right. And she laughed, and she said, "Well, my dear, they certainly put one over on you. That's wheat if I ever saw wheat. But it's lovely, just the same." And then she walked off. She's a dreadful woman, you don't know her; she has dreadful taste, two dreadful children, a dreadful house, and an absolutely adorable husband who sits in a wheel chair all the time. You don't know him. You don't know anybody, do you? She's just a dreadful woman, but she *is* chairman of our woman's club, so naturally I'm terribly fond of her. So, I went right back into the hat shop, and I said, "Look here; what do you mean selling me a hat that you say is beige, when it's wheat all the time . . . wheat! I can tell beige from wheat any day in the week, but not in this artificial light of yours." They have artificial light, Daddy.

DADDY. Have they!

MOMMY. And I said, "The minute I got outside I could tell that it wasn't a beige hat at all; it was a wheat hat." And they said to me, "How could you tell that when you had the hat on the top of your head?" Well, that made me angry, and so I made a scene right there; I screamed as hard as I could; I took my hat off and I threw it down on the counter, and oh, I made a terrible scene. I said, I made a terrible scene.

DADDY *(Snapping to)*. Yes . . . yes . . . good for you!

MOMMY. And I made an absolutely terrible scene; and they became frightened, and they said, "Oh, madam; oh, madam." But I kept right on, and finally they admitted that they might have made a mistake; so they took my hat into the back, and then they came out again with a hat that looked exactly like it. I took one look at it, and I said, "This hat is wheat-colored; wheat." Well, of course, they said, "Oh, no, madam, this hat is beige; you go outside and see." So, I went outside, and lo and behold, it *was* beige. So I bought it.

DADDY *(Clearing his throat)*. I would imagine that it was the same hat they tried to sell you before.

MOMMY *(With a little laugh)*. Well, of course it was!

DADDY. That's the way things are today; you just can't get satisfaction; you just try.

MOMMY. Well, *I* got satisfaction.

DADDY. That's right, Mommy. *You did* get satisfaction, didn't you?

MOMMY. Why are they so late? I don't know what can be keeping them.

DADDY. I've been trying for two weeks to have the leak in the johnny fixed.

MOMMY. You can't get satisfaction; just try. *I* can get satisfaction, but you can't.

DADDY. I've been trying for two weeks and it isn't so much for my sake; I can always go to the club.

MOMMY. It isn't so much for my sake, either; I can always go shopping.

DADDY. It's really for Grandma's sake.

MOMMY. Of course it's for Grandma's sake. Grandma cries every time she goes to the johnny as it is; but now that it doesn't work it's even worse, it makes Grandma think she's getting feeble-headed.

DADDY. Grandma *is* getting feeble-headed.

MOMMY. Of course Grandma is getting feeble-headed, but not about her johnny-do's.

DADDY. No; that's true. I must have it fixed.

MOMMY. WHY are they so late? I don't know what can be keeping them.

DADDY. When they came here the first time, they were ten minutes early; they were quick enough about it then.

(Enter GRANDMA *from the archway, stage left. She is loaded down with boxes, large and small, neatly wrapped and tied.)*

MOMMY. Why Grandma, look at you! What *is* all that you're carrying?

GRANDMA. They're boxes. What do they look like?

MOMMY. Daddy! Look at Grandma; look at all the boxes she's carrying!

DADDY. My goodness, Grandma; look at all those boxes.

GRANDMA. Where'll I put them?

MOMMY. Heavens! I don't know. Whatever are they for?

GRANDMA. That's nobody's damn business.

MOMMY. Well, in that case, put them down next to Daddy; there.

GRANDMA *(Dumping the boxes down, on and around* DADDY's *feet).* I sure wish you'd get the john fixed.

DADDY. Oh, I do wish they'd come and fix it. We hear you . . . for hours . . . whimpering away. . . .

MOMMY. Daddy! What a terrible thing to say to Grandma!

GRANDMA. Yeah. For shame, talking to me that way.

DADDY. I'm sorry, Grandma.

MOMMY. Daddy's sorry, Grandma.

GRANDMA. Well, all right. In that case I'll go get the rest of the boxes. I suppose I deserve being talked to that way. I've gotten so old. Most people think that when you get so old, you either freeze to death, or you burn up. But you don't. When you get so old, all that happens is that people talk to you that way.

DADDY *(Contrite).* I said I'm sorry, Grandma.

MOMMY. Daddy said he was sorry.

GRANDMA. Well, that's all that counts. People being sorry. Makes you feel better; gives you a sense of dignity, and that's all that's important . . . a sense of dignity. And it doesn't matter if you don't care, or not, either. You got to have a sense of dignity, even if you don't care, 'cause, if you don't have that, civilization's doomed.

MOMMY. You've been reading my book club selections again!

DADDY. How dare you read Mommy's book club selections, Grandma!

GRANDMA. Because I'm old! When you're old you gotta do something. When you get old, you can't talk to people because people snap at you. When you get so old, people talk to you that way. That's why you become deaf, so you won't be able to hear people talking to you that way. And that's why you go and hide under the covers in the big soft bed, so you won't feel the house shaking from people talking to you that way. That's why old people die, eventually. People talk to them that way. I've got to go and get the rest of the boxes.

(GRANDMA *exits*)

DADDY. Poor Grandma, I didn't mean to hurt her.

MOMMY. Don't you worry about it; Grandma doesn't know what she means.

DADDY. She knows what she says, though.

MOMMY. Don't you worry about it; she won't know that soon. I love Grandma.

DADDY. I love her, too. Look how nicely she wrapped these boxes.

MOMMY. Grandma has always wrapped boxes nicely. When I was a little girl, I was very poor, and Grandma was very poor, too, because Grandpa was in heaven. And every day, when I went to school, Grandma used to wrap a box for me, and I used to take it with me to school; and when it was lunchtime, all the little boys and girls used to take out their boxes of lunch, and they weren't wrapped nicely at all, and they used to open them and eat their chicken legs and chocolate cakes; and I used to say, "Oh, look at my lovely lunch box; it's so nicely wrapped it would break my heart to open it." And so, I wouldn't open it.

DADDY. Because it was empty.

MOMMY. Oh no. Grandma always filled it up, because she never ate the dinner she cooked the evening before; she gave me all her food for my lunch box the next day. After school, I'd take the box back to Grandma, and she'd open it and eat the chicken legs and chocolate cake that was inside. Grandma used to say, "I love day-old cake." That's where the expression day-old cake came from. Grandma always ate everything a day late. I used to eat all the other little boys' and girls' food at school, because they thought my lunch box was empty. They thought my lunch box was empty, and that's why I wouldn't open it. They thought I suffered from the sin of pride, and since that made them better than me, they were very generous.

DADDY. You were a very deceitful little girl.

MOMMY. We were very poor! But then I married you, Daddy, and now we're very rich.

DADDY. Grandma isn't rich.

MOMMY. No, but you've been so good to Grandma she feels rich. She doesn't know you'd like to put her in a nursing home.

DADDY. I wouldn't!

MOMMY. Well, heaven knows, *I* would! I can't stand it, watching her do the cooking and the housework, polishing the silver, moving the furniture. . . .

DADDY. She likes to do that. She says it's the least she can do to earn her keep.

MOMMY. Well, she's right. You can't live off people. I can live off you, because I married you. And aren't you lucky all I brought with me was Grandma. A lot of women I know would have brought their whole families to live off you. All I brought was Grandma. Grandma is all the family I have.

DADDY. I feel very fortunate.

MOMMY. You should. I have a right to live off of you because I married you, and because I used to let you get on top of me and bump your uglies; and I have a right to all your money when you die. And when you do, Grandma and I can live by ourselves . . . if she's still here. Unless you have her put away in a nursing home.

DADDY. I have no intention of putting her in a nursing home.

MOMMY. Well, I wish somebody would do something with her!

DADDY. At any rate, you're very well provided for.

MOMMY. You're my sweet Daddy; that's very nice.

DADDY. I love my Mommy.

(Enter GRANDMA *again, laden with more boxes)*

GRANDMA *(Dumping the boxes on and around* DADDY*'s feet).* There; that's the lot of them.

DADDY. They're wrapped so nicely.

GRANDMA *(To* DADDY*).* You won't get on my sweet side that way . . . .

MOMMY. Grandma!

GRANDMA. . . . telling me how nicely I wrap boxes. Not after what you said: how I whimpered for hours. . . .

MOMMY. Grandma!

GRANDMA *(To* MOMMY*).* Shut up!

(To DADDY*)*

You don't have any feelings, that's what's wrong with you. Old people make all sorts of noises, half of them they can't help. Old people whimper, and cry, and belch, and make great hollow rumbling sounds at the table; old people wake up in the middle of the night screaming, and find out they haven't even been asleep; and when old people *are* asleep, they try to wake up, and they can't . . . not for the longest time.

MOMMY. Homilies, homilies!

GRANDMA. And there's more, too.

DADDY. I'm really very sorry, Grandma.

GRANDMA. I know you are, Daddy; it's Mommy over there makes all the trouble. If you'd listened to me, you wouldn't have married her in the first place. She was a tramp and a trollop and a trull to boot, and she's no better now.

MOMMY. Grandma!

GRANDMA *(To* MOMMY*)*. Shut up!

(To DADDY*)*

When she was no more than eight years old she used to climb up on my lap and say, in a sickening little voice, "When I gwo up, I'm going to mahwy a wich old man; I'm going to set my wittle were end right down in a tub o' butter, that's what I'm going to do." And I warned you, Daddy; I told you to stay away from her type. I told you to. I did.

MOMMY. You stop that! You're my mother, not his!

GRANDMA. I am?

DADDY. That's right, Grandma. Mommy's right.

GRANDMA. Well, how would you expect somebody as old as I am to re-member a thing like that? You don't make allowances for people. I want an allowance. I want an allowance!

DADDY. All right, Grandma; I'll see to it.

MOMMY. Grandma! I'm ashamed of you.

GRANDMA. Humf! It's a fine time to say that. You should have gotten rid of me a long time ago if that's the way you feel. You should have had Daddy set me up in business somewhere . . . I could have gone into the fur business, or I could have been a singer. But no; not you. You wanted me around so you could sleep in my room when Daddy got fresh. But now it isn't important, because Daddy doesn't want to get fresh with you any more, and I don't blame him. You'd rather sleep with me, wouldn't you, Daddy?

MOMMY. Daddy doesn't want to sleep with anyone. Daddy's been sick.

DADDY. I've been sick. I don't even want to sleep in the apartment.

MOMMY. You see? I told you.

DADDY. I just want to get everything over with.

MOMMY. That's right. Why are they so late? Why can't they get here on time?

GRANDMA *(An owl)*. Who? Who? . . . Who? Who?

39

MOMMY. You know, Grandma.

GRANDMA. No, I don't.

MOMMY. Well, it doesn't really matter whether you do or not.

DADDY. Is that true?

MOMMY. Oh, more or less. Look how pretty Grandma wrapped these boxes.

GRANDMA. I didn't really like wrapping them; it hurt my fingers, and it frightened me. But it had to be done.

MOMMY. Why, Grandma?

GRANDMA. None of your damn business.

MOMMY. Go to bed.

GRANDMA. I don't want to go to bed. I just got up. I want to stay here and watch. Besides . . .

MOMMY. Go to bed.

DADDY. Let her stay up, Mommy; it isn't noon yet.

GRANDMA. I want to watch; besides . . .

DADDY. Let her watch, Mommy.

MOMMY. Well all right, you can watch; but don't you dare say a word.

GRANDMA. Old people are very good at listening; old people don't like to talk; old people have colitis and lavender perfume. Now I'm going to be quiet.

DADDY. She never mentioned she wanted to be a singer.

MOMMY. Oh, I forgot to tell you, but it was ages ago.

(The doorbell rings)

Oh, goodness! Here they are!

GRANDMA. Who? Who?

MOMMY. Oh, just some people.

GRANDMA. The van people? Is it the van people? Have you finally done it? Have you called the van people to come and take me away?

DADDY. Of course not, Grandma!

GRANDMA. Oh, don't be too sure. She'd have you carted off too, if she thought she could get away with it.

MOMMY. Pay no attention to her, Daddy.

(An aside to GRANDMA)

My God, you're ungrateful!

(The doorbell rings again)

DADDY *(Wringing his hands)*. Oh dear; oh dear.

MOMMY *(Still to GRANDMA)*. Just you wait; I'll fix your wagon.

40

(Now to DADDY*)*

Well, go let them in Daddy. What are you waiting for?

DADDY. I think we should talk about it some more. Maybe we've been hasty . . . a little hasty, perhaps.

(Doorbell rings again)

I'd like to talk about it some more.

MOMMY. There's no need. You made up your mind; you were firm; you were masculine and decisive.

DADDY. We might consider the pros and the . . .

MOMMY. I won't argue with you; it has to be done; you were right. Open the door.

DADDY. But I'm not sure that . . .

MOMMY. Open the door.

DADDY. Was I firm about it?

MOMMY. Oh, so firm; so firm.

DADDY. And was I decisive?

MOMMY. SO decisive! Oh, I shivered.

DADDY. And masculine? Was I really masculine?

MOMMY. Oh, Daddy, you were so masculine; I shivered and fainted.

GRANDMA. Shivered and fainted, did she? Humf!

MOMMY. You be quiet.

GRANDMA. Old people have a right to talk to themselves; it doesn't hurt the gums, and it's comforting.

(Doorbell rings again)

DADDY. I shall now open the door.

MOMMY. WHAT a masculine Daddy! Isn't he a masculine Daddy?

GRANDMA. Don't expect me to say anything. Old people are obscene.

MOMMY. Some of your opinions aren't so bad. You know that?

DADDY *(Backing off from the door)*. Maybe we can send them away.

MOMMY. Oh, look at you! You're turning into jelly; you're indecisive; you're a woman.

DADDY. All right. Watch me now; I'm going to open the door. Watch. Watch!

MOMMY. We're watching; we're watching.

GRANDMA. *I'm* not.

DADDY. Watch now; it's opening.

(He opens the door)

It's open!

41

(MRS. BARKER *steps into the room*)
Here they are!

MOMMY. Here they are!

GRANDMA. Where?

DADDY. Come in. You're late. But, of course, we expected you to be late; we were saying that we expected you to be late.

MOMMY. Daddy, don't be rude! We were saying that you just can't get satisfaction these days, and we were talking about you, of course. Won't you come in?

MRS. BARKER. Thank you. I don't mind if I do.

MOMMY. We're very glad that you're here, late as you are. You do remember us, don't you? You were here once before. I'm Mommy, and this is Daddy, and that's Grandma, doddering there in the corner.

MRS. BARKER. Hello, Mommy; hello, Daddy; and hello there, Grandma.

DADDY. Now that you're here, I don't suppose you could go away and maybe come back some other time.

MRS. BARKER. Oh no; we're much too efficient for that. I said, hello there, Grandma.

MOMMY. Speak to them, Grandma.

GRANDMA. I don't see them.

DADDY. For shame, Grandma; they're here.

MRS. BARKER. Yes, we're here, Grandma. I'm Mrs. Barker. I remember you; don't you remember me?

GRANDMA. I don't recall. Maybe you were younger, or something.

MOMMY. Grandma! What a terrible thing to say!

MRS. BARKER. Oh now, don't scold her, Mommy; for all she knows she may be right.

DADDY. Uh . . . Mrs. Barker, is it? Won't you sit down?

MRS. BARKER. I don't mind if I do.

MOMMY. Would you like a cigarette, and a drink, and would you like to cross your legs?

MRS. BARKER. You forget yourself, Mommy; I'm a professional woman. But I will cross my legs.

DADDY. Yes, make yourself comfortable.

MRS. BARKER. I don't mind if I do.

GRANDMA. Are they still here?

MOMMY. Be quiet, Grandma.

MRS. BARKER. Oh, we're still here. My, what an unattractive apartment you have!

MOMMY. Yes, but you don't know what a trouble it is. Let me tell you . . .

DADDY. I was saying to Mommy . . .

MRS. BARKER. Yes, I know. I was listening outside.

DADDY. About the icebox, and . . . the doorbell . . . and the . . .

MRS. BARKER. . . . and the johnny. Yes, we're very efficient; we have to know everything in our work.

DADDY. Exactly what do you do?

MOMMY. Yes, what is your work?

MRS. BARKER. Well, my dear, for one thing, I'm chairman of your woman's club.

MOMMY. Don't be ridiculous. I was talking to the chairman of my woman's club just yester— Why, so you are. You remember, Daddy, the lady I was telling you about? The lady with the husband who sits in the *swing?* Don't you remember?

DADDY. No . . . no. . . .

MOMMY. Of course you do. I'm sorry, Mrs. Barker. I would have known you anywhere, except in this artificial light. And look! You have a hat just like the one I bought yesterday.

MRS. BARKER *(With a little laugh)*. No, not really; this hat is cream.

MOMMY. Well, my dear, that may look like a cream hat to you, but I can . . .

MRS. BARKER. Now, now; you seem to forget who I am.

MOMMY. Yes, I do, don't I? Are you sure you're comfortable? Won't you take off your dress?

MRS. BARKER. I don't mind if I do.
(She removes her dress)

MOMMY. There. You must feel a great deal more comfortable.

MRS. BARKER. Well, I certainly *look* a great deal more comfortable.

DADDY. I'm going to blush and giggle.

MOMMY. Daddy's going to blush and giggle.

MRS. BARKER *(Pulling the hem of her slip above her knees)*. You're lucky to have such a man for a husband.

MOMMY. Oh, don't I know it!

DADDY. I just blushed and giggled and went sticky wet.

MOMMY. Isn't Daddy a caution, Mrs. Barker?

43

MRS. BARKER. Maybe if I smoked . . . ?

MOMMY. Oh, that isn't necessary.

MRS. BARKER. I don't mind if I do.

MOMMY. No; no, don't. Really.

MRS. BARKER. I don't mind . . .

MOMMY. I won't have you smoking in my house, and that's that! You're a professional woman.

DADDY. Grandma drinks AND smokes; don't you, Grandma?

GRANDMA. No.

MOMMY. Well, now, Mrs. Barker; suppose you tell us why you're here.

GRANDMA *(As* MOMMY *walks through the boxes).* The boxes . . . the boxes . . .

MOMMY. Be quiet, Grandma.

DADDY. What did you say, Grandma?

GRANDMA *(As* MOMMY *steps on several of the boxes).* The boxes, damn it!

MRS. BARKER. Boxes; she said boxes. She mentioned the boxes.

DADDY. What about the boxes, Grandma? Maybe Mrs. Barker is here because of the boxes. Is that what you meant, Grandma?

GRANDMA. I don't know if that's what I meant or not. It's certainly not what I *thought* I meant.

DADDY. Grandma is of the opinion that . . .

MRS. BARKER. Can we assume that the boxes are for us? I mean, can we assume that you had us come here for the boxes?

MOMMY. Are you in the habit of receiving boxes?

DADDY. A very good question.

MRS. BARKER. Well, that would depend on the reason we're here. I've got my fingers in so many little pies, you know. Now, I can think of one of my little activities in which we are in the habit of receiving *baskets;* but more in a literary sense than really. We *might* receive boxes, though, under very special circumstances. I'm afraid that's the best answer I can give you.

DADDY. It's a very interesting answer.

MRS. BARKER. *I* thought so. But, does it help?

MOMMY. No; I'm afraid not.

DADDY. I wonder if it might help us any if I said I feel misgivings, that I have definite qualms.

MOMMY. Where, Daddy?

DADDY. Well, mostly right here, right around where the stitches were.

44

MOMMY. Daddy had an operation, you know.

MRS. BARKER. Oh, you poor Daddy! I didn't know; but then, how could I?

GRANDMA. You might have asked; it wouldn't have hurt you.

MOMMY. Dry up, Grandma.

GRANDMA. There you go. Letting your true feelings come out. Old people aren't dry enough, I suppose. My sacks are empty, the fluid in my eyeballs is all caked on the inside edges, my spine is made of sugar candy, I breathe ice; but you don't hear me complain. Nobody hears old people complain because people think that's all old people do. And *that's* because old people are gnarled and sagged and twisted into the shape of a complaint.

(Signs off)

That's all.

MRS. BARKER. What was wrong, Daddy?

DADDY. Well, you know how it is: the doctors took out something that was there and put in something that wasn't there. An operation.

MRS. BARKER. You're very fortunate, I should say.

MOMMY. Oh, he is; he is. All his life, Daddy has wanted to be a United States Senator; but now . . . why now he's changed his mind, and for the rest of his life he's going to want to be Governor . . . it would be nearer the apartment, you know.

MRS. BARKER. You *are* fortunate, Daddy.

DADDY. Yes, indeed; except that I get these qualms now and then, definite ones.

MRS. BARKER. Well, it's just a matter of things settling; you're like an old house.

MOMMY. Why Daddy, thank Mrs. Barker.

DADDY. Thank you.

MRS. BARKER. Ambition! That's the ticket. I have a brother who's very much like you, Daddy . . . ambitious. Of course, he's a great deal younger than you; he's even younger than I am . . . if such a thing is possible. He runs a little newspaper. Just a little newspaper . . . but he runs it. He's chief cook and bottle washer of that little newspaper, which he calls *The Village Idiot*. He has such a sense of humor; he's so self-deprecating, so modest. And he'd never admit it himself, but he *is* the Village Idiot.

MOMMY. Oh, I think that's just grand. Don't you think so, Daddy?

DADDY. Yes, just grand.

MRS. BARKER. My brother's a dear man, and he has a dear little wife, whom he loves, dearly. He loves her so much he just can't get a sentence out without mentioning her. He wants everybody to know he's married. He's really a stickler on that point; he can't be introduced to anybody and say hello without adding, "Of course, I'm married." As far as I'm concerned, he's the chief exponent of Woman Love in this whole country; he's even been written up in psychiatric journals because of it.

DADDY. Indeed!

MOMMY. Isn't that lovely.

MRS. BARKER. Oh, I think so. There's too much woman hatred in this country, and that's a fact.

GRANDMA. Oh, I don't know.

MOMMY. Oh, I think that's just grand. Don't you think so, Daddy?

DADDY. Yes, just grand.

GRANDMA. In case anybody's interested . . .

MOMMY. Be quiet, Grandma.

GRANDMA. Nuts!

MOMMY. Oh, Mrs. Barker, you *must* forgive Grandma. She's rural.

MRS. BARKER. I don't mind if I do.

DADDY. Maybe Grandma has something to say.

MOMMY. Nonsense. Old people have nothing to say; and if old people *did* have something to say, nobody would listen to them.

(To GRANDMA*)*

You see? I can pull that stuff just as easy as you can.

GRANDMA. Well, you got the rhythm, but you don't really have the quality. Besides, you're middle-aged.

MOMMY. I'm proud of it!

GRANDMA. Look. I'll show you how it's really done. Middle-aged people think they can do anything, but the truth is that middle-aged people can't do most things as well as they used to. Middle-aged people think they're special because they're like everybody else. We live in the age of deformity. You see? Rhythm *and* content. You'll learn.

DADDY. I do wish I weren't surrounded by women; I'd like some men around here.

MRS. BARKER. You can say that again!

GRANDMA. I don't hardly count as a woman, so can I say my piece?

MOMMY. Go on. Jabber away.

GRANDMA. It's very simple; the fact is, these boxes don't have anything to do with why this good lady is come to call. Now, if you're interested in knowing why these boxes *are* here . . .

DADDY. I'm sure that must be all very true, Grandma, but what does it have to do with why . . . pardon me, what is that name again?

MRS. BARKER. Mrs. Barker.

DADDY. Exactly. What does it have to do with why . . . that name again?

MRS. BARKER. Mrs. Barker.

DADDY. Precisely. What does it have to do with why what's-her-name is here?

MOMMY. They're here because we asked them.

MRS. BARKER. Yes. That's why.

GRANDMA. Now if you're interested in knowing why these boxes *are* here . . .

MOMMY. Well, nobody *is* interested!

GRANDMA. You can be as snippety as you like for all the good it'll do you.

DADDY. You two will have to stop arguing.

MOMMY. I don't argue with her.

DADDY. It will just have to stop.

MOMMY. Well, why don't you call a van and have her taken away?

GRANDMA. Don't bother; there's no need.

DADDY. No, now, perhaps I can go away myself. . . .

MOMMY. Well, one or the other; the way things are now it's impossible. In the first place, it's too crowded in this apartment.

(To GRANDMA*)*

And it's you that takes up all the space, with your enema bottles, and your Pekinese, and God-only-knows-what-else . . . and now all these boxes. . . .

GRANDMA. These boxes are . . .

MRS. BARKER. I've never heard of enema *bottles.* . . .

GRANDMA. She means enema bags, but she doesn't know the difference. Mommy comes from extremely bad stock. And besides, when Mommy was born . . . well, it was a difficult delivery, and she had a head shaped like a banana.

MOMMY. You ungrateful— Daddy? Daddy, you see how ungrateful she is after all these years, after all the things we've done for her?

(To GRANDMA*)*

One of these days you're going away in a van; that's what's going to happen to you!

GRANDMA. Do tell!

MRS. BARKER. Like a banana?

GRANDMA. Yup, just like a banana.

MRS. BARKER. My word!

MOMMY. You stop listening to her; she'll say anything. Just the other night she called Daddy a hedgehog.

MRS. BARKER. She didn't!

GRANDMA. That's right, baby; you stick up for me.

MOMMY. I don't know where she gets the words; on the television, maybe.

MRS. BARKER. Did you really call him a hedgehog?

GRANDMA. Oh look; what difference does it make whether I did or not?

DADDY. Grandma's right. Leave Grandma alone.

MOMMY *(To DADDY)*. How dare you!

GRANDMA. Oh, leave her alone, Daddy; the kid's all mixed up.

MOMMY. You see? I told you. It's all those television shows. Daddy, you go right into Grandma's room and take her television and shake all the tubes loose.

DADDY. Don't mention tubes to me.

MOMMY. Oh! Mommy forgot!

(To MRS. BARKER)

Daddy has tubes now, where he used to have tracts.

MRS. BARKER. Is that a fact!

GRANDMA. I know why this dear lady is here.

MOMMY. You be still.

MRS. BARKER. Oh, I do wish you'd tell me.

MOMMY. No! No! That wouldn't be fair at all.

DADDY. Besides, she knows why she's here; she's here because we called them.

MRS. BARKER. La! But that still leaves me puzzled. I know I'm here because you called us, but I'm such a busy girl, with this committee and that committee, and the Responsible Citizens Activities I indulge in.

MOMMY. Oh my; busy, busy.

MRS. BARKER. Yes, indeed. So I'm afraid you'll have to give me some help.

MOMMY. Oh, no. No, you must be mistaken. I can't believe we asked you here to give you any help. With the way taxes are these days, and the way you can't get satisfaction in ANYTHING . . . no, I don't believe so.

DADDY. And if you need help . . . why, I should think you'd apply for a Fulbright Scholarship. . . .

MOMMY. And if not that . . . why, then a Guggenheim Fellowship. . . .

GRANDMA. Oh, come on; why not shoot the works and try for the Prix de Rome.

(Under her breath to MOMMY *and* DADDY)

Beasts!

MRS. BARKER. Oh, what a jolly family. But let me think. I'm knee-deep in work these days; there's the Ladies' Auxiliary Air Raid Committee, for one thing; how do you feel about air raids?

MOMMY. Oh, I'd say we're hostile.

DADDY. Yes, definitely; we're hostile.

MRS. BARKER. Then, you'll be no help there. There's too much hostility in the world these days as it is; but I'll not badger you! There's a surfeit of badgers as well.

GRANDMA. While we're at it, there's been a run on old people, too. The Department of Agriculture, or maybe it wasn't the Department of Agriculture—anyway, it was some department that's run by a girl—put out figures showing that ninety per cent of the adult population of the country is over eighty years old . . . or eighty per cent is over ninety years old . . .

MOMMY. You're such a liar! You just finished saying that everyone is middle-aged.

GRANDMA. I'm just telling you what the government says . . . that doesn't have anything to do with what . . .

MOMMY. It's that television! Daddy, go break her television.

GRANDMA. You won't find it.

DADDY *(Wearily getting up).* If I must . . . I must.

MOMMY. And don't step on the Pekinese; it's blind.

DADDY. It may be blind, but Daddy isn't.

(He exits, through the archway, stage left)

GRANDMA. You won't find *it*, either.

MOMMY. Oh, I'm so fortunate to have such a husband. Just think; I could have a husband who was poor, or argumentative, or a husband who sat in a wheel chair all day . . . OOOOHHHH! *What* have I said? *What have* I said?

GRANDMA. You said you could have a husband who sat in a wheel . . .

49

MOMMY. I'm mortified! I could die! I could cut my tongue out! I could . . .

MRS. BARKER *(Forcing a smile).* Oh, now . . . now . . . don't think about it . . .

MOMMY. I could . . . why, I could . . .

MRS. BARKER. . . . don't think about it . . . really. . . .

MOMMY. You're quite right. I won't think about it, and that way I'll forget that I ever said it, and that way it will be all right.

(Pause)

There . . . I've forgotten. Well, now, now that Daddy is out of the room we can have some girl talk.

MRS. BARKER. I'm not sure that I . . .

MOMMY. You *do* want to have some girl talk, don't you?

MRS. BARKER. I was going to say I'm not sure that I wouldn't care for a glass of water. I feel a little faint.

MOMMY. Grandma, go get Mrs. Barker a glass of water.

GRANDMA. Go get it yourself. I quit.

MOMMY. Grandma loves to do little things around the house; it gives her a false sense of security.

GRANDMA. I quit! I'm through!

MOMMY. Now, you be a good Grandma, or you know what will happen to you. You'll be taken away in a van.

GRANDMA. You don't frighten me. I'm too old to be frightened. Besides . . .

MOMMY. WELL! I'll tend to you later. I'll hide your teeth . . . I'll . . .

GRANDMA. Everything's hidden.

MRS. BARKER. I *am* going to faint. I *am.*

MOMMY. Good heavens! I'll go myself.

(As she exits, through the archway, stage-left)

I'll fix you, Grandma. I'll take care of you later.

(She exits)

GRANDMA. Oh, go soak your head.

(To MRS. BARKER*)*

Well, dearie, how do you feel?

MRS. BARKER. A little better, I think. Yes, much better, thank you, Grandma.

GRANDMA. That's good.

MRS. BARKER. But . . . I feel so lost . . . not knowing why I'm here . . . and, on top of it, they say I was here before.

GRANDMA. Well, you were. You weren't *here*, exactly, because we've moved around a lot, from one apartment to another, up and down the social ladder like mice, if you like similes.

MRS. BARKER. I don't . . . particularly.

GRANDMA. Well, then, I'm sorry.

MRS. BARKER *(Suddenly)*. Grandma, I feel I can trust you.

GRANDMA. Don't be too sure; it's every man for himself around this place. . . .

MRS. BARKER. Oh . . . is it? Nonetheless, I really do feel that I can trust you. *Please* tell me why they called and asked us to come. I implore you!

GRANDMA. Oh my; that feels good. It's been so long since anybody implored me. Do it again. Implore me some more.

MRS. BARKER. You're your daughter's mother, all right!

GRANDMA. Oh, I don't mean to be hard. If you won't implore me, then beg me, or ask me, or entreat me . . . just anything like that.

MRS. BARKER. You're a dreadful old woman!

GRANDMA. You'll understand some day. Please!

MRS. BARKER. Oh, for heaven's sake! . . . I implore you . . . I beg you . . . I beseech you!

GRANDMA. Beseech! Oh, that's the nicest word I've heard in ages. You're a dear, sweet woman. . . . You . . . beseech . . . me. I can't resist that.

MRS. BARKER. Well, then . . . please tell me why they asked us to come.

GRANDMA. Well, I'll give you a hint. That's the best I can do, because I'm a muddleheaded old woman. Now listen, because it's important. Once upon a time, not too very long ago, but a long enough time ago . . . oh, about twenty years ago . . . there was a man very much like Daddy, and a woman very much like Mommy, who were married to each other, very much like Mommy and Daddy are married to each other; and they lived in an apartment very much like one that's very much like this one, and they lived there with an old woman who was very much like yours truly, only younger, because it was some time ago; in fact, they were all somewhat younger.

MRS. BARKER. How fascinating!

GRANDMA. Now, at the same time, there was a dear lady very much like you, only younger then, who did all sorts of Good Works. . . . And

51

one of the Good Works this dear lady did was in something very much like a volunteer capacity for an organization very much like the Bye-Bye Adoption Service, which is nearby and which was run by a terribly deaf old lady very much like the Miss Bye-Bye who runs the Bye-Bye Adoption Service nearby.

MRS. BARKER. How enthralling!

GRANDMA. Well, be that as it may. Nonetheless, one afternoon this man, who was very much like Daddy, and this woman who was very much like Mommy came to see this dear lady who did all the Good Works, who was very much like you, dear, and they were very sad and very hopeful, and they cried and smiled and bit their fingers, and they said all the most intimate things.

MRS. BARKER. How spellbinding! What did they say?

GRANDMA. Well, it was very sweet. The woman, who was very much like Mommy, said that she and the man who was very much like Daddy had never been blessed with anything very much like a bumble of joy.

MRS. BARKER. A what?

GRANDMA. A bumble; a bumble of joy.

MRS. BARKER. Oh, like bundle.

GRANDMA. Well, yes; very much like it. Bundle, bumble; who cares? At any rate, the woman, who was very much like Mommy, said that they wanted a bumble of their own, but that the man, who was very much like Daddy, couldn't have a bumble; and the man, who was very much like Daddy, said that yes, they had wanted a bumble of their own, but that the woman, who was very much like Mommy, couldn't have one, and that now they wanted to buy something very much like a bumble.

MRS. BARKER. How engrossing!

GRANDMA. Yes. And the dear lady, who was very much like you, said something that was very much like, "Oh, what a shame; but take heart . . . I think we have just the bumble *for* you." And, well, the lady, who was very much like Mommy, and the man, who was very much like Daddy, cried and smiled and bit their fingers, and said some more intimate things, which were totally irrelevant but which were pretty hot stuff, and so the dear lady, who was very much like you, and who had something very much like a penchant for pornography, listened with something very much like enthusiasm. "Whee," she said. "Whoooopeeeeee!" But that's beside the point.

MRS. BARKER. I suppose *so*. But how gripping!

GRANDMA. Anyway . . . they *bought* something very much like a bumble, and they took it away with them. But . . . things didn't work out very well.

MRS. BARKER. You mean there was trouble?

GRANDMA. You got it.

(With a glance through the archway)

But, I'm going to have to speed up now because I think I'm leaving soon.

MRS. BARKER. Oh. Are you really?

GRANDMA. Yup.

MRS. BARKER. But old people don't go anywhere; they're either taken places, or put places.

GRANDMA. Well, this old person is different. Anyway . . . things started going badly.

MRS. BARKER. Oh yes. Yes.

GRANDMA. Weeeeellll . . . in the first place, it turned out the bumble didn't look like either one of its parents. That was enough of a blow, but things got worse. One night, it cried its heart out, if you can imagine such a thing.

MRS. BARKER. Cried its heart out! Well!

GRANDMA. But that was only the beginning. Then it turned out it only had eyes for its Daddy.

MRS. BARKER. For its Daddy! Why, any self-respecting woman would have gouged those eyes right out of its head.

GRANDMA. Well, she did. That's exactly what she did. But then, it kept its nose up in the air.

MRS. BARKER. Ufggh! How disgusting!

GRANDMA. That's what they thought. But *then*, it began to develop an interest in its you-know-what.

MRS. BARKER. In its you-know-what! Well! I hope they cut its hands off at the wrists!

GRANDMA. Well, yes, they did that eventually. But first, they cut off its you-know-what.

MRS. BARKER. A much better idea!

GRANDMA. That's what they thought. But after they cut off its you-know-what, it *still* put its hands under the covers, *looking* for its you-know-what. So, finally, they *had* to cut off its hands at the wrists.

MRS. BARKER. Naturally!

GRANDMA. And it was such a resentful bumble. Why, one day it called its Mommy a dirty name.

MRS. BARKER. Well, I hope they cut its tongue out!

GRANDMA. Of course. And then, as it got bigger, they found out all sorts of terrible things about it, like: it didn't have a head on its shoulders, it had no guts, it was spineless, its feet were made of clay . . . just dreadful things.

MRS. BARKER. Dreadful!

GRANDMA. So you can understand how they became discouraged.

MRS. BARKER. I certainly can! And what did they do?

GRANDMA. What did they do? Well, for the last straw, it finally up and died; and you can imagine how *that* made them feel, their having paid for it, and all. So, they called up the lady who sold them the bumble in the first place and told her to come right over to their apartment. They wanted satisfaction; they wanted their money back. That's what they wanted.

MRS. BARKER. My, my, my.

GRANDMA. How do you like *them* apples?

MRS. BARKER. My, my, my.

DADDY *(Off stage)*. Mommy! I can't find Grandma's television, and I can't find the Pekinese, either.

MOMMY *(Off stage)*. Isn't that funny! And I can't find the water.

GRANDMA. Heh, heh, heh. I told them everything was hidden.

MRS. BARKER. Did you hide the water, too?

GRANDMA *(Puzzled)*. No. No, I didn't do *that*.

DADDY *(Off stage)*. The truth of the matter is, I can't even find Grandma's room.

GRANDMA. Heh, heh, heh.

MRS. BARKER. My! You certainly did hide things, didn't you?

GRANDMA. Sure, kid, sure.

MOMMY *(Sticking her head in the room)*. Did you ever hear of such a thing, Grandma? Daddy can't find your television, and he can't find the Pekinese, and the truth of the matter is he can't even find your room.

GRANDMA. I told you. I hid everything.

MOMMY. Nonsense, Grandma! Just wait until I get my hands on you. You're a troublemaker . . . that's what you are.

GRANDMA. Well, I'll be out of here pretty soon, baby.

MOMMY. Oh, you don't know how right you are! Daddy's been wanting to send you away for a long time now, but I've been restraining him. I'll tell you one thing, though . . . I'm getting sick and tired of this fighting, and I might just let him have his way. Then you'll see what'll happen. Away you'll go; in a van, too. I'll let Daddy call the van man.

GRANDMA. I'm way ahead of you.

MOMMY. How can you be so old and so smug at the same time? You have no sense of proportion.

GRANDMA. You just answered your own question.

MOMMY. Mrs. Barker, I'd much rather you came into the kitchen for that glass of water, what with Grandma out here, and all.

MRS. BARKER. I don't see what Grandma has to do with it; and besides, I don't think you're very polite.

MOMMY. You seem to forget that you're a guest in this house . . .

GRANDMA. Apartment!

MOMMY. Apartment! And that you're a professional woman. So, if you'll be so good as to come into the kitchen, I'll be more than happy to show you where the water is, and where the glass is, and then you can put two and two together, if you're clever enough.

(She vanishes)

MRS. BARKER *(After a moment's consideration)*. I suppose she's right.

GRANDMA. Well, that's how it is when people call you up and ask you over to do something for them.

MRS. BARKER. I suppose you're right, too. Well, Grandma, it's been very nice talking to you.

GRANDMA. And I've enjoyed listening. Say, don't tell Mommy or Daddy that I gave you that hint, will you?

MRS. BARKER. Oh, dear me, the hint! I'd forgotten about it, if you can imagine such a thing. No, I won't breathe a word of it to them.

GRANDMA. I don't know if it helped you any . . .

MRS. BARKER. I can't tell, yet. I'll have to . . . what *is* the word I want? . . . I'll have to relate it . . . that's it . . . I'll have to relate it to certain things that I *know*, and . . . draw . . . conclusions. . . . What I'll really have to do is to see if it applies to anything. I mean, after all, I *do* do volunteer work for an adoption service, but it isn't very much *like* the Bye-Bye Adoption Service . . . it *is* the Bye-Bye Adoption Service . . . and while I can remember Mommy and Daddy coming to see me, oh, about twenty years ago, about buying a bumble, I can't quite remember anyone very much *like* Mommy and Daddy coming to see me about buying a bumble. Don't you see? It really presents quite a problem. . . . I'll have to think about it . . . mull it . . . but at any rate, it was truly first-class of you to try to help me. Oh, will you still be here after I've had my drink of water?

GRANDMA. Probably . . . I'm not as spry as I used to be.

MRS. BARKER. Oh. Well, I won't say good-by then.

GRANDMA. No. Don't.

(MRS. BARKER *exits through the archway*)

People don't say good-by to old people because they think they'll frighten them. Lordy! If they only knew how awful "hello" and "My, you're looking chipper" sounded, they wouldn't say those things either. The truth is, there isn't much you *can* say to old people that doesn't sound just terrible.

(The doorbell rings)

Come on in!

(The YOUNG MAN *enters*. GRANDMA *looks him over*)

Well, now, aren't you a breath of fresh air!

YOUNG MAN. Hello there.

GRANDMA. My, my, my. Are you the van man?

YOUNG MAN. The what?

GRANDMA. The van man. The van man. Are you coming to take me away?

YOUNG MAN. I don't know what you're talking about.

GRANDMA. Oh.

(Pause)

Well.

(Pause)

My, my, aren't you something!

YOUNG MAN. Hm?

GRANDMA. I said, my, my, aren't you something.

YOUNG MAN. Oh. Thank you.

GRANDMA. You don't sound very enthusiastic.

YOUNG MAN. Oh, I'm . . . I'm used to it.

GRANDMA. Yup . . . yup. You know, if I were about a hundred and fifty years younger I could go for you.

YOUNG MAN. Yes, I imagine so.

GRANDMA. Unh-hunh . . . will you look at those muscles!

YOUNG MAN (Flexing his muscles). Yes, they're quite good, aren't they?

GRANDMA. Boy, they sure are. They natural?

YOUNG MAN. Well the basic structure was there, but I've done some work, too . . . you know, in a gym.

GRANDMA. I'll bet you have. You ought to be in the movies, boy.

YOUNG MAN. I know.

GRANDMA. Yup! Right up there on the old silver screen. But I suppose you've heard that before.

YOUNG MAN. Yes, I have.

GRANDMA. You ought to try out for them . . . the movies.

YOUNG MAN. Well, actually, I may have a career there yet. I've lived out on the West Coast almost all my life . . . and I've met a few people who . . . might be able to help me. I'm not in too much of a hurry, though. I'm almost as young as I look.

GRANDMA. Oh, that's nice. And will you look at that face!

YOUNG MAN. Yes, it's quite good, isn't it? Clean-cut, midwest farm boy type, almost insultingly good-looking in a typically American way. Good profile, straight nose, honest eyes, wonderful smile . . .

GRANDMA. Yup. Boy, you know what you are, don't you? You're the American Dream, that's what you are. All those other people, they don't know what they're talking about. You . . . *you* are the American Dream.

YOUNG MAN. Thanks.

MOMMY *(Off stage)*. Who rang the doorbell?

GRANDMA *(Shouting off-stage)*. The American Dream!

MOMMY *(Off stage)*. What? What was that, Grandma?

GRANDMA *(Shouting)*. The American Dream! The American Dream! Damn it!

DADDY *(Off stage)*. How's that, Mommy?

MOMMY *(Off stage)*. Oh, some gibberish; pay no attention. Did you find Grandma's room?

DADDY *(Off stage)*. No. I can't even find Mrs. Barker.

YOUNG MAN. What was all that?

GRANDMA. Oh, that was just the folks, but let's not talk about them, honey; let's talk about you.

YOUNG MAN. All right.

GRANDMA. Well, let's see. If you're not the van man, what are you doing here?

YOUNG MAN. I'm looking for work.

GRANDMA. Are you! Well, what kind of work?

YOUNG MAN. Oh, almost anything . . . almost anything that pays. I'll do almost anything for money.

GRANDMA. Will you . . . will you? Hmmmm. I wonder if there's anything you could do around here?

YOUNG MAN. There might be. It looked to be a likely building.

GRANDMA. It's always looked to be a rather unlikely building to me, but I suppose you'd know better than I.

YOUNG MAN. I can sense these things.

GRANDMA. There *might* be something you could do around here. Stay there! Don't come any closer.

YOUNG MAN. Sorry.

GRANDMA. I don't mean I'd *mind*. I don't know whether I'd mind, or not. . . . But it wouldn't look well; it would look just *awful*.

YOUNG MAN. Yes; I suppose so.

GRANDMA. Now, stay there, let me concentrate. What could you do? The folks have been in something of a quandary around here today, sort of a dilemma, and I wonder if you mightn't be some help.

YOUNG MAN. I hope so . . . if there's money in it. Do you have any money?

GRANDMA. Money! Oh, there's more money around here than you'd know what to do with.

YOUNG MAN. I'm not so sure.

GRANDMA. Well, maybe not. Besides, I've got money of my own.

YOUNG MAN. You have?

GRANDMA. Sure. Old people quite often have lots of money; more often than most people expect. Come here, so I can whisper to you . . . not too close. I might faint.

YOUNG MAN. Oh, I'm sorry.

GRANDMA. It's all right, dear. Anyway . . . have you ever heard of that big baking contest they run? The one where all the ladies get together in a big barn and bake away?

YOUNG MAN. I'm . . . not . . . sure. . . .

GRANDMA. Not so close. Well, it doesn't matter whether you've heard of it or not. The important thing is—and I don't want anybody to hear this . . . the folks think I haven't been out of the house in eight years—the important thing is that I won first prize in that baking contest this year. Oh, it was in all the papers; not under my own name, though. I used a *nom de boulangère;* I called myself Uncle Henry.

YOUNG MAN. Did you?

GRANDMA. Why not? I didn't see any reason not to. I look just as much like an old man as I do like an old woman. And you know what I called it . . . what I won for?

YOUNG MAN. No. What did you call it?

GRANDMA. I called it Uncle Henry's Day-Old Cake.

YOUNG MAN. That's a very nice name.

GRANDMA. And it wasn't any trouble, either. All I did was go out and get a store-bought cake, and keep it around for a while, and then slip it in, unbeknownst to anybody. Simple.

YOUNG MAN. You're a very resourceful person.

GRANDMA. Pioneer stock.

YOUNG MAN. Is all this true? Do you want me to believe all this?

GRANDMA. Well, you can believe it or not . . . it doesn't make any difference to me. All *I* know is, Uncle Henry's Day-Old Cake won me twenty-five thousand smackerolas.

YOUNG MAN. Twenty-five thou—

GRANDMA. Right on the old loggerhead. Now . . . how do you like them apples?

YOUNG MAN. Love 'em.

GRANDMA. I thought you'd be impressed.

YOUNG MAN. Money talks.

GRANDMA. Hey! You look familiar.

YOUNG MAN. Hm? Pardon?

GRANDMA. I said, you look familiar.

YOUNG MAN. Well, I've done some modeling.

GRANDMA. No . . . no. I don't mean that. You look familiar.

YOUNG MAN. Well, I'm a type.

GRANDMA. Yup; you sure are. Why do you say you'd do anything for money . . . if you don't mind my being nosy?

YOUNG MAN. No, no. It's part of the interviews. I'll be happy to tell you. It's that I have no talents at all, except what you see . . . my person; my body, my face. In every other way I am incomplete, and I must therefore . . . compensate.

GRANDMA. What do you mean, incomplete? You look pretty complete to me.

YOUNG MAN. I think I can explain it to you, partially because you're very old, and very old people have perceptions they keep to themselves, because if they expose them to other people . . . well, you know what ridicule and neglect are.

GRANDMA. I do, child, I do.

YOUNG MAN. Then listen. My mother died the night that I was born, and I never knew my father; I doubt my mother did. But, I wasn't alone, because lying with me . . . in the placenta . . . there was someone else . . . my brother . . . my twin.

GRANDMA. Oh, my child.

YOUNG MAN. We were identical twins . . . he and I . . . not fraternal . . . identical; we were derived from the same ovum; and in *this,* in that we were twins not from separate ova but from the same one, we had a kinship such as you cannot imagine. We . . . we felt each other breathe . . . his heartbeats thundered in my temples . . . mine in his . . . our stomachs ached and we cried for feeding at the same time . . . are you old enough to understand?

GRANDMA. I think so, child; I think I'm nearly old enough.

YOUNG MAN. I hope so. But we were separated when we were still very young, my brother, my twin and I . . . inasmuch as you can separate one being. We were torn apart . . . thrown to opposite ends of the continent. I don't know what became of my brother . . . to the rest of myself . . . except that, from time to time, in the years that have passed, I have suffered losses . . . that I can't explain. A fall from grace . . . a departure of innocence . . . loss . . . loss. How can I put it to you? All right; like this: Once . . . it was as if all at once my heart . . . became numb . . . almost as though I . . . almost as though . . . just like that . . . it had been wrenched from my body . . . and from that time I have been unable to love. Once . . . I was asleep at the time . . . I awoke, and my eyes were burning. And since that time I have been unable to see anything, *anything,* with pity, with affection . . . with anything but . . . cool disinterest. And my groin . . . even there . . . since one time . . . one specific agony . . . since then I have not been able to *love* anyone with my body. And even my hands . . . I cannot touch another person and feel love. And there is more . . . there are more losses, but it all comes down to this: I no longer have the capacity to feel anything. I have no emotions. I have been drained, torn asunder . . . disemboweled. I have, now, only my person . . . my body, my face. I use what I have . . . I let people love me . . . I accept the syntax around me, for while I know I cannot

60

relate . . . I know I must be related *to*. I let people love me . . . I let
people touch me . . . I let them draw pleasure from my groin . . .
from my presence . . . from the fact of me . . . but, that is all it
comes to. As I told you, I am incomplete . . . I can feel nothing. I can
feel nothing. And so . . . here I am . . . as you see me. I am . . .
but this . . . what you see. And it will always be thus.

GRANDMA. Oh, my child; my child.

(Long pause; then)

I was mistaken . . . before. I don't know you from somewhere, but I
knew . . . once . . . someone very much like you . . . or, very
much as perhaps you were.

YOUNG MAN. Be careful; be very careful. What I have told you may not be
true. In my profession . . .

GRANDMA. Shhhhhh.

(The YOUNG MAN *bows his head, in acquiescence)*

Someone . . . to be more precise . . . who might have turned out to
be very much like you might have turned out to be. And . . . unless
I'm terribly mistaken . . . you've found yourself a job.

YOUNG MAN. What are my duties?

MRS. BARKER *(Off stage)*. Yoo-hoo! Yoo-hoo!

GRANDMA. Oh-oh. You'll . . . you'll have to play it by ear, my dear . . .
unless I get a chance to talk to you again. I've got to go into my act,
now.

YOUNG MAN. But, I . . .

GRANDMA. Yoo-hoo!

MRS. BARKER *(Coming through archway)*. Yoo-hoo . . . . oh, there you
are, Grandma. I'm glad to see somebody. I can't find Mommy or
Daddy.

(Double takes)

Well . . . who's this?

GRANDMA. This? Well . . . un . . . oh, this is the . . . uh . . . the
van man. That's who it is . . . the van man.

MRS. BARKER. So! It's true! They *did* call the van man. They *are* having
you carted away.

GRANDMA *(Shrugging)*. Well, you know. It figures.

MRS. BARKER *(To* YOUNG MAN*)*. How dare you cart this poor old woman
away!

YOUNG MAN *(After a quick look at* GRANDMA, *who nods)*. I do what I'm paid to do. I don't ask any questions.

MRS. BARKER *(After a brief pause)*. Oh.

(Pause)

Well, you're quite right, of course, and I shouldn't meddle.

GRANDMA *(To* YOUNG MAN). Dear, will you take my things out to the van?

(She points to the boxes)

YOUNG MAN *(After only the briefest hesitation)*. Why certainly.

GRANDMA *(As the* YOUNG MAN *takes up half the boxes, exits by the front door)*. Isn't that a nice young van man?

MRS. BARKER *(Shaking her head in disbelief, watching the* YOUNG MAN *exit)*. Unh-hunh . . . some things have changed for the better. I remember when I had *my* mother carted off . . . the van man who came for her wasn't anything near as nice as this one.

GRANDMA. Oh, did you have your mother carted off, too?

MRS. BARKER *(Cheerfully)*. Why certainly! Didn't you?

GRANDMA *(Puzzling)*. No . . . no, I didn't. At least, I can't remember. Listen dear; I got to talk to you for a second.

MRS. BARKER. Why certainly, Grandma.

GRANDMA. Now, listen.

MRS. BARKER. Yes, Grandma. Yes.

GRANDMA. Now listen carefully. You got this dilemma here with Mommy and Daddy . . .

MRS. BARKER. Yes! I wonder where they've gone to?

GRANDMA. They'll be back in. Now, LISTEN!

MRS. BARKER. Oh, I'm sorry.

GRANDMA. Now, you got this dilemma here with Mommy and Daddy, and I think I got the way out for you.

(The YOUNG MAN *re-enters through the front door)*

Will you take the rest of my things out now, dear?

(To MRS. BARKER, *while the* YOUNG MAN *takes the rest of the boxes, exits again by the front door)*

Fine. Now listen, dear.

(She begins to whisper in MRS. BARKER's *ear)*

MRS. BARKER. Oh! Oh! Oh! I don't think I could . . . do you really think I could? Well, why not? What a wonderful idea . . . what an absolutely wonderful idea!

GRANDMA. Well, yes, I thought it was.

MRS. BARKER. And you so old!

GRANDMA. Heh, heh, heh.

MRS. BARKER. Well, I think it's absolutely marvelous, anyway. I'm going to find Mommy and Daddy right now.

GRANDMA. Good. You do that.

MRS. BARKER. Well, now. I think I will say good-by. I can't thank you enough.

(She starts to exit through the archway)

GRANDMA. You're welcome. Say it!

MRS. BARKER. Huh? What?

GRANDMA. Say good-by.

MRS. BARKER. Oh. Good-by.

(She exits)

Mommy! I say, Mommy! Daddy!

GRANDMA. Good-by.

(By herself now, she looks about)

Ah me.

(Shakes her head)

Ah me.

(Takes in the room)

Good-by.

(The YOUNG MAN *re-enters)*

GRANDMA. Oh, hello, there.

YOUNG MAN. All the boxes are outside.

GRANDMA *(A little sadly)*. I don't know why I bother to take them with me. They don't have much in them . . . some old letters, a couple of regrets . . . Pekinese . . . blind at that . . . the television . . . my Sunday teeth . . . eighty-six years of living . . . some sounds . . . a few images, a little garbled by now . . . and, well . . .

(She shrugs)

. . . you know . . . the things one accumulates.

YOUNG MAN. Can I get you . . . a cab, or something?

GRANDMA. Oh no, dear . . . thank you just the same. I'll take it from here.

YOUNG MAN. And what shall I do now?

GRANDMA. Oh, you stay here, dear. It will all become clear to you. It will be explained. You'll understand.

YOUNG MAN. Very well.

GRANDMA *(After one more look about).* Well . . .

YOUNG MAN. Let me see you to the elevator.

GRANDMA. Oh . . . that *would* be nice, dear.

(They both exit by the front door, slowly)

(Enter MRS. BARKER, *followed by* MOMMY *and* DADDY)

MRS. BARKER. . . . and I'm happy to tell you that the whole thing's set-tled. Just like that.

MOMMY. Oh, we're so glad. We were afraid there might be a problem, what with delays, and all.

DADDY. Yes, we're very relieved.

MRS. BARKER. Well, now; that's what professional women are for.

MOMMY. Why . . . where's Grandma? Grandma's not here! Where's Grandma? And look! The boxes are gone, too. Grandma's gone, and so are the boxes. She's taken off, and she's stolen something! Daddy!

MRS. BARKER. Why, Mommy, the van man was here.

MOMMY *(Startled).* The what?

MRS. BARKER. The van man. The van man was here.

(The lights might dim a little, suddenly)

MOMMY *(Shakes her head).* No, that's impossible.

MRS. BARKER. Why, I saw him with my own two eyes.

MOMMY *(Near tears).* No, no, that's impossible. No. There's no such thing as the van man. There is no van man. We . . . we made him up. Grandma? Grandma?

DADDY *(Moving to* MOMMY). There, there, now.

MOMMY. Oh Daddy . . . where's Grandma?

DADDY. There, there, now.

(While DADDY *is comforting* MOMMY, GRANDMA *comes out, stage right, near the footlights)*

GRANDMA *(To the audience).* Shhhhhh! I want to watch this.

(She motions to MRS. BARKER *who, with a secret smile, tiptoes to the front door and opens it. The* YOUNG MAN *is framed therein. Lights up full again as he steps into the room)*

MRS. BARKER. Surprise! Surprise! Here we are!

MOMMY. What? What?

DADDY. Hm? What?

MOMMY *(Her tears merely sniffles now).* What surprise?

MRS. BARKER. Why, I told you. The surprise I told you about.

DADDY. You . . . you know, Mommy.

64

MOMMY. Sur . . . prise?

DADDY *(Urging her to cheerfulness)*. You remember, Mommy; why we asked . . . uh . . . what's-her-name to come here?

MRS. BARKER. Mrs. Barker, if you don't mind.

DADDY. Yes. Mommy? You remember now? About the bumble . . . about wanting satisfaction?

MOMMY *(Her sorrow turning into delight)*. Yes. Why yes! Of course! Yes! Oh, how wonderful!

MRS. BARKER *(To the* YOUNG MAN*)*. This is Mommy.

YOUNG MAN. How . . . how do you do?

MRS. BARKER *(Stage whisper)*. Her name's Mommy.

YOUNG MAN. How . . . how do you do, Mommy?

MOMMY. Well! Hello there!

MRS. BARKER *(To the* YOUNG MAN*)*. And that is Daddy.

YOUNG MAN. How do you do, sir?

DADDY. How do you do?

MOMMY *(Herself again, circling the* YOUNG MAN, *feeling his arm, poking him)*. Yes, sir! Yes, sirree! Now this is more like it. Now this is a great deal more like it! Daddy! Come see. Come see if this isn't a great deal more like it.

DADDY. I . . . I can see from here, Mommy. It does look a great deal more like it.

MOMMY. Yes, sir. Yes sirree! Mrs. Barker, I don't know *how* to thank you.

MRS. BARKER. Oh, don't worry about that. I'll send you a bill in the mail.

MOMMY. What this really calls for is a celebration. It calls for a drink.

MRS. BARKER. Oh, what a nice idea.

MOMMY. There's some sauterne in the kitchen.

YOUNG MAN. I'll go.

MOMMY. Will you? Oh, how nice. The kitchen's through the archway there.

(As the YOUNG MAN *exits: to* MRS. BARKER*)*

He's very nice. Really top notch; much better than the other one.

MRS. BARKER. I'm glad you're pleased. And I'm glad everything's all straightened out.

MOMMY. Well, at least we know why we sent for you. We're glad that's cleared up. By the way, what's his name?

MRS. BARKER. Ha! Call him whatever you like. He's yours. Call him what you called the other one.

MOMMY. Daddy? What did we call the other one?

DADDY *(Puzzles)*. Why . . . .

YOUNG MAN *(Re-entering with a tray on which are a bottle of sauterne and five glasses)*. Here we are!

MOMMY. Hooray! Hooray!

MRS. BARKER. Oh, good!

MOMMY *(Moving to the tray)*. So, let's— Five glasses? Why five? There are only four of us. Why five?

YOUNG MAN *(Catches GRANDMA's eye; GRANDMA indicates she is not there)*. Oh, I'm sorry.

MOMMY. You must learn to count. We're a wealthy family, and you must learn to count.

YOUNG MAN. I will.

MOMMY. Well, everybody take a glass.
(They do)
And we'll drink to celebrate. To satisfaction! Who says you can't get satisfaction these days!

MRS. BARKER. What dreadful sauterne!

MOMMY. Yes, isn't it?
(To YOUNG MAN, her voice already a little fuzzy from the wine)
You don't know how happy I am to see you! Yes sirree. Listen, that time we had with . . . with the other one. I'll tell you about it some time.
(Indicates MRS. BARKER)
After she's gone. She was responsible for all the trouble in the first place. I'll tell you all about it.
(Sidles up to him a little)
Maybe . . . maybe later tonight.

YOUNG MAN *(Not moving away)*. Why yes. That would be very nice.

MOMMY *(Puzzles)*. Something familiar about you . . . you know that? I can't quite place it. . . .

GRANDMA *(Interrupting . . . to audience)*. Well, I guess that just about wraps it up. I mean, for better or worse, this is a comedy, and I don't think we'd better go any further. No, definitely not. So, let's leave things as they are right now . . . while everybody's happy . . . while everybody's got what he wants . . . or everybody's got what he thinks he wants. Good night, dears.

CURTAIN

66

WHO'S AFRAID
OF
VIRGINIA WOOLF?
A Play in Three Acts (1961–1962)

For
Richard Barr
and
Clinton Wilder

FIRST PERFORMANCE
October 13, 1962, New York City, Billy Rose Theatre

UTA HAGEN *as* MARTHA

ARTHUR HILL *as* GEORGE

GEORGE GRIZZARD *as* NICK

MELINDA DILLON *as* HONEY

Directed by ALAN SCHNEIDER

The Players

MARTHA: A large, boisterous woman, 52, looking somewhat younger. Ample, but not fleshy.
GEORGE: Her husband, 46. Thin; hair going gray.
HONEY: 26, a petite blond girl, rather plain.
NICK: 30, her husband. Blond, well put-together, good-looking.

The Scene

The living room of a house on the campus of a small New England college..

ACT ONE
Fun and Games

(Set in darkness. Crash against front door. MARTHA'S *laughter heard. Front door opens, lights are switched on.* MARTHA *enters, followed by* GEORGE*)*

MARTHA. *Jesus.* . . .

GEORGE. . . . Shhhhhhh. . . .

MARTHA. . . . H. Christ. . . .

GEORGE. For God's sake, Martha, it's two o'clock in the. . . .

MARTHA. Oh, George!

GEORGE. Well, I'm *sorry*, but. . . .

MARTHA. What a cluck! What a cluck you are.

GEORGE. It's late, you know? Late.

MARTHA. *(Looks about the room. Imitates Bette Davis).* What a dump. Hey, what's that from? "What a dump!"

GEORGE. How would I know what. . . .

MARTHA. Aw, come on! What's it from? *You* know. . . .

GEORGE. . . . Martha. . . .

MARTHA. WHAT'S IT FROM, FOR CHRIST'S SAKE?

GEORGE *(Wearily).* What's what from?

MARTHA. I just told you; I just did it. "What a dump!" Hunh? What's that from?

GEORGE. I haven't the faintest idea what. . . .

MARTHA. Dumbbell! It's from some goddamn Bette Davis picture . . . some goddamn Warner Brothers epic. . . .

GEORGE. *I* can't remember all the pictures that. . . .

MARTHA. Nobody's asking you to remember every single goddamn Warner Brothers epic . . . just one! One single little epic! Bette Davis gets peritonitis in the end . . . she's got this big black fright wig she wears all through the picture and she gets peritonitis, and she's married to Joseph Cotten or something. . . .

GEORGE. . . . Some*body*. . . .

MARTHA. . . . some*body* . . . and she wants to go to Chicago all the time, 'cause she's in love with that actor with the scar. . . . But she gets sick, and she sits down in front of her dressing table. . . .

GEORGE. What actor? What scar?

MARTHA. *I* can't remember his name, for God's sake. What's the name of

71

the *picture?* I want to know what the name of the *picture* is. She sits down in front of her dressing table . . . and she's got this peritonitis . . . and she tries to put her lipstick on, but she can't . . . and she gets it all over her face . . . but she decides to go to Chicago anyway, and. . . .

GEORGE. *Chicago!* It's called *Chicago.*

MARTHA. Hunh? What . . . what is?

GEORGE. The picture . . . it's called *Chicago.* . . .

MARTHA. Good grief! Don't you know *anything? Chicago* was a 'thirties musical, starring little Miss Alice *Faye.* Don't you know *anything?*

GEORGE. Well, that was probably before my *time,* but. . . .

MARTHA. Can it! Just cut that out! This picture . . . Bette Davis comes home from a hard day at the grocery store. . . .

GEORGE. She works in a grocery store?

MARTHA. She's a housewife; she buys things . . . and she comes home with the groceries, and she walks into the modest living room of the modest cottage modest Joseph Cotten has set her up in. . . .

GEORGE. Are they married?

MARTHA *(Impatiently).* Yes. They're married. To each other. Cluck! And she comes in, and she looks around, and she puts her groceries down, and she says, "What a dump!"

GEORGE *(Pause).* Oh.

MARTHA *(Pause).* She's discontent.

GEORGE *(Pause).* Oh.

MARTHA *(Pause).* Well, what's the name of the picture?

GEORGE. I really don't know, Martha. . . .

MARTHA. Well, think!

GEORGE. I'm tired, dear . . . it's late . . . and besides. . . .

MARTHA. I don't know what you're so tired about . . . you haven't *done* anything all day; you didn't have any classes, or anything. . . .

GEORGE. Well, I'm tired. . . . If your father didn't set up these goddamn Saturday night orgies all the time. . . .

MARTHA. Well, that's too bad about you, George. . . .

GEORGE *(Grumbling).* Well, that's how it is, anyway.

MARTHA. You didn't *do* anything; you never *do* anything; you never *mix.* You just sit around and *talk.*

GEORGE. What do you want me to do? Do you want me to act like you?

Do you want me to go around all night *braying* at everybody, the way you do?

MARTHA *(Braying)*. I DON'T BRAY!

GEORGE *(Softly)*. All right . . . you don't bray.

MARTHA *(Hurt)*. I do not *bray*.

GEORGE. All right. I said you didn't bray.

MARTHA *(Pouting)*. Make me a drink.

GEORGE. What?

MARTHA *(Still softly)*. I said, make me a drink.

GEORGE *(Moving to the portable bar)*. Well, I don't suppose a nightcap'd kill either one of us. . . .

MARTHA. A nightcap! Are you kidding? We've got guests.

GEORGE *(Disbelieving)*. We've got what?

MARTHA. Guests. GUESTS.

GEORGE. GUESTS!

MARTHA. Yes . . . guests . . . people. . . . We've got guests coming over.

GEORGE. When?

MARTHA. NOW!

GEORGE. Good Lord, Martha . . . do you know what time it. . . . *Who's* coming over?

MARTHA. What's-their-name.

GEORGE. Who?

MARTHA. WHAT'S-THEIR-NAME!

GEORGE. Who what's-their-name?

MARTHA. I don't know what their name is, George. . . . You met them tonight . . . they're new . . . he's in the math department, or something. . . .

GEORGE. Who . . . who are these people?

MARTHA. You met them tonight, George.

GEORGE. I don't remember meeting anyone tonight. . . .

MARTHA. Well you did . . . Will you give me my drink, please. . . . He's in the math department . . . about thirty, blond, and. . . .

GEORGE. . . . and good-looking. . . .

MARTHA. Yes . . . and good-looking. . . .

GEORGE. It figures.

MARTHA. . . . and his wife's a mousey little type, without any hips, or anything.

73

GEORGE *(Vaguely)*. Oh.

MARTHA. You remember them now?

GEORGE. Yes, I guess so, Martha. . . . But why in God's name are they coming over here now?

MARTHA *(In a so-there voice)*. Because Daddy said we should be nice to them, that's why.

GEORGE *(Defeated)*. Oh, Lord.

MARTHA. May I have my drink, please? Daddy said we should be nice to them. Thank you.

GEORGE. But why now? It's after two o'clock in the morning, and. . . .

MARTHA. Because Daddy said we should be nice to them!

GEORGE. Yes. But I'm sure your father didn't mean we were supposed to stay up all *night* with these people. I mean, we could have them over some Sunday or something. . . .

MARTHA. Well, never mind. . . . Besides, it *is* Sunday. Very early Sunday.

GEORGE. I mean . . . it's ridiculous. . . .

MARTHA. Well, it's *done!*

GEORGE *(Resigned and exasperated)*. All right. Well . . . where are they? If we've got guests where are they?

MARTHA. They'll be here soon.

GEORGE. What did they do . . . go home and get some sleep first, or something?

MARTHA. They'll *be* here!

GEORGE. I wish you'd *tell* me about something sometime. . . . I wish you'd stop *springing* things on me all the time.

MARTHA. I don't *spring* things on you all the time.

GEORGE. Yes, you do . . . you really do . . . you're always *springing* things on me.

MARTHA *(Friendly-patronizing)*. Oh, George!

GEORGE. Always.

MARTHA. Poor Georgie-Porgie, put-upon pie! *(As he sulks)* Awwwwww . . . what are you doing? Are you sulking? Hunh? Let me see . . . are you sulking? Is that what you're doing?

GEORGE *(Very quietly)*. Never mind, Martha. . . .

MARTHA. AWWWWWWWWWW!

GEORGE. Just don't bother yourself. . . .

MARTHA. AWWWWWWWWWW! *(No reaction)* Hey! *(No reaction)* HEY!

   (GEORGE looks at her, put-upon)

Hey. *(She sings)* Who's afraid of Virginia Woolf,
                    Virginia Woolf,
                    Virginia Woolf. . . .

Ha, ha, ha, HA! *(No reaction)* What's the matter . . . didn't you think that was funny? Hunh? *(Defiantly)* I thought it was a scream . . . a real scream. You didn't like it, hunh?

GEORGE. It was all right, Martha. . . .

MARTHA. You laughed your head off when you heard it at the party.

GEORGE. I smiled. I didn't laugh my head off . . . I smiled, you know? . . . it was all right.

MARTHA *(Gazing into her drink)*. You laughed your goddamn head off.

GEORGE. It was all right. . . .

MARTHA *(Ugly)*. It was a scream!

GEORGE *(Patiently)*. It was very funny; yes.

MARTHA *(After a moment's consideration)*. You make me puke!

GEORGE. What?

MARTHA. Uh . . . you make me puke!

GEORGE *(Thinks about it . . . then . . .)*. That wasn't a very nice thing to say, Martha.

MARTHA. That wasn't *what?*

GEORGE. . . . a very nice thing to say.

MARTHA. I like your anger. I think that's what I like about you most . . . your anger. You're such a . . . such a simp! You don't even have the . . . the what? . . .

GEORGE. . . . guts? . . .

MARTHA. PHRASEMAKER! *(Pause . . . then they both laugh)* Hey, put some more ice in my drink, will you? You never put any ice in my drink. Why is that, hunh?

GEORGE *(Takes her drink)*. I always put ice in your drink. You eat it, that's all. It's that habit you have . . . chewing your ice cubes . . . like a cocker spaniel. You'll crack your big teeth.

MARTHA. THEY'RE MY BIG TEETH!

GEORGE. Some of them . . . some of them.

MARTHA. I've got more teeth than you've got.

GEORGE. Two more.

MARTHA. Well, two more's a lot more.

GEORGE. I suppose it is. I suppose it's pretty remarkable . . . considering how old you are.

MARTHA. YOU CUT THAT OUT! *(Pause)* You're not so young yourself.

GEORGE *(With boyish pleasure . . . a chant)*. I'm six years younger than you are. . . . I always have been and I always will be.

MARTHA *(Glumly)*. Well . . . you're going bald.

GEORGE. So are you. *(Pause . . . they both laugh)* Hello, honey.

MARTHA. Hello. C'mon over here and give your Mommy a big sloppy kiss.

GEORGE. . . . oh, now. . . .

MARTHA. I WANT A BIG SLOPPY KISS!

GEORGE *(Preoccupied)*. I don't *want* to kiss you, Martha. Where *are* these people? Where are these *people* you invited over?

MARTHA. They stayed on to talk to Daddy. . . . They'll be here. . . . *Why* don't you want to kiss me?

GEORGE *(Too matter-of-fact)*. Well, dear, if I kissed you I'd get all excited . . . I'd get beside myself, and I'd take you, by force, right here on the living room rug, and then our little guests would walk in, and . . . well, just think what your father would say about *that*.

MARTHA. You pig!

GEORGE *(Haughtily)*. Oink! Oink!

MARTHA. Ha, ha, ha, HA! Make me another drink . . . lover.

GEORGE *(Taking her glass)*. My God, you can swill it down, can't you?

MARTHA *(Imitating a tiny child)*. I'm firsty.

GEORGE. Jesus!

MARTHA *(Swinging around)*. Look, sweetheart, I can drink you under any goddamn table you want . . . so don't worry about me!

GEORGE. Martha, I gave you the prize years ago. . . . There isn't an abomination award going that you. . . .

MARTHA. I swear . . . if you existed I'd divorce you. . . .

GEORGE. Well, just stay on your feet, that's all. . . . These people are your guests, you know, and. . . .

MARTHA. I can't even see you . . . I haven't been able to see you for years. . . .

GEORGE. . . . if you pass out, or throw up, or something. . . .

MARTHA. . . . I mean, you're a blank, a cipher. . . .

GEORGE. . . . and try to keep your clothes on, too. There aren't many more sickening sights than you with a couple of drinks in you and your skirt up over your head, you know. . . .

MARTHA. . . . a zero. . . .

GEORGE. . . . your *heads*, I should say. . . .

(The front doorbell chimes)

MARTHA. Party! Party!

GEORGE *(Murderously)*. I'm really looking forward to this, Martha. . . .

MARTHA *(Same)*. Go answer the door.

GEORGE *(Not moving)*. You answer it.

MARTHA. Get to that door, you.

(He does not move)

I'll fix you, you. . . .

GEORGE *(Fake-spits)*. . . . to you. . . .

(Door chime again)

MARTHA *(Shouting . . . to the door)*. C'MON IN! *(To* GEORGE, *between her teeth)* I said, get over there!

GEORGE *(Moves a little toward the door, smiling slightly)*. All right, love . . . whatever love wants. *(Stops)* Just don't start on the bit, that's all.

MARTHA. The bit? The bit? What kind of language is that? What are you talking about?

GEORGE. The bit. Just don't start in on the bit.

MARTHA. You imitating one of your students, for God's sake? What are you trying to do? WHAT BIT?

GEORGE. Just don't start in on the bit about the kid, that's all.

MARTHA. What do you take me for?

GEORGE. Much too much.

MARTHA *(Really angered)*. Yeah? Well, I'll start in on the kid if I want to.

GEORGE. Just leave the kid out of this.

MARTHA *(Threatening)*. He's mine as much as he is yours. I'll talk about him if I want to.

GEORGE. I'd advise against it, Martha.

MARTHA. Well, good for you. *(Knock)* C'mon in. Get over there and open the door!

GEORGE. You've been advised.

MARTHA. Yeah . . . sure. Get over there!

GEORGE *(Moving toward the door)*. All right, love . . . whatever love wants. Isn't it nice the way some people have manners, though, even in this day and age? Isn't it nice that some people won't just come breaking into other people's houses even if they *do* hear some subhuman monster yowling at 'em from inside . . . ?

MARTHA. SCREW YOU!

(Simultaneously with MARTHA's *last remark,* GEORGE *flings open the*

front door. HONEY *and* NICK *are framed in the entrance. There is a
brief silence, then. . . .)*

GEORGE *(Ostensibly a pleased recognition of* HONEY *and* NICK, *but really
satisfaction at having* MARTHA's *explosion overheard).* Ahhhhhhhhh!

MARTHA *(A little too loud . . . to cover).* HI! Hi, there . . . c'mon in!

HONEY *and* NICK *(ad lib).* Hello, here we are . . . hi . . . *etc.*

GEORGE *(Very matter-of-factly).* You must be our little guests.

MARTHA. Ha, ha, ha, HA! Just ignore old sour-puss over there. C'mon in,
kids . . . give your coats and stuff to sour-puss.

NICK *(Without expression).* Well, now, perhaps we shouldn't have
come. . . .

HONEY. Yes . . . it *is* late, and. . . .

MARTHA. Late! Are you kidding? Throw your stuff down anywhere and
c'mon in.

GEORGE *(Vaguely . . . walking away).* Anywhere . . . furniture, floor
. . . doesn't make any difference around this place.

NICK *(To* HONEY). I told you we shouldn't have come.

MARTHA *(Stentorian).* I said c'mon in! Now c'mon!

HONEY *(Giggling a little as she and* NICK *advance).* Oh, dear.

GEORGE *(Imitating* HONEY's *giggle).* Hee, hee, hee, hee.

MARTHA *(Swinging on* GEORGE). Look, muckmouth . . . you cut that out!

GEORGE *(Innocence and hurt).* Martha! *(To* HONEY *and* NICK) Martha's a
devil with language; she really is.

MARTHA. Hey, *kids* . . . sit down.

HONEY *(As she sits).* Oh, isn't this lovely!

NICK *(Perfunctorily).* Yes indeed . . . very handsome.

MARTHA. Well, thanks.

NICK *(Indicating the abstract painting).* Who . . . who did the . . . ?

MARTHA. That? Oh, that's by. . . .

GEORGE. . . . some Greek with a mustache Martha attacked one night
in. . . .

HONEY *(To save the situation).* Oh, ho, ho, ho, HO.

NICK. It's got a . . . a. . . .

GEORGE. A quiet intensity?

NICK. Well, no . . . a. . . .

GEORGE. Oh. *(Pause)* Well, then, a certain noisy relaxed quality, maybe?

NICK *(Knows what* GEORGE *is doing, but stays grimly, coolly polite).* No.
What I meant was. . . .

GEORGE. How about . . . uh . . . a quietly noisy relaxed intensity.
HONEY. Dear! You're being joshed.
NICK *(Cold)*. I'm aware of that.
(A brief, awkward silence)
GEORGE *(Truly)*. I *am* sorry.
(NICK *nods condescending forgiveness)*
GEORGE. What it is, actually, is it's a pictorial representation of the order of Martha's mind.
MARTHA. Ha, ha, ha, HA! Make the kids a drink, George. What do you want, kids? What do you want to drink, hunh?
NICK. Honey? What would you like?
HONEY. I don't know, dear . . . A little brandy, maybe. "Never mix— never worry." *(She giggles)*
GEORGE. Brandy? Just brandy? Simple; simple. *(Moves to the portable bar)* What about you . . . uh. . . .
NICK. Bourbon on the rocks, if you don't mind.
GEORGE *(As he makes drinks)*. Mind? No, I don't mind. I don't think I mind. Martha? Rubbing alcohol for you?
MARTHA. Sure. "Never mix—never worry."
GEORGE. Martha's tastes in liquor have come down . . . simplified over the years . . . crystallized. Back when I was courting Martha—well, I don't know if that's exactly the right word for it—but back when I was courting Martha. . . .
MARTHA *(Cheerfully)*. Screw, sweetie!
GEORGE *(Returning with* HONEY *and* NICK's *drinks)*. At any rate, back when I was courting Martha, she'd order the damnedest things! You wouldn't believe it! We'd go into a bar . . . you know, a *bar* . . . a whiskey, beer, and bourbon *bar* . . . and what she'd do would be, she'd screw up her face, think real hard, and come up with . . . brandy Alexanders, creme de cacao frappes, gimlets, flaming punch bowls . . . seven-layer liqueur things.
MARTHA. They were good . . . I liked them.
GEORGE. Real lady-like little drinkies.
MARTHA. Hey, where's my rubbing alcohol?
GEORGE *(Returning to the portable bar)*. But the years have brought to Martha a sense of essentials . . . the knowledge that cream is for coffee, lime juice for pies . . . and alcohol *(Brings* MARTHA *her drink)* pure and simple . . . here you are, angel . . . for the pure and sim-

ple. *(Raises his glass)* For the mind's blind eye, the heart's ease, and the liver's craw. Down the hatch, all.

MARTHA *(To them all)*. Cheers, dears. *(They all drink)* You have a poetic nature, George . . . a Dylan Thomas-y quality that gets me right where I live.

GEORGE. Vulgar girl! With guests here!

MARTHA. Ha, ha ha, HA! *(To* HONEY *and* NICK) Hey; hey!

(Sings, conducts with her drink in her hand. HONEY *joins in toward the end)*

Who's afraid of Virginia Woolf,

Virginia Woolf,

Virginia Woolf,

Who's afraid of Virginia Woolf. . . .

(MARTHA *and* HONEY *laugh;* NICK *smiles)*

HONEY. Oh, wasn't that funny? That was so funny. . . .

NICK *(Snapping to)*. Yes . . . yes, it was.

MARTHA. I thought I'd bust a gut; I really did. . . . I really thought I'd bust a gut laughing. George didn't like it. . . . George didn't think it was funny at all.

GEORGE. Lord, Martha, do we have to go through this again?

MARTHA. I'm trying to shame you into a sense of humor, angel, that's all.

GEORGE *(Over-patiently, to* HONEY *and* NICK). Martha didn't think I laughed loud enough. Martha thinks that unless . . . as she demurely puts it . . . that unless you "bust a gut" you aren't amused. You know? Unless you carry on like a hyena you aren't having any fun.

HONEY. Well, I certainly had fun . . . it was a *wonderful* party.

NICK *(Attempting enthusiasm).* Yes . . . it certainly was.

HONEY *(To* MARTHA). And your father! Oh! He is so marvelous!

NICK *(As above)*. Yes . . . yes, he is.

HONEY. Oh, I tell you.

MARTHA *(Genuinely proud)*. He's quite a guy, isn't he? Quite a guy.

GEORGE *(At* NICK). And you'd better believe it!

HONEY *(Admonishing* GEORGE). Ohhhhhhhhh! He's a wonderful man.

GEORGE. I'm not trying to tear him down. He's a god, we all know that.

MARTHA. You lay off my father!

GEORGE. Yes, love. *(To* NICK) All I mean is . . . when you've had as many of these faculty parties as I have. . . .

NICK *(Killing the attempted rapport)*. I rather appreciated it. I mean, aside from enjoying it, I appreciated it. You know, when you're new at a place. . . .

(GEORGE *eyes him suspiciously*)

Meeting everyone, getting introduced around . . . getting to know some of the men. . . . When I was teaching in Kansas. . . .

HONEY. You won't believe it, but we had to make our way all by *ourselves* . . . isn't that right, dear?

NICK. Yes, it is. . . . We. . . .

HONEY. . . . We had to make our own way. . . . I had to go up to wives . . . in the library, or at the supermarket . . . and say, "Hello, I'm new here . . . you must be Mrs. So-and-so, Doctor So-and-so's wife." It really wasn't very nice at all.

MARTHA. Well, *Daddy* knows how to run things.

NICK *(Not enough enthusiasm)*. He's a remarkable man.

MARTHA. You bet your sweet life.

GEORGE *(To* NICK . . . *a confidence, but not whispered)*. Let me tell you a secret, baby. There are easier things in the world, if you happen to be teaching at a university, there are easier things than being married to the daughter of the president of that university. There are easier things in this world.

MARTHA *(Loud . . . to no one in particular)*. It *should* be an extraordinary opportunity . . . for *some* men it would be the chance of a life-time!

GEORGE *(To* NICK . . . *a solemn wink)*. There are, believe me, easier things in this world.

NICK. Well, I can understand how it might make for some . . . awkward-ness, perhaps . . . conceivably, but. . . .

MARTHA. *Some* men would give their right arm for the chance!

GEORGE *(Quietly)*. Alas, Martha, in reality it works out that the sacrifice is usually of a somewhat more private portion of the anatomy.

MARTHA *(A snarl of dismissal and contempt)*. NYYYYAAAAHHHHH!

HONEY *(Rising quickly)*. I wonder if you could show me where the . . . *(Her voice trails off)*

GEORGE *(To* MARTHA, *indicating* HONEY). Martha. . . .

NICK *(To* HONEY). Are you all right?

HONEY. Of course, dear. I want to . . . put some powder on my nose.

GEORGE *(As* MARTHA *is not getting up)*. Martha, won't you show her where we keep the . . . euphemism?

MARTHA. Hm? What? Oh! Sure! *(Rises)* I'm sorry, c'mon. I want to show you the house.

HONEY. I think I'd like to. . . .

MARTHA. . . . wash up? Sure . . . c'mon with me. *(Takes* HONEY *by the arm. To the men)* You two do some men talk for a while.

HONEY *(To* NICK*).* We'll be back, dear.

MARTHA *(To* GEORGE*).* Honestly, George, you burn me up!

GEORGE *(Happily).* All right.

MARTHA. You really do, George.

GEORGE. O.K., Martha . . . O.K. Just . . . trot along.

MARTHA. You really do.

GEORGE. Just don't shoot your mouth off . . . about . . . you-know-what.

MARTHA *(Surprisingly vehement).* I'll talk about any goddamn thing I want to, George!

GEORGE. O.K. O.K. Vanish.

MARTHA. Any goddamn thing I want to! *(Practically dragging* HONEY *out with her)* C'mon. . . .

GEORGE. Vanish. *(The women have gone)* So? What'll it be?

NICK. Oh, I don't know . . . I'll stick to bourbon, I guess.

GEORGE *(Takes* NICK's *glass, goes to portable bar).* That what you were drinking over at Parnassus?

NICK. Over at. . . . ?

GEORGE. Parnassus.

NICK. I don't understand. . . .

GEORGE. Skip it. *(Hands him his drink)* One bourbon.

NICK. Thanks.

GEORGE. It's just a private joke between li'l ol' Martha and me. *(They sit)* So? *(Pause)* So . . . you're in the math department, eh?

NICK. No . . . uh, no.

GEORGE. Martha said you were. I think that's what she said. *(Not too friendly)* What made you decide to be a teacher?

NICK. Oh . . . well, the same things that . . . uh . . . motivated you, I imagine.

GEORGE. What were they?

NICK *(Formal).* Pardon?

GEORGE. I said, what were they? What were the things that motivated me?

NICK *(Laughing uneasily).* Well . . . I'm sure I don't know.

GEORGE. You just finished saying that the things that motivated you were the same things that motivated me.

NICK *(With a little pique)*. I said I *imagined* they were.

GEORGE. Oh *(Off-hand)* Did you? *(Pause)* Well. . . . *(Pause)* You like it here?

NICK *(Looking about the room)*. Yes . . . it's . . . it's fine.

GEORGE. I mean the University.

NICK. Oh. . . . I thought you meant. . . .

GEORGE. Yes . . . I can see you did. *(Pause)* I meant the University.

NICK. Well, I . . . I like it . . . fine. *(As GEORGE just stares at him)* Just fine. *(Same)* You . . . you've been here quite a long time, haven't you?

GEORGE *(Absently, as if he had not heard)*. What? Oh . . . yes. Ever since I married . . . uh, What's-her-name . . . uh, Martha. Even before that. *(Pause)* Forever. *(To himself)* Dashed hopes, and good intentions. Good, better, best, bested. *(Back to NICK)* How do you like that for a declension, young man? Eh?

NICK. Sir, I'm sorry if we. . . .

GEORGE *(With an edge in his voice)*. You didn't answer my question.

NICK. Sir?

GEORGE. Don't you condescend to me! *(Toying with him)* I asked you how you liked that for a declension: Good; better; best; bested. Hm? Well?

NICK *(With some distaste)*. I really don't know what to say.

GEORGE *(Feigned incredulousness)* You really don't know what to say?

NICK *(Snapping it out)*. All right . . . what do you want me to say? Do you want me to say it's funny, so you can contradict me and say it's sad? Or do you want me to say it's sad so you can turn around and say no, it's funny. You can play that damn little game any way you want to, you know!

GEORGE *(Feigned awe)*. Very good! Very good!

NICK *(Even angrier than before)*. And when my wife comes back, I think we'll just. . . .

GEORGE *(Sincere)*. Now, now . . . calm down, my boy. Just . . . calm . . . down. *(Pause)* All right? *(Pause)* You want another drink? Here, give me your glass.

NICK. I still have one. I *do* think that when my wife comes downstairs. . . .

GEORGE. Here . . . I'll freshen it. Give me your glass. *(Takes it)*

NICK. What I mean is . . . you two . . . you and your wife . . . seem to be having *some* sort of a. . . .

GEORGE. Martha and I are having . . . nothing. Martha and I are merely . . . exercising . . . that's all . . . we're merely walking what's left of our wits. Don't pay any attention to it.

NICK *(Undecided)*. Still. . . .

GEORGE *(An abrupt change of pace)*. Well, now . . . let's sit down and talk, hunh?

NICK *(Cool again)*. It's just that I don't like to . . . become involved . . . *(An afterthought)* uh . . . in other people's affairs.

GEORGE *(Comforting a child)*. Well, you'll get over that . . . small college and all. Musical beds is the faculty sport around here.

NICK. Sir?

GEORGE. I said, musical beds is the faculty. . . . Never mind. I wish you wouldn't go "Sir" like that . . . not with the question mark at the end of it. You know? Sir? I know it's meant to be a sign of respect for your *(Winces)* elders . . . but . . . uh . . . the way you do it . . . Uh . . . Sir? . . . Madam?

NICK *(With a small, noncommittal smile)*. No disrespect intended.

GEORGE. How old *are* you?

NICK. Twenty-eight.

GEORGE. I'm forty something. *(Waits for reaction . . . gets none)* Aren't you surprised? I mean . . . don't I look older? Doesn't this . . . *gray* quality suggest the fifties? Don't I sort of fade into backgrounds . . . get lost in the cigarette smoke? Hunh?

NICK *(Looking around for an ash tray)*. I think you look . . . fine.

GEORGE. I've always been lean . . . I haven't put on five pounds since I was your age. I don't have a paunch, either. . . . What I've got . . . I've got this little distension just below the belt . . . but it's hard . . . It's not soft flesh. I use the handball courts. How much do *you* weigh?

NICK. I. . . .

GEORGE. Hundred and fifty-five, sixty . . . something like that? Do you play handball?

NICK. Well, yes . . . no . . . I mean, not very well.

GEORGE. Well, then . . . we shall play sometime. Martha is a hundred and eight . . . years *old*. She weighs somewhat more than that. How old is *your* wife?

NICK *(A little bewildered)*. She's twenty-six.

GEORGE. Martha is a remarkable woman. I would imagine she weighs around a hundred and ten.

NICK. Your . . . wife . . . weighs . . . ?

GEORGE. No, no, my boy. Yours! *Your* wife. My wife is Martha.

NICK. Yes . . . I know.

GEORGE. If you were married to Martha you would know what it means. *(Pause)* But then, if I were married to your wife I would know what that means, too . . . wouldn't I?

NICK *(After a pause).* Yes.

GEORGE. Martha says you're in the Math Department, or something.

NICK *(As if for the hundredth time).* No . . . I'm not.

GEORGE. Martha is seldom mistaken . . . maybe you *should* be in the Math Department, or something.

NICK. I'm a biologist. I'm in the Biology Department.

GEORGE *(After a pause).* Oh. *(Then, as if remembering something)* OH!

NICK. Sir?

GEORGE. You're the one! You're the one's going to make all that trouble . . . making everyone the same, rearranging the chromozones, or whatever it is. Isn't that right?

NICK *(With that small smile).* Not exactly: chromo*somes.*

GEORGE. I'm very mistrustful. Do you believe . . . *(Shifting in his chair)* . . . do you believe that people learn nothing from history? Not that there is nothing to learn, mind you, but that people learn nothing? I am in the History Department.

NICK. Well. . . .

GEORGE. I am a Doctor. A.B. . . . M.A. . . . PH.D. . . . ABMAPHID! Abmaphid has been variously described as a wasting disease of the frontal lobes, and as a wonder drug. It is actually both. I'm really very mistrusting. Biology, hunh?

(NICK does not answer . . . nods . . . looks)

I read somewhere that science fiction is really not fiction at all . . . that you people are rearranging my genes, so that everyone will be like everyone else. Now, I won't have that! It would be a . . . shame. I mean . . . look at me! Is it really such a good idea . . . if everyone was forty something and looked fifty-five? You didn't answer my question about history.

NICK. This genetic business you're talking about. . . .

GEORGE. Oh, that. *(Dismisses it with a wave of his hand.)* That's very

upsetting . . . very . . . disappointing. But history is a great deal
more . . . disappointing. I am in the History Department.

NICK. Yes . . . you told me.

GEORGE. I know I told you . . . I shall probably tell you several more
times. Martha tells me often, that I am *in* the History Department
. . . as opposed to *being* the History Department . . . in the sense of
running the History Department. I do not run the History Department.

NICK. Well, I don't run the Biology Department.

GEORGE. You're twenty-one!

NICK. Twenty-eight.

GEORGE. Twenty-eight! Perhaps when you're forty something and look
fifty-five, you will run the History Department. . . .

NICK. . . . Biology. . . .

GEORGE. . . . the Biology Department. I *did* run the History Department, for four years, during the war, but that was because everybody
was away. Then . . . everybody came back . . . because nobody got
killed. That's New England for you. Isn't that amazing? Not one single
man in this whole place got his head shot off. That's pretty irrational.
(Broods) Your wife *doesn't* have any hips . . . has she . . . does she?

NICK. What?

GEORGE. I don't mean to suggest that I'm hip-happy. . . . I'm not one of
those thirty-six, twenty-two, seventy-eight men. Nosiree . . . not me.
Everything in proportion. I was implying that your wife is . . . slim-
hipped.

NICK. Yes . . . she is.

GEORGE *(Looking at the ceiling).* What are they *doing* up there? I assume
that's where they are.

NICK *(False heartiness).* You know women.

GEORGE *(Gives NICK a long stare, of feigned incredulity . . . then his attention moves).* Not one son-of-a-bitch got killed. Of course, nobody
bombed Washington. No . . . that's not fair. You have any kids?

NICK. Uh . . . no . . . not yet. *(Pause)* You?

GEORGE *(A kind of challenge).* That's for me to know and you to find out.

NICK. Indeed?

GEORGE. No kids, hunh?

NICK. Not yet.

GEORGE. People do . . . uh . . . have kids. That's what I meant about
history. You people are going to make them in test tubes, aren't you?

You biologists. Babies. Then the rest of us . . . them as wants to . . . can screw to their heart's content. What will happen to the tax deduction? Has anyone figured that out yet?

(NICK, *who can think of nothing better to do, laughs mildly*)

But you *are* going to have kids . . . anyway. In spite of history.

NICK *(Hedging)*. Yes . . . certainly. We . . . want to wait . . . a little . . . until we're settled.

GEORGE. And this . . . *(With a handsweep taking in not only the room, the house, but the whole countryside)* . . . this is your heart's content —Illyria . . . Penguin Island . . . Gomorrah. . . . You think you're going to be happy here in New Carthage, eh?

NICK *(A little defensively)*. I hope we'll stay here.

GEORGE. And every definition has its boundaries, eh? Well, it isn't a bad college, I guess. I mean . . . it'll do. It isn't M.I.T. . . . it isn't U.C.L.A. . . . it isn't the Sorbonne . . . or Moscow U. either, for that matter.

NICK. I don't mean . . . forever.

GEORGE. Well, don't you let that get bandied about. The old man wouldn't like it. Martha's father expects loyalty and devotion out of his . . . staff. I was going to use another word. Martha's father expects his . . . staff . . . to cling to the walls of this place, like the ivy . . . to come here and grow old . . . to fall in the line of service. One man, a professor of Latin and Elocution, actually fell in the cafeteria line, one lunch. He was buried, as many of us have been, and as many more of us will be, under the shrubbery around the chapel. It is said . . . and I have no reason to doubt it . . . that we make excellent fertilizer. But the old man is not going to be buried under the shrubbery . . . the old man is not going to die. Martha's father has the staying power of one of those Micronesian tortoises. There are rumors . . . which you must not breathe in front of Martha, for she foams at the mouth . . . that the old man, her father, is over two hundred years old. There is probably an irony involved in this, but I am not drunk enough to figure out what it is. How many kids you going to have?

NICK. I . . . I don't know . . . My wife is. . . .

GEORGE. Slim-hipped. *(Rises)* Have a drink.

NICK. Yes.

GEORGE. MARTHA! *(No answer)* DAMN IT! *(To NICK)* You asked me if I knew women . . . Well, one of the things I do *not* know about them is what they talk about while the men are talking. *(Vaguely)* I must find out some time.

MARTHA'S VOICE. WHADD'YA WANT?

GEORGE. Isn't that a wonderful sound? What I mean is . . . what do you think they really *talk* about . . . or don't you care?

NICK. Themselves, I would imagine.

MARTHA'S VOICE. GEORGE?

GEORGE *(To* NICK*)*. Do you find women . . . puzzling?

NICK. Well . . . yes and no.

GEORGE *(With a knowing nod)*. Unh-hunh. *(Moves toward the hall, almost bumps into* HONEY, *reentering)* Oh! Well, here's one of you, at least. *(*HONEY *moves toward* NICK. GEORGE *goes to the hall)*

HONEY *(To* GEORGE*)*. She'll be right down. *(To* NICK*)* You must see this house, dear . . . this is such a wonderful old house.

NICK. Yes, I. . . .

GEORGE. MARTHA!

MARTHA'S VOICE. FOR CHRIST'S SAKE, HANG ON A MINUTE, WILL YOU?

HONEY *(To* GEORGE*)*. She'll be right down . . . she's changing.

GEORGE *(Incredulous)*. She's *what?* She's changing?

HONEY. Yes.

GEORGE. Her clothes?

HONEY. Her dress.

GEORGE *(Suspicious)*. Why?

HONEY *(With a nervous little laugh)*. Why, I imagine she wants to be . . . comfortable.

GEORGE. *(With a threatening look toward the hall)*. Oh she does, does she?

HONEY. Well, heavens, I should think. . . .

GEORGE. YOU DON'T KNOW!

NICK *(As* HONEY *starts)*. You feel all right?

HONEY *(Reassuring, but with the echo of a whine. A long-practiced tone)*. Oh, yes, dear . . . perfectly fine.

GEORGE *(Fuming . . . to himself)*. So she wants to be comfortable, does she? Well, we'll see about that.

HONEY *(To* GEORGE, *brightly)*. I didn't know until just a minute ago that you had a *son.*

GEORGE *(Wheeling, as if struck from behind)*. WHAT?

HONEY. A son! I hadn't known.

NICK. You to know and me to find out. Well, he must be quite a big. . . .

HONEY. Twenty-one . . . twenty-one tomorrow . . . tomorrow's his birthday.

NICK *(A victorious smile)*. Well!

GEORGE *(To HONEY)*. She told you about him?

HONEY *(Flustered)*. Well, *yes*. Well, I mean. . . .

GEORGE *(Nailing it down)*. She told you about him.

HONEY *(A nervous giggle)*. Yes.

GEORGE *(Strangely)*. You say she's changing?

HONEY. Yes. . . .

GEORGE. And she mentioned . . . ?

HONEY *(Cheerful, but a little puzzled)*. . . . your son's birthday . . . yes.

GEORGE *(More or less to himself)*. O.K., Martha . . . O.K.

NICK. You look pale, Honey. Do you want a . . . ?

HONEY. Yes, dear . . . a little more brandy, maybe. Just a drop.

GEORGE. O.K., Martha.

NICK. May I use the . . . uh . . . bar?

GEORGE. Hm? Oh, yes . . . yes . . . by all means. Drink away . . . you'll need it as the years go on. *(For MARTHA, as if she were in the room)* You goddamn destructive. . . .

HONEY *(To cover)*. What time is it, dear?

NICK. Two-thirty.

HONEY. Oh, it's so late . . . we *should* be getting home.

GEORGE *(Nastily, but he is so preoccupied he hardly notices his own tone)*. For what? You keeping the babysitter up, or something?

NICK *(Almost a warning)*. I told you we didn't have children.

GEORGE. Hm? *(Realizing)* Oh, I'm sorry. I wasn't even listening . . . or thinking . . . *(With a flick of his hand)* . . . whichever one applies.

NICK *(Softly, to HONEY)*. We'll go in a little while.

GEORGE *(Driving)*. Oh no, now . . . you mustn't. Martha is changing . . . and Martha is not changing for *me*. Martha hasn't changed for *me* in years. If Martha is changing, it means we'll be here for . . . days. You are being accorded an honor, and you must not forget that Martha is the daughter of our beloved boss. She is his . . . right ball, you might say.

NICK. You might not understand this . . . but I wish you wouldn't talk that way in front of my wife.

HONEY. Oh, now. . . .

89

GEORGE *(Incredulous)*. Really? Well, you're quite right. . . . We'll leave that sort of talk to Martha.

MARTHA *(Entering)*. What sort of talk?

(MARTHA *has changed her clothes, and she looks, now, more comfortable and . . . and this is most important . . . most voluptuous)*

GEORGE. There you are, my pet.

NICK *(Impressed; rising)*. Well, now. . . .

GEORGE. Why, Martha . . . your Sunday chapel dress!

HONEY *(Slightly disapproving)*. Oh, that's most attractive.

MARTHA *(Showing off)*. You like it? Good! *(To* GEORGE*)* What the hell do you mean screaming up the stairs at me like that?

GEORGE. We got lonely, darling . . . we got lonely for the soft purr of your little voice.

MARTHA *(Deciding not to rise to it)*. Oh. Well, then, you just trot over to the barie-poo. . . .

GEORGE *(Taking the tone from her)*. . . . and make your little mommy a gweat big dwink.

MARTHA *(Giggles)*. That's right. *(To* NICK*)* Well, did you two have a nice little talk? You men solve the problems of the world, as usual?

NICK. Well, no, we . . .

GEORGE *(Quickly)*. What we did, actually, if you really want to know, what we did actually is try to figure out what you two were talking about.

(HONEY *giggles,* MARTHA *laughs)*

MARTHA *(To* HONEY*)*. Aren't they something? Aren't these . . . *(Cheerfully disdainful)* . . . men the absolute end? *(To* GEORGE*)* Why didn't you sneak upstairs and listen in?

GEORGE. Oh, I wouldn't have *listened*, Martha. . . . I would have *peeked*.

(HONEY *giggles,* MARTHA *laughs)*

NICK *(To* GEORGE, *with false heartiness)*. It's a conspiracy.

GEORGE. And now we'll never know. Shucks!

MARTHA *(To* NICK, *as* HONEY *beams)*. Hey, you must be quite a boy, getting your Masters when you were . . . what? . . . twelve? You hear that, George?

NICK. Twelve-and-a-half, actually. No, nineteen really. *(To* HONEY*)* Honey, you needn't have mentioned that. It. . . .

HONEY. Ohhhh . . . I'm *proud* of you. . . .

GEORGE *(Seriously, if sadly)*. That's very . . . impressive.

MARTHA *(Aggressively)*. You're damned right!

GEORGE *(Between his teeth)*. I said I was impressed, Martha. I'm beside myself with jealousy. What do you want me to do, throw up? *(To NICK)* That really is very impressive. *(To HONEY)* You should be right proud.

HONEY *(Coy)*. Oh, he's a pretty nice fella.

GEORGE *(To NICK)*. I wouldn't be surprised if you *did* take over the History Department one of these days.

NICK. The Biology Department.

GEORGE. The *Biology* Department . . . of course. I seem preoccupied with history. Oh! What a remark. *(He strikes a pose, his hand over his heart, his head raised, his voice stentorian)* "I am preoccupied with history."

MARTHA *(As HONEY and NICK chuckle)*. Ha, ha, ha, HA!

GEORGE *(With some disgust)*. I think I'll make *myself* a drink.

MARTHA. George is not preoccupied with *history*. . . . George is preoccupied with the *History Department*. George is preoccupied with the History Department because. . . .

GEORGE. . . . because he is *not* the History Department, but is only *in* the History Department. We know, Martha . . . we went all through it while you were upstairs . . . getting up. There's no need to go through it again.

MARTHA. That's right, baby . . . keep it clean. *(To the others)* George is bogged down in the History Department. He's an old bog in the History Department, that's what George is. A bog. . . . A fen. . . . A G.D. swamp. Ha, ha, ha HA! A SWAMP! Hey, swamp! Hey, SWAMPY!

GEORGE *(With a great effort controls himself . . . then, as if she had said nothing more than "George, dear" . . . . .)*. Yes, Martha? Can I get you something?

MARTHA *(Amused at his game)*. Well . . . uh . . . sure, you can light my cigarette, if you're of a mind to.

GEORGE *(Considers, then moves off)*. No . . . there are limits. I mean, man can put up with only so much without he descends a rung or two on the old evolutionary ladder . . . *(Now a quick aside to NICK)* . . . which is up your line . . . *(Then back to MARTHA)* . . . sinks, Martha, and it's a funny ladder . . . you can't reverse yourself . . . start back up once you're descending.

(MARTHA blows him an arrogant kiss)

Now . . . I'll hold your hand when it's dark and you're afraid of the bogey man, and I'll tote your gin bottles out after midnight, so no one'll see . . . but I will not light your cigarette. And that, as they say, is that.

(Brief silence)

MARTHA *(Under her breath)*. Jesus! *(Then, immediately, to* NICK) Hey, you played football, hunh?

HONEY *(As* NICK *seems sunk in thought)*. Dear. . . .

NICK. Oh! Oh, yes . . . I was a . . . quarterback . . . but I was much more . . . adept . . . at boxing, really.

MARTHA *(With great enthusiasm)*. BOXING! You hear that, George?

GEORGE *(Resignedly)*. Yes, Martha.

MARTHA *(To* NICK, *with peculiar intensity and enthusiasm)*. You musta been pretty good at it . . . I mean, you don't look like you got hit in the face at all.

HONEY *(Proudly)*. He was intercollegiate state middleweight champion.

NICK *(Embarrassed)*. Honey. . . .

HONEY. Well, you were.

MARTHA. You look like you still got a pretty good body *now*, too . . . is that right? Have you?

GEORGE *(Intensely)*. Martha . . . decency forbids. . . .

MARTHA *(To* GEORGE . . . *still staring at* NICK, *though)*. SHUT UP! *(Now, back to* NICK) Well, have you? Have you kept your body?

NICK. *(Unselfconscious . . . almost encouraging her)*. It's still pretty good. I work out.

MARTHA *(With a half-smile)*. Do you!

NICK. Yeah.

HONEY. Oh, yes . . . he has a very . . . firm body.

MARTHA. *(Still with that smile . . . a private communication with* NICK). Have you! Oh, I think that's very nice.

NICK *(Narcissistic, but not directly for* MARTHA). Well, you never know . . . *(shrugs)* . . . you know . . . once you have it. . . .

MARTHA. . . . you never know when it's going to come in handy.

NICK. I was going to say . . . why give it up until you have to.

MARTHA. I couldn't agree with you more.

(They both smile, and there is a rapport of some unformed sort, established)

I couldn't agree with you more.

GEORGE. Martha, your obscenity is more than. . . .

MARTHA. George, here, doesn't cotton much to body talk . . . do you, sweetheart? *(No reply)* George isn't too happy when we get to muscle. You know . . . flat bellies, pectorals . . .

GEORGE *(To* HONEY*)*. Would you like to have a walk around the garden?

HONEY *(Chiding)*. Oh, now. . . .

GEORGE *(Incredulous)*. You're amused? *(Shrugs)* All right.

MARTHA. Paunchy over there isn't too happy when the conversation moves to muscle. How much do you weigh?

NICK. A hundred and fifty-five, a hundred and. . . .

MARTHA. Still at the old middleweight limit, eh? That's pretty good. *(Swings around)* Hey George, tell 'em about the boxing match *we* had.

GEORGE *(Slamming his drink down, moving toward the hall)*. Christ!

MARTHA. George! Tell 'em about it!

GEORGE *(With a sick look on his face)*. You tell them, Martha. You're good at it.
(Exits)

HONEY. Is he . . . all right?

MARTHA *(Laughs)*. Him? Oh, sure. George and I had this boxing match . . . Oh, Lord, twenty years ago . . . a couple of years after we were married.

NICK. A boxing match? The two of you?

HONEY. Really?

MARTHA. Yup . . . the two of us . . . really.

HONEY *(With a little shivery giggle of anticipation)*. I can't imagine it.

MARTHA. Well, like I say, it was twenty years ago, and it wasn't in a ring, or anything like that, you know what I mean. It was wartime, and Daddy was on this physical fitness kick . . . Daddy's always admired physical fitness . . . says a man is only part brain . . . he has a body, too, and it's his responsibility to keep both of them up . . . you know?

NICK. Unh-hunh.

MARTHA. Says the brain can't work unless the body's working, too.

NICK. Well, that's not exactly so. . . .

MARTHA. Well, maybe that *isn't* what he says . . . something like it. *But* . . . it was wartime, and Daddy got the idea all the men should learn how to box . . . self-defense. I suppose the idea was if the Germans landed on the coast, or something, the whole faculty'd go out and punch 'em to death. . . . I don't know.

NICK. It was probably more the principle of the thing.

MARTHA. No kidding. Anyway, so Daddy had a couple of us over one

Sunday and we went out in the back, and Daddy put on the gloves himself. Daddy's a strong man. . . . Well, *you* know.

NICK. Yes . . . yes.

MARTHA. And he asked George to box with him. Aaaaannnnd . . . George didn't *want* to . . . probably something about not wanting to bloody-up his meal ticket. . . .

NICK. Unh-hunh.

MARTHA. . . . Anyway, George said he didn't want to, and Daddy was saying, "Come on, young man . . . what sort of son-in-law *are* you?" . . . and stuff like that.

NICK. Yeah.

MARTHA. So, while this was going on . . . I don't know why I *did* it . . . I got into a pair of gloves myself . . . you know, I didn't lace 'em up, or anything . . . and I snuck up behind George, just kidding, and I yelled "Hey George!" and at the same time I let go sort of a round-house right . . . just kidding, you know?

NICK. Unh-hunh.

MARTHA. . . . and George wheeled around real quick, and he caught it right in the jaw . . . POW! (NICK *laughs*) I hadn't meant it . . . honestly. Anyway . . . POW! Right in the jaw . . . and he was off balance . . . he must have been . . . and he stumbled back a few steps, and then, CRASH, he landed . . . flat . . . in a huckleberry bush!

(NICK *laughs.* HONEY *goes tsk, tsk, tsk, tsk, and shakes her head*)
It was awful, really. It was funny, but it was awful.

(*She thinks, gives a muffled laugh in rueful contemplation of the incident*)
I think it's colored our whole life. Really I do! It's an excuse, anyway.

(GEORGE *enters now, his hands behind his back. No one sees him*)
It's what he uses for being bogged down, anyway . . . why he hasn't *gone* anywhere.

(GEORGE *advances,* HONEY *sees him*)

MARTHA. And it was an *accident* . . . a real, goddamn accident!

(GEORGE *takes from behind his back a short-barreled shotgun, and calmly aims it at the back of* MARTHA'S *head.* HONEY *screams . . . rises.* NICK *rises, and, simultaneously,* MARTHA *turns her head to face* GEORGE. GEORGE *pulls the trigger*)

GEORGE. POW!!!

(*Pop! From the barrel of the gun blossoms a large red and yellow*

Chinese parasol. HONEY *screams again, this time less, and mostly from relief and confusion)*

You're dead! Pow! You're dead!

NICK *(Laughing).* Good Lord.

(HONEY *is beside herself.* MARTHA *laughs too . . . almost breaks down, her great laugh booming.* GEORGE *joins in the general laughter and confusion. It dies, eventually)*

HONEY. Oh! My goodness!

MARTHA *(Joyously).* Where'd you get that, you bastard?

NICK *(His hand out for the gun).* Let me see that, will you?

(GEORGE *hands him the gun)*

HONEY. I've never been so frightened in my life! Never!

GEORGE *(A trifle abstracted).* Oh, I've had it awhile. Did you like that?

MARTHA *(Giggling).* You bastard.

HONEY *(Wanting attention).* I've *never* been so frightened . . . never.

NICK. This is quite a gadget.

GEORGE *(Leaning over* MARTHA*).* You liked that, did you?

MARTHA. Yeah . . . that was pretty good. *(Softer)* C'mon . . . give me a kiss.

GEORGE *(Indicating* NICK *and* HONEY*).* Later, sweetie.

(But MARTHA *will not be dissuaded. They kiss,* GEORGE *standing, leaning over* MARTHA's *chair. She takes his hand, places it on her stageside breast. He breaks away)*

Oh-ho! That's what you're after, is it? What are we going to have . . . blue games for the guests? Hunh? Hunh?

MARTHA *(Angry-hurt).* You . . . prick!

GEORGE *(A Pyrrhic victory).* Everything in its place, Martha . . . everything in its own good time.

MARTHA *(An unspoken epithet).* You. . . .

GEORGE *(Over to* NICK, *who still has the gun).* Here, let me show you . . . it goes back in, like this.

(Closes the parasol, reinserts it in the gun)

NICK. That's damn clever.

GEORGE *(Puts the gun down.)* Drinks now! Drinks for all!

(Takes NICK's *glass without question . . . goes to* MARTHA*)*

MARTHA *(Still angry-hurt).* I'm not finished.

HONEY *(As* GEORGE *puts out his hand for her glass).* Oh, I think I need something.

(He takes her glass, moves back to the portable bar)

NICK. Is that Japanese?

GEORGE. Probably.

HONEY *(To* MARTHA*).* I was never so frightened in my life. Weren't you frightened? Just for a second?

MARTHA *(Smothering her rage at* GEORGE*).* I don't remember.

HONEY. Ohhhh, now . . . I bet you were.

GEORGE. Did you really think I was going to kill you, Martha?

MARTHA *(Dripping contempt).* You? . . . Kill me? . . . That's a laugh.

GEORGE. Well, now, I might . . . some day.

MARTHA. Fat chance.

NICK *(As* GEORGE *hands him his drink).* Where's the john?

GEORGE. Through the hall there . . . and down to your left.

HONEY. Don't you come back with any guns, or anything, now.

NICK *(Laughs).* Oh, no.

MARTHA. You don't need any props, do you, baby?

NICK. Unh-unh.

MARTHA *(Suggestive).* I'll bet not. No fake Jap gun for you, eh?

NICK *(Smiles at* MARTHA*. Then, to* GEORGE*, indicating a side table near the hall).* May I leave my drink here?

GEORGE *(As* NICK *exits without waiting for a reply).* Yeah . . . sure . . . why not? We've got half-filled glasses everywhere in the house, wherever Martha forgets she's left them . . . in the linen closet, on the edge of the bathtub. . . . I even found one in the freezer, once.

MARTHA *(Amused in spite of herself).* You did not!

GEORGE. *Yes* I did.

MARTHA *(Ibid).* You did *not!*

GEORGE *(Giving* HONEY *her brandy).* Yes I *did.* *(To* HONEY*)* Brandy doesn't give you a hangover?

HONEY. I never mix. And then, I don't drink very much, either.

GEORGE *(Grimaces behind her back).* Oh . . . that's good. Your . . . your husband was telling me all about the . . . chromosomes.

MARTHA *(Ugly).* The what?

GEORGE. The chromosomes, Martha . . . the genes, or whatever they are. *(To* HONEY*)* You've got quite a . . . terrifying husband.

HONEY *(As if she's being joshed).* Ohhhhhhhhhh. . . .

GEORGE. No, really. He's quite terrifying, with his chromosomes, and all.

MARTHA. He's in the Math Department.

GEORGE. No, Martha . . . he's a biologist.

MARTHA *(Her voice rising).* He's in the *Math* Department!

HONEY *(Timidly).* Uh . . . biology.

MARTHA *(Unconvinced).* Are you *sure?*

HONEY *(With a little giggle).* Well, I ought to. *(Then as an afterthought)* Be.

MARTHA *(Grumpy).* I suppose so. I don't know who said he was in the Math Department.

GEORGE. You did, Martha.

MARTHA *(By way of irritable explanation).* Well, I can't be expected to remember *everything.* I meet fifteen new teachers and their goddamn wives . . . present company outlawed, of course . . . (HONEY *nods, smiles sillily)* . . . and I'm supposed to remember *everything. (Pause)* So? He's a biologist. Good for him. Biology's even better. It's less . . . abstruse.

GEORGE. Abstract.

MARTHA. ABSTRUSE! In the sense of recondite. *(Sticks her tongue out at* GEORGE*)* Don't you tell me words. Biology's even better. It's . . . right at the *meat* of things.

(NICK *reenters)*

You're right at the meat of things, baby.

NICK *(Taking his drink from the side table).* Oh?

HONEY *(With that giggle).* They thought you were in the Math Department.

NICK. Well, maybe I ought to be.

MARTHA. You stay right where you are . . . you stay right at the . . . *meat* of things.

GEORGE. You're obsessed with that phrase, Martha. . . . It's ugly.

MARTHA *(Ignoring* GEORGE . . . *to* NICK*).* You stay right there. *(Laughs)* Hell, you can take over the History Department just as easy from there as anywhere else. God knows, *some*body's going to take over the History Department, *some* day, and it ain't going to be Georgie-boy, there . . . that's for sure. Are ya, swampy . . . are ya, hunh?

GEORGE. In my mind, Martha, you are buried in cement, right up to your neck. (MARTHA *giggles)* No . . . right up to your nose. . . . that's much quieter.

MARTHA *(To* NICK*).* Georgie-boy, here, says you're terrifying. Why are you terrifying?

NICK *(With a small smile).* I didn't know I was.

HONEY *(A little thickly).* It's because of your chromosomes, dear.

NICK. Oh, the chromosome business.

MARTHA *(To NICK).* What's all this about chromosomes?

NICK. Well, chromosomes are. . . .

MARTHA. I know what chromosomes are, sweetie, I love 'em.

NICK. Oh. . . . Well, then.

GEORGE. Martha eats them . . . for breakfast . . . she sprinkles them on her cereal. *(To MARTHA, now)* It's very simple, Martha, this young man is working on a system whereby chromosomes can be altered . . . well not all by himself—he probably has one or two co-conspirators— the genetic makeup of a sperm cell changed, reordered . . . *to* order, actually . . . for hair and eye color, stature, potency . . . I imagine . . . hairiness, features, health . . . and *mind.* Most important . . . Mind. All imbalances will be corrected, sifted out . . . propensity for various diseases will be gone, longevity assured. We will have a race of men . . . test-tube-bred . . . incubator-born . . . superb and sub- lime.

MARTHA *(Impressed).* Hunh!

HONEY. How exciting!

GEORGE. *But!* Everyone will tend to be rather the same. . . . Alike. Ev- eryone . . . and I'm sure I'm not wrong here . . . will tend to look like this young man *here.*

MARTHA. *That's* not a bad idea.

NICK *(Impatient).* All right, now. . . .

GEORGE. It will, on the surface of it, be all rather pretty . . . quite jolly. But of course there will be a dank side to it, too. A certain amount of regulation will be necessary . . . uh . . . for the experiment to suc- ceed. A certain number of sperm tubes will have to be cut.

MARTHA. Hunh! . . .

GEORGE. Millions upon millions of them . . . millions of tiny little slicing operations that will leave just the smallest scar, on the underside of the scrotum (MARTHA *laughs)* but which will assure the sterility of the im- perfect . . . the ugly, the stupid . . . the . . . unfit.

NICK *(Grimly).* Now look . . . !

GEORGE. . . . with this, we will have, in time, a race of glorious men.

MARTHA. Hunh!

GEORGE. I suspect we will not have much music, much painting, but we will have a civilization of men, smooth, blond, and right at the middle-weight limit.

MARTHA. Awww. . . .

GEORGE. . . . a race of scientists and mathematicians, each dedicated to and working for the greater glory of the super-civilization.

MARTHA. Goody.

GEORGE. There will be a certain . . . loss of liberty, I imagine, as a result of this experiment . . . but diversity will no longer be the goal. Cultures and races will eventually vanish . . . the ants will take over the world.

NICK. Are you finished?

GEORGE *(Ignoring him)*. And I, naturally, am rather opposed to all this. History, which is my field . . . history, of which I am one of the most famous bogs. . . .

MARTHA. Ha, ha, HA!

GEORGE. . . . will lose its glorious variety and unpredictability. I, and with me the . . . the surprise, the multiplexity, the sea-changing rhythm of . . . history, will be eliminated. There will be order and constancy . . . and I am unalterably opposed to it. I will not give up Berlin!

MARTHA. You'll give up Berlin, sweetheart. You going to defend it with your paunch?

HONEY. I don't see what Berlin has to *do* with anything.

GEORGE. There is a saloon in West Berlin where the barstools are five feet high. And the earth . . . the floor . . . is . . . so . . . far . . . below you. I will not give up things like that. No . . . I won't. I will fight you, young man . . . one hand on my scrotum, to be sure . . . but with my free hand I will battle you to the death.

MARTHA *(Mocking, laughing)*. Bravo!

NICK *(To GEORGE)*. That's right. And I am going to be the wave of the future.

MARTHA. You bet you are, baby.

HONEY *(Quite drunk—to NICK)*. I don't see why you want to do all those things, dear. You never told me.

NICK *(Angry)*. Oh for God's sake!

HONEY *(Shocked)*. OH!

GEORGE. The most profound indication of a social malignancy . . . no sense of humor. None of the monoliths could take a joke. Read history. I know something about history.

NICK *(To* GEORGE, *trying to make light of it all).* You . . . you don't know much about science, do you?

GEORGE. I know something about history. I know when I'm being threatened.

MARTHA *(Salaciously—to* NICK*).* So, everyone's going to look like you, eh?

NICK. Oh, sure. I'm going to be a personal screwing machine!

MARTHA. Isn't that nice.

HONEY *(Her hands over her ears).* Dear, you mustn't . . . you mustn't . . . you mustn't.

NICK *(Impatiently).* I'm sorry, Honey.

HONEY. Such language. It's. . . .

NICK. I'm *sorry.* All right?

HONEY *(Pouting).* Well . . . all right. *(Suddenly she giggles insanely, subsides. To* GEORGE*)* . . . When is your son? *(Giggles again)*

GEORGE. What?

NICK *(Distastefully).* Something about your son.

GEORGE. SON!

HONEY. When is . . . where is your son . . . coming home? *(Giggles)*

GEORGE. Ohhhh. *(Too formal)* Martha? When is our son coming home?

MARTHA. Never mind.

GEORGE. No, no . . . I want to know . . . you brought it out into the open. When is he coming home, Martha?

MARTHA. I said never mind. I'm sorry I brought it up.

GEORGE. Him up . . . not it. You brought *him* up. Well, more or less. When's the little bugger going to appear, hunh? I mean isn't tomorrow meant to be his birthday, or something?

MARTHA. I don't want to talk about it!

GEORGE *(Falsely innocent).* But Martha. . . .

MARTHA. I DON'T WANT TO TALK ABOUT IT!

GEORGE. I'll bet you don't. *(To* HONEY *and* NICK*)* Martha does not want to talk about it . . . him. Martha is sorry she brought it up . . . him.

HONEY *(Idiotically).* When's the little bugger coming home? *(Giggles)*

GEORGE. Yes, Martha . . . since you had the bad taste to bring the matter up in the first place . . . when *is* the little bugger coming home?

NICK. Honey, do you think you . . . ?

MARTHA. George talks disparagingly about the little bugger because . . . well, because he has problems.

GEORGE. The little bugger has problems? What problems has the little bugger got?

MARTHA. Not the little bugger . . . stop calling him that! You! You've got problems.

GEORGE *(Feigned disdain)*. I've never heard of anything more ridiculous in my life.

HONEY. Neither have I!

NICK. Honey. . . .

MARTHA. George's biggest problem about the little . . . ha, ha, ha, HA! . . . about our son, about our great big son, is that deep down in the private-most pit of his gut, he's not completely sure it's his own kid.

GEORGE *(Deeply serious)*. My God, you're a wicked woman.

MARTHA. And I've told you a million times, baby . . . I wouldn't conceive with anyone but you . . . you know that, baby.

GEORGE. A deeply wicked person.

HONEY *(Deep in drunken grief)*. My, my, my, my. Oh, my.

NICK. I'm not sure that this is a subject for. . . .

GEORGE. Martha's lying. I want you to know that, right now. Martha's lying. (MARTHA *laughs)* There are very few things in this world that I *am* sure of . . . national boundaries, the level of the ocean, political allegiances, practical morality . . . none of these would I stake my stick on any more . . . but the one thing in this whole sinking world that I am sure of is my partnership, my chromosomological partnership in the . . . creation of our . . . blond-eyed, blue-haired . . . son.

HONEY. Oh, I'm so glad!

MARTHA. That was a very pretty speech, George.

GEORGE. Thank you, Martha.

MARTHA. You rose to the occasion . . . good. Real good.

HONEY. Well . . . real well.

NICK. Honey. . . .

GEORGE. Martha knows . . . she knows better.

MARTHA *(Proudly)*. I know better. I been to college like everybody else.

GEORGE. Martha been to college. Martha been to a convent when she were a little twig of a thing, too.

MARTHA. And I was an atheist. *(Uncertainly)* I still am.

GEORGE. Not an atheist, Martha . . . a pagan. *(To* HONEY *and* NICK) Martha is the only true pagan on the eastern seaboard. (MARTHA *laughs)*

HONEY. Oh, that's nice. Isn't that nice, dear?

NICK *(Humoring her)*. Yes . . . wonderful.

GEORGE. And Martha paints blue circles around her things.

NICK. You do?

MARTHA *(Defensively, for the joke's sake)*. Sometimes. *(Beckoning)* You wanna see?

GEORGE *(Admonishing)*. Tut, tut, tut.

MARTHA. Tut, tut yourself . . . you old floozie!

HONEY. He's not a floozie . . . he can't be a floozie . . . you're a floozie. *(Giggles)*

MARTHA *(Shaking a finger at* HONEY). Now you watch yourself!

HONEY *(Cheerfully)*. All right. I'd like a nipper of brandy, please.

NICK. Honey, I think you've had enough, now. . . .

GEORGE. Nonsense! Everybody's ready, I think. *(Takes glasses, etc.)*

HONEY *(Echoing* GEORGE). Nonsense.

NICK *(Shrugging)*. O.K.

MARTHA *(To* GEORGE). Our son does *not* have blue hair . . . or blue eyes, for that matter. He has green eyes . . . like me.

GEORGE. He has blue eyes, Martha.

MARTHA *(Determined)*. Green.

GEORGE *(Patronizing)*. Blue, Martha.

MARTHA *(Ugly)*. GREEN! *(To* HONEY *and* NICK) He has the loveliest green eyes . . . they aren't all flaked with brown and gray, you know . . . hazel . . . they're real green . . . deep, pure green eyes . . . like mine.

NICK *(Peers)*. Your eyes are . . . brown, aren't they?

MARTHA. Green! *(A little too fast)* Well, in some lights they *look* brown, but they're green. Not green like his . . . more hazel. George has watery blue eyes . . . milky blue.

GEORGE. Make up your mind, Martha.

MARTHA. I was giving you the benefit of the doubt. *(Now back to the others)* Daddy has green eyes, too.

GEORGE. He does not! Your father has tiny red eyes . . . like a white mouse. In fact, he *is* a white mouse.

MARTHA. You wouldn't dare say a thing like that if he was here! You're a coward!

GEORGE *(To* HONEY *and* NICK). You know . . . that great shock of white hair, and those little beady red eyes . . . a great big white mouse.

MARTHA. George hates Daddy . . . not for anything Daddy's done to him, but for his own.

GEORGE *(Nodding . . . finishing it for her).* . . . inadequacies.

MARTHA *(Cheerfully).* That's right. You hit it . . . right on the snout. *(Seeing* GEORGE *exiting)* Where do you think *you're* going?

GEORGE. We need some more booze, angel.

MARTHA. Oh. *(Pause)* So, go.

GEORGE *(Exiting).* Thank you.

MARTHA *(Seeing that* GEORGE *has gone).* He's a good bartender . . . a good bar nurse. The S.O.B., he hates my father. You know that?

NICK *(Trying to make light of it).* Oh, come on.

MARTHA *(Offended).* You think I'm kidding? You think I'm joking? I never joke . . . I don't have a sense of humor. *(Almost pouting)* I have a fine sense of the ridiculous, but no sense of humor. *(Affirmatively)* I have no sense of humor!

HONEY *(Happily).* I haven't, either.

NICK *(Half-heartedly).* Yes, you have, Honey . . . a quiet one.

HONEY *(Proudly).* Thank you.

MARTHA. You want to know *why* the S.O.B. hates my father? You want me to tell you? All right . . . I will tell you why the S.O.B. hates my father.

HONEY *(Swinging to some sort of attention).* Oh, good!

MARTHA *(Sternly, to* HONEY). *Some* people feed on the calamities of others.

HONEY *(Offended).* They do not!

NICK. Honey. . . .

MARTHA. All right! Shut up! Both of you! *(Pause)* All right, now. Mommy died early, see, and I sort of grew up with Daddy. *(Pause—thinks)* . . . I went away to school, and stuff, but I more or less grew up with him. Jesus, I admired that guy! I worshipped him . . . I absolutely worshipped him. I still do. And he was pretty fond of me, too . . . you know? We had a real . . . rapport going . . . a real rapport.

NICK. Yeah, yeah.

MARTHA. And Daddy built this college . . . I mean, he built it up from what it was . . . it's his whole life. He *is* the college.

NICK. Unh-hunh.

MARTHA. The college is him. You know what the endowment was when he took over, and what it is *now?* You look it up some time.

NICK. I know . . . I read about it. . . .

MARTHA. Shut up and listen . . . *(As an afterthought)* . . . cutie. So after I got done with college and stuff, I came back here and sort of . . . sat around, for a while. I wasn't married, or anything. Welllllll, I'd *been* married . . . sort of . . . for a week, my sophomore year at Miss Muff's Academy for Young Ladies . . . college. A kind of junior Lady Chatterly arrangement, as it turned out . . . the marriage. (NICK *laughs)* He mowed the lawn at Miss Muff's, sitting up there, all naked, in a big power mower, mowing away. But Daddy and Miss Muff got together and put an end to that . . . real quick . . . annulled . . . which is a laugh . . . because theoretically you can't get an annulment if there's entrance. Ha! Anyway, so I was revirginized, finished at Miss Muff's . . . where they had one less gardener's boy, and a real shame, that was . . . and I came back here and sort of sat around for a while. I was hostess for Daddy and I took care of him . . . and it was . . . nice. It was very nice.

NICK. Yes . . . yes.

MARTHA. What do you mean, yes, yes? How would you know?
   (NICK *shrugs helplessly)*
   Lover.
   (NICK *smiles a little)*
   And I got the idea, about then, that I'd marry into the college . . . which didn't seem to be quite as stupid as it turned out. I mean, Daddy had a sense of history . . . of . . . continuation. . . . Why don't you come over here and sit by me?

NICK *(Indicating* HONEY, *who is barely with it).* I . . . don't think I . . . should. . . . I. . . .

MARTHA. Suit yourself. A sense of continuation . . . history . . . and he'd always had it in the back of his mind to . . . *groom* someone to take over . . . some time, when he quit. A succession . . . you know what I mean?

NICK. Yes, I do.

MARTHA. Which is natural enough. When you've made something, you want to pass it on, to somebody. So, I was sort of on the lookout, for . . . prospects with the new men. An heir-apparent. *(Laughs)* It wasn't *Daddy's* idea that I had to necessarily marry the guy. I mean, I wasn't the albatross . . . you didn't have to take me to get the prize, or any-thing like that. It was something *I* had in the back of *my* mind. And a lot of the new men were married . . . naturally.

NICK. Sure.

MARTHA *(With a strange smile)*. Like you, baby.

HONEY *(A mindless echo)*. Like you, baby.

MARTHA *(Ironically)*. But then George came along . . . along come George.

GEORGE *(Reentering, with liquor)*. And along came George, bearing hooch. What are you doing now, Martha?

MARTHA *(Unfazed)*. I'm telling a story. Sit down . . . you'll learn some-thing.

GEORGE *(Stays standing. Puts the liquor on the portable bar)*. All rightie.

HONEY. You've come back!

GEORGE. That's right.

HONEY. Dear! He's come back!

NICK. Yes, I see . . . I see.

MARTHA. Where was I?

HONEY. I'm *so* glad.

NICK. Shhhhh.

HONEY *(Imitating him)*. Shhhhh.

MARTHA. Oh yeah. And along came George. That's right. WHO was young . . . intelligent . . . and . . . bushy-tailed, and . . . sort of cute . . . if you can imagine it.

GEORGE. . . . and younger than you. . . .

MARTHA. . . . and younger than me. . . .

GEORGE. . . . by six years. . . .

MARTHA. . . . by six years. . . . It doesn't bother me, George. . . . And along he came, bright-eyed, into the History Department. And you know what I did, dumb cluck that I am? You know what I did? I fell for him.

HONEY *(Dreamy)*. Oh, that's nice.

GEORGE. Yes, she did. You should have seen it. She'd sit outside of my room, on the lawn, at night, and she'd howl and claw at the turf . . . I couldn't work.

MARTHA *(Laughs, really amused)*. I actually fell for him . . . it . . . that, there.

GEORGE. Martha's a Romantic at heart.

MARTHA. That I am. So, I actually fell for him. And the match seemed . . . practical, too. You know, Daddy was looking for someone to. . . .

GEORGE. Just a minute, Martha. . . .

MARTHA. . . . take over, some time, when he was ready to . . .

GEORGE *(Stony)*. Just a minute, Martha.

MARTHA. . . . retire, and so I thought. . . .

GEORGE. STOP IT, MARTHA!

MARTHA *(Irritated)*. Whadda you want?

GEORGE *(Too patiently)*. I'd thought you were telling the story of our courtship, Martha . . . I didn't know you were going to start in on the other business.

MARTHA *(So-thereish)*. Well, I am!

GEORGE. I wouldn't, if I were you.

MARTHA. Oh . . . you wouldn't? Well, you're not!

GEORGE. Now, you've already sprung a leak about you-know-what. . . .

MARTHA *(A duck)*. What? What?

GEORGE. . . . about the apple of our eye . . . the sprout . . . the little bugger . . . *(spits it out)* . . . our *son* . . . and if *you start* in on this other business, I warn you, Martha, it's going to make me angry.

MARTHA *(Laughing at him)*. Oh, it is, is it?

GEORGE. I warn you.

MARTHA *(Incredulous)*. You *what?*

GEORGE *(Very quietly)*. I warn you.

NICK. Do you really think we have to go through . . . ?

MARTHA. I stand warned! *(Pause . . . then, to* HONEY *and* NICK*)* So, anyway, I married the S.O.B., and I had it all planned out. . . . He was the groom . . . he was going to be groomed. He'd take over some day . . . first, he'd take over the History Department, and then, when Daddy retired, he'd take over the college . . . you know? That's the way it was supposed to be.

(To GEORGE, *who is at the portable bar with his back to her)*

You getting angry, baby? Hunh? *(Now back)* That's the way it was *supposed* to be. Very simple. And Daddy seemed to think it was a pretty good idea, too. For a while. Until he watched for a couple of years! *(To* GEORGE *again)* You getting angrier? *(Now back)* Until he watched for a couple of years and started thinking maybe it wasn't such a good idea after all . . . that maybe Georgie-boy didn't have the *stuff* . . . that he didn't have it in him!

106

GEORGE *(Still with his back to them all)*. Stop it, Martha.

MARTHA *(Viciously triumphant)*. The hell I will! You see, George didn't have much . . . push . . . he wasn't particularly . . . aggressive. In fact he was sort of a . . . *(Spits the word at* GEORGE's *back)* . . . a FLOP! A great . . . big . . . fat . . . FLOP!

(CRASH! *Immediately after* FLOP! GEORGE *breaks a bottle against the portable bar and stands there, still with his back to them all, holding the remains of the bottle by the neck. There is a silence, with everyone frozen. Then. . . .)*

GEORGE *(Almost crying)*. I said stop, Martha.

MARTHA *(After considering what course to take)*. I hope that was an empty bottle, George. You don't want to waste good liquor . . . not on your salary.

(GEORGE *drops the broken bottle on the floor, not moving)*

Not on an Associate Professor's salary. *(To* NICK *and* HONEY) I mean, he'd be . . . no good . . . at trustees' dinners, fund raising. He didn't have any . . . personality, you know what I mean? Which was disappointing to Daddy, as you can imagine. So, here I am, stuck with this flop. . . .

GEORGE *(Turning around)*. . . . don't go on, Martha. . . .

MARTHA. . . . this BOG in the History Department. . . .

GEORGE. . . . don't, Martha, don't. . . .

MARTHA *(Her voice rising to match his)*. . . . who's married to the President's daughter, who's expected to *be* somebody, not just some nobody, some bookworm, somebody who's so damn . . . contemplative, he can't make anything out of himself, somebody without the *guts* to make anybody proud of him . . . ALL RIGHT, GEORGE!	GEORGE *(Under her, then covering, to drown her)*. I said, don't. All right . . . all right: *(Sings)* Who's afraid of Virginia Woolf, Virginia Woolf, Virginia Woolf, Who's afraid of Virginia Woolf, early in the morning.

GEORGE *and* HONEY *(Who join him drunkenly)*. Who's afraid of
Virginia Woolf,
Virginia Woolf,
Virginia Woolf . . . *(etc.)*

MARTHA. STOP IT!

107

(A brief silence)

HONEY *(Rising, moving toward the hall).* I'm going to be sick . . . I'm going to be sick . . . I'm going to vomit.
(Exits)

NICK *(Going after her).* Oh, for God's sake!
(Exits)

MARTHA *(Going after them, looks back at* GEORGE, *contemptuously).* Jesus!
(Exits. GEORGE *is alone on the stage)*

CURTAIN

ACT TWO
Walpurgisnacht

GEORGE, *by himself:* NICK *reenters.*

NICK *(After a silence).* I . . . guess . . . she's all right. *(No answer)* She . . . really shouldn't drink. *(No answer)* She's . . . frail. *(No answer)* Uh . . . slim-hipped, as you'd have it. (GEORGE *smiles vaguely*) I'm really very sorry.

GEORGE *(Quietly).* Where's my little yum yum? Where's Martha?

NICK. She's making coffee . . . in the kitchen. She . . . gets sick quite easily.

GEORGE *(Preoccupied).* Martha? Oh no, Martha hasn't been sick a day in her life, unless you count the time she spends in the rest home. . . .

NICK *(He, too, quietly).* No, no; *my* wife . . . *my* wife gets sick quite easily. Your wife is Martha.

GEORGE *(With some rue).* Oh, yes . . . I know.

NICK *(A statement of fact).* She doesn't really spend any time in a rest home.

GEORGE. Your wife?

NICK. No. Yours.

GEORGE. Oh! Mine. *(Pause)* No, no, she doesn't . . . *I* would; I mean if I were . . . her . . . she . . . *I* would. But I'm not . . . and so I don't. *(Pause)* I'd like to, though. It gets pretty bouncy around here sometimes.

NICK *(Coolly).* Yes . . . I'm sure.

GEORGE. Well, you saw an example of it.

NICK. I try not to. . . .

GEORGE. Get involved. Um? Isn't that right?

NICK. Yes . . . that's right.

GEORGE. I'd imagine not.

NICK. I find it . . . embarrassing.

GEORGE *(Sarcastic).* Oh, you do, hunh?

NICK. Yes. Really. Quite.

GEORGE *(Mimicking him).* Yes. Really. Quite. *(Then aloud, but to himself)* IT'S DISGUSTING!

NICK. Now look! I didn't have anything. . . .

GEORGE. DISGUSTING! *(Quietly, but with great intensity)* Do you think I like

109

having that . . . whatever-it-is . . . ridiculing me, tearing me down, in front of . . . *(Waves his hand in a gesture of contemptuous dismissal)* YOU? Do you think I *care* for it?

NICK *(Cold—unfriendly)*. Well, no . . . I don't imagine you care for it at all.

GEORGE. Oh, you don't imagine it, hunh?

NICK *(Antagonistic)*. No . . . I don't. I don't imagine you do!

GEORGE *(Withering)*. Your sympathy disarms me . . . your . . . your compassion makes me weep! Large, salty, unscientific tears!

NICK *(With great disdain)*. I just don't see why you feel you have to subject *other* people to it.

GEORGE. *I?*

NICK. If you and your . . . wife . . . want to go at each other, like a couple of. . . .

GEORGE. *I!* Why *I* want to!

NICK. . . . animals, I don't see why you don't do it when there aren't any. . . .

GEORGE *(Laughing through his anger)*. Why, you smug, self-righteous little. . . .

NICK *(A genuine threat)*. CAN . . . IT . . . MISTER!

(Silence)

Just . . . watch it!

GEORGE. . . . scientist.

NICK. I've never hit an older man.

GEORGE *(Considers it)*. Oh. *(Pause)* You just hit younger men . . . and children . . . women . . . birds. *(Sees that NICK is not amused)* Well, you're quite right, of course. It isn't the prettiest spectacle . . . seeing a couple of middle-age types hacking away at each other, all red in the face and winded, missing half the time.

NICK. Oh, you two don't miss . . . you two are pretty good. Impressive.

GEORGE. And impressive things impress you, don't they? You're . . . easily impressed . . . sort of a . . . pragmatic idealism.

NICK *(A tight smile)*. No, it's that sometimes I can admire things that I don't admire. Now, flagellation isn't my idea of good times, but. . . .

GEORGE. . . . but you can admire a good flagellator . . . a real pro.

NICK. Unh-hunh . . . yeah.

GEORGE. Your wife throws up a lot, eh?

NICK. I didn't say that. . . . I said she gets sick quite easily.

GEORGE. Oh. I thought by sick you meant. . . .

NICK. Well, it's true . . . She . . . she does throw up a lot. Once she starts . . . there's practically no stopping her. . . . I mean, she'll go right on . . . for hours. Not all the time, but . . . regularly.

GEORGE. You can tell time by her, hunh?

NICK. Just about.

GEORGE. Drink?

NICK. Sure. *(With no emotion, except the faintest distaste, as* GEORGE *takes his glass to the bar)* I married her because she was pregnant.

GEORGE. *(Pause).* Oh? *(Pause)* But you said you didn't have any children . . . When I asked you, you said. . . .

NICK. She wasn't . . . really. It was a hysterical pregnancy. She blew up, and then she went down.

GEORGE. And while she was up, you married her.

NICK. And then she went down.

(They both laugh, and are a little surprised that they do)

GEORGE. Uh . . . Bourbon *is* right.

NICK. Uh . . . yes, Bourbon.

GEORGE *(At the bar, still).* When I was sixteen and going to prep school, during the Punic Wars, a bunch of us used to go into New York on the first day of vacations, before we fanned out to our homes, and in the evening this bunch of us used to go to this gin mill owned by the gangster-father of one of us—for this was during the Great Experiment, or Prohibition, as it is more frequently called, and it was a bad time for the liquor lobby, but a fine time for the crooks and the cops—and we would go to this gin mill, and we would drink with the grown-ups and listen to the jazz. And one time, in the bunch of us, there was this boy who was fifteen, and he had killed his mother with a shotgun some years before—accidentally, completely accidentally, without even an unconscious motivation, I have no doubt, no doubt at all—and this one evening this boy went with us, and we ordered our drinks, and when it came his turn he said, I'll have bergin . . . give me some bergin, please . . . bergin and water. Well, we all laughed . . . he was blond and he had the face of a cherub, and we all laughed, and his cheeks went red and the color rose in his neck, and the assistant crook who had taken our order told people at the next table what the boy had said, and then they laughed, and then more people were told and the laughter grew, and more people and more laughter, and no one was laughing more than us, and none of us more than the boy who had shot his mother. And soon, everyone in the gin mill knew what the laughter was about, and everyone started ordering bergin, and laughing when they ordered it. And soon, of course, the laughter became less general, but it did not subside, entirely, for a very long time, for always at this table or that someone would order bergin and a new area of laughter would rise. We drank free that night, and we were bought champagne by the management, by the gangster-father of one of us. And, of course, we suffered the next day, each of us, alone, on his train, away from New York, each of us with a grown-up's hangover . . . but it was the grandest day of my . . . youth.

(Hands NICK *a drink on the word)*

NICK *(Very quietly)*. Thank you. What . . . what happened to the boy . . . the boy who had shot his mother?

GEORGE. I won't tell you.

NICK. All right.

GEORGE. The following summer, on a country road, with his learner's permit in his pocket and his father on the front seat to his right, he swerved the car, to avoid a porcupine, and drove straight into a large tree.

NICK *(Faintly pleading)*. No.

GEORGE. He was not killed, of course. And in the hospital, when he was conscious and out of danger, and when they told him that his father *was* dead, he began to laugh, I have been told, and his laughter grew and he would not stop, and it was not until after they jammed a needle in his arm, not until after that, until his consciousness slipped away from him, that his laughter subsided . . . stopped. And when he was recovered from his injuries enough so that he could be moved without damage should he struggle, he was put in an asylum. That was thirty years ago.

NICK. Is he . . . still there?

GEORGE. Oh, yes. And I'm told that for these thirty years he has . . . not . . . uttered . . . one . . . sound.

(A rather long silence; five seconds, please)

MARTHA! *(Pause)* MARTHA!

NICK. I told you . . . she's making coffee.

GEORGE. For your hysterical wife, who goes up and down.

NICK. Went. Up and down.

GEORGE. Went. No more?

NICK. No more. Nothing.

GEORGE *(After a sympathetic pause)*. The saddest thing about men. . . . Well, no, one of the saddest things about men is the way they age . . . some of them. Do you know what it is with insane people? Do you? . . . the quiet ones?

NICK. No.

GEORGE. They don't change . . . they don't grow old.

NICK. They must.

GEORGE. Well, eventually, probably, yes. But they don't . . . in the usual sense. They maintain a . . . a firm-skinned serenity . . . the . . . the under-use of everything leaves them . . . quite whole.

NICK. Are you recommending it?

GEORGE. No. Some things are sad, though. *(Imitates a pep-talker)* But ya jest gotta buck up an' face 'em, 'at's all. Buck up! *(Pause)* Martha doesn't have hysterical pregnancies.

NICK. My wife had *one*.

GEORGE. Yes. Martha doesn't have pregnancies at all.

NICK. Well, no . . . I don't imagine so . . . now. Do you have any other kids? Do you have any daughters, or anything?

GEORGE *(As if it's a great joke)*. Do we have any *what?*

NICK. Do you have any . . . I mean, do you have only one . . . kid . . . uh . . . your son?

GEORGE *(With a private knowledge)*. Oh no . . . just one . . . one boy . . . our son.

NICK. Well . . . *(Shrugs)* . . . that's nice.

GEORGE. Oh ho, ho. Yes, well, he's a . . . comfort, a bean bag.

NICK. A what?

GEORGE. A bean bag. Bean bag. You wouldn't understand. *(Overdistinct)* Bean . . . bag.

NICK. I *heard* you . . . I didn't say I was deaf . . . I said I didn't understand.

GEORGE. You didn't say that at all.

NICK. I meant I was *implying* I didn't understand. *(Under his breath)* For Christ's sake!

GEORGE. You're getting testy.

NICK *(Testy)*. I'm sorry.

GEORGE. All I said was, our son . . . the apple of our three eyes, Martha being a Cyclops . . . our son is a bean bag, and you get testy.

NICK. I'm sorry! It's late, I'm tired, I've been drinking since nine o'clock, my wife is vomiting, there's been a lot of screaming going on around here. . . .

GEORGE. And so you're testy. Naturally. Don't . . . worry about it. Anybody who comes here ends up getting . . . testy. It's expected . . . don't be upset.

NICK *(Testy).* I'm not upset!

GEORGE. You're testy.

NICK. Yes.

GEORGE. I'd like to set you straight about something . . . while the little ladies are out of the room . . . I'd like to set you straight about what Martha said.

NICK. I don't . . . make judgments, so there's no need, really, unless you. . . .

GEORGE. Well, I want to. I know you don't like to become involved . . . I know you like to . . . preserve your scientific detachment in the face of—for lack of a better word—Life . . . and all . . . but still, I want to tell you.

NICK *(A tight, formal smile).* I'm a . . . guest. You go right ahead.

GEORGE *(Mocking appreciation).* Oh . . . well, thanks. Now! That makes me feel all warm and runny inside.

NICK. Well, if you're going to . . .

MARTHA'S VOICE. HEY!

NICK. . . . if you're going to start that kind of stuff again. . . .

GEORGE. Hark! Forest sounds.

NICK. Hm?

GEORGE. Animal noises.

MARTHA *(Sticking her head in).* Hey!

NICK. Oh!

GEORGE. Well, here's nursie.

MARTHA *(To NICK).* We're sitting up . . . we're having coffee, and we'll be back in.

NICK *(Not rising).* Oh . . . is there anything I should do?

MARTHA. Nyah. You just stay here and listen to George's side of things. Bore yourself to death.

GEORGE. Monstre!

MARTHA. Cochon!

GEORGE. Bête!

114

MARTHA. Canaille!

GEORGE. Putain!

MARTHA *(With a gesture of contemptuous dismissal).* Yaaaahhhh! You two types amuse yourselves . . . we'll be in. *(As she goes)* You clean up the mess you made, George?

GEORGE (MARTHA *goes.* GEORGE *speaks to the empty hallway).* No, Martha, I did not clean up the mess I made. I've been trying for years to clean up the mess I made.

NICK. Have you?

GEORGE. Hm?

NICK. *Have* you been trying for years?

GEORGE *(After a long pause . . . looking at him).* Accommodation, malleability, adjustment . . . those do seem to be in the order of things, don't they?

NICK. Don't try to put me in the same class with you!

GEORGE *(Pause).* Oh. *(Pause)* No, of course not. Things are simpler with you . . . you marry a woman because she's all blown up . . . while I, in my clumsy, old-fashioned way. . . .

NICK. There was more to it than that!

GEORGE. Sure! I'll bet she has money, too!

NICK *(Looks hurt. Then, determined, after a pause).* Yes.

GEORGE. Yes? *(Joyfully)* YES! You mean I was right? I hit it?

NICK. Well, you see. . . .

GEORGE. My God, what archery! First try, too. How about that!

NICK. You see. . . .

GEORGE. There were other things.

NICK. Yes.

GEORGE. To compensate.

NICK. Yes.

GEORGE. There always are. *(Sees that* NICK *is reacting badly)* No, I'm sure there are. I didn't mean to be . . . flip. There are *always* compensating factors . . . as in the case of Martha and myself. . . . Now, on the surface of it. . . .

NICK. We sort of grew up together, you know. . . .

GEORGE. . . . it looks to be a kind of knock-about, drag-out affair, on the *surface* of it. . . .

NICK. We knew each other from, oh God, I don't know, when we were *six*, or something. . . .

115

GEORGE. . . . but somewhere back there, at the beginning of it, right when I first came to New Carthage, back then. . . .

NICK *(With some irritation).* I'm *sorry.*

GEORGE. Hm? Oh. No, no . . . *I'm* sorry.

NICK. No . . . it's . . . it's all right.

GEORGE. No . . . you go ahead.

NICK. No . . . please.

GEORGE. I insist . . . You're a guest. You go first.

NICK. Well, it seems a little silly . . . now.

GEORGE. Nonsense! *(Pause)* But if you were six, she must have been four, or something.

NICK. Maybe I was eight . . . she was six. We . . . we used to play . . . doctor.

GEORGE. That's a good healthy heterosexual beginning.

NICK *(Laughing).* Yup.

GEORGE. The scientist even then, eh?

NICK *(Laughs).* Yeah. And it was . . . always taken for granted . . . you know . . . by our families, and by us, too, I guess. And . . . so, we did.

GEORGE *(Pause).* Did what?

NICK. We got married.

GEORGE. When you were eight?

NICK. No. No, of course not. Much later.

GEORGE. I wondered.

NICK. I wouldn't say there was any . . . particular *passion* between us, even at the beginning . . . of our marriage, I mean.

GEORGE. Well, certainly no surprise, no earth-shaking discoveries, after Doctor, and all.

NICK *(Uncertainly).* No. . . .

GEORGE. Everything's all pretty much the same, anyway . . . in *spite* of what they say about Chinese women.

NICK. What is that?

GEORGE. Let me freshen you up. *(Takes* NICK's *glass)*

NICK. Oh, thanks. After a while you don't get any drunker, do you?

GEORGE. Well, you *do* . . . but it's different . . . everything slows down. . . . you get sodden. . . . unless you can up-chuck . . . like your wife . . . then you can sort of start all over again.

116

NICK. Everybody drinks a lot here in the East. *(Thinks about it)* Everybody drinks a lot in the middle-west, too.

GEORGE. We drink a great deal in this country, and I suspect we'll be drinking a great deal more, too . . . if we survive. We should be Arabs or Italians . . . the Arabs don't drink, and the Italians don't get drunk much, except on religious holidays. We should live on Crete, or something.

NICK *(Sarcastically . . . as if killing a joke)*. And that, of course, would make us cretins.

GEORGE *(Mild surprise)*. So it would. *(Hands* NICK *his drink)* Tell me about your wife's money.

NICK *(Suddenly suspicious)*. Why?

GEORGE. Well . . . don't then.

NICK. What do you want to know about my wife's money for? *(Ugly)* Hunh?

GEORGE. Well, I thought it would be nice.

NICK. No you didn't.

GEORGE *(Still deceptively bland)*. All right. . . . I want to know about your wife's money because . . . well, because I'm fascinated by the methodology . . . by the pragmatic accommodation by which you wave-of-the-future boys are going to take over.

NICK. You're starting in again.

GEORGE. Am I? No I'm not. Look . . . Martha has money too. I mean, her father's been robbing this place blind for years, and. . . .

NICK. No, he hasn't. He has not.

GEORGE. He hasn't?

NICK. No.

GEORGE *(Shrugs)*. Very well. . . . Martha's father has *not* been robbing this place blind for years, and Martha does not have any money. O.K.?

NICK. We were talking about *my* wife's money . . . not yours.

GEORGE. O.K. . . . talk.

NICK. No. *(Pause)* My father-in-law . . . was a man of the Lord, and he was very rich.

GEORGE. What faith?

NICK. He . . . my father-in-law . . . was called by God when he was six, or something, and he started preaching, and he baptized people, and he saved them, and he traveled around a lot, and he became pretty famous

. . . not like some of them, but he became pretty famous . . . and when he died he had a lot of money.

GEORGE. God's money.

NICK. No . . . his own.

GEORGE. What happened to God's money?

NICK. He spent God's money . . . and he saved his own. He built hospitals, and he sent off Mercy ships, and he brought the outhouses indoors, and he brought the people outdoors, into the sun, and he built three churches, or whatever they were, and two of them burned down . . . and he ended up pretty rich.

GEORGE *(After considering it).* Well, I think that's very nice.

NICK. Yes. *(Pause. Giggles a little)* And so, my wife's got some money.

GEORGE. But not God's money.

NICK. No. Her own.

GEORGE. Well, I think that's very nice.

(NICK *giggles a little)*

Martha's got money because Martha's father's second wife . . . not Martha's mother, but after Martha's mother died . . . was a very old lady with warts who was very rich.

NICK. She was a witch.

GEORGE. She was a *good* witch, and she married the white mouse . . .

(NICK *begins to giggle)*

. . . with the tiny red eyes . . . and he must have nibbled her warts, or something like that, because she went up in a puff of smoke almost immediately. POUF!

NICK. POUF!

GEORGE. POUF! And all that was left, aside from some wart medicine, was a big fat will. . . . A peach pie, with some for the township of New Carthage, some for the college, some for Martha's daddy, and just this much for Martha.

NICK *(Quite beside himself).* Maybe . . . maybe my father-in-law and the witch with the warts should have gotten together, because he was a mouse, too.

GEORGE *(Urging NICK on).* He was?

NICK *(Breaking down).* Sure . . . he was a church mouse! *(They both laugh a great deal, but it is sad laughter . . . eventually they subside, fall silent)* Your wife never mentioned a stepmother.

GEORGE *(Considers it).* Well . . . maybe it isn't true.

NICK *(Narrowing his eyes).* And maybe it is.

GEORGE. Might be . . . might not. Well, I think your story's a lot nicer . . . about your pumped-up little wife, and your father-in-law who was a priest. . . .

NICK. He was not a priest . . . he was a man of God.

GEORGE. Yes.

NICK. And my wife wasn't pumped up . . . she blew up.

GEORGE. Yes, yes.

NICK *(Giggling).* Get things straight.

GEORGE. I'm sorry . . . I will. I'm sorry.

NICK. O.K.

GEORGE. You realize, of course, that I've been drawing you out on this stuff, not because I'm interested in your terrible lifehood, but only because you represent a direct and pertinent threat to my lifehood, and I want to get the goods on you.

NICK *(Still amused).* Sure . . . sure.

GEORGE. I mean . . . I've warned you . . . you stand warned.

NICK. I stand warned. *(Laughs)* It's you sneaky types worry me the most, you know. You ineffectual sons of bitches . . . you're the worst.

GEORGE. Yes . . . we are. Sneaky. An elbow in your steely-blue eye . . . a knee in your solid gold groin . . . we're the worst.

NICK. Yup.

GEORGE. Well, I'm glad you don't believe me. . . . I know you've got history on your side, and all. . . .

NICK. Unh-unh. *You've* got history on *your* side. . . . I've got biology on mine. History, biology.

GEORGE. I know the difference.

NICK. You don't act it.

GEORGE. No? I thought we'd decided that you'd take over the History Department first, before you took over the whole works. You know . . . a step at a time.

NICK *(Stretching . . . luxuriating . . . playing the game).* Nyaah . . . what I thought I'd do is . . . I'd sort of insinuate myself generally, play around for a while, find all the weak spots, shore 'em up, but with my own name plate on 'em . . . become sort of a fact, and then turn into a . . . a what . . . ?

GEORGE. An inevitability.

NICK. Exactly. . . . An inevitability. You know. . . . Take over a few courses from the older men, start some special groups for myself . . . plow a few pertinent wives. . . .

GEORGE. Now that's it! You can take over all the courses you want to, and get as much of the young elite together in the gymnasium as you like, but until you start plowing pertinent wives, you really aren't working. The way to a man's heart is through his wife's belly, and don't you forget it.

NICK *(Playing along)*. Yeah. . . . I know.

GEORGE. And the women around here are no better than puntas—you know, South American ladies of the night. You know what they do in South America . . . in Rio? The puntas? Do you know? They hiss . . . like geese. . . . They stand around in the street and they hiss at you . . . like a bunch of geese.

NICK. Gangle.

GEORGE. Hm?

NICK. Gangle . . . gangle of geese . . . not bunch . . . gangle.

GEORGE. Well, if you're going to get all cute about it, all ornithological, it's gaggle . . . not gangle, *gaggle*.

NICK. Gaggle? Not Gangle?

GEORGE. Yes, gaggle.

NICK *(Crestfallen)*. Oh.

GEORGE. Oh. Yes. . . . Well they stand around on the street and they hiss at you, like a bunch of geese. All the faculty wives, downtown in New Carthage, in front of the A&P, hissing away like a bunch of geese. That's the way to power—plow 'em all!

NICK *(Still playing along)*. I'll bet you're right.

GEORGE. Well, I am.

NICK. And I'll bet your wife's the biggest goose in the gangle, isn't she . . . ? Her father president, and all.

GEORGE. You bet your historical inevitability she is!

NICK. Yessirree. *(Rubs his hands together)* Well now, I'd just better get her off in a corner and mount her like a goddam dog, eh?

GEORGE. Why, you'd certainly better.

NICK *(Looks at GEORGE a minute, his expression a little sick)*. You know, I almost think you're serious.

GEORGE *(Toasting him)*. No, baby . . . *you* almost think you're serious, and it scares the hell out of you.

NICK *(Exploding in disbelief)*. ME!

GEORGE *(Quietly)*. Yes . . . you.

NICK. You're kidding!

GEORGE *(Like a father)*. I wish I were. . . . I'll give you some good advice if you want me to. . . .

NICK. Good advice! From you? Oh boy! *(Starts to laugh)*

GEORGE. You haven't learned yet. . . . Take it wherever you can get it. . . . Listen to me, now.

NICK. Come off it!

GEORGE. I'm giving you good advice, now.

NICK. Good God . . . !

GEORGE. There's quicksand here, and you'll be dragged down, just as. . . .

NICK. Oh boy . . . !

GEORGE. . . . before you know it . . . sucked down. . . .

(NICK *laughs derisively*)

You disgust me on principle, and you're a smug son of a bitch personally, but I'm trying to give you a survival kit. DO YOU HEAR ME?

NICK *(Still laughing)*. I hear you. You come in loud.

GEORGE. ALL RIGHT!

NICK. Hey, Honey.

GEORGE *(Silence. Then quietly)*. All right . . . O.K. You want to play it by ear, right? Everything's going to work out anyway, because the timetable's history, right?

NICK. Right . . . right. You just tend to your knitting, grandma . . . I'll be O.K.

GEORGE *(After a silence)*. I've tried to . . . tried to reach you . . . to. . . .

NICK *(Contemptuously)*. . . . make contact?

GEORGE. Yes.

NICK *(Still)*. . . . communicate?

GEORGE. Yes. Exactly.

NICK. Aw . . . that *is* touching . . . that is . . . downright moving . . . that's what it is. *(With sudden vehemence)* UP YOURS!

GEORGE *(Brief pause)*. Hm?

NICK *(Threatening)*. You heard me!

GEORGE *(At Nick, not to him)*. You take the trouble to construct a civilization . . . to . . . to build a society, based on the principles of . . . of principle . . . you endeavor to make communicable sense out of natural order, morality out of the unnatural disorder of man's mind

121

. . . you make government and art, and realize that they are, must be, both the same . . . you bring things to the saddest of all points . . . to the point where there *is* something to lose . . . then all at once, through all the music, through all the sensible sounds of men building, attempting, comes the *Dies Irae*. And what is it? What does the trumpet sound? Up yours. I suppose there's justice to it, after all the years. . . . Up yours.

NICK *(Brief pause . . . then applauding)*. Ha, ha! Bravo! Ha, ha! *(Laughs on)*

(And MARTHA *reenters, leading* HONEY, *who is wan but smiling bravely)*

HONEY *(Grandly)*. Thank you . . . thank you.

MARTHA. Here we are, a little shaky, but on our feet.

GEORGE. Goodie.

NICK. What? Oh . . . OH! Hi, Honey . . . you better?

HONEY. A little bit, dear. . . . I'd better sit down, though.

NICK. Sure . . . c'mon . . . you sit by me.

HONEY. Thank you, dear.

GEORGE *(Beneath his breath)*. Touching . . . touching.

MARTHA *(To* GEORGE*)*. Well? Aren't you going to apologize?

GEORGE *(Squinting)*. For what, Martha?

MARTHA. For making the little lady throw up, what else?

GEORGE. I did not make her throw up.

MARTHA. You most certainly did!

GEORGE. I did not!

HONEY *(Papal gesture)*. No, now . . . no.

MARTHA *(To* GEORGE*)*. Well, who do you think did . . . Sexy over there? You think he made his *own* little wife sick?

GEORGE *(Helpfully)*. Well, you make *me* sick.

MARTHA. THAT'S DIFFERENT!

HONEY. No, now. I . . . I throw up . . . I mean, I get sick . . . occasionally, all by myself . . . without any reason.

GEORGE. Is that a fact?

NICK. You're . . . you're delicate, Honey.

HONEY *(Proudly)*. I've always done it.

GEORGE. Like Big Ben.

NICK *(A warning)*. Watch it!

HONEY. And the doctors say there's nothing wrong with me . . . organically. You know?

NICK. Of course there isn't.

HONEY. Why, just before we got married, I developed . . . appendicitis . . . or everybody *thought* it was appendicitis . . . but it turned out to be . . . it was a . . . *(laughs briefly)* . . . false alarm.

(GEORGE *and* NICK *exchange glances)*

MARTHA *(To* GEORGE). Get me a drink.

(GEORGE *moves to the bar)*

George makes everybody sick. . . . When our son was just a little boy, he used to. . . .

GEORGE. Don't Martha. . . .

MARTHA. . . . he used to throw up all the time, because of George. . . .

GEORGE. I said, don't!

MARTHA. It got so bad that whenever George came into the room he'd start right in retching, and. . . .

GEORGE. . . . the real reason *(Spits out the words)* our son . . . used to throw up all the time, wife and lover, was nothing more complicated than that he couldn't stand you fiddling at him all the time, breaking into his bedroom with your kimono flying, fiddling at him all the time, with your liquor breath on him, and your hands all over his. . . .

MARTHA. YEAH? And I suppose that's why he ran away from home twice in one month, too. *(Now to the guests)* Twice in one month! Six times in one year!

GEORGE *(Also to the guests)*. Our son ran away from home all the time because Martha here used to corner him.

MARTHA *(Braying)*. I NEVER CORNERED THE SON OF A BITCH IN MY LIFE!

GEORGE *(Handing* MARTHA *her drink)*. He used to run up to me when I'd get home, and he'd say, "Mama's always coming at me." That's what he'd say.

MARTHA. Liar!

GEORGE *(Shrugging)*. Well, that's the way it was . . . you were always coming at him. I thought it was very embarrassing.

NICK. If you thought it was so embarrassing, what are you talking about it for?

HONEY *(Admonishing)*. Dear . . . !

MARTHA. Yeah! *(To* NICK) Thanks, sweetheart.

GEORGE *(To them all)*. I didn't want to talk about him at all . . . I would

123

have been perfectly happy not to discuss the whole subject. . . . I never want to talk about it.

MARTHA. Yes you do.

GEORGE. When we're alone, maybe.

MARTHA. We're alone!

GEORGE. Uh . . . no, love . . . we've got guests.

MARTHA *(With a covetous look at* NICK*).* We sure have.

HONEY. Could I have a little brandy? I think I'd like a little brandy.

NICK. Do you think you should?

HONEY. Oh yes . . . yes, dear.

GEORGE *(Moving to the bar again).* Sure! Fill 'er up!

NICK. Honey, I don't think you. . . .

HONEY *(Petulance creeping in).* It will steady me, *dear.* I feel a little unsteady.

GEORGE. Hell, you can't walk steady on half a bottle . . . got to do it right.

HONEY. Yes. *(To* MARTHA*)* I love brandy . . . I really do.

MARTHA *(Somewhat abstracted).* Good for you.

NICK *(Giving up).* Well, if you think it's a good idea. . . .

HONEY *(Really testy).* I know what's best for me, dear.

NICK *(Not even pleasant).* Yes . . . I'm sure you do.

HONEY (GEORGE *hands her a brandy).* Oh, goodie! Thank you. *(To* NICK*)* Of course I do, dear.

GEORGE *(Pensively).* I used to drink brandy.

MARTHA *(Privately).* You used to drink bergin, too.

GEORGE *(Sharp).* Shut up, Martha!

MARTHA *(Her hand over her mouth in a little girl gesture).* Oooooops.

NICK *(Something having clicked, vaguely).* Hm?

GEORGE *(Burying it).* Nothing . . . nothing.

MARTHA *(She, too).* You two men have it out while we were gone? George tell you his side of things? He bring you to tears, hunh?

NICK. Well . . . no. . . .

GEORGE. No, what we did, actually, was . . . we sort of danced around.

MARTHA. Oh, yeah? Cute!

HONEY. Oh, I love dancing.

NICK. He didn't mean that, Honey.

HONEY. Well, I didn't think he did! Two grown men dancing . . . heavens!

124

MARTHA. You mean he didn't start in on how he would have amounted to
something if it hadn't been for Daddy? How his high moral sense
wouldn't even let him *try* to better himself? No?

NICK *(Qualified)*. No. . . .

MARTHA. And he didn't run on about how he tried to publish a goddam
book, and Daddy wouldn't let him.

NICK. A book? No.

GEORGE. Please, Martha. . . .

NICK *(Egging her on)*. A book? What book?

GEORGE *(Pleading)*. Please. Just a book.

MARTHA *(Mock incredulity)*. Just a book!

GEORGE. *Please*, Martha!

MARTHA *(Almost disappointed)*. Well, I guess you didn't get the whole sad
story. What's the matter with you, George? You given up?

GEORGE *(Calm . . . serious)*. No . . . no. It's just I've got to figure out
some new way to fight you, Martha. Guerilla tactics, maybe . . . inter-
nal subversion . . . I don't know. Something.

MARTHA. Well, you figure it out, and you let me know when you do.

GEORGE *(Cheery)*. All right, love.

HONEY. Why don't we dance? I'd love some dancing.

NICK. Honey. . . .

HONEY. I would! I'd love some dancing.

NICK. Honey. . . .

HONEY. I *want* some! I want some dancing!

GEORGE. All right . . . ! For heaven's sake . . . we'll have some dancing.

HONEY *(All sweetness again) (To* MARTHA*)*. Oh, I'm so glad . . . I just
love dancing. Don't you?

MARTHA *(With a glance at* NICK*)*. Yeah . . . yeah, that's not a bad idea.

NICK *(Genuinely nervous)*. Gee.

GEORGE. Gee.

HONEY. I dance like the wind.

MARTHA *(Without comment)*. Yeah?

GEORGE *(Picking a record)*. Martha had her daguerrotype in the paper once
. . . oh 'bout twenty-five years ago. . . . Seems she took second prize
in one o' them seven-day dancin' contest things . . . biceps all bulg-
ing, holding up her partner.

MARTHA. Will you put a record on and shut up?

GEORGE. Certainly, love. *(To all)* How are we going to work this? Mixed doubles?

MARTHA. Well, you certainly don't think I'm going to dance with *you*, do you?

GEORGE *(Considers it)*. Noooooo . . . not with him around . . . that's for sure. And not with twinkle-toes here, either.

HONEY. I'll dance with anyone. . . . I'll dance by myself.

NICK. Honey. . . .

HONEY. I dance like the wind.

GEORGE. All right, kiddies . . . choose up and hit the sack.

(Music starts. . . . Second movement, Beethoven's 7th Symphony)

HONEY *(Up, dancing by herself)*. De, de de *da* da, da-da de, da *da*-da de da . . . wonderful . . . !

NICK. Honey. . . .

MARTHA. All right, George . . . cut that out!

HONEY. Dum, de de da da, da-da de, dum de *da* da da. . . . Wheeeee . . . !

MARTHA. Cut it out, George!

GEORGE *(Pretending not to hear)*. What, Martha? What?

NICK. Honey . . .

MARTHA *(As* GEORGE *turns up the volume)*. CUT IT OUT, GEORGE!

GEORGE. WHAT?

MARTHA *(Gets up, moves quickly, threateningly, to* GEORGE*)*. All right, you son of a bitch. . . .

GEORGE *(Record off, at once. Quietly)*. What did you say, love?

MARTHA. You son of a. . . .

HONEY *(In an arrested posture)*. You stopped! Why did you stop?

NICK. Honey. . . .

HONEY *(To* NICK, *snapping)*. Stop that!

GEORGE. I thought it was fitting, Martha.

MARTHA. Oh you did, hunh?

HONEY. You're always *at* me when I'm having a good time.

NICK *(Trying to remain civil)*. I'm sorry, Honey.

HONEY. Just . . . leave me alone!

GEORGE. Well, why don't *you* choose, Martha? *(Moves away from the phonograph . . . leaves it to* MARTHA*)* Martha's going to run things . . . the little lady's going to lead the band.

HONEY. I like to dance and you don't want me to.

126

NICK. *I* like you to dance.

HONEY. Just . . . leave me alone. *(She sits . . . takes a drink)*

GEORGE. Martha's going to put on some rhythm she understands . . .
Sacre du Printemps, maybe. *(Moves . . . sits by* HONEY*)* Hi, sexy.

HONEY *(A little giggle-scream)*. Oooooohhhhh!

GEORGE *(Laughs mockingly)*. Ha, ha, ha, ha, ha. Choose it, Martha . . .
do your stuff!

MARTHA *(Concentrating on the machine)*. You're damn right!

GEORGE *(To* HONEY*)*. You want to dance with me, angel-tits?

NICK. What did you call my wife?

GEORGE *(Derisively)*. Oh boy!

HONEY *(Petulantly)*. No! If I can't do my interpretive dance, I don't want
to dance with anyone. I'll just sit here and. . . . *(Shrugs . . . drinks)*

MARTHA *(Record on . . . a jazzy slow pop tune)*. O.K. stuff, let's go.
(Grabs NICK*)*

NICK. Hm? Oh . . . hi.

MARTHA. Hi. *(They dance, close together, slowly)*

HONEY *(Pouting)*. We'll just sit here and watch.

GEORGE. That's *right!*

MARTHA *(To* NICK*)*. Hey, you *are* strong, aren't you?

NICK. Unh-hunh.

MARTHA. I like that.

NICK. Unh-hunh.

HONEY. They're dancing like they've danced before.

GEORGE. It's a familiar dance . . . they both know it. . . .

MARTHA. Don't be shy.

NICK. I'm . . . not. . . .

GEORGE *(To* HONEY*)*. It's a very old ritual, monkey-nipples . . . old as
they come.

HONEY. I . . . I don't know what you mean.

(NICK *and* MARTHA *move apart now, and dance on either side of where*
GEORGE *and* HONEY *are sitting; they face each other, and while their
feet move but little, their bodies undulate congruently. . . . It is as if
they were pressed together)*

MARTHA. I like the way you move.

NICK. I like the way you move, too.

GEORGE *(To* HONEY*)*. They like the way they move.

HONEY *(Not entirely with it)*. That's nice.

127

MARTHA *(To* NICK). I'm surprised George didn't give you his side of things.
GEORGE *(To* HONEY). Aren't they cute?
NICK. Well, he didn't.
MARTHA. That surprises me.

(Perhaps MARTHA's *statements are more or less in time to the music)*
NICK. Does it?
MARTHA. Yeah . . . he usually does . . . when he gets the chance.
NICK. Well, what do you know.
MARTHA. It's really a very sad story.
GEORGE. You have ugly talents, Martha.
NICK. Is it?
MARTHA. It would make you weep.
GEORGE. Hideous gifts.
NICK. Is that so?
GEORGE. Don't encourage her.
MARTHA. Encourage me.
NICK. Go on.

(They may undulate toward each other and then move back)
GEORGE. I warn you . . . don't encourage her.
MARTHA. He warns you . . . don't encourage me.
NICK. I heard him . . . tell me more.
MARTHA *(Consciously making rhymed speech).* Well, Georgie-boy had lots
of big ambitions
In spite of something funny in his past. . . .
GEORGE *(Quietly warning).* Martha. . . .
MARTHA. Which Georgie-boy here turned into a novel. . . .
His first attempt and also his last. . . .
Hey! I rhymed! I rhymed!
GEORGE. I warn you, Martha.
NICK. Yeah . . . you rhymed. Go on, go on.
MARTHA. But Daddy took a look at Georgie's novel. . . .
GEORGE. You're looking for a punch in the mouth. . . . You know that,
Martha.
MARTHA. Do tell! . . . and he was very shocked by what he read.
NICK. He was?
MARTHA. Yes . . . he was. . . . A novel all about a naughty boy-
child. . . .
GEORGE *(Rising).* I will not tolerate this!

128

NICK *(Offhand, to* GEORGE). Oh, can it.

MARTHA. . . . ha, ha!
naughty boychild
who . . . uh . . . who killed his mother and his father dead.

GEORGE. STOP IT, MARTHA!

MARTHA. And Daddy said . . . Look here, I will not let you publish such
a thing. . . .

GEORGE *(Rushes to phonograph . . . rips the record off).* That's it! The
dancing's over. That's it. Go on now!

NICK. What do you think you're doing, hunh?

HONEY *(Happily).* Violence! Violence!

MARTHA *(Loud: a pronouncement).* And Daddy said . . . Look here, kid,
you don't think for a second I'm going to let you publish this crap, do
you? Not on your life, baby . . . not while you're teaching here. . . .
You publish that goddam book and you're out . . . on your ass!

GEORGE. DESIST! DESIST!

MARTHA. Ha, ha, ha, HA!

NICK *(Laughing).* De . . . sist!

HONEY. Oh, violence . . . violence!

MARTHA. Why, the idea! A teacher at a respected, conservative institution
like this, in a town like New Carthage, publishing a book like that? If
you respect your position here, young man, young . . . whippersnap-
per, you'll just withdraw that manuscript. . . .

GEORGE. I will not be made mock of!

NICK. He will not be made mock of, for Christ's sake. *(Laughs)*
(HONEY *joins in the laughter, not knowing exactly why)*

GEORGE. I will not!
(All three are laughing at him)
(Infuriated) THE GAME IS OVER!

MARTHA *(Pushing on).* Imagine such a thing! A book about a boy who
murders his mother and kills his father, and pretends it's all an accident!

HONEY *(Beside herself with glee).* An accident!

NICK *(Remembering something related).* Hey . . . wait a minute . . .

MARTHA *(Her own voice now).* And you want to know the clincher? You
want to know what big brave Georgie said to Daddy?

GEORGE. NO! NO! NO! NO!

NICK. Wait a minute now. . . .

MARTHA. Georgie said . . . but Daddy . . . I mean . . . ha, ha, ha, ha
. . . but *Sir*, it isn't a *novel* at all . . . *(Other voice)* Not a novel?
(Mimicking GEORGE's *voice)* No, sir . . . it isn't a novel at all. . . .
GEORGE *(Advancing on her).* You will not say this!
NICK *(Sensing the danger).* Hey.
MARTHA. The hell I won't. Keep away from me, you bastard!
(Backs off a little . . . uses GEORGE's *voice again)*
No, Sir, this isn't a novel at all . . . this is the truth . . . this really
happened. . . . TO ME!
GEORGE *(On her).* I'LL KILL YOU!
(Grabs her by the throat. They struggle)
NICK. HEY! *(Comes between them)*
HONEY *(Wildly).* VIOLENCE! VIOLENCE!
*(*GEORGE, MARTHA, *and* NICK *struggle . . . yells, etc.)*
MARTHA. IT HAPPENED! TO ME! TO ME!
GEORGE. YOU SATANIC BITCH!
NICK. STOP THAT! STOP THAT!
HONEY. VIOLENCE! VIOLENCE!
(The other three struggle. GEORGE's *hands are on* MARTHA's *throat.*
NICK *grabs him, tears him from* MARTHA, *throws him on the floor.*
GEORGE, *on the floor;* NICK *over him;* MARTHA *to one side, her hand on
her throat)*
NICK. That's enough now!
HONEY *(Disappointment in her voice).* Oh . . . oh . . . oh. . . .
*(*GEORGE *drags himself into a chair. He is hurt, but it is more a pro-
found humiliation than a physical injury)*
GEORGE *(They watch him . . . a pause. . . .).* All right . . . all right
. . . very quiet now . . . we will all be . . . very quiet.
MARTHA *(Softly, with a slow shaking of her head).* Murderer. Mur . . .
der . . . er.
NICK *(Softly to* MARTHA*).* O.K. now . . . that's enough.
*(A brief silence. They all move around a little, self-consciously, like
wrestlers flexing after a fall)*
GEORGE *(Composure seemingly recovered, but there is a great nervous inten-
sity).* Well! That's one game. What shall we do now, hunh?
*(*MARTHA *and* NICK *laugh nervously)*
Oh come on . . . let's think of something else. We've played Humili-

ate the Host . . . we've gone through that one . . . what shall we do now?

NICK. Aw . . . look. . . .

GEORGE. AW LOOK! *(Whines it)* Awww . . . looooook. *(Alert)* I mean, come on! We must know other games, college-type types like us . . . that can't be the . . . limit of our vocabulary, can it?

NICK. I think maybe. . . .

GEORGE. Let's see now . . . what else can we do? There are other games. How about . . . how about . . . Hump the Hostess? HUNH?? How about that? How about Hump the Hostess? *(To NICK)* You wanna play that one? You wanna play Hump the Hostess? HUNH? HUNH?

NICK *(A little frightened).* Calm down, now.

(MARTHA *giggles quietly*)

GEORGE. Or is that for later . . . mount her like a goddamn dog?

HONEY *(Wildly toasting everybody).* Hump the Hostess!

NICK *(To* HONEY . . . *sharply).* Just shut up . . . will you?

(HONEY *does, her glass in mid-air*)

GEORGE. You don't wanna play that now, hunh? You wanna save that game till later? Well, what'll we play now? We gotta play a game.

MARTHA *(Quietly).* Portrait of a man drowning.

GEORGE *(Affirmatively, but to none of them).* I am not drowning.

HONEY *(To* NICK, *tearfully indignant).* You told me to shut up!

NICK *(Impatiently).* I'm sorry.

HONEY *(Between her teeth).* No you're not.

NICK *(To* HONEY, *even more impatiently).* I'm sorry.

GEORGE *(Claps his hands together, once, loud).* I've got it! I'll tell you what game we'll play. We're done with Humiliate the Host . . . this round, anyway . . . we're done with that . . . and we don't want to play Hump the Hostess, yet . . . not yet . . . so I know what we'll play. . . . We'll play a round of Get the Guests. How about that? How about a little game of Get the Guests?

MARTHA *(Turning away, a little disgusted).* Jesus, George.

GEORGE. Book dropper! Child mentioner!

HONEY. I don't like these games.

NICK. Yeah. . . . I think maybe we've had enough of games, now. . . .

GEORGE. Oh, no . . . oh, no . . . we haven't. We've had only one game. . . . Now we're going to have another. You can't fly on one game.

NICK. I think maybe. . . .

GEORGE *(With great authority)*. SILENCE! *(It is respected)* Now, how are we going to play Get the Guests?

MARTHA. For God's sake, George. . . .

GEORGE. You be quiet!

(MARTHA *shrugs*)

I wonder. . . . I wonder. *(Puzzles . . . then. . . .)* O.K.! Well . . . Martha . . . in her indiscreet way . . . well, not really indiscreet, because Martha is a naive, at heart . . . anyway, Martha told you all about my first novel. True or false? Hunh? I mean, true or false that there ever was such a thing. HA! But, Martha told you about it . . . my first novel, my . . . memory book . . . which I'd sort of preferred she hadn't, but hell, that's blood under the bridge. BUT! what she didn't do . . . what Martha didn't tell you about is she didn't tell us all about my *second* novel.

(MARTHA *looks at him with puzzled curiosity*)

No, you didn't know about that, did you, Martha? About my second novel, true or false. True or false?

MARTHA *(Sincerely)*. No.

GEORGE. No.

(He starts quietly but as he goes on, his tone becomes harsher, his voice louder)

Well, it's an allegory, really—probably—but it can be read as straight, cozy prose . . . and it's all about a nice young couple who come out of the middle west. It's a bucolic you see. AND, this nice young couple comes out of the middle west, and he's blond and about thirty, and he's a scientist, a teacher, a scientist . . . and his mouse is a wifey little type who gargles brandy all the time . . . and . . .

NICK. Just a minute here. . . .

GEORGE. . . . and they got to know each other when they was only teensie little types, and they used to get under the vanity table and poke around, and. . . .

NICK. I said JUST A MINUTE!

GEORGE. This is my game! You played yours . . . you people. This is my game!

HONEY *(Dreamy)*. I want to hear the story. I love stories.

MARTHA. George, for heaven's sake. . . .

GEORGE. AND! And Mousie's father was a holy man, see, and he ran sort of

a traveling clip joint, based on Christ and all those girls, and he took the
faithful . . . that's all . . . just took 'em. . . .

HONEY *(Puzzling)*. This is familiar. . . .

NICK *(Voice shaking a little)*. No kidding!

GEORGE. . . . and he died eventually, Mousie's pa, and they pried him
open, and all sorts of money fell out. . . . Jesus money, Mary money.
. . . LOOT!

HONEY. *(Dreamy, puzzling)*. I've heard this story before.

NICK. *(With quiet intensity . . . to waken her)*. Honey. . . .

GEORGE. But that's in the backwash, in the early part of the book. Anyway,
Blondie and his frau out of the plain states came. *(Chuckles)*

MARTHA. Very funny, George. . . .

GEORGE. . . . thank you . . . and settled in a town just like nouveau
Carthage here. . . .

NICK *(Threatening)*. I don't think you'd better go on, mister. . . .

GEORGE. Do you not!

NICK *(Less certainly)*. No. I . . . I don't think you'd better.

HONEY. I love familiar stories . . . they're the best.

GEORGE. How right you are. But Blondie was in disguise, really, all got up
as a teacher, 'cause his baggage ticket had bigger things writ on it . . .
H.I. HI! Historical inevitability.

NICK. There's no need for you to go any further, now. . . .

HONEY *(Puzzling to make sense out of what she is hearing)*. Let them go
on.

GEORGE. We shall. And he had this baggage with him, and part of this
baggage was in the form of his mouse. . . .

NICK. We don't have to listen to this!

HONEY. Why not?

GEORGE. Your bride has a point. And one of the things nobody could
understand about Blondie was his baggage . . . his mouse, I mean,
here he was, pan-Kansas swimming champeen, or something, and he
had this mouse, of whom he was solicitous to a point that faileth human
understanding . . . given that she was sort of a simp, in the long
run. . . .

NICK. This isn't fair of you. . . .

GEORGE. Perhaps not. Like, as I said, his mouse, she tooted brandy immod-
estly and spent half of her time in the upchuck. . . .

HONEY *(Focussing)*. I know these people. . . .

GEORGE. Do you! . . . But she was a money baggage amongst other things . . . Godly money ripped from the golden teeth of the unfaithful, a pragmatic extension of the big dream . . . and she was put up with. . . .

HONEY *(Some terror)*. I don't like this story. . . .

NICK *(Surprisingly pleading)*. Please . . . please don't.

MARTHA. Maybe you better stop, George. . . .

GEORGE. . . . and she was put up with. . . . STOP? Ha-ha.

NICK. Please . . . please don't.

GEORGE. Beg, baby.

MARTHA. George. . . .

GEORGE. . . . and . . . oh, we get a flashback here, to How They Got Married.

NICK. NO!

GEORGE *(Triumphant)*. YES!

NICK *(Almost whining)*. Why?

GEORGE. How They Got Married. Well, how they got married is this. . . . The Mouse got all puffed up one day, and she went over to Blondie's house, and she stuck out her puff, and she said . . . look at me.

HONEY *(White . . . on her feet)*. I . . . don't . . . like this.

NICK *(To GEORGE)*. Stop it!

GEORGE. Look at me . . . I'm all puffed up. Oh my goodness, said Blondie. . . .

HONEY *(As from a distance)*. . . . and so they were married. . . .

GEORGE. . . . and so they were married. . . .

HONEY. . . . and then. . . .

GEORGE. . . . and then. . . .

HONEY *(Hysteria)*. WHAT? . . . and then, WHAT?

NICK. NO! No!

GEORGE *(As if to a baby)*. . . . and then the puff went *away* . . . like magic . . . pouf!

NICK *(Almost sick)*. Jesus God. . . .

HONEY. . . . the puff went away. . . .

GEORGE *(Softly)*. . . . pouf.

NICK. Honey . . . I didn't mean to . . . honestly, I didn't mean to. . . .

HONEY. You . . . you told them. . . .

NICK. Honey . . . I didn't mean to. . . .

HONEY *(With outlandish horror)*. You . . . told them! You told them! OOOOHHHH! Oh, no, no, no, no! You couldn't have told them . . . oh, noooo!

NICK. Honey, I didn't mean to . . .

HONEY *(Grabbing at her belly)*. Ohhhhh . . . nooooo.

NICK. Honey . . . baby . . . I'm sorry . . . I didn't mean to. . . .

GEORGE *(Abruptly and with some disgust)*. And that's how you play Get the Guests.

HONEY. I'm going to . . . I'm going to be . . . sick. . . .

GEORGE. Naturally!

NICK. Honey. . . .

HONEY *(Hysterical)*. Leave me alone . . . I'm going . . . to . . . be . . . sick.

(She runs out of the room)

MARTHA *(Shaking her head, watching* HONEY's *retreating form)*. God Almighty.

GEORGE *(Shrugging)*. The patterns of history.

NICK *(Quietly shaking)*. You shouldn't have done that . . . you shouldn't have done that at all.

GEORGE *(Calmly)*. I hate hypocrisy.

NICK. That was cruel . . . and vicious. . . .

GEORGE. . . . she'll get over it . . .

NICK. . . . and damaging . . . !

GEORGE. . . . she'll recover. . . .

NICK. DAMAGING!! TO ME!!

GEORGE *(With wonder)*. To you!

NICK. TO ME!!

GEORGE. To you!!

NICK. YES!!

GEORGE. Oh beautiful . . . beautiful. By God, you gotta have a swine to show you where the truffles are. *(So calmly)* Well, you just rearrange your alliances, boy. You just pick up the pieces where you can . . . you just look around and make the best of things . . . you scramble back up on your feet.

MARTHA *(Quietly, to* NICK*)*. Go look after your wife.

GEORGE. Yeah . . . go pick up the pieces and plan some new strategy.

NICK *(To* GEORGE, *as he moves toward the hall)*. You're going to regret this.

GEORGE. Probably. I regret everything.

NICK. I mean, I'm going to make you regret this.

GEORGE *(Softly)*. No doubt. Acute embarrassment, eh?

NICK. I'll play the charades like you've got 'em set up. . . . I'll play in your language. . . . I'll be what you say I am.

GEORGE. You are already . . . you just don't know it.

NICK *(Shaking within)*. No . . . no. Not really. But I'll *be* it, mister. . . . I'll show you something come to life you'll wish you hadn't set up.

GEORGE. Go clean up the mess.

NICK *(Quietly . . . intensely)*. You just wait, mister.

(He exits. Pause. GEORGE *smiles at* MARTHA*)*

MARTHA. Very good, George.

GEORGE. Thank you, Martha.

MARTHA. Really good.

GEORGE. I'm glad you liked it.

MARTHA. I mean. . . . You did a good job . . . you really fixed it.

GEORGE. Unh-hunh.

MARTHA. It's the most . . . life you've shown in a long time.

GEORGE. You bring out the best in me, baby.

MARTHA. Yeah . . . pigmy hunting!

GEORGE. PIGMY!

MARTHA. You're really a bastard.

GEORGE. I? I?

MARTHA. Yeah . . . you.

GEORGE. Baby, if quarterback there is a pigmy, you've certainly changed your style. What are you after now . . . giants?

MARTHA. You make me sick.

GEORGE. It's perfectly all right for you. . . . I mean, you can make your own rules . . . you can go around like a hopped-up Arab, slashing away at everything in sight, scarring up half the world if you want to. But somebody else try it . . . no sir!

MARTHA. You miserable. . . .

GEORGE *(Mocking)*. Why baby, I did it all for you. I thought you'd like it, sweetheart . . . it's sort of to your taste . . . blood, carnage and all. Why, I thought you'd get all excited . . . sort of heave and pant and come running at me, your melons bobbling.

MARTHA. You've really screwed up, George.

GEORGE *(Spitting it out)*. Oh, for God's sake, Martha!

MARTHA. I mean it . . . you really have.

GEORGE *(Barely contained anger now).* You can sit there in that chair of yours, you can sit there with the gin running out of your mouth, and you can humiliate me, you can tear me apart . . . ALL NIGHT . . . and that's perfectly all right . . . that's O.K. . . .

MARTHA. YOU CAN STAND IT!

GEORGE. I CANNOT STAND IT!

MARTHA. YOU CAN STAND IT!! YOU MARRIED ME FOR IT!!

(A silence)

GEORGE *(Quietly).* That is a desperately sick lie.

MARTHA. DON'T YOU KNOW IT, EVEN YET?

GEORGE *(Shaking his head).* Oh . . . . . Martha.

MARTHA. My arm has gotten tired whipping you.

GEORGE *(Stares at her in disbelief).* You're mad.

MARTHA. For twenty-three years!

GEORGE. You're deluded . . . Martha, you're deluded.

MARTHA. IT'S NOT WHAT I'VE WANTED!

GEORGE. I thought at least you were . . . on to yourself. I didn't know. I . . . didn't know.

MARTHA *(Anger taking over).* I'm on to myself.

GEORGE *(As if she were some sort of bug).* No . . . no . . . you're . . . sick.

MARTHA *(Rises—screams).* I'LL SHOW YOU WHO'S SICK!

GEORGE. All right, Martha . . . you're going too far.

MARTHA *(Screams again).* I'LL SHOW YOU WHO'S SICK. I'LL SHOW YOU.

GEORGE *(He shakes her).* Stop it! *(Pushes her back in her chair)* Now, stop it!

MARTHA *(Calmer).* I'll show you who's sick. *(Calmer)* Boy, you're really having a field day, hunh? Well, I'm going to finish you . . . before I'm through with you. . . .

GEORGE. . . . you and the quarterback . . . you both gonna finish me . . . ?

MARTHA. . . . before I'm through with you you'll wish you'd died in that automobile, you bastard.

GEORGE *(Emphasizing with his forefinger).* And you'll wish you'd never mentioned our son!

MARTHA *(Dripping contempt).* You. . . .

GEORGE. Now, I said I warned you.

MARTHA. I'm impressed.

137

GEORGE. I warned you not to go too far.

MARTHA. I'm just beginning.

GEORGE *(Calmly, matter-of-factly).* I'm numbed enough . . . and I don't mean by liquor, though maybe that's been part of the process—a gradual, over-the-years going to sleep of the brain cells—I'm numbed enough, now, to be able to take you when we're alone. I don't listen to you . . . or when I *do* listen to you, I sift everything, I bring everything down to reflex response, so I don't really *hear* you, which is the only way to manage it. But you've taken a new tack, Martha, over the past couple of centuries—or however long it's been I've lived in this house with you—that makes it just too much . . . too much. I don't mind your dirty underthings in public . . . well, I *do* mind, but I've reconciled myself to that . . . but you've moved bag and baggage into your own fantasy world now, and you've started playing variations on your own distortions, and, as a result. . . .

MARTHA. Nuts!

GEORGE. Yes . . . you have.

MARTHA. Nuts!

GEORGE. Well, you can go on like that as long as you want to. And, when you're done. . . .

MARTHA. Have you ever listened to your sentences, George? Have you ever listened to the way you talk? You're so frigging . . . convoluted . . . that's what you are. You talk like you were writing one of your stupid papers.

GEORGE. Actually, I'm rather worried about you. About your mind.

MARTHA. Don't you worry about my mind, sweetheart!

GEORGE. I think I'll have you committed.

MARTHA. You WHAT?

GEORGE *(Quietly . . . distinctly).* I think I'll have you committed.

MARTHA *(Breaks into long laughter).* Oh baby, aren't you something!

GEORGE. I've got to find some way to really get at you.

MARTHA. You've got at me, George . . . you don't have to do anything. Twenty-three years of you has been quite enough.

GEORGE. Will you go quietly, then?

MARTHA. You know what's happened, George? You want to know what's *really happened? (Snaps her fingers)* It's snapped, finally. Not me . . . *it.* The whole arrangement. You can go along . . . forever, and everything's . . . manageable. You make all sorts of excuses to yourself . . .

you know . . . this is life . . . the hell with it . . . maybe tomorrow he'll be dead . . . maybe tomorrow *you'll* be dead . . . all sorts of excuses. But then, one day, one night, something happens . . . and SNAP! It breaks. And you just don't give a damn anymore. I've tried with you, baby . . . really, I've tried.

GEORGE. Come off it, Martha.

MARTHA. I've tried . . . I've really tried.

GEORGE *(With some awe).* You're a monster . . . you *are.*

MARTHA. I'm loud, and I'm vulgar, and I wear the pants in this house because somebody's got to, but I am *not* a monster. I am *not.*

GEORGE. You're a spoiled, self-indulgent, willful, dirty-minded, liquor-ridden. . . .

MARTHA. SNAP! It went snap. Look, I'm not going to try to get through to you anymore. . . . I'm not going to try. There was a second back there, maybe, there was a second, just a second, when I could have gotten through to you, when maybe we could have cut through all this crap. But that's past, and now I'm not going to try.

GEORGE. Once a month, Martha! I've gotten used to it . . . once a month and we get misunderstood Martha, the good-hearted girl underneath the barnacles, the little Miss that the touch of kindness'd bring to bloom again. And I've believed it more times than I want to remember, because I don't want to think I'm that much of a sucker. I don't believe you . . . I just don't believe you. There is no moment . . . there is no moment anymore when we could . . . come together.

MARTHA *(Armed again).* Well, maybe you're right, baby. You can't come together with nothing, and you're nothing! SNAP! It went snap tonight at Daddy's party. *(Dripping contempt, but there is fury and loss under it)* I sat there at Daddy's party, and I watched you . . . I watched you sitting there, and I watched the younger men around you, the men who were going to go somewhere. And I sat there and I watched you, and *you* weren't *there!* And it snapped! It finally snapped! And I'm going to howl it out, and I'm not going to give a damn what I do, and I'm going to make the damned biggest explosion you ever heard.

GEORGE *(Very pointedly).* You try it and I'll beat you at your own game.

MARTHA *(Hopefully).* Is that a threat, George! Hunh?

GEORGE. That's a threat, Martha.

MARTHA *(Fake-spits at him).* You're going to get it, baby.

GEORGE. Be careful, Martha . . . I'll rip you to pieces.

MARTHA. You aren't man enough . . . you haven't got the guts.

GEORGE. Total war?

MARTHA. Total.

(Silence. They both seem relieved . . . elated. NICK reenters)

NICK *(Brushing his hands off)*. Well . . . she's . . . resting.

GEORGE *(Quietly amused at NICK's calm, off-hand manner)*. Oh?

MARTHA. Yeah? She all right?

NICK. I think so . . . now. I'm . . . terribly sorry. . . .

MARTHA. Forget about it.

GEORGE. Happens all the time around here.

NICK. She'll be all right.

MARTHA. She lying down? You put her upstairs? On a bed?

NICK *(Making himself a drink)*. Well, no, actually. Uh . . . may I? She's . . . in the bathroom . . . on the bathroom floor . . . she's lying there.

GEORGE *(Considers it)*. Well . . . that's not very nice.

NICK. She likes it. She says it's . . . cool.

GEORGE. Still, I don't think. . . .

MARTHA *(Overruling him)*. If she wants to lie on the bathroom floor, let her. *(To NICK seriously)* Maybe she'd be more comfortable in the tub?

NICK *(He, too, seriously)*. No, she says she likes the floor . . . she took up the mat, and she's lying on the tiles. She . . . she lies on the floor a lot . . . she really does.

MARTHA *(Pause)*. Oh.

NICK. She . . . she gets lots of headaches and things, and she always lies on the floor. *(To GEORGE)* Is there . . . ice?

GEORGE. What?

NICK. Ice. Is there ice?

GEORGE *(As if the word were unfamiliar to him)*. Ice?

NICK. Ice. Yes.

MARTHA. Ice.

GEORGE *(As if he suddenly understood)*. Ice!

MARTHA. Attaboy.

GEORGE *(Without moving)*. Oh, yes . . . I'll get some.

MARTHA. Well, go. *(Mugging . . . to NICK)* Besides, we want to be alone.

GEORGE *(Moving to take the bucket)*. I wouldn't be surprised, Martha . . . I wouldn't be surprised.

MARTHA *(As if insulted)*. Oh, you wouldn't, hunh?

140

GEORGE. Not a bit, Martha.

MARTHA *(Violent)*. NO?

GEORGE *(He too)*. NO! *(Quietly again)* You'll try anything, Martha.
(Picks up the ice bucket)

NICK *(To cover)*. Actually, she's very . . . frail, and.

GEORGE. . . . slim-hipped.

NICK *(Remembering)*. Yes . . . exactly.

GEORGE *(At the hallway . . . not kindly)*. That why you don't have any
kids?
(He exits)

NICK *(To GEORGE's retreating form)*. Well, I don't know that that's . . .
(Trails off) . . . if that has anything to do with any . . . thing.

MARTHA. Well, if it does, who cares? Hunh?

NICK. Pardon?

(MARTHA *blows him a kiss*)

NICK *(Still concerned with GEORGE's remark)*. I . . . what? . . . I'm
sorry.

MARTHA. I said . . . *(Blows him another kiss)*

NICK *(Uncomfortable)*. Oh . . . yes.

MARTHA. Hey . . . hand me a cigarette . . . lover. (NICK *fishes in his
pocket)* That's a good boy. *(He gives her one)* Unh . . . thanks.
*(He lights it for her. As he does, she slips her hand between his legs,
somewhere between the knee and the crotch, bringing her hand around
to the outside of his leg)*
Ummmmmmmm.
*(He seems uncertain, but does not move. She smiles, moves her hand a
little)*
Now, for being such a good boy, you can give me a kiss. C'mon.

NICK *(Nervously)*. Look . . . I don't think we should. . . .

MARTHA. C'mon, baby . . . a friendly kiss.

NICK *(Still uncertain)*. Well. . . .

MARTHA. . . . you won't get hurt, little boy. . . .

NICK. . . . not so little. . . .

MARTHA. I'll bet you're not. C'mon. . . .

NICK *(Weakening)*. But what if he should come back in, and . . .
or . . . ?

MARTHA *(All the while her hand is moving up and down his leg)*. George?

Don't worry about him. Besides, who could object to a friendly little kiss? It's all in the faculty.

(They both laugh, quietly . . . NICK *a little nervously)*

We're a close-knit family here . . . Daddy always says so. . . . Daddy wants us to get to know each other . . . that's what he had the party for tonight. So c'mon . . . let's get to know each other a little bit.

NICK. It isn't that I don't want to . . . believe me. . . .

MARTHA. You're a scientist, aren't you? C'mon . . . make an experiment . . . make a little experiment. Experiment on old Martha.

NICK *(Giving in).* . . . not very old. . . .

MARTHA. That's right, not very old, but lots of good experience . . . lots of it.

NICK. I'll . . . I'll bet.

MARTHA *(As they draw slowly closer).* It'll be a nice change for you, too.

NICK. Yes, it would.

MARTHA. And you could go back to your little wife all refreshed.

NICK *(Closer . . . almost whispering).* She wouldn't know the difference.

MARTHA. Well, nobody else's going to know, either.

(They come together. What might have been a joke rapidly becomes serious, with MARTHA *urging it in that direction. There is no frenetic quality, but rather a slow, continually involving intertwining. Perhaps* MARTHA *is still more or less in her chair, and* NICK *is sort of beside and on the chair.)*

*(*GEORGE *enters . . . stops . . . watches a moment . . . smiles . . . laughs silently, nods his head, turns, exits, without being noticed.)*

*(*NICK, *who has already had his hand on* MARTHA's *breast, now puts his hand inside her dress)*

MARTHA *(Slowing him down).* Hey . . . hey. Take it easy, boy. Down, baby. Don't rush it, hunh?

NICK *(His eyes still closed).* Oh, c'mon, now. . . .

MARTHA *(Pushing him away).* Unh-unh. Later, baby . . . later.

NICK. I told you . . . I'm a biologist.

MARTHA *(Soothing him).* I know. I can tell. Later, Hunh?

*(*GEORGE *is heard off-stage, singing "Who's afraid of Virginia Woolf?"* MARTHA *and* NICK *go apart,* NICK *wiping his mouth,* MARTHA *checking her clothes. Safely later,* GEORGE *reenters with the ice bucket)*

GEORGE. . . . . of Virginia Woolf,
   Virginia Woolf,
   Virginia. . . .
   . . . ah! Here we are . . . ice for the lamps of China, Manchuria
   thrown in. *(To* NICK) You better watch those yellow bastards, my love
   . . . they aren't amused. Why don't you come on over to our side, and
   we'll blow the hell out of 'em. Then we can split up the money between
   us and be on Easy Street. What d'ya say?

NICK *(Not at all sure what is being talked about).* Well . . . sure. Hey!
   Ice!

GEORGE *(With hideously false enthusiasm).* Right! *(Now to* MARTHA, *purr-
   ing)* Hello, Martha . . . my dove. . . . You look . . . radiant.

MARTHA *(Off-hand).* Thank you.

GEORGE *(Very cheerful).* Well now, let me see. I've got the ice. . . .

MARTHA. . . . gotten. . . .

GEORGE. *Got,* Martha. Got is perfectly correct . . . it's just a little . . .
   archaic, like you.

MARTHA *(Suspicious).* What are you so cheerful about?

GEORGE *(Ignoring the remark).* Let's see now . . . I've got the ice. Can I
   make someone a drink? Martha, can I make you a drink?

MARTHA *(Bravura).* Yeah, why not?

GEORGE *(Taking her glass).* Indeed . . . why not? *(Examines the glass)*
   Martha! You've been nibbling away at the glass.

MARTHA. I have not!

GEORGE *(To* NICK, *who is at the bar).* I see you're making your own, which
   is fine . . . fine. I'll just hootch up Martha, here, and then we'll be all
   set.

MARTHA *(Suspicious).* All set for what?

GEORGE *(Pause . . . considers).* Why, I don't know. We're having a
   party, aren't we? *(To* NICK, *who has moved from the bar)* I passed your
   wife in the hall. I mean, I passed the john and I looked in on her.
   Peaceful . . . so peaceful. Sound asleep . . . and she's actually . . .
   sucking her thumb.

MARTHA. Awwwwww!

GEORGE. Rolled up like a fetus, sucking away.

NICK *(A little uncomfortably).* I suppose she's all right.

GEORGE *(Expansively).* Of course she is! *(Hands* MARTHA *her drink)* There
   you are.

MARTHA *(Still on her guard)*. Thanks.

GEORGE. And now one for me. It's my turn.

MARTHA. Never baby . . . it's never your turn.

GEORGE *(Too cheerful)*. Oh, now, I wouldn't say that, Martha.

MARTHA. You moving on the principle the worm turns? Well, the worm part's O.K. . . . cause that fits you fine, but the turning part . . . unh-unh! You're in a straight line, buddy-boy, and it doesn't lead anywhere . . . *(A vague afterthought)* . . . except maybe the grave.

GEORGE *(Chuckles, takes his drink)*. Well, you just hold that thought, Martha . . . hug it close . . . run your hands over it. Me, I'm going to sit down . . . if you'll excuse me. . . . I'm going to sit down over there and read a book.

(He moves to a chair facing away from the center of the room, but not too far from the front door)

MARTHA. You're gonna do *what?*

GEORGE *(Quietly, distinctly)*. I am going to read a book. Read. Read. Read? You've heard of it? *(Picks up a book)*

MARTHA *(Standing)*. Whaddya mean you're gonna read? What's the matter with you?

GEORGE *(Too calmly)*. There's nothing the matter with me, Martha. . . . I'm going to read a book. That's all.

MARTHA *(Oddly furious)*. We've got company!

GEORGE *(Over-patiently)*. I know, my dear . . . *(Looks at his watch)* . . . but . . . it's after four o'clock, and I always read around this time. Now, you . . . *(Dismisses her with a little wave)* . . . go about your business . . . I'll sit here very quietly. . . .

MARTHA. You read in the afternoon! You read at four o'clock in the afternoon . . . you don't read at four o'clock in the morning! Nobody reads at four o'clock in the morning!

GEORGE *(Absorbing himself in his book)*. Now, now, now.

MARTHA *(Incredulously, to NICK)*. He's going to read a book. . . . The son of a bitch is going to read a book!

NICK *(Smiling a little)*. So it would seem.

(Moves to MARTHA, puts his arm around her waist. GEORGE cannot see this, of course)

MARTHA *(Getting an idea)*. Well, we can amuse ourselves, can't we?

NICK. I imagine so.

MARTHA. We're going to amuse ourselves, George.

GEORGE *(Not looking up)*. Unh-hunh. That's nice.

MARTHA. You might not like it.

GEORGE *(Never looking up)*. No, no, now . . . you go right ahead . . . you entertain your guests.

MARTHA. I'm going to entertain myself, too.

GEORGE. Good . . . good.

MARTHA. Ha, ha. You're a riot, George.

GEORGE. Unh-hunh.

MARTHA. Well, I'm a riot, too, George.

GEORGE. Yes you are, Martha.

(NICK *takes* MARTHA'S *hand, pulls her to him. They stop for a moment, then kiss, not briefly)*

MARTHA *(After)*. You know what I'm doing, George?

GEORGE. No, Martha . . . what are you doing?

MARTHA. I'm entertaining. I'm entertaining one of the guests. I'm necking with one of the guests.

GEORGE *(Seemingly relaxed and preoccupied, never looking)*. Oh, that's nice. Which one?

MARTHA *(Livid)*. Oh, by God you're funny! *(Breaks away from* NICK . . . *moves into* GEORGE's *side-line of vision by herself. Her balance is none too good, and she bumps into or brushes against the door chimes by the door. They chime)*

GEORGE. Someone at the door, Martha.

MARTHA. Never mind that. I said I was necking with one of the guests.

GEORGE. Good . . . good. You go right on.

MARTHA *(Pauses . . . not knowing quite what to do)*. Good?

GEORGE. Yes, good . . . good for you.

MARTHA *(Her eyes narrowing, her voice becoming hard)*. Oh, I see what you're up to, you lousy little. . . .

GEORGE. I'm up to page a hundred and. . . .

MARTHA. Cut it! Just cut it out! *(She hits against the door chimes again; they chime)* Goddam bongs.

GEORGE. They're chimes, Martha. Why don't you go back to your necking and stop bothering me? I want to read.

MARTHA. Why, you miserable. . . . I'll show *you*.

GEORGE *(Swings around to face her . . . says, with great loathing)*. No . . . show him, Martha . . . he hasn't seen it. *Maybe* he hasn't seen it. *(Turns to* NICK) You haven't seen it yet, have you?

145

NICK *(Turning away, a look of disgust on his face).* I . . . I have no respect for you.

GEORGE. And none for yourself, either. . . . *(Indicating* MARTHA*)* I don't
know what the younger generation's coming to.

NICK. You don't . . . you don't even. . . .

GEORGE. Care? You're quite right. . . . I couldn't care less. So, you just
take this bag of laundry here, throw her over your shoulder, and. . . .

NICK. You're disgusting.

GEORGE *(Incredulous).* Because *you're* going to hump Martha, *I'm* disgusting?

(He breaks down in ridiculing laughter)

MARTHA *(To* GEORGE*).* You Mother! *(To* NICK*)* Go wait for me, hunh? Go
wait for me in the kitchen. *(But* NICK *does not move.* MARTHA *goes to
him, puts her arms around him)* C'mon, baby . . . please. Wait for me
. . . in the kitchen . . . be a good baby.

(NICK *takes her kiss, glares at* GEORGE . . . *who has turned his back
again . . . and exits.)*

(MARTHA *swings around to* GEORGE*)*

Now you listen to me. . . .

GEORGE. I'd rather read, Martha, if you don't mind. . . .

MARTHA *(Her anger has her close to tears, her frustration to fury).* Well, I
do mind. Now, you pay attention to me! You come off this kick you're
on, or I swear to God I'll do it. I swear to God I'll follow that guy into
the kitchen, and then I'll take him upstairs, and. . . .

GEORGE *(Swinging around to her again . . . loud . . . loathing).* SO
WHAT, MARTHA?

MARTHA *(Considers him for a moment . . . then, nodding her head, backing off slowly).* O.K. . . . O.K. . . . You asked for it . . . and you're
going to get it.

GEORGE *(Softly, sadly).* Lord, Martha, if you want the boy that much . . .
have him . . . but do it honestly, will you? Don't cover it over with all
this . . . all this . . . footwork.

MARTHA *(Hopeless).* I'll make you sorry you made me want to marry you.
(At the hallway) I'll make you regret the day you ever decided to come
to this college. I'll make you sorry you ever let yourself down.
(She exits)
(Silence. GEORGE *sits still, staring straight ahead. Listening . . . but*

there is no sound. Outwardly calm, he returns to his book, reads a moment, then looks up . . . considers. . . .)

GEORGE. "And the west, encumbered by crippling alliances, and burdened with a morality too rigid to accommodate itself to the swing of events, must . . . eventually . . . fall."

(He laughs, briefly, ruefully . . . rises, with the book in his hand. He stands still . . . then, quickly, he gathers all the fury he has been containing within himself . . . he shakes . . . he looks at the book in his hand and, with a cry that is part growl, part howl, he hurls it at the chimes. They crash against one another, ringing wildly. A brief pause, then HONEY enters)

HONEY *(The worse for wear, half asleep, still sick, weak, still staggering a little . . . vaguely, in something of a dream world).* Bells. Ringing. I've been hearing bells.

GEORGE. Jesus!

HONEY. I couldn't sleep . . . for the bells. Ding-ding, bong . . . it woke me up. What time is it?

GEORGE *(Quietly beside himself).* Don't bother me.

HONEY *(Confused and frightened).* I was asleep, and the bells started . . . they BOOMED! Poe-bells . . . they were Poe-bells . . . Bing-bing-bong-BOOM!

GEORGE. BOOM!

HONEY. I was asleep, and I was dreaming of . . . something . . . and I heard the sounds coming, and I didn't know what it was.

GEORGE *(Never quite to her).* It was the sound of bodies. . . .

HONEY. And I didn't want to wake up, but the sound kept coming. . . .

GEORGE. . . . go back to sleep. . . .

HONEY. . . . and it FRIGHTENED ME!

GEORGE *(Quietly . . . to MARTHA, as if she were in the room).* I'm going to get you . . . Martha.

HONEY. And it was so . . . cold. The wind was . . . the wind was so cold! And I was lying somewhere, and the covers kept slipping away from me, and I didn't want them to. . . .

GEORGE. Somehow, Martha.

HONEY. . . . and there was someone there . . . !

GEORGE. There was no one there.

HONEY *(Frightened).* And I didn't want someone there . . . I was . . . naked . . . !

147

GEORGE. You don't know what's going on, do you?

HONEY *(Still with her dream)*. I DON'T WANT ANY . . . NO . . . !

GEORGE. You don't know what's been going on around here while you been having your snoozette, do you.

HONEY. NO! . . . I DON'T WANT ANY . . . I DON'T WANT THEM. . . . GO 'WAY. . . . *(Begins to cry)* I DON'T WANT . . . ANY . . . CHILDREN . . . I . . . don't . . . want . . . any . . . children. I'm afraid! I don't want to be hurt . . . PLEASE!

GEORGE *(Nodding his head . . . speaks with compassion)*. I should have known.

HONEY *(Snapping awake from her reverie)*. What! What?

GEORGE. I should have known . . . the whole business . . . the head-aches . . . the whining . . . the. . . .

HONEY *(Terrified)*. What are you talking about?

GEORGE *(Ugly again)*. Does *he* know that? Does that . . . stud you're married to know about that, hunh?

HONEY. About what? Stay away from me!

GEORGE. Don't worry, baby . . . I wouldn't. . . . Oh, my God, that *would* be a joke, wouldn't it! But don't worry, baby. HEY! How you do it? Hunh? How do you make your secret little murders stud-boy doesn't know about, hunh? Pills? PILLS? You got a secret supply of pills? Or what? Apple jelly? WILL POWER?

HONEY. I feel sick.

GEORGE. You going to throw up again? You going to lie down on the cold tiles, your knees pulled up under your chin, your thumb stuck in your mouth . . . ?

HONEY *(Panicked)*. Where is he?

GEORGE. Where's who? There's nobody here, baby.

HONEY. I want my husband! I want a drink!

GEORGE. Well, you just crawl over to the bar and make yourself one. *(From off-stage comes the sound of* MARTHA'S *laughter and the crashing of dishes)* *(Yelling)* That's right! Go at it!

HONEY. I want . . . something. . . .

GEORGE. You know what's going on in there, little Miss? Hunh? You hear all that? You know what's going on in there?

HONEY. I don't want to know anything!

GEORGE. There are a couple of people in there. . . .

148

(MARTHA's *laughter again*)

. . . they are in there, in the kitchen. . . . Right there, with the onion skins and the coffee grounds . . . sort of . . . sort of a . . . sort of a dry run for the wave of the future.

HONEY *(Beside herself)*. I . . . don't . . . understand . . . you. . . .

GEORGE *(A hideous elation)*. It's very simple. . . . When people can't abide things as they are, when they can't abide the present, they do one of two things . . . either they . . . either they turn to a contemplation of the past, as I have done, or they set about to . . . alter the future. And when you want to change something . . . YOU BANG! BANG! BANG! BANG!

HONEY. Stop it!

GEORGE. And you, you simpering bitch . . . you don't want *children?*

HONEY. You leave me . . . alone. Who . . . WHO RANG?

GEORGE. What?

HONEY. What were the bells? Who rang?

GEORGE. You don't want to know, do you? You don't want to listen to it, hunh?

HONEY *(Shivering)*. I don't want to listen to you. . . . I want to know who rang.

GEORGE. Your husband is . . . and you want to know who *rang?*

HONEY. Who rang? Someone rang!

GEORGE *(His jaw drops open . . . he is whirling with an idea)*. . . . Someone. . . .

HONEY. RANG!

GEORGE. . . . someone . . . rang . . . yes . . . yessss . . .

HONEY. The . . . bells . . . rang. . . .

GEORGE *(His mind racing ahead)*. The bells rang . . . and it was someone. . . .

HONEY. Somebody. . . .

GEORGE *(He is home, now)*. . . . somebody rang . . . it was somebody . . . with . . . I'VE GOT IT! I'VE GOT IT, MARTHA . . . ! Somebody with a message . . . and the message was . . . our son . . . OUR SON! *(Almost whispered)* It was a message . . . the bells rang and it was a message, and it was about . . . our son . . . and the message . . . was . . . and the message was . . . our . . . son . . . is . . . DEAD!

HONEY *(Almost sick)*. Oh . . . no.

GEORGE *(Cementing it in his mind)*. Our son is . . . dead . . . And . . . Martha doesn't know. . . . I haven't told . . . Martha.

HONEY. No . . . no . . . no.

GEORGE *(Slowly, deliberately)*. Our son is dead, and Martha doesn't know.

HONEY. Oh. God in heaven . . . no.

GEORGE *(To* HONEY . . . *slowly, deliberately, dispassionately)*. And you're not going to tell her.

HONEY *(In tears)*. Your son is dead.

GEORGE. I'll tell her myself . . . in good time. I'll tell her myself.

HONEY *(So faintly)*. I'm going to be sick.

GEORGE *(Turning away from her . . . he, too, softly)*. Are you? That's nice.

(MARTHA's *laugh is heard again)*

Oh, listen to that.

HONEY. I'm going to die.

GEORGE *(Quite by himself now)*. Good . . . good . . . you go right ahead.

(Very softly, so MARTHA *could not possibly hear)*

Martha? Martha? I have some . . . terrible news for you.

(There is a strange half-smile on his lips)

It's about our . . . son. He's dead. Can you hear me, Martha? Our boy is dead.

(He begins to laugh, very softly . . . it is mixed with crying)

CURTAIN

ACT THREE
The Exorcism

MARTHA *enters, talking to herself.*

MARTHA. Hey, hey. . . . Where is everybody . . . ? *(It is evident she is not bothered)* So? Drop me; pluck me like a goddamn . . . whatever-it-is . . . creeping vine, and throw me over your shoulder like an old shoe . . . George? *(Looks about her)* George? *(Silence)* George! What are you doing: Hiding, or something? *(Silence)* GEORGE!! *(Silence)* Oh, fa Chri . . . . . . *(Goes to the bar, makes herself a drink and amuses herself with the following performance)* Deserted! Abandon-ed! Left out in the cold like an old pussycat. HA! Can I get you a drink, Martha? Why, thank you, George; that's very kind of you. No, Martha, no; why I'd do anything for you. Would you, George? Why, I'd do anything for you, too. Would you, Martha? Why, certainly, George. Martha, I've misjudged you. And I've misjudged you, too, George. WHERE IS EVERY-BODY!!! Hump the Hostess! *(Laughs greatly at this, falls into a chair; calms down, looks defeated, says, softly)* Fat chance. *(Even softer)* Fat chance. *(Baby-talk now)* Daddy? Daddy? Martha is abandon-ed. Left to her own vices at . . . *(Peers at a clock)* . . . something o'clock in the old A.M. Daddy White-Mouse; do you really have red eyes? Do you? Let me see. Ohhhhh! You do! You do! Daddy, you have red eyes . . . because you cry all the time, don't you, Daddy. Yes; you do. You cry alllll the time. I'LL GIVE ALL YOU BASTARDS FIVE TO COME OUT FROM WHERE YOU'RE HIDING!! *(Pause)* I cry all the time too, Daddy. I cry alllll the time; but deep inside, so no one can see me. I cry all the time. And Georgie cries all the time, too. We both cry all the time, and then, what we do, we cry, and we take our tears, and we put 'em in the ice box, in the goddamn ice trays *(Begins to laugh)* until they're all frozen *(Laughs even more)* and then . . . we put them . . . in our . . . drinks. *(More laughter, which is something else, too. After sobering silence)* Up the drain, down the spout, dead, gone and forgotten. . . . Up the spout, not down the spout; *Up* the spout: THE POKER NIGHT. Up the spout. . . . *(Sadly)* I've got windshield wipers on my eyes, because I married you . . . baby! . . . Martha, you'll be a song-writer yet. *(Jiggles the ice in her glass)* CLINK! *(Does it again)* CLINK! *(Giggles, repeats it several times)* CLINK! . . . CLINK! . . . CLINK! . . . CLINK!

(NICK *enters while* MARTHA *is clinking; he stands in the hall entrance and watches her; finally he comes in*)

NICK. My God, you've gone crazy too.

MARTHA. Clink?

NICK. I said, you've gone crazy too.

MARTHA *(Considers it)*. Probably . . . probably.

NICK. You've all gone crazy: I come downstairs, and what happens. . . .

MARTHA. What happens?

NICK. . . . my wife's gone into the can with a liquor bottle, and she winks at me . . . winks at me! . . .

MARTHA *(Sadly)*. She's never wunk at you; what a shame. . . .

NICK. She is lying down on the floor again, the tiles, all curled up, and she starts peeling the label off the liquor bottle, the brandy bottle. . . .

MARTHA. . . . we'll never get the deposit back that way. . . .

NICK. . . . and I ask her what she's doing, and she goes: shhhhhh!, nobody knows I'm here; and I come back in here, and you're sitting there going Clink!, for God's sake. Clink!

MARTHA. CLINK!

NICK. You've all gone crazy.

MARTHA. Yes. Sad but true.

NICK. Where is your husband?

MARTHA. He is vanish-ed. Pouf!

NICK. You're all crazy: nuts.

MARTHA *(Affects a brogue)*. Awww, 'tis the refuge we take when the unreality of the world weighs too heavy on our tiny heads. *(Normal voice again)* Relax; sink into it; you're no better than anybody else.

NICK *(Wearily)*. I think I am.

MARTHA *(Her glass to her mouth)*. You're certainly a flop in some departments.

NICK *(Wincing)*. I beg your pardon . . . ?

MARTHA *(Unnecessarily loud)*. I said, you're certainly a flop in some. . . .

NICK *(He, too, too loud)*. I'm sorry you're disappointed.

MARTHA *(Braying)*. I didn't say I was disappointed! Stupid!

NICK. You should try me some time when we haven't been drinking for ten hours, and maybe. . . .

MARTHA *(Still braying)*. I wasn't talking about your potential; I was talking about your goddamn performance.

NICK *(Softly)*. Oh.

MARTHA *(She softer, too)*. Your potential's fine. It's dandy. *(Wiggles her eyebrows)* Absolutely dandy. I haven't seen such a dandy potential in a long time. Oh, but baby, you sure are a flop.

NICK *(Snapping it out)*. Everybody's a flop to you! Your husband's a flop, *I'm* a flop. . . .

MARTHA *(Dismissing him)*. You're all flops. I am the Earth Mother, and you're all flops. *(More or less to herself)* I disgust me. I pass my life in crummy, totally pointless infidelities . . . *(Laughs ruefully) would*-be infidelities. Hump the Hostess? That's a laugh. A bunch of boozed-up . . . impotent lunk-heads. Martha makes goo-goo eyes, and the lunk-heads grin, and roll their beautiful, beautiful eyes back, and grin some more, and Martha licks her chops, and the lunk-heads slap over to the bar to pick up a little courage, *and* they pick up a little courage, and they bounce back over to old Martha, who does a little dance for them, which heats them all up . . . mentally . . . and so they slap over to the bar again, and pick up a little more courage, and their wives and sweethearts stick their noses up in the air . . . right through the ceiling, sometimes . . . which sends the lunk-heads back to the soda fountain again where they fuel up some more, while Martha-poo sits there with her dress up over her head . . . suffocating—you don't know how *stuffy* it is with your dress up over your head—suffocating! waiting for the lunk-heads; so, *finally* they get their courage up . . . but that's all, baby! Oh my, there is sometimes some very nice potential, but, oh my! My, my, my. *(Brightly)* But that's how it is in civilized society. *(To herself again)* All the gorgeous lunk-heads. Poor babies. *(To* NICK, *now; earnestly)* There is only one man in my life who has ever . . . made me happy. Do you know that? One!

NICK. The . . . the what-do-you-call-it? . . . uh . . . the lawn mower, or something?

MARTHA. No; I'd forgotten him. But when I think about him and me it's almost like being a voyeur. Hunh. No; I didn't mean him; I meant George, of course. *(No response from* NICK*)* Uh . . . George; my husband.

NICK *(Disbelieving)*. You're kidding.

MARTHA. Am I?

NICK. You must be. Him?

MARTHA. Him.

NICK *(As if in on a joke)*. Sure; sure.

MARTHA. You don't believe it.

NICK *(Mocking)*. Why, of course I do.

MARTHA. You always deal in appearances?

NICK *(Derisively)*. Oh, for God's sake. . . .

MARTHA. . . . George who is out somewhere there in the dark. . . .
George who is good to me, and whom I revile; who understands me,
and whom I push off; who can make me laugh, and I choke it back in
my throat; who can hold me, at night, so that it's warm, and whom I
will bite so there's blood; who keeps learning the games we play as
quickly as I can change the rules; who can make me happy and I do not
wish to be happy, and yes I do wish to be happy. George and Martha:
sad, sad, sad.

NICK *(Echoing, still not believing)*. Sad.

MARTHA. . . . whom I will not forgive for having come to rest; for having
seen me and having said: yes, this will do; who has made the hideous,
the hurting, the insulting mistake of loving me and must be punished
for it. George and Martha: sad, sad, sad.

NICK *(Puzzled)*. Sad.

MARTHA. . . . who tolerates, which is intolerable; who is kind, which is
cruel; who understands, which is beyond comprehension. . . .

NICK. George and Martha: sad, sad, sad.

MARTHA. Some day . . . hah! some *night* . . . some stupid, liquor-ridden night . . . I will go too far . . . and I'll either break the man's
back . . . or push him off for good . . . which is what I deserve.

NICK. I don't think he's got a vertebra intact.

MARTHA *(Laughing at him)*. You don't, huh? You don't think so. Oh, little
boy, you got yourself hunched over that microphone of yours. . . .

NICK. Microscope. . . .

MARTHA. . . . yes . . . and you don't see anything, do you? You see everything but the goddamn mind; you see all the little specks and crap,
but you don't see what goes on, do you?

NICK. I know when a man's had his back broken; I can see that.

MARTHA. Can you!

NICK. You're damn right.

MARTHA. Oh . . . you know so little. And you're going to take over the
world, hunh?

NICK. All right, now. . . .

MARTHA. You think a man's got his back broken 'cause he makes like a clown and walks bent, hunh? Is that *really* all you know?

NICK. I said, all *right!*

MARTHA. Ohhhh! The stallion's mad, hunh. The gelding's all upset. Ha, ha, ha, HA!

NICK *(Softly; wounded)*. You . . . you swing wild, don't you.

MARTHA *(Triumphant)*. HAH!

NICK. Just . . . anywhere.

MARTHA. HAH! I'm a gattling gun. Hahahahahahahahaha!

NICK *(In wonder)*. Aimless . . . butchery. Pointless.

MARTHA. Aw! You poor little bastard.

NICK. Hit out at everything.

(The door chimes chime)

MARTHA. Go answer the door.

NICK *(Amazed)*. What did you say?

MARTHA. I said, go answer the door. What are you, deaf?

NICK *(Trying to get it straight)*. You . . . want me . . . to go answer the door?

MARTHA. That's right, lunk-head; answer the door. There must be something you can do well; or, are you too drunk to do that, too? Can't you get the latch up, either?

NICK. Look, there's no need. . . .

(Door chimes again)

MARTHA *(Shouting)*. Answer it! *(Softer)* You can be houseboy around here for a while. You can start off being houseboy right now.

NICK. Look, lady, I'm no flunky to you.

MARTHA *(Cheerfully)*. Sure you are! You're ambitious, aren't you, boy? You didn't chase me around the kitchen and up the goddamn stairs out of mad, driven passion, did you now? You were thinking a little bit about your career, weren't you? Well, you can just houseboy your way up the ladder for a while.

NICK. There's no limit to you, is there?

(Door chimes again)

MARTHA *(Calmly, surely)*. No, baby; none. Go answer the door. (NICK *hesitates*) Look, boy; once you stick your nose in it, you're not going to pull out just whenever you feel like it. You're in for a while. Now, git!

NICK. Aimless . . . wanton . . . pointless. . . .

MARTHA. Now, now, now; just do what you're told; show old Martha there's something you *can* do. Hunh? Atta boy.

NICK *(Considers, gives in, moves toward the door. Chimes again).* I'm coming, for Christ's sake!

MARTHA *(Claps her hands).* Ha HA! Wonderful; marvelous. *(Sings)* "Just a gigolo, everywhere I go, people always say. . . ."

NICK. STOP THAT!

MARTHA *(Giggles).* Sorry, baby; go on now; open the little door.

NICK *(With great rue).* Christ.

(He flings open the door, and a hand thrusts into the opening a great bunch of snapdragons; they stay there for a moment. NICK *strains his eyes to see who is behind them)*

MARTHA. Oh, how lovely!

GEORGE *(Appearing in the doorway, the snapdragons covering his face; speaks in a hideously cracked falsetto).* Flores; flores para los muertos. Flores.

MARTHA. Ha, ha, ha, HA!

GEORGE *(A step into the room; lowers the flowers; sees* NICK; *his face becomes gleeful; he opens his arms).* Sonny! You've come home for your birthday! At last!

NICK *(Backing off).* Stay away from me.

MARTHA. Ha, ha, ha, HA! That's the houseboy, for God's sake.

GEORGE. Really? That's not our own little sonny-Jim? Our own little all-American something-or-other?

MARTHA *(Giggling).* Well, I certainly hope not; he's been acting awful funny, if he is.

GEORGE *(Almost manic).* Ohhhh! I'll bet! Chippie-chippie-chippie, hunh? *(Affecting embarrassment)* I . . . I brungya dese flowers, Mart'a, 'cause I . . . wull, 'cause you'se . . . awwwwww hell. Gee.

MARTHA. Pansies! Rosemary! Violence! My wedding bouquet!

NICK *(Starting to move away).* Well, if you two kids don't mind, I think I'll just. . . .

MARTHA. Ach! You just stay where you are. Make my hubby a drink.

NICK. I don't think I will.

GEORGE. No, Martha, no; that would be too much; he's your houseboy, baby, not mine.

NICK. I'm nobody's houseboy. . . .

GEORGE *and* MARTHA. . . . Now! *(Sing)* I'm nobody's houseboy now. . . . *(Both laugh)*

NICK. Vicious. . . .

GEORGE *(Finishing it for him)*. . . . children. Hunh? That's right? Vicious children, with their oh-so-sad games, hopscotching their way through life, etcetera, etcetera. Is that it?

NICK. Something like it.

GEORGE. Screw, baby.

MARTHA. Him can't. Him too fulla booze.

GEORGE. Weally? *(Handing the snapdragons to* NICK) Here; dump these in some gin. (NICK *takes them, looks at them, drops them on the floor at his feet)*

MARTHA *(Sham dismay)*. Awwwwwww.

GEORGE. What a terrible thing to do . . . to Martha's snapdragons.

MARTHA. Is that what they are?

GEORGE. Yup. And here I went out into the moonlight to pick 'em for Martha tonight, and for our sonny-boy tomorrow, for his birfday.

MARTHA *(Passing on information)*. There is no moon now. I saw it go down from the bedroom.

GEORGE *(Feigned glee)*. From the bedroom! *(Normal tone)* Well, there was a moon.

MARTHA *(Too patient; laughing a little)*. There couldn't have been a moon.

GEORGE. Well, there was. There is.

MARTHA. There is no moon; the moon went down.

GEORGE. There is a moon; the moon is up.

MARTHA *(Straining to keep civil)*. I'm afraid you're mistaken.

GEORGE *(Too cheerful)*. No; no.

MARTHA *(Between her teeth)*. There is no goddamn moon.

GEORGE. My dear Martha . . . I did not pick snapdragons in the stony dark. I did not go stumbling around Daddy's greenhouse in the pitch.

MARTHA. Yes . . . you did. You would.

GEORGE. Martha, I do not pick flowers in the blink. I have never robbed a hothouse without there is a light from heaven.

MARTHA *(With finality)*. There is no moon; the moon went down.

GEORGE *(With great logic)*. That may very well be, Chastity; the moon may very well have gone down . . . but it came back up.

MARTHA. The moon does *not* come back up; when the moon has gone down it stays down.

157

GEORGE *(Getting a little ugly)*. You don't know anything. IF the moon went down, then it came back up.

MARTHA. BULL!

GEORGE. Ignorance! Such . . . ignorance.

MARTHA. Watch who you're calling ignorant!

GEORGE. Once . . . once, when I was sailing past Majorca, drinking on deck with a correspondent who was talking about Roosevelt, the moon went down, thought about it for a little . . . considered it, you know what I mean? . . . and then, POP, came up again. Just like that.

MARTHA. That is not true! That is such a lie!

GEORGE. You must not call everything a lie, Martha. *(To NICK)* Must she?

NICK. Hell, I don't know when you people are lying, or what.

MARTHA. You're damned right!

GEORGE. You're not supposed to.

MARTHA. Right!

GEORGE. At any rate, I was sailing past Majorca. . . .

MARTHA. You never sailed past Majorca. . . .

GEORGE. Martha. . . .

MARTHA. You were never in the goddamn Mediterranean at all . . . ever. . . .

GEORGE. I certainly was! My Mommy and Daddy took me there as a college graduation present.

MARTHA. Nuts!

NICK. Was this after you killed them?

(GEORGE *and* MARTHA *swing around and look at him; there is a brief, ugly pause*)

GEORGE *(Defiantly)*. Maybe.

MARTHA. Yeah; maybe not, too.

NICK. Jesus!

(GEORGE *swoops down, picks up the bunch of snapdragons, shakes them like a feather duster in* NICK'S *face, and moves away a little*)

GEORGE. HAH!

NICK. Damn you.

GEORGE *(To* NICK*)*. Truth and illusion. Who knows the difference, eh, toots? Eh?

MARTHA. You were never in the Mediterranean . . . truth or illusion . . . either way.

158

GEORGE. If I wasn't in the Mediterranean, how did I get to the Aegean? Hunh?

MARTHA. OVERLAND!

NICK. Yeah!

GEORGE. Don't you side with her, houseboy.

NICK. I am not a houseboy.

GEORGE. Look! I know the game! You don't make it in the sack, you're a houseboy.

NICK. I AM NOT A HOUSEBOY!

GEORGE. No? Well then, you must have made it in the sack. Yes? *(He is breathing a little heavy; behaving a little manic)* Yes? Someone's lying around here; somebody isn't playing the game straight. Yes? Come on; come on; who's lying? Martha? Come on!

NICK *(After a pause; to* MARTHA, *quietly with intense pleading).* Tell him I'm not a houseboy.

MARTHA *(After a pause, quietly, lowering her head).* No; you're not a house-boy.

GEORGE *(With great, sad relief).* So be it.

MARTHA *(Pleading).* Truth and illusion, George; you don't know the difference.

GEORGE. No; but we must carry on as though we did.

MARTHA. Amen.

GEORGE *(Flourishing the flowers).* SNAP WENT THE DRAGONS!! (NICK *and* MARTHA *laugh weakly)* Hunh? Here we go round the mulberry bush, Hunh?

NICK *(Tenderly, to* MARTHA). Thank you.

MARTHA. Skip it.

GEORGE *(Loud).* I said, here we go round the mulberry bush!

MARTHA *(Impatiently).* Yeah, yeah; we know; snap go the dragons.

GEORGE *(Taking a snapdragon, throwing it, spear-like, stem-first at* MARTHA). SNAP!

MARTHA. Don't, George.

GEORGE *(Throws another).* SNAP!

NICK. Don't do that.

GEORGE. Shut up, stud.

NICK. I'm not a stud!

GEORGE *(Throws one at* NICK). SNAP! Then you're a houseboy. Which is it?

159

Which are you? Hunh? Make up your mind. Either way. . . . *(Throws another at him)* SNAP! . . . *you disgust me.*

MARTHA. Does it matter to you, George!?

GEORGE *(Throws one at her)*. SNAP! No, actually, it doesn't. Either way . . . I've had it.

MARTHA. Stop throwing those goddamn things at me!

GEORGE. Either way. *(Throws another at her)* SNAP!

NICK *(To* MARTHA). Do you want me to . . . do something to him?

MARTHA. You leave him alone!

GEORGE. If you're a houseboy, baby, you can pick up after me; if you're a stud, you can protect your plow. Either way. Either way. . . . Everything.

NICK. Oh for God's. . . .

MARTHA *(A little afraid)*. Truth or illusion, George. Doesn't it matter to you . . . at all?

GEORGE *(Without throwing anything)*. SNAP! *(Silence)* You got your answer, baby?

MARTHA *(Sadly)*. Got it.

GEORGE. You just gird your blue-veined loins, girl *(Sees* NICK *moving toward the hall)* Now; we got one more game to play. And it's called bringing up baby.

NICK *(More-or-less under his breath)*. Oh, for Lord's sake. . . .

MARTHA. George. . . .

GEORGE. I don't want any fuss. *(To* NICK) You don't want any scandal around here, do you, big boy? You don't want to wreck things, do you? Hunh? You want to keep to your time table, don't you? Then sit! (NICK *sits) (To* MARTHA) And you, pretty Miss, you like fun and games, don't you? You're a sport from way back, aren't you?

MARTHA *(Quietly, giving in)*. All right, George; all right.

GEORGE *(Seeing them both cowed; purrs)*. Goooooooood; gooooood. *(Looks about him)* But, we're not all here. *(Snaps his fingers a couple of times at* NICK) You; you . . . uh . . . you; your little wifelet isn't here.

NICK. Look; she's had a rough night, now; she's in the can, and she's. . . .

GEORGE. Well, we can't play without everyone here. Now that's a fact. We gotta have your wife. *(Hog-calls toward the hall)* SOOOWWWIIIEEE!! SOOOWWWIIIEEE!!

NICK *(As* MARTHA *giggles nervously)*. Cut that!

GEORGE *(Swinging around, facing him)*. Then get your butt out of that chair and bring the little dip back in here. *(As* NICK *does not move)* Now be a good puppy. Fetch, good puppy, go fetch.

(NICK *rises, opens his mouth to say something, thinks better of it, exits)* One more game.

MARTHA *(After* NICK *goes).* I don't like what's going to happen.

GEORGE *(Surprisingly tender).* Do you know what it is?

MARTHA *(Pathetic).* No. But I don't like it.

GEORGE. Maybe you will, Martha.

MARTHA. No.

GEORGE. Oh, it's a real fun game, Martha.

MARTHA *(Pleading).* No more games.

GEORGE *(Quietly triumphant).* One more, Martha. One more game, and then beddie-bye. Everybody pack up his tools and baggage and stuff and go home. And you and me, well, we gonna climb them well-worn stairs.

MARTHA *(Almost in tears).* No, George; no.

GEORGE *(Soothing).* Yes, baby.

MARTHA. No, George; please?

GEORGE. It'll all be done with before you know it.

MARTHA. No, George.

GEORGE. No climb stairs with Georgie?

MARTHA *(A sleepy child).* No more games . . . please. It's games I don't want. No more games.

GEORGE. Aw, sure you do, Martha . . . original game-girl and all, 'course you do.

MARTHA. Ugly games . . . ugly. And now this new one?

GEORGE *(Stroking her hair).* You'll love it, baby.

MARTHA. No, George.

GEORGE. You'll have a ball.

MARTHA *(Tenderly; moves to touch him).* Please, George, no more games; I . . .

GEORGE *(Slapping her moving hand with vehemence).* Don't you touch me! You keep your paws clean for the undergraduates!

MARTHA *(A cry of alarm, but faint).*

GEORGE *(Grabbing her hair, pulling her head back).* Now, you listen to me, Martha; you have had quite an evening . . . quite a night for yourself, and you can't just cut it off whenever you've got enough blood in your mouth. We are going on, and I'm going to have at you, and it's going to make your performance tonight look like an Easter pageant. Now I want you to get yourself a little alert. *(Slaps her lightly with his free hand)* I want a little life in you, baby. *(Again)*

MARTHA *(Struggling)*. Stop it!

GEORGE *(Again)*. Pull yourself together! *(Again)* I want you on your feet and slugging, sweetheart, because I'm going to knock you around, and I want you up for it. *(Again; he pulls away, releases her; she rises)*

MARTHA. All right, George. What do you want, George?

GEORGE. An equal battle, baby; that's all.

MARTHA. You'll get it!

GEORGE. I want you mad.

MARTHA. I'M MAD!!

GEORGE. Get madder!

MARTHA. DON'T WORRY ABOUT IT!

GEORGE. Good for you, girl; now, we're going to play this one to the death.

MARTHA. Yours!

GEORGE. You'd be surprised. Now, here comes the tots; you be ready for this.

MARTHA *(She paces, actually looks a bit like a fighter)*. I'm ready for you. *(NICK and HONEY reenter; NICK supporting HONEY, who still retains her brandy bottle and glass)*

NICK *(Unhappily)*. Here we are.

HONEY *(Cheerfully)*. Hip, hop. Hip, hop.

NICK. You a bunny, Honey? *(She laughs greatly, sits)*

HONEY. I'm a bunny, Honey.

GEORGE *(To HONEY)*. Well, now; how's the bunny?

HONEY. Bunny funny! *(She laughs again)*

NICK *(Under his breath)*. Jesus.

GEORGE. Bunny funny? Good for bunny!

MARTHA. Come on, George!

GEORGE *(To MARTHA)*. Honey funny bunny! *(HONEY screams with laughter)*

NICK. Jesus God. . . .

GEORGE *(Slaps his hands together, once)*. All right! Here we go! Last game! All sit. *(NICK sits)* Sit down, Martha. This is a civilized game.

MARTHA *(Cocks her fist, doesn't swing) (Sits)*. Just get on with it.

HONEY *(To GEORGE)*. I've decided I don't remember anything. *(To NICK)* Hello, Dear.

GEORGE. Hunh? What?

MARTHA. It's almost dawn, for God's sake. . . .

HONEY *(Ibid).* I don't remember anything, and you don't remember anything, either. Hello, Dear.

GEORGE. You what?

HONEY *(Ibid) (An edge creeping into her voice).* You heard me, nothing. Hello, Dear.

GEORGE *(To* HONEY, *referring to* NICK). You do know that's your husband, there, don't you?

HONEY *(With great dignity).* Well, I certainly know *that.*

GEORGE *(Close to* HONEY'S *ear).* It's just some things you can't remember . . . hunh?

HONEY *(A great laugh to cover; then quietly, intensely to* GEORGE). *Don't* remember; not *can't.* *(At* NICK, *cheerfully)* Hello, Dear.

GEORGE *(To* NICK). Well, speak to your little wifelet, your little bunny, for God's sake.

NICK *(Softly, embarrassed).* Hello, Honey.

GEORGE. Awww, that was nice. I think we've been having a . . . a real good evening . . . all things considered. . . . We've sat around, and got to know each other, and had fun and games . . . curl-up-on-the-floor, for example. . . .

HONEY. . . . the tiles. . . .

GEORGE. . . . the tiles . . . Snap the Dragon.

HONEY. . . . peel the label. . . .

GEORGE. . . . peel the . . . what?

MARTHA. Label. Peel the label.

HONEY *(Apologetically, holding up her brandy bottle).* I peel labels.

GEORGE. We all peel labels, sweetie; and when you get through the skin, all three layers, through the muscle, slosh aside the organs *(An aside to* NICK) them which is still sloshable—*(Back to* HONEY) and get down to bone . . . you know what you do then?

HONEY *(Terribly interested).* No!

GEORGE. When you get down to bone, you haven't got all the way, yet. There's something inside the bone . . . the marrow . . . and that's what you gotta get at. *(A strange smile at* MARTHA)

HONEY. Oh! I see.

GEORGE. The marrow. But bones are pretty resilient, especially in the young. Now, take our son. . . .

HONEY *(Strangely).* Who?

GEORGE. Our son. . . . Martha's and my little joy!

NICK *(Moving toward the bar)*. Do you mind if I . . . ?

GEORGE. No, no; you go right ahead.

MARTHA. George. . . .

GEORGE *(Too kindly)*. Yes, Martha?

MARTHA. Just what are you doing?

GEORGE. Why love, I was talking about our son.

MARTHA. Don't.

GEORGE. Isn't Martha something? Here we are, on the eve of our boy's home-coming, the eve of his twenty-first birfday, the eve of his majority . . . and Martha says don't talk about him.

MARTHA. Just . . . don't.

GEORGE. But I want to, Martha! It's very important we talk about him. Now bunny and the . . . well, whichever he is . . . here don't know much about junior, and I think they should.

MARTHA. Just . . . don't.

GEORGE *(Snapping his fingers at NICK)*. You. Hey, you! You want to play bringing up baby, don't you!

NICK *(Hardly civil)*. Were you snapping at me?

GEORGE. That's right. *(Instructing him)* You want to hear about our bouncey boy.

NICK *(Pause; then, shortly)*. Yeah; sure.

GEORGE *(To HONEY)*. And you, my dear? You want to hear about him, too, don't you.

HONEY *(Pretending not to understand)*. Whom?

GEORGE. Martha's and my son.

HONEY *(Nervously)*. Oh, you have a child?

(MARTHA *and* NICK *laugh uncomfortably*)

GEORGE. Oh, indeed; do we ever! Do you want to talk about him, Martha, or shall I? Hunh?

MARTHA *(A smile that is a sneer)*. Don't, George.

GEORGE. All rightie. Well, now; let's see. He's a nice kid, really, in spite of his home life; I mean, most kids'd grow up neurotic, what with Martha here carrying on the way she does; sleeping 'till four in the P.M., climbing all over the poor bastard, trying to break the bathroom door down to wash him in the tub when he's sixteen, dragging strangers into the house at all hours. . . .

MARTHA *(Rising)*. O.K. YOU!

GEORGE *(Mock concern)*. Martha!

164

MARTHA. That's enough!

GEORGE. Well, do you want to take over?

HONEY *(To* NICK*)*. Why would anybody want to wash somebody who's sixteen years old?

NICK *(Slamming his drink down)*. Oh, for Christ's sake, Honey!

HONEY *(Stage whisper)*. Well, why?!

GEORGE. Because it's her baby-poo.

MARTHA. ALL RIGHT!!

(By rote; a kind of almost-tearful recitation)

Our son. You want our son? You'll have it.

GEORGE. You want a drink, Martha?

MARTHA *(Pathetically)*. Yes.

NICK *(To* MARTHA *kindly)*. We don't have to hear about it . . . if you don't want to.

GEORGE. Who says so? You in a position to set the rules around here?

NICK *(Pause; tight-lipped)*. No.

GEORGE. Good boy; you'll go far. All right, Martha; your recitation, please.

MARTHA *(From far away)*. What, George?

GEORGE *(Prompting)*. "Our son. . . ."

MARTHA. All right. Our son. Our son was born in a September night, a night not unlike tonight, though tomorrow, and twenty . . . one . . . years ago.

GEORGE *(Beginning of quiet asides)*. You see? I told you.

MARTHA. It was an easy birth. . . .

GEORGE. Oh, Martha; no. You labored . . . how you labored.

MARTHA. It was an easy birth . . . once it had been . . . accepted, relaxed into.

GEORGE. Ah . . . yes. Better.

MARTHA. It was an easy birth, once it had been accepted, and I was young.

GEORGE. And I was younger. . . . *(Laughs quietly to himself)*

MARTHA. And I was young, and he was a healthy child, a red, bawling child, with slippery firm limbs. . . .

GEORGE. . . . Martha thinks she saw him at delivery. . . .

MARTHA. . . . with slippery, firm limbs, and a full head of black, fine, fine hair which, oh, later, later, became blond as the sun, our son.

GEORGE. He was a healthy child.

MARTHA. And I had wanted a child . . . oh, I had wanted a child.

GEORGE *(Prodding her)*. A son? A daughter?

165

MARTHA. A child! *(Quieter)* A child. And I had my child.

GEORGE. Our child.

MARTHA *(With great sadness)*. Our child. And we raised him . . . *(Laughs, briefly, bitterly)* yes, we did; we raised him. . . .

GEORGE. With teddy bears and an antique bassinet from Austria . . . and *no nurse.*

MARTHA. . . . with teddy bears and transparent floating goldfish, and a pale blue bed with cane at the headboard when he was older, cane which he wore through . . . finally . . . with his little hands . . . in his . . . sleep. . . .

GEORGE. . . . nightmares. . . .

MARTHA. . . . *sleep.* . . . He was a restless child. . . .

GEORGE. . . . *(Soft chuckle, head-shaking of disbelief)* . . . Oh Lord. . . .

MARTHA. . . . sleep . . . and a croup tent . . . a pale green croup tent, and the shining kettle hissing in the one light of the room that time he was sick . . . those four days . . . and animal crackers, and the bow and arrow he kept under his bed. . . .

GEORGE. . . . the arrows with rubber cups at their tip. . . .

MARTHA. . . . at their tip, which he kept beneath his bed. . . .

GEORGE. Why? Why, Martha?

MARTHA. . . . for fear . . . for fear of. . . .

GEORGE. For fear. Just that: for fear.

MARTHA *(Vaguely waving him off; going on)*. . . . and . . . and sandwiches on Sunday night, and Saturdays . . . *(Pleased recollection)* . . . and Saturdays the banana boat, the whole peeled banana, scooped out on top, with green grapes for the crew, a double line of green grapes, and along the sides, stuck to the boat with toothpicks, orange slices . . . SHIELDS.

GEORGE. And for the oar?

MARTHA *(Uncertainly)*. A . . . carrot?

GEORGE. Or a swizzle stick, whatever was easier.

MARTHA. No. A carrot. And his eyes were green . . . green with . . . if you peered so deep into them . . . so deep . . . bronze . . . bronze parentheses around the irises . . . such green eyes!

GEORGE. . . . blue, green, brown. . . .

MARTHA. . . . and he loved the sun! . . . He was tan before and after everyone . . . and in the sun his hair . . . became . . . fleece.

166

GEORGE *(Echoing her)*. . . . fleece. . . .

MARTHA. . . . beautiful, beautiful boy.

GEORGE. Absolve, Domine, animas omnium fidelium defunctorum ab omni vinculo delictorum.

MARTHA. . . . and school . . . and summer camp . . . and sledding . . . and swimming. . . .

GEORGE. Et gratia tua illis succurrente, mereantur evadere judicium ultionis.

MARTHA *(Laughing, to herself)*. . . . and how he broke his arm . . . how funny it was . . . oh, no, it hurt him! . . . but, oh, it was funny . . . in a field, his very first cow, the first he'd ever seen . . . and he went into the field, to the cow, where the cow was grazing, head down, busy . . . and he moo'd at it! *(Laughs ibid)* He moo'd at it . . . and the beast, oh, surprised, swung its head up and moo'd at him, all three years of him, and he ran, startled, and he stumbled . . . fell . . . and broke his poor arm. *(Laughs, ibid)* Poor lamb.

GEORGE. Et lucis aeternae beatitudine perfrui.

MARTHA. George cried! Helpless . . . George . . . cried. I carried the poor lamb. George snuffling beside me, I carried the child, having fashioned a sling . . . and across the great fields.

GEORGE. In Paradisum deducant te Angeli.

MARTHA. And as he grew . . . and as he grew . . . oh! so wise! . . . he walked evenly between us . . . *(She spreads her hands)* . . . a hand out to each of us for what we could offer by way of support, affection, teaching, even love . . . and these hands, still, to hold us off a bit, for mutual protection, to protect us all from George's . . . weakness . . . and my . . . necessary greater strength . . . to protect himself . . . and *us*.

GEORGE. In memoria aeterna erit justus: ab auditione mala non timebit.

MARTHA. So wise; so wise.

NICK *(To GEORGE)*. What is this? What are you doing?

GEORGE. Shhhhh.

HONEY. Shhhhh.

NICK *(Shrugging)*. O.K.

MARTHA. So beautiful; so wise.

GEORGE *(Laughs quietly)*. All truth being relative.

MARTHA. It was true! Beautiful; wise; perfect.

GEORGE. There's a real mother talking.

HONEY *(Suddenly; almost tearfully)*. I want a child.

NICK. Honey. . . .

HONEY *(More forcefully)*. I want a child!

GEORGE. On principle?

HONEY *(In tears)*. I want a child. I want a baby.

MARTHA *(Waiting out the interruption, not really paying it any mind)*. Of course, this state, this perfection . . . couldn't last. Not with George . . . not with George around.

GEORGE *(To the others)*. There; you see? I knew she'd shift.

HONEY. Be still!

GEORGE *(Mock awe)*. Sorry . . . mother.

NICK. Can't you be still?

GEORGE *(Making a sign at NICK)*. Dominus vobiscum.

MARTHA. Not with George around. A drowning man takes down those nearest. George tried, but, oh, God, how I fought him. God, how I fought him.

GEORGE *(A satisfied laugh)*. Ahhhhhhh.

MARTHA. Lesser states can't stand those above them. Weakness, imperfection cries out against strength, goodness and innocence. And George tried.

GEORGE. How did I try, Martha? How did I try?

MARTHA. How did you . . . what? . . . No! No . . . he grew . . . our son grew . . . up; he is grown up; he is away at school, college. He is fine, everything is fine.

GEORGE *(Mocking)*. Oh, come on, Martha!

MARTHA. No. That's all.

GEORGE. Just a minute! You can't cut a story off like that, sweetheart. You started to say something . . . now you say it!

MARTHA. No!

GEORGE. Well, I will.

MARTHA. No!

GEORGE. You see, Martha, here, stops just when the going gets good . . . just when things start getting a little rough. Now, Martha, here, is a misunderstood little girl; she really is. Not only does she have a husband who is a bog . . . a younger-than-she-is bog albeit . . . not only does she have a husband who is a bog, she has as well a tiny problem with spiritous liquors—like she can't get enough. . . .

MARTHA *(Without energy)*. No more, George.

GEORGE. . . . and on top of all that, poor weighed-down girl, PLUS a
father who really doesn't give a damn whether she lives or dies, who
couldn't care less *what* happens to his only daughter . . . on top of all
that she has a *son*. She has a son who fought her every inch of the way,
who didn't want to be turned into a weapon against his father, who
didn't want to be used as a goddamn club whenever Martha didn't get
things like she wanted them!

MARTHA *(Rising to it)*. Lies! Lies!!

GEORGE. Lies? All right. A son who would *not* disown his father, who came
to him for advice, for information, for love that wasn't mixed with
sickness—and you know what I mean, Martha!—who could not tolerate
the slashing, braying residue that called itself his MOTHER. MOTHER?
HAH!!

MARTHA *(Cold)*. All right, you. A son who was so ashamed of his father he
asked me once if it—possibly—wasn't true, as he had heard, from some
cruel boys, maybe, that he was not our child; who could not tolerate the
shabby failure his father had become. . . .

GEORGE. Lies!

MARTHA. Lies? Who would not bring his girl friends to the house. . . .

GEORGE. . . . in shame of his mother. . . .

MARTHA. . . . of his father! Who writes letters only to me!

GEORGE. Oh, so you think! To me! At my office!

MARTHA. Liar!

GEORGE. I have a stack of them!

MARTHA. YOU HAVE NO LETTERS!

GEORGE. And you have?

MARTHA. He has no letters. A son . . . a son who spends his summers
away . . . away from his family . . . ON ANY PRETEXT . . . because
he can't stand the shadow of a man flickering around the edges of a
house. . . .

GEORGE. . . . who spends his summers away . . . and he does! . . .
who spends his summers away because there isn't room for him in a
house full of empty bottles, lies, strange men, and a harridan who. . . .

MARTHA. Liar!!

GEORGE. Liar?

MARTHA. . . . A son who I have raised as best I can against . . . vicious
odds, against the corruption of weakness and petty revenges. . . .

169

GEORGE. . . . A son who is, deep in his gut, sorry to have been born. . . .
(BOTH TOGETHER)

MARTHA. I have tried, oh God I have tried; the one thing . . . the one thing I've tried to carry pure and unscathed through the sewer of this marriage; through the sick nights, and the pathetic, stupid days, through the derision and the laughter . . . *God*, the laughter, through one failure after another, one failure compounding another failure, each attempt more sickening, more numbing than the one before; the one thing, the one *person* I have tried to protect, to raise above the mire of this vile, crushing marriage; the one light in all this hopeless . . . *dark*ness . . . OUR SON.
(End together)

GEORGE. Libera me, Domine, de morte aeterna, in die illa tremenda: Quando caeli movendi sunt et terra: Dum veneris judicare saeculum per ignem. Tremens factus sum ego, et timeo, dum discussio venerit, atque ventura ira. Quando caeli movendi sunt et terra. Dies illa, dies irae, calamitatis et miseriae; dies magna et amara valde. Dum veneris judicare saeculum per ignem. Requiem aeternam dona eis, Domine: et lux perpetua luceat eis. Libera me Domine de morte aerterna in die illa tremenda: quando caeli mo vendi sunt et terra: Dum veneris judicare saeculum per ignem.

HONEY *(Her hands to her ears)*. STOP IT!! STOP IT!!

GEORGE *(With a hand sign)*. Kyrie, eleison. Christe, eleison. Kyrie, eleison.

HONEY. JUST STOP IT!!

GEORGE. Why, baby? Don't you like it?

HONEY *(Quite hysterical)*. You . . . can't . . . do . . . this!

GEORGE *(Triumphant)*. Who says!

HONEY. I! Say!

GEORGE. Tell us why, baby.

HONEY. No!

NICK. Is this game over?

HONEY. Yes! Yes, it is.

GEORGE. Ho-ho! Not by a long shot. *(To* MARTHA*)* We got a little surprise for you, baby. It's about sunny-Jim.

MARTHA. No more, George.

GEORGE. YES!

NICK. Leave her be!

GEORGE. I'M RUNNING THIS SHOW! *(To* MARTHA*)* Sweetheart, I'm afraid I've got some bad news for you . . . for us, of course. Some rather sad news.

(HONEY *begins weeping, head in hands*)

MARTHA *(Afraid, suspicious).* What is this?

GEORGE *(Oh, so patiently).* Well, Martha, while you were out of the room, while the . . . two of you were out of the room . . . I mean, I don't know where, hell, you both must have been somewhere *(Little laugh).* . . . While you were out of the room, for a while . . . well, Missey and I were sittin' here havin' a little talk, you know: a chaw and a talk . . . and the doorbell rang. . . .

HONEY *(Head still in hands).* Chimed.

GEORGE. Chimed . . . and . . . well, it's hard to tell you, Martha. . . .

MARTHA *(A strange throaty voice).* Tell me.

HONEY. Please . . . don't.

MARTHA. Tell me.

GEORGE. . . . and . . . what it was . . . it was good old Western Union, some little boy about seventy.

MARTHA *(Involved).* Crazy Billy?

GEORGE. Yes, Martha, that's right . . . crazy Billy . . . and he had a telegram, and it was for us, and I have to tell you about it.

MARTHA *(As if from a distance).* Why didn't they phone it? Why did they bring it; why didn't they telephone it?

GEORGE. Some telegrams you have to deliver, Martha; some telegrams you can't phone.

MARTHA *(Rising).* What do you mean?

GEORGE. Martha . . . I can hardly bring myself to say it. . . .

HONEY. Don't.

GEORGE *(To* HONEY*).* Do you want to do it?

HONEY *(Defending herself against an attack of bees).* No no no no no.

GEORGE *(Sighing heavily).* All right. Well, Martha . . . I'm afraid our boy isn't coming home for his birthday.

MARTHA. Of course he is.

GEORGE. No, Martha.

MARTHA. Of course he is. I say he is!

GEORGE. He . . . can't.

MARTHA. He is! I say so!

GEORGE. Martha . . . *(Long pause)* . . . our son is . . . dead.

(Silence)

He was . . . killed . . . late in the afternoon. . . .

(Silence)

(A tiny chuckle) on a country road, with his learner's permit in his pocket, he swerved, to avoid a porcupine, and drove straight into a. . . .

MARTHA *(Rigid fury)*. YOU . . . CAN'T . . . DO . . . THAT!

GEORGE. . . . large tree.

MARTHA. YOU CANNOT DO THAT!

NICK *(Softly)*. Oh my God. (HONEY *is weeping louder)*

GEORGE *(Quietly, dispassionately)*. I thought you should know.

NICK. Oh my God; no.

MARTHA *(Quivering with rage and loss)*. NO! NO! YOU CANNOT DO THAT! YOU CAN'T DECIDE THAT FOR YOURSELF! I WILL NOT LET YOU DO THAT!

GEORGE. We'll have to leave around noon, I suppose. . . .

MARTHA. I WILL NOT LET YOU DECIDE THESE THINGS!

GEORGE. . . . because there are matters of identification, naturally, and arrangements to be made. . . .

MARTHA *(Leaping at GEORGE, but ineffectual)*. YOU CAN'T DO THIS! (NICK *rises, grabs hold of* MARTHA, *pins her arms behind her back)* I WON'T LET YOU DO THIS, GET YOUR HANDS OFF ME!

GEORGE *(As NICK holds on; right in MARTHA'S face)*. You don't seem to understand, Martha; I haven't done anything. Now, pull yourself together. Our son is DEAD! Can you get that into your head?

MARTHA. YOU CAN'T DECIDE THESE THINGS.

NICK. Lady, please.

MARTHA. LET ME GO!

GEORGE. Now listen, Martha; listen carefully. We got a telegram; there was a car accident, and he's dead. POUF! Just like that! Now, how do you like it?

MARTHA *(A howl which weakens into a moan)*. NOOOOOOooooooo.

GEORGE *(To NICK)*. Let her go. (MARTHA *slumps to the floor in a sitting position)* She'll be all right now.

MARTHA *(Pathetic)*. No; no, he is *not* dead; he is not *dead*.

GEORGE. He is dead. Kyrie, eleison. Christe, eleison. Kyrie, eleison.

MARTHA. You can*not*. You may not decide these things.

NICK *(Leaning over her; tenderly)*. He hasn't decided anything, lady. It's not his doing. He doesn't have the power. . . .

172

GEORGE. That's right, Martha; I'm not a god. I don't have the power over life and death, do I?

MARTHA. YOU CAN'T KILL HIM! YOU CAN'T HAVE HIM DIE!

HONEY. Lady . . . please. . . .

MARTHA. YOU CAN'T!

GEORGE. There was a telegram, Martha.

MARTHA *(Up; facing him).* Show it to me! Show me the telegram!

GEORGE *(Long pause; then, with a straight face).* I ate it.

MARTHA *(A pause; then with the greatest disbelief possible, tinged with hysteria).* What did you just say to me?

GEORGE *(Barely able to stop exploding with laughter).* I . . . ate . . . it.

(MARTHA *stares at him for a long moment, then spits in his face*)

GEORGE *(With a smile).* Good for you, Martha.

NICK *(To* GEORGE). Do you think that's the way to treat her at a time like this? Making an ugly goddamn joke like that? Hunh?

GEORGE *(Snapping his fingers at* HONEY). Did I eat the telegram or did I not?

HONEY *(Terrified).* Yes; yes, you ate it. I watched . . . I watched you . . . you . . . you ate it all down.

GEORGE *(Prompting).* . . . like a good boy.

HONEY. . . . like a . . . g-g-g-good . . . boy. Yes.

MARTHA *(To* GEORGE, *coldly).* You're not going to get away with this.

GEORGE *(With disgust).* YOU KNOW THE RULES, MARTHA! FOR CHRIST'S SAKE, YOU KNOW THE RULES!

MARTHA. NO!

NICK *(With the beginnings of a knowledge he cannot face).* What are you two talking about?

GEORGE. I can kill him, Martha, if I want to.

MARTHA. HE IS OUR CHILD!

GEORGE. Oh yes, and you bore him, and it was a good delivery. . . .

MARTHA. HE IS OUR CHILD!

GEORGE. AND I HAVE KILLED HIM!

MARTHA. NO!

GEORGE. YES!

(Long silence)

NICK *(Very quietly).* I think I understand this.

GEORGE *(Ibid).* Do you?

NICK *(Ibid).* Jesus Christ, I think I understand this.

173

GEORGE *(Ibid)*. Good for you, buster.

NICK *(Violently)*. JESUS CHRIST I THINK I UNDERSTAND THIS!

MARTHA *(Great sadness and loss)*. You have no right . . . you have no right at all. . . .

GEORGE *(Tenderly)*. I have the right, Martha. We never spoke of it; that's all. I could kill him any time I wanted to.

MARTHA. But why? Why?

GEORGE. You broke our rule, baby. You mentioned him . . . you mentioned him to someone else.

MARTHA *(Tearfully)*. I did *not.* I never did.

GEORGE. Yes, you did.

MARTHA. Who? WHO?!

HONEY *(Crying)*. To me. You mentioned him to me.

MARTHA *(Crying)*. I FORGET! Sometimes . . . sometimes when it's night, when it's late, and . . . and everybody else is . . . talking . . . I forget and I . . . want to mention him . . . but I . . . HOLD ON . . . I hold on . . . but I've wanted to . . . so often . . . oh, George, you've *pushed* it . . . there was no need . . . there was no need for *this.* I *men*tioned him . . . all right . . . but you didn't have to push it over the EDGE. You didn't have to . . . kill him.

GEORGE. Requiescat in pace.

HONEY. Amen.

MARTHA. You didn't have to have him die, George.

GEORGE. Requiem aeternam dona eis, Domine.

HONEY. Et lux perpetua luceat eis.

MARTHA. That wasn't . . . needed.

(A long silence)

GEORGE *(Softly)*. It will be dawn soon. I think the party's over.

NICK *(To GEORGE; quietly)*. You couldn't have . . . any?

GEORGE. *We* couldn't.

MARTHA *(A hint of communion in this)*. *We* couldn't.

GEORGE *(To NICK and HONEY)*. Home to bed, children; it's way past your bedtime.

NICK *(His hand out to HONEY)*. Honey?

HONEY *(Rising, moving to him)*. Yes.

GEORGE (MARTHA *is sitting on the floor by a chair now)*. You two go now.

NICK. Yes.

HONEY. Yes.

NICK. I'd like to. . . .

GEORGE. Good night.

NICK *(Pause)*. Good night.

(NICK *and* HONEY *exit;* GEORGE *closes the door after them; looks around the room; sighs, picks up a glass or two, takes it to the bar) (This whole last section very softly, very slowly)*

GEORGE. Do you want anything, Martha?

MARTHA *(Still looking away)*. No . . . nothing.

GEORGE. All right. *(Pause)* Time for bed.

MARTHA. Yes.

GEORGE. Are you tired?

MARTHA. Yes.

GEORGE. I am.

MARTHA. Yes.

GEORGE. Sunday tomorrow; all day.

MARTHA. Yes.

(A long silence between them)

Did you . . . did you . . . have to?

GEORGE *(Pause)*. Yes.

MARTHA. It was . . . ? You had to?

GEORGE *(Pause)*. Yes.

MARTHA. I don't know.

GEORGE. It was . . . time.

MARTHA. Was it?

GEORGE. Yes.

MARTHA *(Pause)*. I'm cold.

GEORGE. It's late.

MARTHA. Yes.

GEORGE *(Long silence)*. It will be better.

MARTHA *(Long silence)*. I don't . . . know.

GEORGE. It will be . . . maybe.

MARTHA. I'm . . . not . . . sure.

GEORGE. No.

MARTHA. Just . . . us?

GEORGE. Yes.

MARTHA. I don't suppose, maybe, we could. . . .

GEORGE. No, Martha.

MARTHA. Yes. No.

GEORGE. Are you all right?

MARTHA. Yes. No.

GEORGE *(Puts his hand gently on her shoulder; she puts her head back and he sings to her, very softly).* Who's afraid of Virginia Woolf
Virginia Woolf
Virginia Woolf,

MARTHA. I . . . am . . . George. . . .

GEORGE. Who's afraid of Virginia Woolf. . . .

MARTHA. I . . . am . . . George. . . . I . . . am. . . .

   (GEORGE *nods, slowly*)

   (Silence; tableau)

CURTAIN

176

A
DELICATE
BALANCE
A Play (1966)

For
John Steinbeck
Affection and Admiration

FIRST PERFORMANCE

September 12, 1966, New York City, Martin Beck Theatre

JESSICA TANDY *as* AGNES

HUME CRONYN *as* TOBIAS

ROSEMARY MURPHY *as* CLAIRE

CARMEN MATHEWS *as* EDNA

HENDERSON FORSYTHE *as* HARRY

MARIAN SELDES *as* JULIA

Directed by ALAN SCHNEIDER

The Players:

AGNES: A handsome woman in her late 50's
TOBIAS: Her husband, a few years older
CLAIRE: Agnes' sister, several years younger
JULIA: Agnes' and Tobias' daughter, 36, angular
EDNA AND HARRY: Very much like Agnes and Tobias

The Scene:

The living room of a large and well-appointed suburban house.
Now.

ACT ONE
Friday Night

(In the library-livingroom. AGNES *in a chair,* TOBIAS *at a shelf, looking into cordial bottles)*

AGNES *(Speaks usually softly, with a tiny hint of a smile on her face: not sardonic, not sad . . . wistful, maybe).* What I find most astonishing—aside from that belief of mine, which never ceases to surprise me by the very fact of its surprising lack of unpleasantness, the belief that I might very easily—as they say—lose my mind one day, not that I suspect I am about to, or am even . . . nearby . . .

TOBIAS *(He speaks somewhat the same way).* There is no saner woman on earth, Agnes.

(Putters at the bottles)

AGNES. . . . for I'm not that sort; merely that it is not beyond . . . happening: some gentle loosening of the moorings sending the balloon adrift—and I think that is the only outweighing thing: adrift; the . . . becoming a stranger in . . . the world, quite . . . uninvolved, for I never see it as violent, only a drifting—what are you looking for, Tobias?

TOBIAS. We will all go mad before you. The anisette.

AGNES *(A small happy laugh).* Thank you, darling. But I could never do it —go adrift—for what would become of you? Still, what I find most astonishing, aside, as I said, from that speculation—and I wonder, too, sometimes, if I am the only one of you to admit to it: not that *I* may go mad, but that each of you wonders if each of *you* might not—why on earth do you want anisette?

TOBIAS *(Considers).* I thought it might be nice.

AGNES *(Wrinkles her nose).* Sticky. I will do cognac. It is supposed to be healthy—the speculation, or the assumption, I suppose, that if it occurs to you that you might be, then you are not; but I've never been much comforted by it; it follows, to my mind, that since I speculate I might, some day, or early evening I think more likely—some autumn dusk—go quite mad, then I very well might.

(Bright laugh)

Some autumn dusk: Tobias at his desk, looks up from all those awful

181

bills, and sees his Agnes, mad as a hatter, chewing the ribbons on her dress. . . .

TOBIAS *(Pouring)*. Cognac?

AGNES. Yes; Agnes Sit-by-the-fire, her mouth full of ribbons, her mind aloft, adrift; nothing to do with the poor old thing but put her in a bin somewhere, sell the house, move to Tucson, say, and pine in the good sun, and live to be a hundred and four.

(He gives her her cognac)

Thank you, darling.

TOBIAS *(Kisses her forehead)*. Cognac is sticky, too.

AGNES. Yes, but it's nicer. Sit by me, hm?

TOBIAS *(Does so; raises his glass)*. To my mad lady, ribbons dangling.

AGNES *(Smiles)*. And, of course, I haven't worn the ribbon dress since Julia's remarriage. Are you comfortable?

TOBIAS. For a little.

AGNES. What astonishes me most—aside from my theoretically healthy fear—no, not fear, how silly of me—healthy speculation that I might some day become an embarrassment to you . . . what I find most astonishing in this world, and with all my years . . . is Claire.

TOBIAS *(Curious)*. Claire? Why?

AGNES. That anyone—be they one's sister, or not—can be so . . . well, I don't want to use an unkind word, 'cause we're cozy here, aren't we?

TOBIAS *(Smiled warning)*. Maybe.

AGNES. As the saying has it, the one thing sharper than a serpent's tooth is a sister's ingratitude.

TOBIAS *(Getting up, moving to a chair)*. The saying does not have it that way.

AGNES. Should. Why are you moving?

TOBIAS. It's getting uncomfortable.

AGNES *(Semi-serious razzing)*. Things get hot, move off, huh? Yes?

TOBIAS *(Not rising to it)*. I'm not as young as either of us once was.

AGNES *(Toasting him)*. I'm as young as the day I married you—though I'm certain I don't look it—because you're a very good husband . . . most of the time. But I was talking about Claire, or was beginning to.

TOBIAS *(Knowing shaking of the head)*. Yes, you were.

AGNES. If I were to list the mountain of my burdens—if I had a thick pad and a month to spare—that bending my shoulders *most*, with the possible exception of Julia's trouble with marriage, would be your—it must be instinctive, I think, or *reflex*, that's more like it—your reflex defense of everything that Claire . . .

TOBIAS *(Very nice, but there is steel underneath)*. Stop it, Agnes.

AGNES *(A little laugh)*. Are you going to throw something at me? Your glass? My goodness, I hope not . . . that awful anisette all over everything.

TOBIAS *(Patient)*. No.

AGNES *(Quietly daring him)*. What then?

TOBIAS *(Looking at his hand)*. I shall sit very quietly . . .

AGNES. . . . as always . . .

TOBIAS. . . . yes, and I shall will you to apologize to your sister for what I must in truth tell you I thought a most . . .

AGNES. Apologize! To her? To Claire? I have spent my adult life apologizing *for* her; I will not double my humiliation by apologizing *to* her.

TOBIAS *(Mocking an epigram)*. One does not apologize to those for whom one must?

AGNES *(Winking slowly)*. Neat.

TOBIAS. Succinct, but one of the rules of an aphorism . . .

AGNES. An epigram, I thought.

TOBIAS *(Small smile)*. An epigram is usually satiric, and you . . .

AGNES. . . . and I am grimly serious. Yes?

TOBIAS. I fear so.

AGNES. To revert specifically from Claire to . . . her effect, what *would* you do were I to . . . spill my marbles?

TOBIAS *(Shrugs)*. Put you in a bin somewhere, sell the house and move to Tucson. Pine in the hot sun and live forever.

AGNES *(Ponders it)*. Hmmm, I bet you would.

TOBIAS *(Friendly)*. Hurry, though.

AGNES. Oh, I'll *try*. It won't be simple paranoia, though, I know that. I've tried so hard, to . . . well, you know how little I vary; goodness, I can't even raise my voice except in the most calamitous of events, and I find that both joy and sorrow work their . . . wonders on me more . . . evenly, slowly, with*in*, than most: a suntan rather than a scalding. There are no mountains in my life . . . nor chasms. It is a rolling, pleasant land . . . verdant, my darling, thank you.

TOBIAS *(Cutting a cigar)*. We do what we can.

AGNES *(Little laugh)*. Our motto. If we should ever go downhill, have a crest made, join things, we must have that put in Latin—We do what we can—on your blazers, over the mantel; maybe we could do it on the linen, as well. . . .

TOBIAS. Do you think I should go to Claire's room?

AGNES *(Silence: then stony, firm)*. No.

(TOBIAS *shrugs, lights his cigar*)

Either she will be down, or not.

TOBIAS. We do what we can?

AGNES. Of course.

(Silence)

So, it will not be simple paranoia. Schizophrenia, on the other hand, is far more likely—even given the unlikelihood. I believe it can be chemically induced . . .

(Smiles)

if all else should fail; if sanity, such as it is, should become too much. There are times when I think it would be so . . . proper, if one could take a pill—or even inject—just . . . remove.

TOBIAS *(Fairly dry)*. You should take drugs, my dear.

AGNES. Ah, but those are temporary; even addiction is a repeated temporary . . . stilling. I am concerned with peace . . . not mere relief. And I am not a compulsive—like . . . like some . . . like our dear Claire, say.

TOBIAS. Be kind. Please?

AGNES. I think I should want to have it fully . . . even on the chance I could not . . . come back. Wouldn't that be terrible, though? To have done it, induced, if naturally looked unlikely and the hope was there? *(Wonder in her voice)*

Not be able to come back? Why did you put my cognac in the tiny glass?

TOBIAS *(Rising, going to her)*. Oh . . . I'm sorry. . . .

AGNES *(Holding her glass out to him; he takes it from her)*. I'm not a sipper tonight; I'm a breather: my nose buried in the glass, all the wonder there, and very silent.

TOBIAS *(Getting her a new cognac)*. I thought Claire was much better tonight. I didn't see any need for you to give her such a going-over.

AGNES *(Weary)*. Claire was *not* better tonight. Honestly, Tobias!

TOBIAS *(Clinging to his conviction)*. I thought she was.

AGNES *(Putting an end to it)*. Well, she was *not*.

TOBIAS. Still . . .

AGNES *(Taking her new drink).* Thank you. I have decided, all things considered, that I shall not induce, that all the years we have put up with each other's wiles and crotchets have earned us each other's company. And I promise you as well that I shall think good thoughts—healthy ones, positive—to ward off madness, should it come by . . . uninvited.

TOBIAS *(Smiles).* You mean I have no hope of Tucson?

AGNES. None.

TOBIAS *(Mock sadness). Hélas . . .*

AGNES. You have hope, only, of growing even older than you are in the company of your steady wife, your alcoholic sister-in-law and occasional visits . . . from our melancholy Julia.

(A little sad)

That is what you have, my dear Tobias. Will it do?

TOBIAS *(A little sad, too, but warmth).* It will do.

AGNES *(Happy).* I've never doubted that it would.

(Hears something, says sourly)

Hark.

(CLAIRE *has entered)*

Did I hear someone?

TOBIAS *(Sees* CLAIRE *standing, uncomfortably, away from them).* Ah, there you are. I said to Agnes just a moment ago . . .

CLAIRE *(To* AGNES' *back, a rehearsed speech, gone through but hated).* I must apologize, Agnes; I'm . . . very sorry.

AGNES *(Not looking at her; mock surprise).* But what are you sorry for, Claire?

CLAIRE. I apologize that my nature is such to bring out in you the full force of your brutality.

TOBIAS *(To placate).* Look, now, I think we can do without any of this sort of

AGNES *(Rises from her chair, proceeds toward exiting).* If you come to the dinner table unsteady, *if* when you try to say good evening and weren't the autumn colors lovely today you are nothing but vowels, and *if* one smells the vodka on you from across the room—and *don't* tell me again, *either* of you! that vodka leaves nothing on the breath: if you are expecting it, if you are sadly and wearily expecting it, it *does—if* these conditions exist . . . *persist* . . . then the reaction of one who is burdened by her love is not brutality—though it would be excused, believe me!—not brutality at all, but the souring side of love. If I scold, it is because I wish I needn't. If I am sharp, it is because I am neither less nor more than human, and if I am to be accused once again of making too much of things, let me remind you that it is my manner and not the matter. I apologize for being articulate. Tobias, I'm going to call Julia, I think. Is it one or two hours difference? . . . I can never recall.

TOBIAS *(Dry)*. Three.

AGNES. Ah, yes. Well, be kind to Claire, dear. She is . . . injured.
(Exits. A brief silence)

TOBIAS. Ah, well.

CLAIRE. I have never known whether to applaud or cry. Or, rather, I never know which would be the more appreciated—expected.

TOBIAS *(Rather sadly)*. You are a great damn fool.

CLAIRE *(Sadly)*. Yes. Why is she calling Julia?

TOBIAS. Do you want a quick brandy before she comes back?

CLAIRE *(Laughs some)*. Not at all; a public one. Fill the balloon half up, and I shall sip it ladylike, and when she . . . glides back in, I shall lie on the floor and balance the glass on my forehead. That will give her occasion for another paragraph, and your ineffectual stop-it-now's.

TOBIAS *(Pouring her brandy)*. You *are* a great damn fool.

CLAIRE. Is Julia having another divorce?

TOBIAS. Hell, I don't know.

CLAIRE *(Takes the glass)*. It's only your daughter. Thank you. I should imagine—from all that I have . . . watched, that it is come-home time.
(Offhand)
Why don't you kill Agnes?

TOBIAS *(Very offhand)*. Oh, no, I couldn't do that.

CLAIRE. Better still, why don't you wait till Julia separates and comes back here, all sullen and confused, and take a gun and blow all our heads off? . . . Agnes first—through respect, of course, then poor Julia, and finally—if you have the kindness for it—me?

TOBIAS *(Kind, triste)*. Do you really want me to shoot you?

CLAIRE. I want you to shoot Agnes first. Then I'll think about it.

TOBIAS. But it would have to be an act of passion—out of my head, and all that. I doubt I'd stand around with the gun smoking, Julia locked in her room screaming, wait for you to decide if you wanted it or not.

CLAIRE. But unless you kill Agnes . . . how shall I ever know whether I want to live?

(Incredulous)

An act of passion!?

TOBIAS *(Rather hurt)*. Well . . . yes.

CLAIRE *(Laughs)*. Oh, my; *that's* funny.

TOBIAS *(Same)*. I'm sorry.

CLAIRE *(Friendly laugh)*. Oh, my darling Tobias, *I'm* sorry, but I just don't see you in the role, that's all—outraged, maddened into action, proceeding by reflex . . . Can you see yourself, though? In front of the judge? Predictable, stolid Tobias? "It all went blank, your honor. One moment, there I was, deep in my chair, drinking my . . ." What is that?

TOBIAS. Anisette.

CLAIRE. "Anisette." Really? Anisette?

TOBIAS *(Slightly edgy)*. I *like* it.

CLAIRE *(Wrinkles her nose)*. Sticky. "There I was, your honor, one moment in my chair, sipping at my anisette . . . and the next thing I knew . . . they were all lying about, different rooms, heads blown off, the gun still in my hand. I . . . I have no recollection of it, sir." Can you imagine that, Tobias?

TOBIAS. Of course, with all of you dead, your brains lying around in the rugs, there'd be no one to say it *wasn't* an act of passion.

CLAIRE. Leave me till last. A breeze might rise and stir the ashes. . . .

TOBIAS. Who's that?

CLAIRE. No one, I think. Just sounds like it should be.

TOBIAS. Why don't you go back to your . . . thing . . . to your alcoholics thing?

CLAIRE *(Half serious)*. Because I don't like the people. . . .

TOBIAS. What is it called?

CLAIRE. Anonymous.

TOBIAS. Yes; that. Why don't you go back?

CLAIRE *(Suddenly rather ugly)*. Why don't you mind your own hooting business?

TOBIAS *(Offended)*. I'm sorry, Claire.

CLAIRE *(Kisses at him)*. Because.

TOBIAS. It was better.

CLAIRE *(Holds her glass out; he hesitates)*. Be a good brother-in-law; it's only the first I'm not supposed to have.

TOBIAS *(Pouring for her)*. *I* thought it was better.

187

CLAIRE. Thank you.

(Lies on the floor, balances glass on her forehead, puts it beside her, etc.)

You mean Agnes thought it was better.

TOBIAS *(Kindly, calmly)*. No, I thought so too. That it would be.

CLAIRE. I told you: not our type; nothing in common with them. When you used to go to business—before you became a squire, parading around in jodhpurs, confusing the gardener . . .

TOBIAS *(Hurt)*. I've never done any such thing.

CLAIRE. Before all that . . .

(Smiles, chuckles)

sweet Tobias . . . when you used to spend all your time in town . . . with your business friends, your indistinguishable if not necessarily similar friends . . . what did you have in common with them?

TOBIAS. Well, uh . . . well, everything.

(Maybe slightly on the defensive, but more . . . vague)

Our business; we all mixed well, were friends away from the office, too . . . clubs, our . . . an, an environment, I guess.

CLAIRE. Unh-huh. But what did you have in common with them? Even Harry: your very best friend . . . in all the world—as far as you know; I mean, you haven't met everybody . . . are you switching from anisette?

TOBIAS *(Pouring himself brandy)*. Doesn't go for a long time. All right?

CLAIRE. Doesn't matter to *me*. Your very best friend . . . Tell me, dear Tobias; what do you have in common with him? Hm?

TOBIAS *(Softly)*. Please, Claire . . .

CLAIRE. What do you really have in common with your very best friend . . . 'cept the coincidence of having cheated on your wives in the same summer with the same woman . . . girl . . . woman? What except that? And hardly a distinction. I believe she was upended that whole July.

TOBIAS *(Rather tight-mouthed)*. If you'll forgive me, Claire, common practice is hardly . . .

CLAIRE. Poor girl, poor whatever-she-was that hot and very *wet* July.
(Hard)
The distinction would have been to have not: to have been the one or two of the very, very many and oh, God, similar who did not upend the poor . . . unfamiliar thing that dry and oh, so wet July.

188

TOBIAS. Please! Agnes!

CLAIRE *(Quieter).* Of course, you had the wanton only once, while Harry! Good friend Harry, I have it from the horse's mouth, was on top for good and keeps twice, with a third try not so hot in the gardener's shed, with the mulch, or whatever it is, and the orange pots. . . .

TOBIAS *(Quietly).* Shut your mouth.

CLAIRE *(Stands, faces TOBIAS; softly).* All right.
 (Down again)
 What was her name?

TOBIAS *(A little sad).* I don't remember.

CLAIRE *(Shrugs).* No matter; she's gone.
 (Brighter)
 Would you give friend Harry the shirt off your back, as they say?

TOBIAS *(Relieved to be on something else).* I *suppose* I would. He *is* my best friend.

CLAIRE *(Nicely).* How sad does that make you?

TOBIAS *(Looks at her for a moment, then).* Not much; some; not much.

CLAIRE. No one to listen to Bruckner with you; no one to tell you're sick of golf; no one to admit to that—now and then—you're suddenly frightened and you don't know why?

TOBIAS *(Mild surprise).* Frightened? No.

CLAIRE *(Pause; smile).* All right. Would you like to know what happened last time I climbed the stairs to the fancy alkie club, and why I've not gone back? What I have *not* in common with those people?

TOBIAS *(Not too enthusiastic).* Sure.

CLAIRE *(Chuckle).* Poor Tobias. "Sure." Light me a cigarette?
 (TOBIAS *hesitates a moment, then lights her one)*
 That will give me everything.
 (He hands the lighted cigarette to her; she is still on the floor)
 I need. A smoke, a sip and a good hard surface. Thank you.
 (Laughs a bit at that)

TOBIAS *(Standing over her).* Comfy?

CLAIRE *(Raises her two arms, one with the cigarette, the other the brandy glass; it is a casual invitation.* TOBIAS *looks at her for a moment, moves a little away).* Very. Do you remember the spring I moved out, the time I was *really* sick with the stuff: was drinking like the famous fish? Was a source of great embarrassment? So that you and Agnes set me up in the apartment near the station, and Agnes was *so* good about coming to see me?

(TOBIAS *sighs heavily*)

Sorry.

TOBIAS *(Pleading a little)*. When will it all . . . just go in the past . . . forget itself?

CLAIRE. When all the defeats are done, admitted. When memory takes over and corrects fact . . . makes it tolerable. When Agnes lies on her deathbed.

TOBIAS. Do you know that Agnes has . . . such wonderful control I haven't seen her cry in . . . for the longest time . . . no matter what?

CLAIRE. Warn me when she's coming; I'll act drunk. Pretend you're very sick, Tobias, like you were with the stomach business, but pretend you feel your insides are all green, and stink, and mixed up, and your eyes hurt and you're half deaf and your brain keeps turning off, and you've got peripheral neuritis and you can hardly walk and you hate. You hate with the same green stinking sickness you feel your bowels have turned into . . . yourself, and *everybody*. Hate, and, oh, God!! you want love, l-o-v-e, so badly—comfort and snuggling is what you really mean, of course—but you hate, and you notice—with a sort of detachment that amuses you, you think—that you're more like an animal every day . . . you snarl, and *grab* for things, and hide things and forget where you hid them like not-very-bright dogs, and you wash less, prefer to *be* washed, and once or twice you've actually soiled your bed and laid in it because you can't get up . . . pretend all that. No, you don't like that, Tobias?

TOBIAS. I don't know why you want to . . .

CLAIRE. You want to know what it's like to be an alkie, don't you, boy?

TOBIAS *(Sad)*. Sure.

CLAIRE. Pretend all that. So the guy you're spending your bottles with starts you going to the old A.A. And, you sit there at the alkie club and watch the . . . better ones—not recovered, for once an alkie, always, and you'd better remember it, or you're gone the first time you pass a saloon—you watch the better ones get up and tell their stories.

TOBIAS *(Wistful, triste)*. Once you drop . . . you can come back up part way . . . but never . . . really back again. Always . . . descent.

CLAIRE *(Gently, to a child)*. Well, that's life, baby.

TOBIAS. You are a great, damn fool.

CLAIRE. But, I'm not an alcoholic. I am not now and never was.

TOBIAS *(Shaking his head).* All the promise . . . all the chance . . .

CLAIRE. It would be so much simpler if I *were*. An alcoholic.

(She will rise and re-enact during this)

So, one night, one month, sometime, I'd had one martini—as a Test to see if I could—which, given my . . . stunning self-discipline, had become three, and I felt . . . rather daring and nicely detached and a little bigger than life and not snarling yet. So I marched, more or less straight, straight up to the front of the room, hall, and faced my peers. And I looked them over—all of them, trying so hard, grit and guilt and failing and trying again and loss . . . and I had a moment's—sweeping —pity and disgust, and I almost cried, but I didn't—like sister like sister, by God—and I heard myself say, in my little-girl voice—and there were a lot of different me's by then—"I am a alcoholic."

(Little-girl voice)

"My name is Claire, and I am a alcoholic."

(Directly to TOBIAS*)*

You try it.

TOBIAS *(Rather vague, but not babytalk).* My name is . . . My name is Claire, and I am an alcoholic.

CLAIRE. A alcoholic.

TOBIAS *(Vaguer).* A alcoholic.

CLAIRE. "My name is Claire, and I am a . . . alcoholic." Now, I was supposed to go on, *you* know, say how bad I was, and didn't want to be, and How It Happened, and What I Wanted To Happen, and Would They Help Me Help Myself . . . but I just stood there for a . . . ten seconds maybe, and then I curtsied; I made my little-girl curtsy, and on my little-girl feet I padded back to my chair.

TOBIAS *(After a pause; embarrassedly).* Did they laugh at you?

CLAIRE. Well, an agnostic in the holy of holies doesn't get much camaraderie, a little patronizing, maybe. Oh, they were taken by the *vaude*ville, don't misunderstand me. But the one lady was nice. She came up to me later and said, "You've taken the first step, dear."

TOBIAS *(Hopeful).* That was nice of her.

CLAIRE *(Amused).* She didn't say the first step toward *what*, of course. Sanity, *in*sanity, revelation, self-deception. . . .

TOBIAS *(Not much help).* Change . . . sometimes . . . no matter what . . .

CLAIRE *(Cheerful laugh).* Count on you, Tobias . . . snappy phrase every time. But it *hooked* me—the applause, the stage presence . . . that beginning; no school tot had more gold stars for never missing class. I went; oh, God, I *did.*

TOBIAS. But stopped.

CLAIRE. Until I learned . . .

(AGNES *enters, unobserved by either* TOBIAS *or* CLAIRE)

. . . and being a slow student in my young middle-age, slowly . . . that I was not, nor had ever been . . . a alcoholic . . . or an. Either. What I did not have in common with those people. That they were alcoholics, and I was not. That I was just a drunk. That they couldn't help it; I could, and wouldn't. That they were sick, and I was merely . . . willful.

AGNES. I have talked to Julia.

TOBIAS. Ah! How is she?

AGNES *(Walking by* CLAIRE). My, what an odd glass to put a soft drink in. Tobias, you have a quiet sense of humor, after all.

TOBIAS. Now, Agnes . . .

CLAIRE. He has not!

AGNES *(Rather heavy-handed).* Well, it *can't* be brandy; Tobias is a grown-up, and knows far better than to . . .

CLAIRE *(Harsh, waving her glass).* A toast to you, sweet sister; I drink your —not health; persistence—in good, hard brandy, *âge inconnu.*

AGNES *(Quiet, tight smile, ignoring* CLAIRE). It *would* serve you right, my dear Tobias, were I to go away, drift off. You would not have a woman left about you—only Claire and Julia . . . not even people; it would serve you right.

CLAIRE *(Great mocking).* But I'm not an alcoholic, baby!

TOBIAS. She . . . she can drink . . . a little.

AGNES *(There is true passion here; we see under the calm a little).* I WILL NOT TOLERATE IT!! I WILL NOT HAVE YOU!

(Softer, but tight-lipped)

Oh, God. I wouldn't mind for a moment if you filled your bathtub with it, lowered yourself in it, DROWNED! I rather wish you would. It would give me the peace of mind to know you could do something well, thoroughly. If you want to kill yourself—then do it *right!*

TOBIAS. Please, Agnes . . .

AGNES. What I cannot stand is the selfishness! Those of you who want to die . . . and take your whole lives doing it.

CLAIRE *(Lazy, but with loathing under it)*. Your wife is a perfectionist; they are *very* difficult to live with, these people.

TOBIAS *(To AGNES, a little pleading in it)*. She isn't an alcoholic . . . she says; she can drink some.

CLAIRE *(Little-child statement, but not babytalk)*. I am not a alcoholic!

AGNES. We think that's very nice. We shall all rest easier to know that it is willful; that the vomit and the tears, the muddy mind, the falls and the absences, the cigarettes out on the tabletops, the calls from the club to come and get you please . . . that they are all . . . willful, that it *can* be helped.

(Scathing, but softly)

If you are not an alcoholic, you are beyond forgiveness.

CLAIRE *(Ibid.)*. Well, I've been that for a long time, haven't I, sweetheart?

AGNES *(Not looking at either of them)*. If we change for the worse with drink, we are an alcoholic. It is as simple as that.

CLAIRE. And who is to say!

AGNES. I!

CLAIRE *(A litany)*. If we are to live here, on Tobias' charity, then we are subject to the will of his wife. If we were asked, at our father's dying . . .

AGNES *(Final)*. Those are the ground rules.

CLAIRE *(A sad smile)*. Tobias?

(Pause)

Nothing?

(Pause)

Are those the ground rules? Nothing? Too . . . settled? Too . . . dried up? Gone?

(Nicely)

All right.

(Back to AGNES)

Very well, then, Agnes, you win. I shall be an alcoholic.

(The smile too sweet)

What are you going to do about it?

AGNES *(Regards CLAIRE for a moment, then decides she—CLAIRE—is not in the room with them. AGNES will ignore CLAIRE's coming comments until otherwise indicated. TOBIAS will do this, too, but uncomfortably, embar-*

193

rassedly). Tobias, you will be unhappy to know it, I suppose, or of mixed emotions, certainly, but Julia is coming home.

CLAIRE *(A brief laugh).* Naturally.

TOBIAS. Yes?

AGNES. She is leaving Douglas, which is no surprise to *me.*

TOBIAS. But, wasn't Julia happy? You didn't tell me anything about . . .

AGNES. If Julia were happy, she would not be coming home. I don't want her here, God knows. I mean she's welcome, of course . . .

CLAIRE. Right on schedule, once every three years. . . .

AGNES *(Closes her eyes for a moment, to keep ignoring* CLAIRE*).* . . . it *is* her home, we are her parents, the *two* of us, and we have our obligations to her, and I have reached an age, Tobias, when I wish we were always alone, you and I, without . . . hangers-on . . . or anyone.

CLAIRE *(Cheerful but firm).* Well, I'm not going.

AGNES. . . . but if she and Doug are through—and I'm not suggesting *she* is in the right—then her place is properly here, as for some it is not.

CLAIRE. One, two, three, four, down they go.

TOBIAS. Well, I'd like to talk to Doug.

AGNES *(As if the opposite answer were expected from her).* I wish you would! If you had talked to Tom, or Charlie, yes! even Charlie, or . . . uh . . .

CLAIRE. Phil?

AGNES *(No recognition of* CLAIRE *helping her).* . . . Phil, it might have done some good. If you've decided to assert yourself, finally, too late, I imagine . . .

CLAIRE. Damned if you do, damned if you don't.

AGNES. . . . Julia might, at the very least, come to think her father cares, and that might be consolation—if not help.

TOBIAS. I'll . . . I'll talk to Doug.

CLAIRE. Why don't you invite him *here?* And while you're at it, bring the others along.

AGNES *(Some reproach).* And you might talk to Julia, too. You don't, very much.

TOBIAS. Yes.

CLAIRE *(A mocking sing-song).*
    Philip loved to gamble.
    Charlie loved the boys,

Tom went after women,
Douglas . . .

AGNES *(Turning on* CLAIRE). *Will* you stop that?

CLAIRE. Ooh, I *am* here, after all. I exist!

AGNES. Why don't you go off on a vacation, Claire, now that Julia's coming home again? Why don't you go to Kentucky, or Tennessee, and visit the distilleries? Or why don't you lock yourself in your room, or find yourself a bar with an apartment in the back. . . .

CLAIRE. Or! Agnes; why don't you die?

(AGNES *and* CLAIRE *lock eyes, stay still)*

TOBIAS *(Not rising from his chair, talks more or less to himself)*. If I saw some point to it, I might—if I saw some reason, chance. If I thought I might . . . break through to her, and say, "Julia . . . ," but then what would I say? "Julia . . ." Then, nothing.

AGNES *(Breaking eye contact with* CLAIRE, *says, not looking at either)*. If we do not love someone . . . never have loved them . . .

TOBIAS *(Soft correction)*. No; there can be silence, even having.

AGNES *(More curious than anything)*. Do you really want me dead, Claire?

CLAIRE. Wish, yes. Want? I don't know; probably, though I might regret it if I had it.

AGNES. Remember the serpent's tooth, Tobias.

TOBIAS *(Recollection)*. The cat that I had.

AGNES. Hm?

TOBIAS. The cat that I had . . . when I was—well, a year or so before I *met* you. She was very old; I'd had her since I was a kid; she must have been fifteen, or more. An alley cat. She didn't like people very much, I think; when people came . . . she'd . . . pick up and walk away. She liked *me;* or, rather, when I was alone with her I could see she was content; she'd sit on my lap. I don't know if she was happy, but she was content.

AGNES. Yes.

TOBIAS. And how the thing happened I don't really know. She . . . one day she . . . well, one day I realized she no longer liked me. No, that's not right; one day I realized she must have stopped liking me some time before. One evening I was alone, home, and I was suddenly aware of her absence, not just that she wasn't in the room with me, but that she hadn't been, in rooms with me, watching me shave . . . just *about* . . . for . . . and I couldn't place *how* long. She hadn't gone *away,* you understand; well, she *had*, but she hadn't run off. I knew she was *around*; I remembered I had caught sight of her—from time to time—under a chair, moving out of a room, but it was only when I realized something had happened that I could give any pattern to things that had . . . that I'd noticed. She didn't like me any more. It was that simple.

CLAIRE. Well, she was old.

TOBIAS. No, it wasn't that. She didn't like me any more. I tried to force myself on her.

AGNES. Whatever do you mean?

TOBIAS. I'd close her in a room with me; I'd pick her up, and I'd *make* her sit in my lap; I'd make her stay there when she didn't want to. But it didn't work; she'd abide it, but she'd get down when she could, go away.

CLAIRE. Maybe she was ill.

TOBIAS. No, she wasn't; I had her to the vet. She didn't like me any more. One night—I was *fixed* on it now—I had her in the room with me, and on my lap for the . . . the what, the fifth time the same evening, and she lay there, with her back to me, and she wouldn't purr, and I *knew*: I knew she was just waiting till she could get down, and I said, "Damn you, you like me; God damn it, you stop this! I haven't *done* anything to you." And I shook her; I had my hands around her shoulders, and I shook her . . . and she bit me; hard; and she hissed at me. And so I hit her. With my open hand, I hit her, smack, right across the head. I . . . I *hated* her!

AGNES. Did you hurt her badly?

TOBIAS. Yes; well, not badly; she . . . I must have hurt her ear some; she shook her head a lot for a day or so. And . . . you see, there was no *reason*. She and I had lived together and been, well, you know, friends, and . . . there was no *reason*. And I hated her for that. I hated her, well, I suppose because I was being accused of something, of . . . failing. But, I hadn't been cruel, by design; if I'd been neglectful, well, my life was . . . . I resented it. I resented having a . . . being judged. Being *betrayed*.

CLAIRE. What did you do?

TOBIAS. I had *lived* with her; I had done . . . *everything*. And . . . and if there was a, any responsibility I'd failed in . . . well . . . there was nothing I could *do*. And, and I was being accused.

CLAIRE. Yes; what did you do?

TOBIAS *(Defiance and self-loathing)*. I had her killed.

AGNES *(Kindly correcting)*. You had her put to sleep. She was old. You had her put to sleep.

TOBIAS *(Correcting)*. I had her killed. I took her to the vet and he took her . . . he took her into the back and

(Louder)

he gave her an injection and killed her! I had her *killed!*

AGNES *(After a pause)*. Well, what else could you have done? There was nothing to be done; there was no . . . meeting between you.

TOBIAS. I might have tried longer. I might have gone on, as long as cats live, the same way. I might have worn a hair shirt, locked myself in the house with her, done penance. For *something.* For *what.* God knows.

CLAIRE. You probably did the right *thing.* Distasteful alternatives; the less . . . ugly choice.

TOBIAS. Was it?

(A silence from them all)

AGNES *(Noticing the window)*. Was that a car in the drive?

TOBIAS. "If we do not love someone . . . never have loved some-one . . ."

CLAIRE *(An abrupt, brief laugh)*. Oh, stop it! "Love" is not the problem. You love Agnes and Agnes loves Julia and Julia loves me and I love you. We all love each other; yes we do. We love each other.

TOBIAS. Yes?

CLAIRE *(Something of a sneer)*. Yes; to the depths of our self-pity and our greed. What else but love?

TOBIAS. Error?

CLAIRE *(Laughs)*. Quite possibly: love and error.

(There is a knock at the door; AGNES *answers it)*

AGNES. Edna? Harry? What a surprise! Tobias, it's Harry and Edna. Come in. Why don't you take off your . . .

(HARRY and EDNA enter. They seem somewhat ill at ease, strained for such close friends)

TOBIAS. Edna!

EDNA. Hello, Tobias.

HARRY *(Rubbing his hands; attempt at being bluff)*. Well, now!

TOBIAS. Harry!

CLAIRE *(Too much surprise)*. Edna!

197

(Imitates HARRY'S *gruff voice)*

Hello, there, Harry!

EDNA. Hello, dear Claire!

(A little timid)

Hello, Agnes.

HARRY *(Somewhat distant).* Evening . . . Claire.

AGNES *(Jumping in, just as a tiny silence commences).* Sit *down.* We were just having a cordial. . . .

(Curiously loud)

Have you been . . . out? Uh, to the club?

HARRY *(Is he ignoring* AGNES' *question?).* I like this room.

AGNES. To the club?

CLAIRE *(Exaggerated, but not unkind).* How's the old Harry?

HARRY *(Self-pity entering).* Pretty well, Claire, not as good as I'd like, but . . .

EDNA. Harry's been having his shortness of breath again.

HARRY *(Generally).* I can't breathe sometimes . . . for just a bit.

TOBIAS *(Joining them all).* Well, two sets of tennis, you know.

EDNA *(As if she can't remember something).* What have you done to the room, Agnes?

AGNES *(Looks around with a little apprehension, then relief).* Oh, the summer *things* are off.

EDNA. Of course.

AGNES *(Persisting in it, a strained smile).* Have you been to the club?

HARRY *(To* TOBIAS). I was talking to Edna, 'bout having our books done in leather; bound.

TOBIAS. Oh? Yes?

(Brief silence)

CLAIRE. The question—'less I'm going deaf from all the alcohol—was

(Southern accent)

"Have you-all been to the club?"

AGNES *(Nervous, apologetic covering).* I wondered!

HARRY *(Hesitant).* Why . . . no, no.

EDNA *(Ibid.).* Why, why, no, Agnes. . . .

AGNES. I wondered, for I thought perhaps you'd dropped by here on your way from there.

HARRY. . . . no, no . . .

AGNES. . . . or perhaps that we were having a party, and I'd lost a day. . . .

HARRY. No, we were . . . just sitting home.

EDNA *(Some condolence)*. Agnes.

HARRY *(Looking at his hands)*. Just . . . sitting home.

AGNES *(Cheerful, but lack of anything better to say)*. Well.

TOBIAS. Glad you're here! Party or not!

HARRY *(Relieved)*. Good to see you, Tobias!

EDNA *(All smiles)*. How is Julia?!

CLAIRE. Wrong question.

(Lifts her glass)

May I have some brandy, Tobias?

AGNES *(A savage look to* CLAIRE, *back to* EDNA). She's coming home . . . I'm afraid.

EDNA *(Disappointment)*. Oh . . . not again!

TOBIAS *(Getting* CLAIRE's *glass, attempted levity)*. Just can't keep that one married, I guess.

EDNA. Oh, Agnes, what a shame!

HARRY *(More embarrassed than sorry)*. Gee, that's too bad.

(Silence)

CLAIRE. Why *did* you come?

AGNES. Please! Claire!

(Back, reassuring)

We're *glad* you're here; we're glad you came to surprise us!

TOBIAS *(Quickly)*. Yes!

*(*HARRY *and* EDNA *exchange glances)*

HARRY *(Quite sad and curious about it)*. We were . . . sitting home . . . just sitting home. . . .

EDNA. Yes . . .

AGNES *(Mildly reproving)*. We're *glad* to *see* you.

CLAIRE *(Eyes narrowing)*. What happened, Harry?

AGNES *(Sharp)*. Claire! Please!

TOBIAS *(Wincing a little, shaking his head)*. Claire . . .

EDNA *(Reassuring him)*. It's all right, Tobias.

AGNES. I don't see why people have to be questioned when they've come for a friendly . . .

CLAIRE *(Small victory)*. Harry wants to tell you, Sis.

EDNA. Harry?

HARRY. We . . . well, we were sitting home . . .

TOBIAS. Can I get you a drink, Harry?

HARRY *(Shakes his head)*. . . . I . . . we thought about going to the club, but . . . it's, it's so crowded on a Friday night . . .

EDNA *(Small voice, helpful, quiet)*. . . . with the canasta party, and getting ready for the dance tomorrow . . .

HARRY. . . . we didn't want to do that, and I've . . . been tired, and we didn't want to do that . . .

EDNA. . . . Harry's been tired this whole week.

HARRY. . . . so we had dinner home, and thought we'd stay . . .

EDNA. . . . rest.

AGNES. Of course.

CLAIRE. Shhhhh.

AGNES *(Rather vicious)*. I WILL NOT SHHHH!

HARRY. Please?

(Waits a moment)

TOBIAS *(Kind)*. Go on, Harry.

HARRY. So we were sitting, and Edna was doing that—that panel she works on . . .

EDNA *(Wistful, some loss)*. . . . my needlepoint . . .

HARRY. . . . and I was reading my French; I've got it pretty good now—not the accent, but the . . . the words.

(A brief silence)

CLAIRE *(Quietly)*. And then?

HARRY *(Looks over to her, a little dreamlike, as if he didn't know where he was)*. Hmm?

CLAIRE *(Nicely)*. And then?

HARRY *(Looks at* EDNA*)*. I . . . I don't know quite what happened then; we . . . we were . . . it was all very quiet, and we were all alone . . .

*(*EDNA *begins to weep, quietly;* AGNES *notices, the others do not;* AGNES *does nothing)*

. . . and then . . . nothing happened, but . . .

*(*EDNA *is crying more openly now)*

. . . nothing at all happened, but . . .

EDNA *(Open weeping; loud)*. WE GOT . . . FRIGHTENED.

(Open sobbing; no one moves)

HARRY *(Quiet wonder, confusion)*. We got scared.

EDNA *(Through her sobbing)*. WE WERE . . . FRIGHTENED.

HARRY. There was nothing . . . but we were very scared.

(AGNES *comforts* EDNA, *who is in free sobbing anguish.* CLAIRE *lies slowly back on the floor*)

EDNA. We . . . were . . . terrified.

HARRY. We were scared.

(*Silence;* AGNES *comforting* EDNA. HARRY *stock still. Quite innocent, almost childlike*)

It was like being lost: very young again, with the dark, and lost. There was no . . . thing . . . to be . . . frightened of, but . . .

EDNA (*Tears; quiet hysteria*). WE WERE FRIGHTENED . . . AND THERE WAS NOTHING.

(*Silence in the room*)

HARRY (*Matter-of-fact, but a hint of daring under it*). We couldn't stay there, and so we came here. You're our very best friends.

EDNA (*Crying softly now*). In the whole world.

AGNES (*Comforting, arms around her*). Now, now, Edna.

HARRY (*Apologizing some*). We couldn't go anywhere else, so we came here.

AGNES (*A deep breath, control*). Well, we'll . . . you did the right thing . . . of course.

TOBIAS. Sure.

EDNA. Can I go to bed now? Please?

AGNES (*Pause; then, not quite understanding*). Bed?

HARRY. We can't go back there.

EDNA. Please?

AGNES (*Distant*). Bed?

EDNA. I'm so . . . tired.

HARRY. You're our best friends in the world. Tobias?

TOBIAS (*A little bewilderment; rote*). Of course we are, Harry.

EDNA (*On her feet, moving*). Please?

(*Cries a little again*)

AGNES (*A million things going through her head, seeping through management*). Of . . . of course you can. There's . . . there's Julia's room, and . . .

(*Arm around* EDNA).

Come with me, dear.

(*Reaches doorway; turns to* TOBIAS; *a question that has no answer*)

Tobias?

HARRY *(Rises, begins to follow* EDNA, *rather automaton-like).* Edna?

TOBIAS *(Confused).* Harry?

HARRY *(Shaking his head).* There was no one else we could go to.

    (Exits after AGNES *and* EDNA. CLAIRE *sits up, watches* TOBIAS, *as he stands for a moment, looking at the floor: silence)*

CLAIRE *(A small, sad chuckle).* I was wondering when it would begin . . . when it would start.

TOBIAS *(Hearing her only after a moment).* Start?

    (Louder)

START?

    (Pause)

WHAT?!

CLAIRE *(Raises her glass to him).* Don't you know yet?

    (Small chuckle)

You will.

CURTAIN

ACT TWO
Scene One
Early Saturday Evening

(Same set; before dinner, next evening. JULIA *and* AGNES *alone.* AGNES *sitting,* JULIA *on her feet, pacing, maybe)*

JULIA *(Anger and self-pity; too loud).* Do you think I like it? Do you?
AGNES *(No pleading).* Julia! Please!
JULIA. DO YOU!? Do you think I enjoy it?
AGNES. Julia!
JULIA. Do you think it gives me some kind of . . . martyr's pleasure? Do you?
AGNES. Will you be still?
JULIA. WELL!?
AGNES. THERE IS A HOUSE FULL OF PEOPLE!
JULIA. Yes! What *about* that! I come home: my room is full of Harry and Edna. I have no place to put my things. . . .
AGNES *(Placating).* They'll go to Tobias' room, he'll sleep with me. . . .
JULIA *(Muttered).* That'll be different.
AGNES. What did you say, young lady?
JULIA. I SAID, THAT WILL BE NICE.
AGNES. You did *not* say any such thing. You said . . .
JULIA. What are they *doing* here? Don't they have a house any more? Has the market gone bust without my knowing it? I may have been out of touch, but . . .
AGNES. Just . . . let it be.
JULIA *(Between her teeth; controlled hysteria).* Why are they here?
AGNES *(Weary; head back; calm).* They're . . . frightened. Haven't you heard of it?
JULIA *(Incredulous).* They're . . . what!?
AGNES *(Keeping her voice down).* They're frightened. Now, will you let it be!
JULIA *(Offended).* What are they frightened of? Harry and *Edna?* Frightened?
AGNES. I don't . . . I don't know yet.
JULIA. Well, haven't you *talked* to them about it? I mean, for God's sake. . . .

AGNES *(Trying to stay calm)*. No. I haven't.

JULIA. What have they done: stayed up in their room all day—*my* room!—not come down? Locked in?

AGNES. Yes.

JULIA. Yes what?

AGNES. Yes, they have stayed up in their room all day.

JULIA. My room.

AGNES. Your room. Now, let it be.

JULIA *(Almost goes on in the same tone; doesn't; very nice, now)*. No, I . . .

AGNES. Please?

JULIA. I'm sorry, Mother, sorry for screeching.

AGNES. I am too old—as I remember—to remember what it is like to be a daughter, if my poor parents, in their separate heavens, will forgive me, but I am sure it is simpler than being a mother.

JULIA *(Slight edge)*. I said I was sorry.

AGNES *(All of this more for her own bemusement and amusement than anything else)*. I don't recall if I ever asked my poor mother that. I do wish sometimes that I had been born a man.

JULIA *(Shakes her head; very matter-of-fact)*. Not so hot.

AGNES. Their concerns are so simple: money and death—making ends meet until they meet the end.

(Great self-mockery and exaggeration)

If they *knew* what it was like . . . to be a wife; a mother; a lover; a homemaker; a nurse; a hostess, an agitator, a pacifier, a truth-teller, a deceiver . . .

JULIA *(Saws away at an invisible violin; sings)*. Da-da-dee; da-da-da.

AGNES *(Laughs softly)*. There is a book out, I believe, a new one by one of the thirty million psychiatrists practicing in this land of ours, a book which opines that the sexes are reversing, or coming to resemble each other too much, at any rate. It is a book to be read and disbelieved, for it disturbs our sense of well-being. If the book is right, and I suspect it is, then I would be no better off as a man . . . would I?

JULIA *(Sober, though tongue-in-cheek agreement; shaking of head)*. No. Not at all.

AGNES *(Exaggerated fret)*. Oh! There is nowhere to rest the weary head . . . or whatever.

ACT TWO

(Hand out; loving, though a little grand)
How are you, my darling?

JULIA *(A little abrupt)*. What?

AGNES *(Hand still out; somewhat strained)*. How are you, my darling?

JULIA *(Gathering energy)*. How is your darling? Well, I was trying to tell
you before you shut me up with Harry and Edna hiding upstairs,
and . . .

AGNES. ALL RIGHT!

(Pause)

JULIA *(Strained control)*. I will try to tell you, Mother—once again—before you've turned into a man. . . .

AGNES. I shall try to hear you out, but if I feel my voice changing, in the
middle of your . . . rant, you will have to forgive my male prerogative,
if I become uncomfortable, look at my watch, or jiggle the change in
my pocket . . .

(Sees JULIA marching toward the archway as TOBIAS enters)
. . . where do you think you're going?

JULIA. *(Head down, muttered)*. . . . you go straight to hell. . . .

TOBIAS *(Attempt at cheer)*. Now, now, what's going on here?

JULIA *(Right in front of him; force)*. Will you shut her up?

TOBIAS *(Overwhelmed)*. Will I . . . what?

AGNES *(Marching toward the archway herself)*. Well, there you are, Julia;
your father may safely leave the room now, I think.

(Kisses TOBIAS on the cheek)
Hello, my darling.

(Back to JULIA)
Your mother has arrived. Talk to *him!*

(To TOBIAS)
Your daughter is in need of consolation or a great cuffing around the
ears. I don't know which to recommend.

TOBIAS *(Confused)*. Have . . . have Harry and Edna . . . ?

AGNES *(Exiting)*. No, they have not.

(Gone)

TOBIAS *(After her, vaguely)*. Well, I thought maybe . . .

(To JULIA, rather timid)
What was that . . . all about?

JULIA. As they say: I haven't the faintest.

TOBIAS *(Willing to let it go)*. Oh.

JULIA *(Rather brittle).* Evening papers?

TOBIAS. Oh, yes; want them?

JULIA. Anything happy?

TOBIAS *(Hopefully).* My daughter's home.

JULIA *(Not giving in).* Any other joys?

TOBIAS. Sorry.

(Sighs)

No; small wars, large anxieties, our dear Republicans as dull as ever, a teen-age marijuana nest not far from here. . . .

(Some wonder)

I've never had marijuana . . . in my entire life.

JULIA. Want some?

TOBIAS. Wasn't fashionable.

JULIA. What the hell do Harry and Edna want?

TOBIAS *(Scratches his head).* Just let it be.

JULIA. Didn't you try to talk to them today? I mean . . .

TOBIAS *(Not embarrassed, but not comfortable either).* Well, no; they weren't down when I went off to the club, and . . .

JULIA. Good old golf?

TOBIAS *(Surprisingly nasty).* Don't ride me, Julia, I warn you.

JULIA *(Nervously nicer).* I've never had any marijuana, either. Aren't I a good old girl?

TOBIAS *(Thinking of something else).* Either that or slow.

JULIA *(Exploding; but anger, not hysteria).* Great Christ! What the hell did I come home to? And why? Both of you? Snotty, mean . . .

TOBIAS. LOOK!

(Silence; softer, but no nonsense)

There are some . . . times, when it all gathers up . . . too much.

JULIA *(Nervously).* Sure, sure.

TOBIAS *(Not put off).* Some *times* when it's going to be Agnes and Tobias, and not just Mother and Dad. Right? Some *times* when the allowances aren't going to be made. What are you doing, biting off your fingernails now?

JULIA *(Not giving in).* It broke off.

TOBIAS. There are some *times* when it's all . . . too much. *I* don't know what the hell Harry and Edna are doing sitting up in that bedroom! Claire is drinking, she and Agnes are at each other like a couple of . . . of . . .

206

ACT TWO

JULIA *(Softly)*. Sisters?

TOBIAS. What? The goddamn government's at me over some deductions, and you!

JULIA *(Head high, defiant)*. And me? Yes?

TOBIAS. This isn't the first time, you know. This isn't the first time you've come back with one of your goddamned marriages on the rocks. Four! Count 'em!

JULIA *(Rage)*. I know how many marriages I've gotten myself into, you . . .

TOBIAS. Four! You expect to come back here, nestle in to being fifteen and misunderstood each time!? You are thirty-six years old, for God's sake! . . .

JULIA. And you are one hundred! Easily!

TOBIAS. Thirty-six! Each time! Dragging your . . . your—I was going to say pride—your marriage with you like some Raggedy Ann doll, by the foot. You, you fill this house with your whining. . . .

JULIA *(Rage)*. I DON'T ASK TO COME BACK HERE!!

TOBIAS. YOU BELONG HERE!

(Heavy breathing from both of them, finally a little rueful giggle;
TOBIAS *speaks rather nonchalantly now)*

Well. Now that I've taken out on my only daughter the . . . disgust of my declining years, I'll mix a very good and very strong martini. Join me?

JULIA *(Rather wistful)*. When I was a very little girl—well, when I was a little girl: after I'd gotten over my two-year burn at suddenly having a brother, may his soul rest, when I was still a little girl, I thought you were a marvel—saint, sage, daddy, everything. And then, as the years turned and I reached my . . . somewhat angular adolescence . . .

TOBIAS *(At the sideboard; unconcerned)*. Five to one? Or more?

JULIA. And then, as the years turned—poor old man—you sank to cipher, and you've stayed there, I'm afraid—very nice but ineffectual, essential, but not-really-thought-of, gray . . . noneminence.

TOBIAS *(Mixing, hardly listening)*. Unh-hunh . . .

JULIA. And now you've changed again, sea monster, ram! Nasty, violent, absolutely human man! Yes, as you make it, five to one, or better.

TOBIAS. I made it about seven, I think.

JULIA. Your transformations amaze me. How can I have changed so much? Or *is* it really you?

207

(He hands her a drink)

Thank you.

TOBIAS *(As they both settle)*. I told Agnes that I'd speak to Doug . . . if you think that would do any good. By golly, Dad, that's a good martini!

JULIA. Do you really want to talk to Doug? You won't get anywhere: the compulsives you can get somewhere with—or the illusion of getting—the gamblers, the fags, the lechers . . .

TOBIAS. . . . of this world . . .

JULIA. . . . yes, you can have the illusion 'cause they're after something, the jackpot, somehow: break the bank, find the boy, climb the babe . . . something.

TOBIAS. You do pick 'em.

JULIA *(Pregnant). Do* I?

TOBIAS. Hm?

JULIA. *Do* I pick 'em? I thought it was fifteen hundred and six, or so, where daughter went with whatever man her parents thought would hold the fief together best, or something. "Love will come after."

TOBIAS *(Grudging)*. Well, you may have been pushed on Charlie. . . .

JULIA. Poor Charlie.

TOBIAS *(Temper rising a little)*. Well, for Christ's sake, if you miss him so much . . .

JULIA. I do not miss him! Well, yes, I do, but not that way. Because he seemed so like what Teddy would have been.

TOBIAS *(Quiet anger and sorrow)*. Your brother would not have grown up to be a fag.

JULIA *(Bitter smile)*. Who is to say?

TOBIAS *(Hard look)*. I!

(Pause. CLAIRE *in the archway)*

CLAIRE. Do I breathe gin?

*(*JULIA *sees her, runs to her, arms out, both of them, they envelop each other)*

Darling!

JULIA. Oh, my sweet Claire!

CLAIRE. Julia Julia.

JULIA *(Semi-mock condemnation)*. I must say the welcome-home committee was pretty skimpy, you and Daddy gone. . . .

CLAIRE. Oh, now.

(To TOBIAS*)*

I said, do I breathe gin?

TOBIAS *(Not rising)*. You do.

CLAIRE *(Appraising* JULIA*)*. Well, you don't look too bad for a quadruple amputee, I must say. Are you going to make me a whatever, Tobias? *(To* JULIA*)*

Besides, my darling, it's getting to be rather a habit, isn't it?

JULIA *(False smile)*. Yes, I suppose so.

CLAIRE *(Sees* TOBIAS *is not moving)*. Then I shall make my own.

TOBIAS *(Getting up; wearily)*. Sit down, Claire, I'll do it.

CLAIRE. I wouldn't want to tax you, now. *(Generally)*

Well, I had an adventure today. Went into town, thought I'd shake 'em up a little, so I tried to find me a topless bathing suit.

JULIA *(Giggling)*. You didn't!

TOBIAS *(At the sideboard, disapproving)*. Really, Claire.

CLAIRE. Yes, I did. I went into what's-their-names', and I went straight up to the swim-wear, as they call it, department and I got me an eighteen-nineties schoolteacher type, who wondered what she could do for me. *(*JULIA *giggles)*

and I felt like telling her, "Not much, sweetheart" . . .

TOBIAS. Are you sure you wouldn't rather have a . . .

CLAIRE. Very. But I said, "Hello, there, I'm in the market for a topless swimsuit."

JULIA. You know! They *are* wearing them on the coast. I've . . .

CLAIRE. Hush. Hurry up there, Toby. "A what, Miss?" she said, which I didn't know whether to take as a compliment or not. "A topless swim-suit," I said. "I don't know what you mean," she said after a beat. "Oh, certainly you do," I said, "no top, stops at the waist, latest thing, lots of freedom." "Oh, yes," she said, looking at me like she was seeing the local madam for the first time, "those." Then a real sniff. "I'm afraid we don't carry . . . those."

JULIA. I could have brought you one! . . . *(Afterthought)*

If I'd known I was coming home.

CLAIRE. "Well, in that case," I told her, "do you have any separates?" "Those we carry," she said, "those we do." And she started going under the counter, and I said, "I'll just buy the bottoms of one of those."

JULIA. No! You didn't!

CLAIRE. Yes, I did. She came up from under the counter, adjusted her spectacles and said, "What did you say?"

TOBIAS. Shall I bring it, or will you come for it?

CLAIRE. You bring. I said, "I said, 'I'll buy the bottom of one of those.' " She thought for a minute, and then she said, with ice in her voice, "And what will we do with the tops?" "Well," I said, "why don't you save 'em? Maybe bottomless swimsuits'll be in *next* year."

(JULIA *laughs openly*)

Then the poor sweet thing gave me a look I couldn't tell was either a D minus, or she was going to send me home with a letter to my mother, and she said, sort of far away, "I think you need the manager." And off she walked.

TOBIAS (*Handing* CLAIRE *her martini; mildly amused throughout*). What were you doing buying a bathing suit in October, anyway?

JULIA. Oh, Dad!

CLAIRE. No, now; it's a man's question.

(*Sips*)

Wow, what a good martini.

TOBIAS (*Still standing over her, rather severe*). Truth will get you nowhere. Why?

CLAIRE. Why? Well . . .

(*Thinks*)

. . . maybe I'll go on a trip somewhere.

TOBIAS. That would please Agnes.

CLAIRE (*Nods*). As few things would. What I meant was, maybe Toby'll walk in one day, trailing travel folders, rip his tie off, announce he's fed up to there with the north, the east, the suburbs, the regulated great gray life, dwindling before him—poor Toby—and has bought him an island off Paraguay . . .

TOBIAS. . . . which has no seacoast . . .

CLAIRE. . . . yes, *way* off—has bought him this island, and is taking us all to *that*, to hack through the whatever, build us an enormous lean-to, all of us. Take us away, to where it is always good and happy.

(*Watches* TOBIAS, *who looks at his drink, frowning a little*)

JULIA (*She, too*). Would you, Dad?

TOBIAS (*Looks up, sees them both looking at him, frowns more*). It's . . . it's too late, or something.

(*Small silence*)

210

ACT TWO

CLAIRE *(To lighten it).* Or, maybe I simply wanted a topless bathing suit. *(Pause)*

No? Well, then . . . maybe it's more complicated yet. I mean, Claire couldn't find herself a man if she tried, and here comes Julia, home from the wars. . . .

TOBIAS *(Quiet contradiction).* You could find a man.

CLAIRE *(Some bitterness).* Indeed, I have found several, briefly, and none my own.

TOBIAS *(To JULIA; terribly offhand).* Julia, don't you think Auntie Claire could find herself a man?

JULIA *(Didactic).* I *don't* like the subject.

CLAIRE. . . . and here comes Julia, home from the wars, four purple hearts . . .

JULIA. Why don't you just have another drink and stop it, Claire?

CLAIRE *(Looks at her empty glass, shrugs).* All right.

JULIA *(Rather defensive).* I have *left* Doug. We are not *divorced*.

CLAIRE. Yet! Are you cooking a second batch, Tobias?

(Back to JULIA)

But you've come back home, haven't you? And didn't you—with the others?

JULIA *(Her back up).* Where else am I supposed to go?

CLAIRE. It's a great big world, baby. There are hotels, new cities. Home is the quickest road to Reno I know of.

JULIA *(Condescending).* You've had a lot of experience in these matters, Claire.

CLAIRE. Sidelines! Good seats, right on the fifty-yard line, objective observer.

(Texas accent, or near it)

I swar! Ef I din't love muh sister so, Ah'd say she got yuh hitched fur the pleasure uh gettin' yuh back.

JULIA. ALL RIGHT!   TOBIAS. THAT WILL DO NOW!

CLAIRE *(In the silence that follows).* Sorry. Very . . . very sorry.

(AGNES appears through the archway)

AGNES *(What she may have overheard she gives no indication of).* "They" tell me in the kitchen . . . "they" tell me we are about to dine. In a bit. Are we having a cocktail? I think one might be nice.

(Puts her arm around JULIA as she passes her)

211

It's one of those days when everything's underneath. But, we are all together . . . which is something.

JULIA. Quite a few of us.

TOBIAS. Any word from . . .

(Points to the ceiling)

. . . up there?

AGNES. No. I dropped upstairs—well, *that* doesn't make very much sense, does it?—I *happened* upstairs, and I knocked at Harry and Edna's *Julia's* room, door, and after a moment I heard Harry say, "It's all right; we're all right." I didn't have the . . . well, I felt such an odd mixture of . . . embarrassment and irritation, and . . . apprehension, I suppose, and . . . fatigue . . . I didn't persevere.

TOBIAS. Well, haven't they been *out?* I mean, haven't they eaten or anything?

AGNES. Will you make me a . . . thing, a martini, please? I am told— *"they"* tell me that while we were all out, at our various whatever-they-may-be's, Edna descended, asked them to make sandwiches, which were brought to the closed door and handed in.

TOBIAS. Well, God, I mean . . .

AGNES *(Rather a recitation).* There is no point in pressing it, they are our very dear friends, they will tell us in good time.

CLAIRE *(Looking through her glass).* I had a glimmer of it last night; thought I knew.

AGNES *(So gracious).* That which we see in the bottom of our glass is most often dregs.

CLAIRE *(Peers into her glass, over-curious).* Really? Truly so?

TOBIAS *(Holding a glass out to AGNES).* Did you say you wanted?

AGNES *(Her eyes still on CLAIRE).* Yes, I did, thank you.

CLAIRE. I have been trying, without very much success, to find out why Miss Julie here is come home.

AGNES. I would imagine Julia is home because she wishes to be, and it is where she belongs if she wants.

TOBIAS. That's logistics, isn't it?

AGNES. You too?

JULIA. He's against everything!

AGNES. Your father?

JULIA. Doug!

AGNES. You needn't make a circus of it; tell me later, when . . . .

JULIA. War, marriage, money, children . . . .

AGNES. You needn't!

JULIA. You! Daddy! Government! Claire—if he'd met her . . . every-thing!

CLAIRE. Well, I doubt he'd dislike *me;* I'm against everything too.

AGNES *(To* JULIA). You're tired; we'll talk about it after . . .

JULIA *(Sick disgust).* I've talked about it! I just talked about it!

AGNES *(Quiet boring in).* I'm sure there's more.

JULIA. There is no more.

AGNES *(Clenched teeth).* There is a great deal more, and I'll hear it from you later, when we're alone. You have not come to us in your fourth debacle . . .

JULIA. HE IS OPPOSED! AND THAT IS ALL! TO EVERYTHING!

AGNES *(After a small silence).* Perhaps after dinner.

JULIA. NO! NOT PERHAPS AFTER DINNER!

TOBIAS. ALL OF YOU! BE STILL!

(Silence)

CLAIRE *(Flat; to* TOBIAS). Are we having our dividend, or are we not?

(Silence; then, a gentle mocking apology)

"All happy families are alike."

*(*HARRY *and* EDNA *appear in the archway, coats on or over arms)*

HARRY *(A little embarrassed).* Well.

CLAIRE *(Exaggerated bonhomie).* Well, look who's here!

TOBIAS *(Embarrassed).* Harry, just in time for a martini. . . .

HARRY. No, no, we're . . . Julia, there you are!

EDNA *(Affectionate commiseration).* Oh, Julia.

JULIA *(Bravely, nicely).* Hello there.

AGNES *(On her feet).* There's just time for a drink before dinner, if my husband will hurry some . . .

HARRY. No, we're . . . . going home now.

AGNES *(Relief peeking through the surprise).* Oh? Yes?

EDNA. Yes.

(Pause)

AGNES. Well.

(Pause)

If we were any help at all, we . . . .

HARRY. To . . . . uh, to get our things.

(Silence)

Our clothes, and things.

EDNA. Yes.

HARRY. We'll be back in . . . well, after dinner, so don't . . .

EDNA. An hour or two. It'll take us a while.

(Silence)

HARRY. We'll let ourselves . . . don't bother.

(They start out, tentatively, see that the others are merely staring at them. Exit. Silence)

JULIA *(Controlled, but near tears)*. I want my room back! I want my room!

AGNES *(Composed, chilly, standing in the archway)*. I believe that dinner is served. . . .

TOBIAS *(Vacant)*. Yes?

AGNES. If any of you have the stomach for it.

CURTAIN

ACT TWO
Scene Two
Later That Night

(Same set, after dinner, the same evening. AGNES *and* TOBIAS *to one side,* AGNES *standing,* TOBIAS *not;* JULIA *in another corner, not facing them)*

JULIA *(A statement, directed to neither of them).* That was, without question, the *ugliest* dinner I have ever sat through.

AGNES *(Seemingly pleased).* What did you say?

(No answer)

Now, what can you mean? Was the ragout not to your pleasure? Did the floating island sink? Watch what you say, for your father is proud of his wines. . . .

JULIA. No! You! Sitting there! Like a combination . . . pope, and . . . "We will not discuss it"; "Claire, be still"; "No, Tobias, the table is not the proper place"; "Julia!" . . . nanny! Like a nanny!

AGNES. When we are dealing with children . . .

JULIA. I must discover, sometime, who you think you are.

AGNES *(Icy).* You will learn . . . one day.

JULIA. No, more like a drill sergeant! *You* will do this, *you* will not say that.

AGNES. "To keep in shape." Have you heard the expression? Most people misunderstand it, assume it means alteration, when it does not. Maintenance. When we keep something in shape, we maintain its shape— whether we are proud of that shape, or not, is another matter—we keep *it* from falling apart. We do not attempt the impossible. We maintain. We hold.

JULIA. Yes? So?

AGNES *(Quietly).* I shall . . . keep this family in shape. I shall maintain it; hold it.

JULIA *(A sneer).* But you won't attempt the impossible.

AGNES *(A smile).* I shall keep it in shape. If I am a drill sergeant . . . so be it. Since nobody . . . *really* wants to talk about your latest . . . marital disorder, really wants to talk *around* it, use it as an excuse for all sorts of horrid little revenges . . . I think we can at least keep the table . . . unlittered of *that.*

JULIA *(Sarcastic salute, not rising though).* Yes, sir.

AGNES *(Reasonable).* And, if I shout, it's merely to be heard . . . above

215

the awful din of your privacies and sulks . . . all of you. I am not being an ogre, am I?

TOBIAS *(Not anxious to argue)*. No, no; very . . . reasonable.

AGNES. If I am a stickler on certain points

(Just as JULIA'S *mouth opens to speak)*

—a martinet, as Julia would have it, would you not, sweet?, in fact, were you not about to?—if I am a stickler on points of manners, timing, tact —the graces, I almost blush to call them—it is simply that I am the one member of this . . . reasonably happy family blessed and burdened with the ability to view a situation objectively while I am in it.

JULIA *(Not really caring)*. What time is it?

AGNES *(A little harder now)*. The double position of seeing not only facts but their implications . . .

TOBIAS. Nearly ten.

AGNES *(Some irritation toward both of them)*. . . . . the longer view as well as the shorter. There *is* a balance to be maintained, after all, though the rest of you teeter, unconcerned, or uncaring, *assuming* you're on level ground . . . by divine right, I gather, though that is hardly so. And if I must be the fulcrum . . .

(Sees neither of them is really listening, says in the same tone)

. . . I think I shall have a divorce.

(Smiles to see that her words have had no effect)

TOBIAS *(It sinks in)*. Have what? A *what?*

AGNES. No fear; merely testing. Everything is taken for granted and no one listens.

TOBIAS *(Wrinkling his nose)*. Have a divorce?

AGNES. No, no; Julia has them for all of us. Not even separation; that is taken care of, and in life: the gradual . . . demise of intensity, the private preoccupations, the substitutions. We become allegorical, my darling Tobias, as we grow older. The individuality we hold so dearly sinks into crotchet; we see ourselves repeated by those we bring into it all, either by mirror or rejection, honor or fault.

(To herself, really)

I'm not a fool; I'm really not.

JULIA *(Leafing a magazine; clear lack of interest but not insulting)*. What's Claire up to?

AGNES *(Walking to* TOBIAS, *a hand on his shoulder)*. Really not at all.

TOBIAS *(Looking up; fondness)*. No; really not.

216

ACT TWO

AGNES *(Surprisingly unfriendly; to* JULIA*).* How would I know what she's doing?

JULIA *(She too).* Well, you are the fulcrum and all around here, the double vision, the great balancing act. . . .

(Lets it slide away)

AGNES *(A little triste; looking away).* I dare say she's in her room.

JULIA *(Little girl).* At least she has one.

AGNES *(Swinging around to face her; quite hard).* Well, why don't you run upstairs and claim your goddamn room back! Barricade yourself in there! Push a bureau in front of the door! Take Tobias' pistol while you're at it! Arm yourself!

(A burst from an accordion; CLAIRE *appears in the archway, wearing it)*

CLAIRE. Barricades? Pistols? Really? So soon?

JULIA *(Giggling in spite of herself).* Oh, Claire . . .

AGNES *(Not amused).* Claire, will you take off that damned thing!

CLAIRE. "They laughed when I sat down to the accordion." Take it off? No, I will not! This is going to be a festive night—from the smell of it, and sister Claire wants to do her part—pay her way, so to speak . . . justify.

AGNES. You're not going to play that dreadful instrument in here, and . . .

(But the rest of what she wants to say is drowned out by a chord from the accordion)

Tobias?

(Calm)

Do something about that.

TOBIAS *(He, too, chuckling).* Oh, now, Agnes . . .

CLAIRE. So . . .

(Another chord)

. . . shall I wait? Shall I start now? A polka? What?

AGNES *(Icy, but to* TOBIAS*).* My sister is not *really* lazy. The things she has learned since leaving the nest!: gaucherie, ingratitude, drunkenness, and even . . . this. She has become a musician, too.

CLAIRE *(A twang in her voice).* Maw used to say: "Claire, girl" . . . she had an uncle named Claire, so she always called me Claire-girl—

AGNES *(No patience with it).* That is not so.

CLAIRE. "Claire girl," she used to say, "when you go out into the world, get dumped outa the nest, or pushed by your sister . . ."

217

AGNES *(Steady, but burning).* Lies.

(Eyes slits)

She kept you, allowed you . . . tolerated! Put up with your filth, your . . . "emancipated womanhood."

(To JULIA, *overly sweet)*

Even in her teens, your Auntie Claire had her own and very special ways, was very . . . advanced.

CLAIRE *(Laughs).* Had a ball, the same as you, 'cept I wasn't puce with socially proper remorse every time.

(To JULIA*)*

Your mommy got her pudenda scuffed a couple times herself 'fore she met old Toby, you know.

TOBIAS. Your what?

AGNES *(Majesty).* My pudenda.

CLAIRE *(A little grumpy).* You can come on all forgetful in your old age, if you want to, but just remember . . .

AGNES *(Quiet anger).* I am not an old woman.

(Sudden thought; to TOBIAS*)*

Am I?

TOBIAS *(No help; great golly-gosh).* Well, you're my old lady . . .

(AGNES *almost says something, changes her mind, shakes her head, laughs softly)*

CLAIRE *(A chord).* Well, what'll it be?

JULIA *(Glum).* Save it for Harry and Edna.

CLAIRE. Save it for Harry and Edna? Save it for them?

(Chord)

AGNES *(Nice).* Please.

CLAIRE. All right; I'll unload.

(Removes accordion)

AGNES. I dare say . . .

(Stops)

TOBIAS. What?

AGNES. No. Nothing.

CLAIRE *(Half-smile).* We're waiting, aren't we?

TOBIAS. Hm?

CLAIRE. Waiting. The room; the doctor's office; beautiful unconcern; intensive study of the dreadful curtains; absorption in *Field and Stream*, waiting for the Bi-op-*see*.

218

ACT TWO

(Looks from one to the other)

No? Don't know what I mean?

JULIA *(Rather defiant).* What *about* Harry and Edna?

CLAIRE *(Echo; half-smile).* We don't want to talk about it.

AGNES. *If* they come back . . .

CLAIRE. *If!?*

AGNES *(Closes her eyes briefly).* If they come back . . . we will . . .
(Shrugs)

CLAIRE. You've only got two choices, Sis. You take 'em in, or you throw
'em out.

AGNES. Ah, how simple it is from the sidelines.

TOBIAS *(Sees through the window).* We'll do neither, I'd imagine. Take in;
throw out.

CLAIRE. Oh?

TOBIAS *(A feeling of nakedness).* Well, yes, they're just . . . passing
through.

CLAIRE. As they have been . . . all these years.

AGNES. Well, we shall know soon enough.
(Not too much pleasure)
They're back.

TOBIAS *(Rises, goes to the window with her).* Yes?

JULIA. I think I'll go up . . .

AGNES. You stay right here!

JULIA. I want to go to my . . .

AGNES. It is their room! For the moment.

JULIA *(Not nice).* Among Doug's opinions, you might like to know, is that
when you and your ilk are blown to pieces by a Chinese bomb, the
world will be a better place.

CLAIRE. Isn't ilk a lovely word?

TOBIAS *(Disbelief).* Oh, come on now!

CLAIRE. It will certainly be a less crowded one.

AGNES *(Dry).* You choose well, Julia.

JULIA *(Retreating into uncertainty).* That's what he says.

AGNES. Have, always. Did he include *you* as ilk, as well? Will you be with
us when "the fatal mushroom" comes, as those dirty boys put it? Are we
to have the pleasure?

JULIA *(After a pause; as much a threat as a promise).* I'll be right here.

TOBIAS. Agnes!

219

JULIA. Would you like to know something else he says?

AGNES *(Patiently)*. No, Julia.

JULIA. Dad?

TOBIAS *(Some apology in it)*. Not . . . right this minute, Julia.

JULIA *(Defiance)*. Claire? You?

CLAIRE. Well, come on! You *know* I'd like to hear about it—love to—but Toby and Ag've got an invasion on their hands, and . . .

AGNES. We have no such thing.

CLAIRE. . . . and maybe you'd better save it for Harry and Edna, too.

AGNES. It does not concern Edna and Harry.

CLAIRE. Best friends.

AGNES. Tobias?

TOBIAS *(Reluctantly on his feet)*. Where . . . what do you want me to do with everything? Every . . . ?

AGNES *(Heading toward the archway)*. Well for God's sake! I'll do it.
(They exit)

JULIA *(As CLAIRE moves to the sideboard)*. What . . . what do they want? Harry and Edna.

CLAIRE *(Pouring for herself)*. Hmm?

JULIA. You'll make Mother mad. Harry and Edna: what do they want?

CLAIRE. Succor.

JULIA *(Tiny pause)*. Pardon?

CLAIRE *(Brief smile)*. Comfort.
(Sees JULIA doesn't understand)
Warmth. A special room with a night light, or the door ajar so you can look down the hall from the bed and see that Mommy's door is open.

JULIA *(No anger; loss)*. But that's my room.

CLAIRE. It's . . . the *room*. Happens you were in it. You're a visitor as much as anyone, now.
(We hear mumbled conversation from the hallway)

JULIA *(Small whine)*. But I *know* that room.

CLAIRE *(Pointed, but kind)*. Are you home for good now?
(JULIA stares at her)
Are you home forever, back from the world? To the sadness *and* reassurance of your parents? Have you come to take my place?

JULIA *(Quiet despair)*. This is my home!

CLAIRE. This . . . ramble? Yes?
(Surprised delight)

220

hide out

You're laying claim to the cave! Well, I don't know how they'll take to that. We're not a communal nation, dear;

(EDNA *appears in the archway, unseen)*

giving, but not sharing, outgoing, but not friendly.

EDNA. Hello.

CLAIRE *(Friendly, but not turning to look at her).* Hello!

(Back to JULIA*)*

We submerge our truths and have our sunsets on untroubled waters. C'mon in, Edna.

EDNA. Yes.

CLAIRE *(Back to* JULIA*).* We live with our truths in the grassy bottom, and we examine aalllll the interpretations of aalllll the implications like we had a life for nothing else, for God's sake.

(Turns to EDNA*)*

Do *you* think we can walk on the water, Edna? Or do you think we sink?

EDNA *(Dry).* We sink.

CLAIRE. And we better develop gills. Right?

EDNA. Right.

JULIA. I didn't see you come in.

EDNA. We drove around the back. Harry is helping Agnes and Tobias get our bags upstairs.

JULIA *(Slight schoolteacher tone).* Don't you mean Agnes and Tobias are helping Harry?

EDNA *(Tired).* If you like.

(To CLAIRE*)*

What were you two up to?

CLAIRE. I think Julia is home for good this time.

JULIA *(Annoyed and embarrassed).* For Christ's sake, Claire!

EDNA *(Rather as if* JULIA *were not in the room).* Oh? Is it come to that?

CLAIRE. I always said she would, finally.

JULIA *(Under her breath, to* CLAIRE*).* This is family business!

EDNA *(Looking around the room).* Yes, but I'm not sure Agnes and Tobias have seen it as clearly. I do wish Agnes would have that chair recovered. Perhaps now . . .

JULIA *(Exploding).* Well, why don't you call the upholsterers! Now that you're living here!

CLAIRE *(Quiet amusement).* All in the family.

EDNA. You're not a child any more, Julia, you're nicely on your way to forty, and you've not helped . . . wedlock's image any, with your . . . shenanigans . . .

JULIA *(Full, quivering rage).* YOU ARE A GUEST IN THIS HOUSE!!

EDNA *(Lets a moment pass, continues quietly).* . . . and if you *have* decided to . . .

(Wistful)

return forever? . . . then it's a matter of some concern for quite a few peo—

JULIA. You are a *guest!*

CLAIRE *(Quietly).* As you.

EDNA. . . . for quite a few people . . . whose lives are . . . moved—if not necessarily touched—by your actions. Claire, where does Agnes have her upholstery done? Does she use . . .

JULIA. NO!

EDNA *(Strict, soft and powerful).* Manners, young lady!

CLAIRE *(Pointed).* Julia, why don't you ask Edna if she'd like something?

JULIA *(Mouth agape for a moment).* NO!

(To EDNA)

You have no rights here. . . .

EDNA. I'll have a cognac, Julia.

(JULIA stands stock still. EDNA continues; precise and pointed)

My husband and I are your parents' best friends. We are, in addition, your godparents.

JULIA. DOES THIS GIVE YOU RIGHTS?!

CLAIRE *(Smile).* Some.

EDNA. Some. Rights and responsibilities. Some.

CLAIRE *(Seeing HARRY in the archway).* Hello, there, Harry; c'mon in. Julia's about to fix us all something. What'll you . . .

HARRY *(Rubbing his hands together; quite at ease).* I'll do it; don't trouble yourself, Julia.

JULIA *(Rushes to the sideboard, her back to it, spreads her arms, protecting it, curiously disturbed and frightened by something).* NO! Don't you come near it! Don't you take a step!

HARRY *(Patiently, moving forward a little).* Now, Julia . . .

JULIA. NO!

EDNA *(Sitting, relaxing).* Let her do it, Harry. She wants to.

JULIA. I DON'T WANT TO!!

222

ACT TWO

HARRY *(Firm)*. Then I'll do it, Julia.

JULIA *(Suddenly a little girl; crying)*. Mother!? MOTHER!?

EDNA *(Shaking her head; not unkindly)*. Honestly.

JULIA. MOTHER!?

CLAIRE *(The way a nurse speaks to a disturbed patient)*. Julia? Will you let me do it? May I get the drinks?

JULIA *(Hissed)*. Stay away from it! All of you!

CLAIRE *(Rising)*. Now, Julia . . .

HARRY. Oh, come on, Julie, now . . .

EDNA. Let her *go*, Harry.

JULIA. MOTHER? FATHER! HELP ME!!

(AGNES *enters*)

AGNES *(Pained)*. Julia? You're shouting?

JULIA. Mother!

AGNES *(Quite conscious of the others)*. What *is* it, dear?

JULIA *(Quite beside herself, seeing no sympathy)*. THEY! THEY WANT!

EDNA. Forget it, Julia.

HARRY *(A tiny, condescending laugh)*. Yes, for God's sake, forget it.

JULIA. THEY WANT!

AGNES *(Kindly, but a little patronizing)*. Perhaps you *had* better go upstairs.

JULIA *(Still semi-hysterical)*. Yes? Where!? What room!?

AGNES *(Patient)*. Go up to my room, lie down.

JULIA *(An ugly laugh)*. Your room!

EDNA *(Calm)*. You may lie down in *our* room, if you prefer.

JULIA *(A trapped woman, surrounded)*. Your room!

(To AGNES)

Your room? MINE!!

(Looks from one to another, sees only waiting faces)

MINE!!

HARRY *(Makes a move toward the sideboard)*. God.

JULIA. Don't you go near *that!*

AGNES. Julia . . .

JULIA. I *want!*

CLAIRE *(Sad smile)*. What do you want, Julia?

JULIA. I . . .

HARRY. Jesus.

JULIA. I WANT . . . WHAT IS MINE!!

223

AGNES *(Seemingly dispassionate; after a pause).* Well, then, my dear, you will have to decide what that is, will you not.

JULIA *(A terrified pause; runs from the room).* Daddy? Daddy?

(A silence; HARRY *moves to the sideboard, begins to make himself a drink)*

AGNES *(As if very little had happened).* Why, I do believe that's the first time she's called on her father in . . . since her childhood.

CLAIRE. When she used to skin her knees?

AGNES *(A little laugh).* Yes, and she would come home bloody. I *assumed* she was clumsy, but it crossed my mind a time or two . . . that she was religious.

EDNA. Praying on the gravel? A penance?

AGNES *(Chuckles, but it covers something else).* Yes. Teddy had just died, I think, and it was an . . . unreal time . . . for a number of us, for me. *(Brief sorrow clearly shown)*

Poor little boy.

EDNA. Yes.

AGNES. It was an unreal time: I thought Tobias was out of love with me— or, rather, was tired of it, when Teddy died, as if that had been the string.

HARRY. Would you like something, Edna?

EDNA *(Her eyes on* AGNES; *rather dreamy).* Um-humh.

AGNES *(Not explaining, and to none of them, really).* Ah, the things I doubted then: that I was loved—that *I* loved, for that matter!—that Teddy had ever lived at all—my mind, you see. That Julia would be with us long. I think . . . I think I thought Tobias was unfaithful to me then. Was he, Harry?

EDNA. Oh, Agnes.

HARRY *(Unsubtle).* Come on, Agnes! Of course not! No!

AGNES *(Faint amusement).* Was he, Claire? That hot summer, with Julia's knees all bloody and Teddy dead? Did my husband . . . cheat on me?

CLAIRE *(Looks at her steadily, toasts her; then).* Ya got me, Sis.

AGNES *(An amen).* And that will have to do.

EDNA. Poor *Julia.*

AGNES *(Shrugs).* Julia is a fool. Will you make me a drink, Harry, since you're being Tobias? A Scotch?

HARRY *(Hands* EDNA *a drink).* Sure thing. Claire?

CLAIRE. Why not.

224

AGNES *(An overly sweet smile).* Claire could tell us so much if she cared to, could you not, Claire. Claire, who watches from the sidelines, has seen so very much, has seen us all so clearly, have you not, Claire. You were not named for nothing.

CLAIRE *(A pleasant warning).* Lay off, Sis.

AGNES *(Eyes level on* EDNA *and* HARRY; *precisely and not too nicely).* What do you *want?*

HARRY *(After a pause and a look at* EDNA*).* I don't know what you mean.

EDNA *(Seemingly puzzled).* Yes.

AGNES *(Eyes narrow).* What do you *really . . . want?*

CLAIRE. You gonna tell her, Harry?

HARRY. I, *I* don't know what you mean, Claire. Scotch, was it, Agnes?

AGNES. I *said.*

HARRY *(Less than pleasant).* Yes, but I don't re*member.*

EDNA *(Her eyes narrowing, too).* Don't talk to Harry like that.

AGNES *(About to attack, thinks better of it).* I . . . I'm sorry, Edna. I forgot that you're . . . very frightened people.

EDNA. DON'T YOU MAKE FUN OF US!

AGNES. My dear Edna, I am not mak—

EDNA. YES YOU ARE! YOU'RE MAKING FUN OF US.

AGNES. I assure you, Edna . . .

HARRY *(Handing* AGNES *a drink; with some disgust).* Here's your drink.

AGNES. I, I assure you.

CLAIRE *(Putting on her accordion).* I think it's time for a little music, don't you, kids! I yodel a little, too, nowadays, if anybody . . .

AGNES *(Exasperated).* We *don't* want music, Claire!

HARRY *(Horrified and amused).* You, you *what!?* You *yodel!?*

CLAIRE *(As if it were the most natural thing in the world).* Well . . . sure.

EDNA *(Dry).* Talent will out.

HARRY *(Continuing disbelief).* You yodel!

CLAIRE *(Emphatic; babytalk).* 'ES!

*(*TOBIAS *has appeared in the archway)*

HARRY. She yodels!

CLAIRE *(Bravura).* What would ya like, Harry? A chorus of "Take me to the greenhouse, lay me down . . ."?

AGNES. Claire!

TOBIAS. I . . . I wonder if, before the concert, one of you would mind telling me why, uh, my daughter is upstairs, in hysterics?

CLAIRE. Envy, baby; she don't sing, or nothin'.

(A chord)

TOBIAS. PLEASE!

TOBIAS. *(To the others).* Well? Will any of you tell me?

AGNES *(Controlled).* What, what was she doing, Tobias?

TOBIAS. I told you! She's in hysterics!

AGNES *(Tight smile).* That is a condition; I inquired about an action.

EDNA *(More sincere than before).* Poor Julia.

HARRY. I don't understand that girl.

TOBIAS *(Quite miffed).* An action? Is that what you want? O.K., how about

(Demonstrates this)

pressed against a corner of the upstairs hall, arms wide, palms back? Eyes darting? Wide?

(EDNA *shakes her head)*

How about tearing into Harry and Edna's room . . . ripping the clothes from the closets, hangers and all on the floor? The same for the bureaus?

AGNES *(Steady).* I see.

TOBIAS. More?

AGNES *(Steady).* All right.

TOBIAS. Or into your room next? Twisted on your bed, lots of breathing and the great wide eyes? The spread all gathered under her, your big lace pillow in her arms—like a lover—her eyes wide open, no tears now? Though if you come near her the sounds start and you think she'll scream if you touch her?

(Pause)

How's that?

CLAIRE *(Pause).* Pretty good.

AGNES *(Pause).* And accurate, I imagine.

TOBIAS *(Daring her).* You're damned right! Now, why?

AGNES *(To* TOBIAS *with a sad smile, ironic).* Would it seem . . . incomplete to you, my darling, were I to tell you Julia is upset that Har— Edna and Harry are here, that . . .

HARRY *(Arms wide, helplessly).* I was making myself a drink, for God's sake. . . .

EDNA. I asked her to *make* me something. . . .

TOBIAS. Oh, come on!

EDNA *(Some pleasure).* She rose . . . like a silent film star, ran to the sideboard, defended it, like a princess in the movies, hiding her lover in the closet from the king.

CLAIRE. That sound incomplete to you, Toby?

TOBIAS *(Stern)*. Somewhat.

AGNES. Julia *has* been through a trying time, Tobias. . . .

HARRY *(A little apologetic)*. I suppose we did upset her some. . . .

EDNA *(Consoling)*. Of course!

TOBIAS *(To AGNES; a kind of wondrous bewilderment)*. Don't you think you should go tend to her?

(The others all look to AGNES)

AGNES *(Shakes her head; lightly)*. No. She will be down or she will not. She will stop, or she will . . . go on.

TOBIAS *(Spluttering)*. Well, for God's sake, Agnes . . . !

AGNES *(An end to it; hard)*. I haven't the time, Tobias.

(Gentler)

I haven't time for the four-hour talk, the soothing recapitulation. You don't go through it, my love: the history. Nothing is calmed by a pat on the hand, a gentle massage, or slowly, slowly combing the hair, no: the history. Teddy's birth, and how she felt unwanted, tricked; his death, and was she more relieved than lost . . . ? All the schools we sent her to, and did she fail in them through hate . . . or love? And when we come to marriage, dear: each one of them, the fear, the happiness, the sex, the stopping, the infidelities . . .

TOBIAS *(Nodding; speaks softly)*. All right, Agnes.

AGNES *(Shakes her head)*. Oh, my dear Tobias . . . my life is gone through more than hers. I see myself . . . growing old each time, see my own life passing. No, I haven't time for it now. At midnight, maybe . . .

(Sad smile)

when you're all in your beds . . . safely sleeping. Then I will comfort our Julia, and lose myself once more.

CLAIRE *(To break an uncomfortable silence)*. I tell ya, there are so many martyrdoms here.

EDNA *(Seeing a hangnail)*. One to a person.

AGNES *(Dry)*. That is the usual,

(A glance at CLAIRE)

though I do believe there are some with none, and others who have

227

known Job. The helpless are the cruelest lot of all: they shift their burdens so.

CLAIRE. If you interviewed a camel, he'd admit he loved his load.

EDNA *(Giving up on the hangnail).* I wish you two would stop having at each other.

HARRY. Hell, yes! Let's have a drink, Tobias?

TOBIAS *(From deep in thought).* Hm?

HARRY. What can I make yuh, buddy?

CLAIRE *(Rather pleased).* Why, Edna; you've actually spoken your mind.

TOBIAS *(Confused as to where he is).* What can *you* make *me?*

EDNA. I do . . . sometimes.

HARRY. Well, sure; I'm here.

EDNA *(Calm).* When an environment is not all that it might be.

TOBIAS. Oh. Yeah; Scotch.

AGNES *(Strained smile).* Is that for you to say?

CLAIRE *(A chord; then).* Here we come!

AGNES. Stop it, Claire, dear.

(To EDNA*)*

I said: Is that for you to say?

EDNA *(To* AGNES; *calm, steady).* We must be helpful when we can, my dear; that is the . . . responsibility, the double demand of friendship . . . is it not?

AGNES *(Slightly schoolteacherish).* But, when we are *asked.*

EDNA *(Shakes her head, smiles gently).* No. Not only.

(This heard by all)

It seemed to me, to us, that since we were living *here* . . .

(Silence, AGNES *and* TOBIAS *look from* EDNA *to* HARRY*)*

CLAIRE. *That's* my cue!

(A chord, then begins to yodel, to an ump-pah base. JULIA *appears in the archway, unseen by the others; her hair is wild, her face is tear-streaked; she carries* TOBIAS' *pistol, but not pointed; awkwardly and facing down)*

JULIA *(Solemnly and tearfully).* Get them out of here, Daddy, getthemout ofheregetthemoutofheregetthemoutofheregetthemoutofheregetthem outofhere. . . .

(They all see JULIA *and the gun simultaneously;* EDNA *gasps but does not panic;* HARRY *retreats a little;* TOBIAS *moves slowly toward* JULIA*)*

AGNES. Julia!

JULIA. Get them out of here, Daddy!

TOBIAS *(Moving toward her, slowly, calmly, speaking in a quiet voice)*. All right, Julia, baby; let's have it now.

JULIA. Get them out of here, Daddy. . . .

TOBIAS *(As before)*. Come on now, Julia.

JULIA *(Calmly, she hands the gun to* TOBIAS, *nods)*. Get them out of here, Daddy.

AGNES *(Soft intensity)*. You ought to be horsewhipped, young lady.

TOBIAS *(Meant for both* JULIA *and* AGNES). All right, now . . .

JULIA. Do it, Daddy? Or give it back?

AGNES *(Turns on* JULIA; *withering)*. How dare you come into this room like that! How dare you embarrass me and your father! How dare you frighten Edna and Harry! How dare you come into this room like that!

JULIA *(To* HARRY *and* EDNA; *venom)*. Are you going?

AGNES. Julia!

TOBIAS *(Pleading)*. Julia, please. . . .

JULIA. ARE YOU!?

(Silence, all eyes on HARRY *and* EDNA)

EDNA *(Finally; curiously unconcerned)*. Going? No, we are not going.

HARRY. No.

JULIA *(To all)*. YOU SEE!?

HARRY. Coming down here with a gun like that . . .

EDNA *(Becoming* AGNES). You return to your nest from your latest disaster, dispossessed, and suddenly dispossessing; screaming the house down, clawing at order . . .

JULIA. STOP HER!

EDNA. . . . willful, wicked, wretched girl . . .

JULIA. You are not my . . . YOU HAVE NO RIGHTS!

EDNA. We have rights here. We belong.

JULIA. MOTHER!

AGNES *(Tentative)*. Julia . . .

EDNA. We belong here, do we not?

JULIA *(Triumphant distaste)*. FOREVER!!

(Small silence)

HAVE YOU COME TO STAY FOREVER??

(Small silence)

EDNA *(Walks over to her, calmly slaps her)*. If need be.

(To TOBIAS *and* AGNES, *calmly)*

229

Sorry; a godmother's duty.

(This next calm, almost daring, addressed at, rather than to the others)

If we come to the point . . . *if* we are at home one evening, and the
. . . terror comes . . . descends . . . if all at once we . . . NEED
. . . we come where we are wanted, where we know we are expected,
not only where we want; we come where the table has been laid for us
in such an event . . . where the bed is turned down . . . and warmed
. . . and has been ready should we need it. We are not . . . transients
. . . like some.

JULIA. NO!

EDNA *(To* JULIA*)*. You must . . . what is the word? . . . coexist, my dear.

(To the others)

Must she not?

(Silence; calm)

Must she not. This is what you have meant by friendship . . . is it
not?

AGNES *(Pause; finally, calmly)*. You have come to live with us, then.

EDNA *(After a pause; calm)*. Why, yes; we have.

AGNES *(Dead calm; a sigh)*. Well, then.

(Pause)

Perhaps it is time for bed, Julia? Come upstairs with me.

JULIA *(A confused child)*. M-mother?

AGNES. Ah-ah; let me comb your hair, and rub your back.

(Arm over JULIA*'s shoulder, leads her out. Exiting)*

And we shall soothe . . . and solve . . . and fall to sleep. Tobias?

(Exits with JULIA. *Silence)*

EDNA. Well, I think it's time for bed.

TOBIAS *(Vague, preoccupied)*. Well, yes; yes, of course.

EDNA *(She and* HARRY *have risen; a small smile)*. We know the way.

(Pauses as she and HARRY *near the archway)*

Friendship *is* something like a marriage, is it not, Tobias? For better and
for worse?

TOBIAS *(Ibid.)*. Sure.

EDNA *(Something of a demand here)*. We *haven't* come to the wrong place,
have we?

HARRY *(Pause; shy)*. Have we, Toby?

TOBIAS *(Pause; gentle, sad)*. No.

(Sad smile)

No; of course you haven't.

EDNA. Good night, dear Tobias. Good night, Claire.

CLAIRE *(A half smile)*. Good night, you two.

HARRY *(A gentle pat at* TOBIAS *as he passes)*. Good night, old man.

TOBIAS *(Watches as the two exit)*. Good . . . good night, you two.

(CLAIRE *and* TOBIAS *alone;* TOBIAS *still holds the pistol)*

CLAIRE *(After an interval)*. Full house, Tobias, every bed and every cupboard.

TOBIAS *(Not moving)*. Good night, Claire.

CLAIRE *(Rising, leaving her accordion)*. Are you going to stay up, Tobias? Sort of a nightwatch, guarding? *I've done it.* The breathing, as you stand in the quiet halls, slow and heavy? And the special . . . warmth, and . . . permeation . . . of a house . . . asleep? When the house is sleeping? When the people *are* asleep?

TOBIAS. Good night, Claire.

CLAIRE *(Near the archway)*. And the difference? The different breathing and the cold, when every bed is awake . . . all night . . . very still, eyes open, staring into the dark? Do you know that one?

TOBIAS. Good night, Claire.

CLAIRE *(A little sad)*. Good night, Tobias.

(Exit as the curtain falls)

ACT THREE
Early Sunday Morning

(Seven-thirty the next morning; same set. TOBIAS alone, in a chair, wearing pajamas and a robe, slippers. Awake. AGNES enters, wearing a dressing gown which could pass for a hostess gown. Her movements are not assertive, and her tone is gentle)

AGNES *(Seeing him)*. Ah; there you are.

TOBIAS *(Not looking at her, but at his watch; there is very little emotion in his voice)*. Seven-thirty A.M., and all's well . . . I guess.

AGNES. So odd.

TOBIAS. Hm?

AGNES. There was a stranger in my room last night.

TOBIAS. Who?

AGNES. You.

TOBIAS. Ah.

AGNES. It was nice to have you there.

TOBIAS *(Slight smile)*. Hm.

AGNES. *Le temps perdu.* I've never understood that; *perdu* means lost, not merely . . . past, but it was nice to have you there, though I remember, when it was a constancy, how easily I would fall asleep, pace my breathing to your breathing, and if we were touching! ah, what a splendid cocoon that was. But last night—what a shame, what sadness —you were a stranger, and I stayed awake.

TOBIAS. *I'm* sorry.

AGNES. Were you asleep at all?

TOBIAS. No.

AGNES. I would go half, then wake—your unfamiliar presence, sir. I *could* get used to it again.

TOBIAS. Yes?

AGNES. I think.

TOBIAS. You didn't have your talk with Julia—your all-night lulling.

AGNES. No; she wouldn't let me stay. "Look to your own house," is what she said. You stay down long?

TOBIAS. When?

AGNES. After . . . before you came to bed.

TOBIAS. Some.

232

(Laughs softly, ruefully)
I almost went into *my* room . . . by habit . . . by mistake, rather, but then I realized that your room is my room because my room is Julia's because Julia's room is . . .

AGNES. . . . yes.

(Goes to him, strokes his temple)
And I was awake when you left my room again.

TOBIAS *(Gentle reproach)*. You could have said.

AGNES *(Curious at the truth)*. I felt shy.

TOBIAS *(Pleased surprise)*. Hm!

AGNES. Did you go to Claire?

TOBIAS. I never go to Claire.

AGNES. Did you go to Claire to talk?

TOBIAS. I never go to Claire.

AGNES. We must always envy someone we should not, be jealous of those who have so much less. You and Claire make so much sense together, talk so well.

TOBIAS. I never go to Claire at night, or talk with her alone—save publicly.

AGNES *(Small smile)*. In public rooms . . . like this.

TOBIAS. Yes.

AGNES. Have *never*.

TOBIAS. Please?

AGNES. Do we dis*like* happiness? We manufacture such a portion of our own despair . . . such busy folk.

TOBIAS. We are a highly moral land: we assume we have done great wrong. We find the things.

AGNES. I shall start missing you again—when you move from my room . . . if you do. I had stopped, I believe.

TOBIAS *(Grudging little chuckle)*. Oh, you're an honest woman.

AGNES. Well, we need *one* . . . in every house.

TOBIAS. It's very strange . . . to be downstairs, in a room where everyone has been, and is gone . . . very late, after the heat has gone—the furnace *and* the bodies: the hour or two before the sun comes up, the furnace starts again. And tonight especially: the cigarettes still in the ashtrays—odd, metallic smell. The odors of a room don't mix, late, when there's no one there, and I think the silence helps it . . . and the lack of bodies. Each . . . thing stands out in its place.

AGNES. What did you decide?

233

TOBIAS. And when you *do* come down . . . if you do, at three, or four, and you've left a light or two—in case someone should come in late, I suppose, but who is there left? The inn is full—it's rather . . . God-like, if I may presume: to look at it all, reconstruct, with such . . . de*tach*ment, see your*self*, you, Julia . . . Look at it all . . . play it out again, *watch*.

AGNES. Judge?

TOBIAS. No; that's being in it. Watch. And if you have a drink or two . . .

AGNES *(Mild surprise)*. Did you?

TOBIAS *(Nods)*. And if you have a drink or two, very late, in the quiet, tired, the mind . . . lets loose.

AGNES. Yes?

TOBIAS. And you watch it as it reasons, all with a kind of . . . grateful delight, at the same time sadly, 'cause you know that when the daylight comes the pressures will be on, and all the insight won't be worth a damn.

AGNES. What did you decide?

TOBIAS. You can sit and watch. You can have . . . so clear a picture, see everybody moving through his own jungle . . . an insight into all the reasons, all the needs.

AGNES. Good. And what did you decide?

TOBIAS *(No complaint)*. Why is the room so dirty? Can't we have better servants, some help who . . . help?

AGNES. They keep far better hours than we, that's all. They are a comment on our habits, a reminder that we are out of step—that is why we pay them . . . so very, very much. Neither a servant nor a master be. Remember?

TOBIAS. I remember when . . .

AGNES *(Picking it right up)*. . . . . you were very young and lived at home, and the servants were awake whenever you were: six A.M. for your breakfast when you wanted it, or five in the morning when you came home drunk and seventeen, washing the vomit from the car, and you, telling no one; stealing just enough each month, by arrangement with the stores, to keep them in a decent wage; generations of them: the laundress, blind and always dying, and the cook, who did a better dinner drunk than sober. Those servants? Those days? When you were young, and lived at home?

TOBIAS *(Memory)*. Hmmm.

AGNES *(Sweet; sad).* Well, my darling, you are not young now, and you do not live at home.

TOBIAS *(Sad question).* Where do I live?

AGNES *(An answer of sorts).* The dark sadness. Yes?

TOBIAS *(Quiet, rhetorical).* What are we going to do?

AGNES. What did you decide?

TOBIAS *(Pause; they smile).* Nothing.

AGNES. Well, you must. Your house is not in order, sir. It's full to bursting.

TOBIAS. Yes. You've got to help me here.

AGNES. No. I don't *think* so.

TOBIAS *(Some surprise).* No?

AGNES. No. I thought a little last night, too: while you were seeing everything so clearly here. I lay in the dark, and I . . . revisited—our life, the years and years. There are many things a woman does: she bears the children—if there *is* that blessing. Blessing? Yes, I suppose, even with the sadness. She runs the house, for what that's worth: makes sure there's food, and not just anything, and decent linen; looks well; assumes whatever duties are demanded—if she is in love, or loves; and plans.

TOBIAS *(Mumbled; a little embarrassed).* I know, I know. . . .

AGNES. And plans. Right to the end of it; expects to be alone one day, abandoned by a heart attack or the cancer, *prepares* for that. And prepares earlier, for the children to become *adult* strangers instead of growing ones, for that loss, and for the body chemistry, the end of what the Bible tells us is our usefulness. The reins we hold! It's a team of twenty horses, and we sit there, and we watch the road and check the leather . . . if our . . . man is so disposed. But there are things we do not do.

TOBIAS *(Slightly edgy challenge).* Yes?

AGNES. Yes.

(Harder)

We don't decide the route.

TOBIAS. You're copping out . . . as they say.

AGNES. No, indeed.

TOBIAS *(Quiet anger).* Yes, you are!

AGNES *(Quiet warning).* Don't you yell at me.

TOBIAS. You're copping *out!*

235

AGNES *(Quiet, calm, and almost smug)*. We follow. We let our . . . men decide the moral issues.

TOBIAS *(Quite angry)*. Never! You've never done that in your life!

AGNES. Always, my darling. Whatever you decide . . . I'll make it work; I'll run it for you so you'll never know there's been a change in anything.

TOBIAS *(Almost laughing; shaking his head)*. No. No.

AGNES *(To end the discussion)*. So, let me know.

TOBIAS *(Still almost laughing)*. I *know* I'm tired. I know I've hardly slept at all: I know I've sat down here, and thought . . .

AGNES. And made your decisions.

TOBIAS. But I have not *judged*. I told you that.

AGNES *(Almost a stranger)*. Well, when you have . . . you let me know.

TOBIAS *(Frustration and anger)*. NO!

AGNES *(Cool)*. You'll wake the house.

TOBIAS *(Angry)*. I'll wake the house!

AGNES. This is not the time for you to lose control.

TOBIAS. I'LL LOSE CONTROL! I have *sat* here . . . in the cold, in the empty cold, I have sat here alone, and . . .

(Anger has shifted to puzzlement, complaint)

I've looked at *every*thing, *all* of it. I thought of you, and Julia, and Claire. . . .

AGNES *(Still cool)*. And Edna? And Harry?

TOBIAS *(Tiny pause; then anger)*. Well, of course! What do you think!

AGNES *(Tiny smile)*. I don't know. I'm listening.

(JULIA appears in the archway; wears a dressing gown; subdued, sleepy)

JULIA. Good morning. I don't suppose there's . . . shall I make some coffee?

AGNES *(Chin high)*. Why don't you do that, darling.

TOBIAS *(A little embarrassed)*. Good morning, Julie.

JULIA *(Hating it)*. I'm sorry about last night, Daddy.

TOBIAS. Oh, well, now . . .

JULIA *(Bite to it)*. I mean I'm sorry for having embarrassed you.

(Starts toward the hallway)

AGNES. Coffee.

JULIA *(Pausing at the archway; to TOBIAS)*. Aren't you sorry for embarrassing me, too?

(Waits a moment, smiles, exits. Pause)

AGNES. Well, isn't that nice that Julia's making coffee? No? If the help aren't up, isn't it nice to have a daughter who can put a pot to boil?

TOBIAS *(Under his breath, disgusted).* "Aren't you sorry for embarrassing me, too."

AGNES. You have a problem there with Julia.

TOBIAS. *I? I* have a problem!

AGNES. Yes.

(Gentle irony)

But at least you have your women with you—crowded 'round, firm arm, support. *That* must be a comfort to you. *Most* explorers go alone, don't have their families with them—pitching tents, tending the fire, shooing off the . . . . the antelopes or the bears or whatever.

TOBIAS *(Wanting to talk about it).* "Aren't you sorry for embarrassing me, too."

AGNES. Are you quoting?

TOBIAS. Yes.

AGNES. Next we'll have my younger sister with us—another porter for the dreadful trip.

(Irony)

Claire has never missed a chance to participate in watching. She'll be here. We'll have us all.

TOBIAS. And you'll all sit down and watch me carefully; smoke your pipes and stir the cauldron; watch.

AGNES *(Dreamy; pleased).* Yes.

TOBIAS. You, who make all the decisions, really rule the game . . .

AGNES *(So patient).* That is an *illusion* you have.

TOBIAS. You'll all sit here—too early for . . . *anything* on this . . . stupid Sunday—all of you and . . . and *dare* me?—when it's just as much your choice as mine?

AGNES. Each time that Julia comes, each clockwork time . . . do you send her back? Do you tell her, "Julia, go home to your husband, try it again"? Do you? No, you let it . . . slip. It's your decision, sir.

TOBIAS. It is not! I . . .

AGNES. . . . and I must live with it, resign myself one marriage more, and wait, and hope that Julia's motherhood will come . . . one day, one marriage.

(Tiny laugh)

I am almost too old to be a grandmother as I'd hoped . . . too young to be one. Oh, I had wanted that: the *youngest* older woman in the block. *Julia* is almost too old to have a child properly, *will* be if she ever does . . . if she marries again. *You* could have pushed her back . . . if you'd wanted to.

TOBIAS *(Bewildered incredulity)*. It's very early yet: that must be it. I've never heard such . . .

AGNES. Or Teddy! No? No stammering here? You'll let this pass?

TOBIAS *(Quiet embarrassment)*. Please.

AGNES *(Remorseless)*. When Teddy died?

(Pause)

We *could* have had another son; we could have tried. But no . . . those months—or was it a year—?

TOBIAS. No more of this!

AGNES. . . . I think it was a year, when you spilled yourself on my belly, sir? "Please? Please, Tobias?" No, you wouldn't even say it out: I don't want another child, another loss. "Please? Please, Tobias?" And guiding you, *trying* to hold you in?

TOBIAS *(Tortured)*. Oh, Agnes! Please!

AGNES. "Don't leave me then, like that. Not again, Tobias. Please? *I* can take care of it: we *won't* have another child, but please don't . . . leave me like that." Such . . . silent . . . sad, disgusted . . . love.

TOBIAS *(Mumbled, inaudible)*. I didn't want you to have to.

AGNES. Sir?

TOBIAS *(Numb)*. I didn't want you to have to . . . you know.

AGNES *(Laughs in spite of herself)*. Oh, that was thoughtful of you! Like a pair of adolescents in a rented room, or in the family car. Doubtless you hated it as much as I.

TOBIAS *(Softly)*. Yes.

AGNES. But wouldn't let me help you.

TOBIAS *(Ibid.)*. No.

AGNES *(Irony)*. Which is why you took to your own sweet room instead.

TOBIAS *(Ibid.)*. Yes.

AGNES. The theory being pat: that a half a loaf is worse than none. That you are racked with guilt—stupidly!—and *I* must *suffer* for it.

TOBIAS *(Ibid.)*. Yes?

AGNES *(Quietly; sadly)*. Well, it was your decision, was it not?

TOBIAS *(Ibid.)*. Yes.

AGNES. And I have made the best of it. Have lived with it. Have I not?

TOBIAS *(Pause; a plea)*. What are we going to do? About everything?

AGNES *(Quietly; sadly; cruelly)*. Whatever you like. Naturally.

(Silence. CLAIRE *enters, she, too, in a dressing gown)*

CLAIRE *(Judges the situation for a moment)*. Morning, kids.

AGNES *(To* TOBIAS, *in reference to* CLAIRE*)*. All I can do, my dear, is run it for you . . . and forecast.

TOBIAS *(Glum)*. Good morning, Claire.

AGNES. Julia is in the kitchen making coffee, Claire.

CLAIRE. Which means, I guess, I go watch Julia grind the beans and drip the water, hunh?

(Exiting)

I tell ya, she's a real pioneer, that girl: coffee pot in one hand, pistol in t'other.

(Exits)

AGNES *(Small smile)*. Claire is a comfort in the early hours . . . I have been told.

TOBIAS *(A dare)*. Yes?

AGNES *(Pretending not to notice his tone)*. That is what I have been *told*.

TOBIAS *(Blurts it out)*. Shall I ask them to leave?

AGNES *(Tiny pause)*. Who?

TOBIAS *(Defiant)*. Harry and Edna?

AGNES *(Tiny laugh)*. Oh. For a moment I thought you meant Julia and Claire.

TOBIAS *(Glum)*. No. Harry and Edna. Shall I throw them out?

AGNES *(Restatement of a fact)*. Harry is your very best friend in the whole . . .

TOBIAS *(Impatient)*. Yes, and Edna is yours. Well?

AGNES. You'll have to live with it either way: do or don't.

TOBIAS *(Anger rising)*. Yes? Well, then, why *don't* I throw Julia and Claire out instead? Or better yet, why don't I throw the whole bunch out!?

AGNES. Or get rid of me! That would be easier: rid yourself of the harridan. Then you can run your mission and take out sainthood papers.

TOBIAS *(Clenched teeth)*. I think you're stating an opinion, a preference.

AGNES. But if you *do* get rid of me . . . you'll no longer have your life the way you want it.

TOBIAS *(Puzzled)*. But that's not my . . . that's not all the choice I've got, is it?

AGNES. I don't care very much what choice you've got, my darling, but I *am* concerned with what choice you *make*.

(JULIA *and* CLAIRE *enter;* JULIA *carries a tray with coffee pot, cups, sugar, cream;* CLAIRE *carries a tray with four glasses of orange juice)*

Ah, here are the helpmeets, what would we do without them.

JULIA *(Brisk, efficient)*. The coffee is instant, I'm afraid; I couldn't find a bean: Those folk must lock them up before they go to bed.

(Finds no place to put her tray down)

Come on, Pop; let's clear away a little of the debris, hunh?

TOBIAS. P-Pop?

AGNES *(Begins clearing)*. It's true: we cannot drink our coffee amidst a sea of last night's glasses. Tobias, do be a help.

(TOBIAS *rises, takes glasses to the sideboard, as* AGNES *moves some to another table)*

CLAIRE *(Cheerful)*. And I didn't have to do a thing; thank God for pre-squeezed orange juice.

JULIA *(Setting the tray down)*. There; now that's much better, isn't it?

TOBIAS *(In a fog)*. Whatever you say, Julie.

(JULIA *pours, knows what people put in)*

CLAIRE. Now, I'll play waiter. Sis?

AGNES. Thank you, Claire.

CLAIRE. Little Julie?

JULIA. Just put it down beside me, Claire. I'm pouring, you can see.

CLAIRE *(Looks at her a moment, does not, offers a glass to* TOBIAS). Pop?

TOBIAS *(Bewildered, apprehensive)*. Thank you, Claire.

CLAIRE *(Puts* JULIA's *glass on the mantel)*. Yours is here, daughter, when you've done with playing early-morning hostess.

JULIA *(Intently pouring; does not rise to the bait)*. Thank you, Claire.

CLAIRE. Now; one for little Claire.

JULIA *(Still pouring; no expression)*. Why don't you have some vodka in it, Claire? To start the Sunday off?

AGNES *(Pleased chuckle)*. Julia!

TOBIAS *(Reproving)*. Please, Julie!

JULIA *(Looks up at him; cold)*. Did I say something wrong, Father?

CLAIRE. Vodka? Sunday? Ten to eight? Well, hell, why not!

TOBIAS *(Quietly, as she moves to the sideboard)*. You don't *have* to, Claire.

JULIA *(Dropping sugar in a cup)*. Let her do what she wants.

CLAIRE *(Pouring vodka into her glass)*. Yes I *do*, Tobias; the rules of the

240

guestbook—be polite. We have our friends and guests for patterns, don't we?—known quantities. The drunks stay drunk; the Catholics go to Mass, the bounders bound. We can't have changes—throws the balance off.

JULIA *(Ibid.)*. Besides; you like to drink.

CLAIRE. Besides, I like to drink. Just think, Tobias, what would happen if the patterns changed: you wouldn't know where you stood, and the world would be full of strangers; that would never do.

JULIA *(Not very friendly)*. Bring me my orange juice, will you please.

CLAIRE *(Getting it for her)*. Oooh, Julia's back for a spell, I think—settling in.

JULIA *(Handing* TOBIAS *his coffee)*. Father?

TOBIAS *(Embarrassed)*. Thank you, Julia.

JULIA. Mother?

AGNES *(Comfortable)*. Thank you, darling.

JULIA. Yours is here, Claire; on the tray.

CLAIRE *(Considers a moment, looks at* JULIA's *orange juice, still in one of her hands, calmly pours it on the rug)*. Your juice is here, Julia, when you want it.

AGNES *(Furious)*. CLAIRE!

TOBIAS *(Mild reproach)*. For God's sake, Claire.

JULIA *(Looks at the mess on the rug; shrugs)*. Well, why not. Nothing changes.

CLAIRE. Besides, our friends upstairs don't like the room; they'll want some alterations.

(CLAIRE sits down)

TOBIAS *(Lurches to his feet; stands, legs apart)*. Now! All of you! Sit down! Shut up. I want to talk to you.

JULIA. Did I give you sugar, Mother?

TOBIAS. BE QUIET, JULIA!

AGNES. Shhh, my darling, yes, you did.

TOBIAS. I want to talk to you.

(Silence)

CLAIRE *(Slightly mocking encouragement)*. Well, go on, Tobias.

TOBIAS *(A plea)*. You, too, Claire? Please.

(Silence. The women stir their coffee or look at him, or at the floor. They seem like children about to be lectured, unwilling, and dangerous, but, for the moment, behaved)

241

Now.

(Pause)

Now, something happened here last night, and I don't mean Julia's hysterics with the gun—be quiet, Julia!—though I *do* mean that, in part. I mean . . .

(Deep sigh)

. . . Harry and Edna . . . coming here . . .

(JULIA *snorts*)

Yes? Did you want to say something, Julia? No? I came down here and I sat, all night—hours—and I did something rather rare for this family: I *thought* about something. . . .

AGNES *(Mild)*. I'm sorry, Tobias, but that's not fair.

TOBIAS *(Riding over)*. I *thought*. I sat down here and I thought about all of us . . . and everything. Now, Harry and Edna have come to us and . . . asked for help.

JULIA. That is not *true*.

TOBIAS. Be quiet!

JULIA. That is not true! They have not *asked* for anything!

AGNES. . . . please, Julia . . .

JULIA. They have *told!* They have come in here and *ordered!*

CLAIRE *(Toasts)*. Just like the family.

TOBIAS. Asked! If you're begging and you've got your pride . . .

JULIA. *If* you're begging, then you may not have your pride!

AGNES *(Quiet contradiction)*. I don't think that's true, Julia.

CLAIRE. Julia wouldn't know. Ask me.

JULIA. *(Adamant)*. Those people have no right!

TOBIAS. No right? All these years? We've known them since . . . for God's sake, Julia, those people are our *friends!*

JULIA *(Hard)*. THEN TAKE THEM IN!

(Silence)

Take these . . . intruders in.

CLAIRE *(To JULIA: hard)*. Look, baby; didn't you get the message on rights last night? Didn't you learn about intrusion, what the score is, who belongs?

JULIA *(To TOBIAS)*. You bring these people in here, Father, and I'm leaving!

TOBIAS *(Almost daring her)*. Yes?

JULIA. I don't mean coming and going, Father; I mean as *family!*

TOBIAS *(Frustration and rage)*. HARRY AND EDNA ARE OUR FRIENDS!!

242

JULIA *(Equal)*. THEY ARE INTRUDERS!!

(Silence)

CLAIRE *(To* TOBIAS, *laughing)*. Crisis sure brings out the best in us, don't it, Tobe? The family circle? Julia standing there . . . *asserting;* perpetual brat, and maybe ready to pull a Claire. *And* poor Claire! Not much help there either, is there? And lookit Agnes, talky Agnes, ruler of the roost, and maître d', *and* licensed wife—silent. All cozy, coffee, thinking of the menu for the week, *planning.* Poor Tobe.

AGNES *(Calm, assured)*. Thank you, Claire; I was merely waiting—until I'd heard, and thought a little, listened to the rest of you. I thought someone should sit back. Especially me: ruler of the roost, licensed wife, midnight . . . nurse. And I've been thinking about Harry and Edna; about disease.

TOBIAS *(After a pause)*. About what?

CLAIRE *(After a swig)*. About disease.

JULIA. Oh, for God's sake . . .

AGNES. About disease—or, if you like, the terror.

CLAIRE *(Chuckles softly)*. Unh, hunh.

JULIA *(Furious)*. TERROR!?

AGNES *(Unperturbed)*. Yes: the terror. Or the plague—they're both the same. Edna and Harry have come to us—dear friends, our very best, though there's a judgment to be made about that, I think—have come to us and brought the plague. Now, poor Tobias has sat up all night and wrestled with the moral problem.

TOBIAS *(Frustration; anger)*. I've not been . . . *wrestling* with some . . . abstract problem! These are *people!* Harry and Edna! These are our friends, God damn it!

AGNES. Yes, but they've brought the plague with them, and that's another matter. Let me tell you something about disease . . . mortal illness; you either are immune to it . . . or you fight it. If you are immune, you wade right in, you treat the patient until he either lives, or dies of it. But if you are *not* immune, you risk infection. Ten centuries ago—and even less—the treatment was quite simple . . . burn them. Burn their bodies, burn their houses, burn their clothes—and move to another town, if you were enlightened. But now, with modern medicine, we merely isolate; we quarantine, we ostracize—if we are not immune ourselves, or unless we are saints. So, your night-long vigil, darling, your reasoning in the cold, pure hours, has been over the patient, and not the illness. It is not Edna and Harry who have come to us—our friends—it is a disease.

TOBIAS *(Quiet anguish, mixed with impatience)*. Oh, for God's sake, Agnes! It is our friends! What am I supposed to do? Say: "Look, you can't stay here, you two, you've got trouble. You're friends, and all, but you come in here *clean.*" Well, I can't do that. No. Agnes, for God's sake, if . . . if that's all Harry and Edna mean to us, then . . . then what about *us?* When we talk to each other . . . what have we meant? Anything? When we touch, when we promise, and say . . . yes, or please . . . with our*selves?* . . . have we meant, yes, but only if . . . if there's any condition, Agnes! Then it's . . . all been empty.

AGNES *(Noncommittal)*. Perhaps. But blood binds us. Blood holds us together when we've no more . . . deep affection for ourselves than others. I am *not* asking you to choose between your family and . . . our friends. . . .

TOBIAS. *Yes* you are!

AGNES *(Eyes closed)*. I am merely saying that there is *disease* here! And I ask you: who in this family is immune?

CLAIRE *(Weary statement of fact)*. I am. I've had it. I'm still alive, I think.

AGNES. Claire is the strongest of us all: the walking wounded often are, the least susceptible; but think about the rest of us. Are we immune to it? The plague, my darling, the terror sitting in the room upstairs? Well, if we are, then . . . on with it! And, if we're not . . .
· *(Shrugs)*
well, why not be infected, why not die of it? We're bound to die of something . . . soon, or in a while. Or shall we burn them out, rid ourselves of it all . . . and wait for the next invasion. You decide, my darling.
(Silence. TOBIAS *rises, walks to the window; the others sit.* HARRY *and* EDNA *appear in the archway, dressed for the day, but not with coats)*

EDNA *(No emotion)*. Good morning.

AGNES *(Brief pause)*. Ah, you're up.

CLAIRE. Good morning, Edna, Harry.

*(*JULIA *does not look at them;* TOBIAS *does, but says nothing)*

EDNA *(A deep breath, rather a recitation)*. Harry wants to talk to Tobias. I think that they should be alone. Perhaps . . .

AGNES. Of course.

Act Three

(The three seated women rise, as at a signal, begin to gather the coffee things)

Why don't we all go in the kitchen, make a proper breakfast.

HARRY. Well, now, no; you don't have to . . .

AGNES. Yes, yes, we want to leave you to your talk. Tobias?

TOBIAS *(Quiet)*. Uh . . . yes.

AGNES *(To TOBIAS; comfortingly)*. We'll be nearby.

(The women start out)

Did you sleep well, Edna? Did you sleep at all? I've never had that bed, but I know that when . . .

(The women have exited)

HARRY *(Watching them go; laughs ruefully)*. Boy, look at 'em go. They got outa *here* quick enough. You'd think there was a . . .

(Trails off, sees TOBIAS is ill at ease; says, gently)

Morning, Tobias.

TOBIAS *(Grateful)*. Morning, Harry.

(Both men stay standing)

HARRY *(Rubs his hands together)*. You, ah . . . you know what I'd like to do? Something I've never done in my life, except once, when I was about twenty-four?

TOBIAS *(Not trying to guess)*. No? What?

HARRY. Have a drink before breakfast? Is, is that all right?

TOBIAS *(Smiles wanly, moves slowly toward the sideboard)*. Sure.

HARRY *(Shy)*. Will you join me?

TOBIAS *(Very young)*. I guess so, yes. There isn't any ice.

HARRY. Well, just some whiskey, then; neat.

TOBIAS. Brandy?

HARRY. No, oh, God, no.

TOBIAS. Whiskey, then.

HARRY. Yes. Thank you.

TOBIAS *(Somewhat glum)*. Well, here's to youth again.

HARRY. Yes.

(Drinks)

Doesn't taste too bad in the morning, does it?

TOBIAS. No, but I had some . . . before.

HARRY. When?

TOBIAS. Earlier . . . oh, three, four, while you all were . . . asleep, or whatever you were doing.

245

HARRY *(Seemingly casual)*. Oh, you were . . . awake, hunh?

TOBIAS. Yes.

HARRY. I slept a *little.*

(Glum laugh)

God.

TOBIAS. What?

HARRY. You know what I did last night?

TOBIAS. No?

HARRY. I got out of bed and I . . . crawled in with Edna?

TOBIAS. Yes?

HARRY. *She* held me. She let me stay awhile, then I could see she wanted to, and I didn't . . . so I went back. But it was funny.

TOBIAS *(Nods)*. Yeah.

HARRY. Do you . . . do you, uh, like Edna . . . Tobias?

TOBIAS *(Embarrassed)*. Well, sure I *like* her, Harry.

HARRY *(Pause)*. Now, Tobias, about last night, and yesterday, and our coming here, now . . .

HARRY. I was talking about it to Edna, last night, and I said, "Look, Edna, what do we think we're doing."

TOBIAS. I sat up all night and I thought about it, Harry and I talked to Agnes this morning, before you all came down.

HARRY. *I'm* sorry.

TOBIAS. I said, I sat up all night and I thought about it, Harry, and I talked to Agnes, too, before you all came down, and . . . By God, it isn't easy, Harry . . . but we can make it . . . if you want us to. . . . *I* can, I mean, I *think* I can.

HARRY. No . . . we're . . . we're going, Tobias.

TOBIAS. I don't know what help . . . I don't know *how* . . .

HARRY. I said: we're going.

TOBIAS. Yes, but . . . you're going?

HARRY *(Nice, shy smile)*. Sure.

TOBIAS. But, but you can *try* it here . . . or we can, God, I don't know, Harry. You can't go back there; you've got to . . .

HARRY. Got to what? Sell the house? Buy another? Move to the club?

TOBIAS. You came *here!*

HARRY *(Sad)*. Do you *want* us here, Tobias?

TOBIAS. You *came* here.

HARRY. Do you *want* us here?

TOBIAS. You *came! Here!*

HARRY *(Too clearly enunciated)*. Do you want us here?

(Subdued, almost apologetic)

Edna and I . . . there's . . . so much . . . over the dam, so many . . . disappointments, evasions, I guess, lies maybe . . . so much we remember we wanted, once . . . so little that we've . . . settled for . . . we talk, sometimes, but mostly . . . no. We don't . . . "like." Oh, sure, we *like* . . . but I've always been a little shy—gruff, you know, and . . . shy. And Edna isn't . . . happy—I suppose that's it. We . . . we like you and . . . and Agnes, and . . . well Claire, and Julia, too, I guess I mean . . . *I* like you, and you like me, I think, and . . . you're our best friends, but . . . I told Edna upstairs, I said: Edna, what if they'd come to us? And she didn't say anything. And I said: Edna, if they'd come to us like this, and even though we don't have . . . Julia, and all of that, I . . . Edna, I wouldn't take them in.

(Brief silence)

I wouldn't take them in, Edna; they don't . . . they don't have any right. And she said: yes, I know; they wouldn't have the right.

(Brief silence)

Toby, I wouldn't let *you* stay.

(Shy, embarrassed)

You . . . you don't *want* us, do you, Toby? You don't want us here.

TOBIAS *(This next is an aria. It must have in its performance all the horror and exuberance of a man who has kept his emotions under control too long.* TOBIAS *will be carried to the edge of hysteria, and he will find himself laughing, sometimes, while he cries from sheer release. All in all, it is genuine and bravura at the same time, one prolonging the other. I shall try to notate it somewhat).*

(Softly, and as if the word were unfamiliar)

Want?

(Same)

What? Do I what?

(Abrupt laugh; joyous)

DO I WANT?

(More laughter; also a sob)

DO I WANT YOU HERE!

(Hardly able to speak from the laughter)

You come in here, you come in here with your . . . wife, and with your . . . terror! And you ask me if I want you here!
(*Great breathing sounds*)
YES! OF COURSE! I WANT YOU HERE! I HAVE BUILT THIS HOUSE! I WANT YOU IN IT! I WANT YOUR PLAGUE! YOU'VE GOT SOME TERROR WITH YOU? BRING IT IN!
(*Pause, then, even louder*)
BRING IT IN!! YOU'VE GOT THE ENTREE, BUDDY, YOU DON'T NEED A KEY! YOU'VE GOT THE ENTREE, BUDDY! FORTY YEARS!
(*Soft, now; soft and fast, almost a monotone*)
You don't need to ask me, Harry, you don't need to ask a thing; you're our friends, our very best friends in the world, and you don't have to ask.
(*A shout*)
WANT? ASK?
(*Soft, as before*)
You come for dinner don't you come for cocktails see us at the club on Saturdays and talk and lie and laugh with us and pat old Agnes on the hand and say you don't know what old Toby'd do without her and we've known you all these years and we love each other don't we?
(*Shout*)
DON'T WE?! DON'T WE LOVE EACH OTHER?
(*Soft again, laughter and tears in it*)
Doesn't friendship grow to that? To love? Doesn't forty years amount to anything? We've cast our lot together, boy, we're friends, we've been through lots of thick OR thin together. Which is it, boy?
(*Shout*)
WHICH IS IT, BOY?!
THICK?!
THIN?!
WELL, WHATEVER IT IS, WE'VE BEEN THROUGH IT, BOY!
(*Soft*)
And you don't have to ask. I like you, Harry, yes, I really do, I don't like Edna, but that's not half the point, I like you fine; I find my liking you has limits . . .
(*Loud*)
BUT THOSE ARE MY LIMITS!
NOT YOURS!

248

(Soft)

The fact I like you well enough, but not enough . . . that best friend in the world should be something else—more—well, that's my poverty. So, bring your wife, and bring your terror, bring your plague.

(Loud)

BRING YOUR PLAGUE!

(The four women appear in the archway, coffee cups in hand, stand, watch)

I DON'T WANT YOU HERE!

YOU ASKED?!

NO! I DON'T

(Loud)

BUT BY CHRIST YOU'RE GOING TO STAY HERE!

YOU'VE GOT THE RIGHT!

THE RIGHT!

DO YOU KNOW THE WORD?

THE RIGHT!

(Soft)

You've put nearly forty years in it, baby; so have I, and if it's nothing, I don't give a damn, you've got the right to be here, you've earned it

(Loud)

AND BY GOD YOU'RE GOING TO TAKE IT!

DO YOU HEAR ME?!

YOU BRING YOUR TERROR AND YOU COME IN HERE AND YOU LIVE WITH US!

YOU BRING YOUR PLAGUE!

YOU STAY WITH US!

I DON'T WANT YOU HERE!

I DON'T LOVE YOU!

BUT BY GOD . . . YOU STAY!!

(Pause)

STAY!

(Softer)

Stay!

(Soft, tears)

Stay. Please? Stay?

(Pause)

Stay? Please? Stay?

(A silence in the room. HARRY, *numb, rises; the women come into the room, slowly, stand. The play is quiet and subdued from now until the end)*

EDNA *(Calm).* Harry, will you bring our bags down? Maybe Tobias will help you. Will you ask him?

HARRY *(Gentle).* Sure.

(Goes to TOBIAS, *who is quietly wiping tears from his face, takes him gently by the shoulder)*

Tobias? Will you help me? Get the bags upstairs?

(TOBIAS *nods, puts his arm around* HARRY. *The two men exit. Silence)*

EDNA *(Stirring her coffee; slightly strained, but conversational).* Poor Harry; he's not a . . . callous man, for all his bluff.

(Relaxing a little, almost a contentment)

He . . . he came to my bed last night, got in with me, I . . . let him stay, and talk. I let him think I . . . wanted to make love; he . . . it pleases him, I think—to know he would be wanted, if he . . . He said to me . . . He . . . he lay there in the dark with me—this man—and he said to me, very softly, and like a little boy, rather: "Do they love us? Do they love us, Edna?" Oh, I let a silence go by. "Well . . . as much as we love them . . . I should think."

(Pause)

The hair on his chest is very gray . . . and soft. "Would . . . would we let them stay, Edna?" Almost a whisper. Then still again.

(Kindly)

Well, I hope he told Tobias something simple, something to help. We mustn't press our luck, must we: test.

(Pause. Slight smile)

It's sad to come to the end of it, isn't it, nearly the end; so much more of it gone by . . . than left, and still not know—still not have learned . . . the boundaries, what we may not do . . . not ask, for fear of looking in a mirror. We *shouldn't* have come.

AGNES *(A bit by rote).* Now, Edna . . .

EDNA. For our own sake; our own . . . lack. It's sad to know you've gone through it all, or most of it, without . . . that the one body you've wrapped your arms around . . . the only skin you've ever known . . . is your own—and that it's dry . . . and not warm.

(Pause. Back to slightly strained conversational tone)

What will you do, Julia? Will you be seeing Douglas?

JULIA *(Looking at her coffee)*. I haven't thought about it; I don't know; I doubt it.

AGNES. Time.

(Pause. They look at her)

Time happens, I suppose.

(Pause. They still look)

To people. Everything becomes . . . too late, finally. You know it's going on . . . up on the hill; you can see the dust, and hear the cries, and the steel . . . but you wait; and time happens. When you *do* go, sword, shield . . . finally . . . there's nothing there . . . save rust; bones; and the wind.

(Pause)

I'm sorry about the coffee, Edna. The help must hide the beans, or take them with them when they go to bed.

EDNA. Oooh. Coffee and wine: they're much the same with me—I can't tell good from bad.

CLAIRE. Would anyone . . . besides Claire . . . care to have a drink?

AGNES *(Muttered)*. Oh, really, Claire.

CLAIRE. Edna?

EDNA *(Little deprecating laugh)*. Oh, good heavens, thank you, Claire. No.

CLAIRE. Julia?

JULIA *(Looks up at her; steadily; slowly)*. All right; thank you. I will.

EDNA *(As AGNES is about to speak; rising)*. I think I hear the men.

(TOBIAS *and* HARRY *appear in the archway, with bags*)

TOBIAS. We'll just take them to the car, now.

(They do so)

EDNA *(Pleasant, but a little strained)*. Thank you, Agnes, you've been . . . well, just thank you. We'll be seeing you.

AGNES *(Rises, too; some worry on her face)*. Yes; well, don't be strangers.

EDNA *(Laughs)*. Oh, good Lord, how could we be? Our lives are . . . the same.

(Pause)

Julia . . . think a little.

JULIA *(A trifle defiant)*. Oh, I will, Edna. I'm fond of marriage.

EDNA. Claire, my darling, *do* be good.

CLAIRE *(Two drinks in her hands; bravura)*. Well, I'll try to be quiet.

EDNA. I'm going into town on Thursday, Agnes. Would you like to come?

(A longer pause than necessary, CLAIRE *and* JULIA *look at* AGNES)

AGNES *(Just a trifle awkward)*. Well . . . no, I don't think so, Edna; I've . . . I've so much to do.

EDNA *(Cooler; sad)*. Oh. Well . . . perhaps another week.

AGNES. Oh, yes; we'll do it.

(The men reappear)

TOBIAS *(Somewhat formal, reserved)*. All done.

HARRY *(Slight sigh)*. All set.

AGNES *(Going to HARRY, embracing him)*. Harry, my darling; take good care.

HARRY *(Kisses her, awkwardly, on the cheek)*. Th-thank you, Agnes; you, too, Julia? You . . . you be good.

JULIA. Goodbye, Harry.

CLAIRE *(Handing JULIA her drink)*. 'Bye, Harry: see you 'round.

HARRY *(Smiles, a little ruefully)*. Sure thing, Claire.

EDNA *(Embraces TOBIAS)*. Goodbye, Tobias . . . thank you.

TOBIAS *(Mumbled)*. Goodbye, Edna.

(Tiny silence)

HARRY *(Puts his hand out, grabs TOBIAS', shakes it hard)*. Thanks, old man.

TOBIAS *(Softly; sadly)*. Please? Stay?

(Pause)

HARRY *(Nods)*. See you at the club. Well? Edna?

(They start out)

AGNES *(After them)*. Drive carefully, now. It's Sunday.

EDNA'S AND HARRY'S VOICES. All right. Goodbye. Thank you.

(The four in the room together. JULIA and CLAIRE have sat down; AGNES moves to TOBIAS, puts her arm around him)

AGNES *(Sigh)*. Well. Here we all are. You all right, my darling?

TOBIAS *(Clears his throat)*. Sure.

AGNES *(Still with her arm around him)*. Your daughter has taken to drinking in the morning, I hope you'll notice.

TOBIAS *(Unconcerned)*. Oh?

(Moves away from her)

I had one here . . . somewhere, one with Harry. Oh, there it is.

AGNES. Well, I would seem to have *three* early-morning drinkers now. I hope it won't become a club. We'd have to get a license, would we not?

TOBIAS. Just think of it as very late at night.

AGNES. All right, I will.

(Silence)

252

TOBIAS. I tried.
(Pause)
I was honest.
(Silence)
Didn't I?
(Pause)
Wasn't I?

JULIA *(Pause)*. You were very honest, Father. And you tried.

TOBIAS. Didn't I try, Claire? Wasn't I honest?

CLAIRE *(Comfort; rue)*. Sure you were. You tried.

TOBIAS. I'm sorry. I apologize.

AGNES *(To fill a silence)*. What I find most astonishing—aside from my belief that I will, one day . . . lose my mind—but when? Never, I begin to think, as the years go by, or that I'll not *know* if it happens, or maybe even *has*—what I find most astonishing, I think, is the wonder of daylight, of the sun. All the centuries, millenniums—all the history— I wonder if that's why we sleep at night, because the darkness still . . . frightens us? They say we sleep to let the demons out—to let the mind go raving mad, our dreams and nightmares all our logic gone awry, the dark side of our reason. And when the daylight comes again . . . comes order with it.
(Sad chuckle)
Poor Edna and Harry.
(Sigh)
Well, they're safely gone . . . and we'll all forget . . . quite soon.
(Pause)
Come now; we can begin the day.

CURTAIN

BOX
and
QUOTATIONS
FROM
CHAIRMAN MAO TSE-TUNG

Two Inter-Related Plays (1968)

FIRST PERFORMANCE: March 7, 1968
Buffalo, New York, Studio Arena Theater

FIRST NEW YORK CITY PERFORMANCE: September 30, 1968
New York City, Billy Rose Theatre

THE VOICE OF RUTH WHITE *as* BOX
WYMAN PENDLETON *as* CHAIRMAN MAO
NANCY KELLY *as* THE LONG-WINDED LADY
SUDIE BOND *as* THE OLD WOMAN
GEORGE BARTENIEFF *as* THE MINISTER

Directed by ALAN SCHNEIDER

AUTHOR'S NOTE

While it is true that *Box* and *Quotations From Chairman Mao Tse-Tung* are separate plays, were conceived at different though not distant moments, stand by themselves, and can be played one without the company of the other, I feel that they are more effective performed enmeshed, as I have suggested herein.

To perform *Box* without *Quotations From Chairman Mao Tse-Tung*, it is necessary merely to perform *Box*, though I feel that *Box* will make its points most effectively if played twice (or even three times) in a row, without intermission, going to black between each playing. The over-all lighting might change—from light blue, to deep blue; from red to green; at any rate, from one color-sense to another.

To perform *Quotations From Chairman Mao Tse-Tung* without *Box* is

256

as simple: merely exclude, from the body of the play, the excerpts from *Box* which have been included in the preferred joint performance.

It is also possible, of course, to perform both plays without doing them in the manner I have indicated—*Box, Quotations From Chairman Mao Tse-Tung,* and then *Box.* In this case, I recommend that *Box* be performed second, and that the excerpts from *Box* remain in the body of *Quotations From Chairman Mao Tse-Tung.*

The ideal performance, then, will be *Box,* followed by *Quotations From Chairman Mao Tse-Tung,* followed by *Box.* Also ideally, there should be no intermission. There will have to be a lowering of the lights, of course, so that the setting for *Quotations From Chairman Mao Tse-Tung* can appear; and again, at the end of *Quotations From Chairman Mao Tse-Tung,* its set must vanish so that *Box* can reappear. But, for the whole play, there will be no intermission necessary.

In the New York production the setting for *Quotations From Chairman Mao Tse-Tung* was on a winch powered platform which was behind a Black Drop upstage of the *Box* set. At the end of *Box* the lights went to Black Out and the Black Drop was raised and the rear floor bottom piece of cube was removed. As lights build Mao came down center and during his first speech the winch powered platform with actors in place slowly came into position inside the *Box* set.

At the end of *Quotations From Chairman Mao Tse-Tung* the winch powered platform was slowly taken upstage leaving the cube empty once again.

CHARACTERS

CHAIRMAN MAO: Should be played, ideally, by an oriental actor who resembles Mao. However, the role can be played either with makeup or a face mask. In any event, an attempt should be made to make the actor resemble Mao as much as possible. Mao speaks rather like a teacher. He does not raise his voice; he is not given to histrionics. His tone is always reasonable, sometimes a little sad; occasionally a half-smile will appear. Mao *always* speaks to the audience. He is aware of the other characters, but he must *never* suggest in any way that anything they say is affecting his words. When I say that Mao always addresses the audience I do not mean that he must look them in the eye constantly. Once he has made it clear that he is addressing them he may keep that intention clear in any way he likes—looking away, speaking to only one person, whatever.

LONG-WINDED LADY: A lady of sixty. I care very little about how she looks so long as she looks very average and upper-middle-class. Nothing exotic; nothing strange. She should, I think, stay pretty much to her deck chair. She never *speaks* to the audience. Sometimes she is clearly speaking to the Minister; more often she is speaking both for his benefit and her own. She can withdraw entirely into self from time to time. She uses the minister as a sounding board.

THE OLD WOMAN: Shabby, poor, without being so in a comedy sense. She has a bag with her. She will eat occasionally. Her bag also contains a small jar of apple sauce and a spoon. She is aware of everybody but speaks *only* to the audience. Her reading of her poem can have some emotion to it, though never too much. It should be made clear, though, that while the subject of her speeches is dear to her heart, a close matter, she *is* reciting a poem. She may look at the other characters from time to time, but what she says must never seem to come from what any of the others has said. She might nod in agreement with Mao now and again, or shake her head over the plight of the Long-Winded Lady. She should stay in one place, up on something.

BOX AND QUOTATIONS FROM CHAIRMAN MAO TSE-TUNG

THE MINISTER: Has no lines, and stays in his deck chair. He must try to pay close attention to the Long-Winded Lady though, nod, shake his head, cluck, put an arm tentatively out, etc. He must also keep busy with his pipe and pouch and matches. He should doze off from time to time. He must *never* make the audience feel he is looking at them or is aware of them. Also, he is not aware of either Mao or the Old Woman. He is seventy or so, has white or gray hair, a clerical collar. A florid face would be nice. If a thin actor is playing the role, however, then make the face sort of gray-yellow-white.

GENERAL COMMENTS

For this play to work according to my intention, careful attention must be paid to what I have written about the characters: to whom they speak; to whom they may and may not react; how they speak; how they move or do not. Alteration from the patterns I have set may be interesting but I fear they will destroy the attempt of the experiment: musical structure—form and counterpoint. Primarily the characters must seem interested in what they, themselves, are doing and saying. While the lines must not read metronome-exact, I feel that a certain set rhythm will come about, quite of itself. No one rushes in on the end of anyone else's speech; no one waits too long. I have indicated, quite precisely, within the speeches of the Long-Winded Lady, by means of commas, periods, semi-colons, colons, dashes and dots (as well as parenthetical stage directions) the speech rhythms. Please observe them carefully, for they were not thrown in, like herbs on a salad, to be mixed about. I have underlined words I want stressed. I have capitalized for loudness, and used exclamation points for emphasis. There are one or two seeming questions that I have left the question mark off of. This was done on purpose, as an out-loud reading will make self-evident. I have appended, at the end of the text of *Box-Mao-Box* the Long-Winded Lady's entire monologue. I have done so for I can think of no other way for the actress to learn it, or for the director to understand it without reading the whole play many, many times.

260

Box

Curtain rises in darkness. Lights go up slowly to reveal the interior of a large cube. The cube should take up almost all of a small stage opening. The sides are open, and we should see the other sides clearly . . . the feeling of a cube. The twelve joins should be painted with glo paint. The lights on the cube stay constant until the final dimout—there should be five seconds' silence.

VOICE. *(The voice should not come from the stage, but should seem to be coming from nearby the spectator—from the back or the sides of the theatre. The voice of a woman, not young, but not ancient, either: fifty-ish. Neither a sharp, crone's voice, but not refined. A middle-western farm woman's voice would be best. Matter-of-fact, announcement of a subject.)* Box. *(Five second silence.)* Box. *(Three second silence.)* Nicely done. Well put . . . *(Pause.)* . . . together. Box. *(Three second silence. More conversational now.)* Room inside for a sedia d'ondalo, which, in English—for that is Italian—would be, is, rocking chair. Room to rock. *And* room to move about in . . . some. Enough. *(Three second silence.)* Carpentry is among the arts going out . . . or crafts, if you're of a nonclassical disposition. There are others: other arts which have gone down to craft and which are going further . . . walls, brick walls, music . . . *(Pause.)* . . . the making of good bread if you won't laugh; living. Many arts: all craft now . . . and going further. But *this* is solid, perfect joins . . . good work. Knock and there's no give—no give of sound, I mean. A thud; no hollow. Oh, very good work; fine timber, and so fastidious, like when they shined the bottoms of the shoes . . . *and* the instep. Not only where you might *expect* they'd shine the bottoms if they *did* . . . but even the instep. *(Two second silence. Grudging, but not very.) And* other crafts have come up . . . if not to replace, then . . . occupy. *(Tiny laugh.)* Nature abhors, among so many, so much else . . . amongst so much, us, itself, they say, vacuum. *(Five second silence. A listing.)* System as conclusion, in the sense of method as an end, the dice so big you can hardly throw them any more. *(Some awe, some sadness.)* Seven hundred million babies dead in the time it takes, took, to knead the dough to make a proper loaf. Well, little wonder so many . . . went . . . cut off, said no instead of hanging on. *(Three second silence.)* Apathy, I think. *(Five second silence.)*

Inevitability. And progress is merely a direction, movement. *(Earnest.)* When it was *simple* . . . *(Light, self-mocking laugh.)* Ah, well, yes, when it was simple. *(Three second silence. Wistful.)* Beautiful, beautiful box. *(Three second silence.) And* room enough to walk around in, take a turn. *(Tiny pause.)* If only they had *told* us! Clearly! When it was clear that we were not only corrupt—for there is nothing that is not, or little —but corrupt to the selfishness, to the corruption that we should die to keep it . . . go under rather than . . . *(Three second silence. Sigh.)* Oh, my. *(Five second silence.)* Or was it the milk? *That* may have been the moment: spilling and spilling and killing all those children to make a point. A penny or two, and a symbol at that, and I suppose the children were symbolic, too, though they died, and couldn't stop. Once it starts—gets to a certain point—the momentum is too much. But spilling milk! *(Two second silence. Firmly felt.)* Oh, shame! *(A little schoolmarmish.)* The *Pope* warned us; *he* said so. There are no posses-sions, he said; so long as there are some with nothing we have no right to anything. *(Two second silence.)* It's the *little* things, the *small* cracks. Oh, for every pound of milk they spill you can send a check to someone, but that does not unspill. That it *can* be *done* is the crack. And if you go back to a partita . . . ahhhhh, what when it makes you cry!? Not from the beauty of it, but from solely that you cry from loss . . . so pre-cious. When art begins to hurt . . . when art begins to hurt it's time to look around. Yes it is. *(Three second silence.)* Yes it is. *(Three second silence.)* No longer just great beauty which takes you more to every-thing, but a reminder! And not of what *can* . . . but what *has.* Yes, when art hurts . . . *(Three second silence.)* Box. *(Two second silence.)* And room enough to move around, except like a fly. That would be *very* good! *(Rue.)* Yes, but so would so much. *(Two second silence. School-marmish.)* Here is the thing about tension and the tonic—the impor-tant thing. *(Pause.)* The release of tension is the return to consonance; no matter how far travelled, one comes back, not circular, not to the starting point, but a . . . setting down again, and the beauty of art is order—not what is familiar, necessarily, but order . . . on its own terms. *(Two second silence. Sigh.)* So much . . . flies. A billion birds at once, black net skimming the ocean, or the monarchs that time, that island, blown by the wind, but going straight . . . in a direction. Or-der! *(Two second silence.)* And six sides to bounce it all off of. *(Three second silence. Brave start again.)* When the beauty of it reminds us of

loss. Instead of the attainable. When it tells us what we cannot have
. . . well, then . . . it no longer relates . . . *does* it. That is the
thing about music. That is why we cannot listen any more. *(Pause.)*
Because we cry. *(Three second silence.)* And *if* he says, or *she* . . . why
are you doing that?, and, and your only honest response is: art hurts
. . . *(Little laugh.)* Well. *(Five second silence.)* Look! More birds! Another . . . sky of them. *(Five second silence.)* It is not a matter of
garden, or straight lines, or even . . . morality. It's only when you
can't come back; when you get in some distant key; that when you say,
the tonic! the tonic! and they say, what is *that?* It's *then. (Three second
silence.)* There! More! A thousand, and one below them, moving fast in
the opposite way! *(Two second silence.)* What was it used to frighten
me? Bell buoys and sea gulls; the *sound* of them, at night, in a fog,
when I was very young. *(A little laugh.)* Before I had ever seen them,
before I had heard them. *(Some wonder.)* But I knew what they *were*
. . . a thousand miles from the sea. Land-locked, never been, and yet
the sea sounds . . . *(Three second silence. Very matter-of-fact.)* Well,
we can exist with *any*thing; with*out.* There's little that we need to have
to go on . . . evolving. Goodness; we all died when we were thirty
once. Now, much younger. Much. *(Suddenly aware of something.)* But
it *couldn't* have been fog, not the sea-fog. Not way back *there.* It was
the memory of it, to be seen and proved later. And more! and more!
they're all moving! The memory of what we have not known. And so it
is with the fog, which I had never seen, yet knew it. And the resolution
of a chord; no difference. *(Three second silence.)* And even that can
happen here, I guess. But unprovable. Ahhhhh. That makes the difference, does it *not.* Nothing can seep here except the memory of what I'll
not prove. *(Two second silence. Sigh.)* Well, we give up something for
something. *(Three second silence. Listing again, pleased.)* Sturdy, light
. . . interesting . . . in its way. Room enough for a sedia d'ondalo,
which is the Italian of . . . or for . . . *of,* I prefer . . . The Italian
of rocking chair. *(Three second silence.)* When art hurts. That is what
to remember. *(Two second silence.)* What to look for. Then corruption
. . . *(Three second silence.)* Then the corruption is complete. *(Five
second silence. The sound of bell buoys and sea gulls begins, faintly,
growing, but never very loud.)* Nothing belongs. *(Three second silence.
Great sadness.)* Look; more of them; a black net . . . skimming.
(Pause.) And just one . . . moving beneath . . . in the opposite way.

(Three second silence. Very sad.) Milk. *(Three second silence.)* Milk. *(Five second silence. Wistful.)* Box. *(Silence, except for the sound of bell buoys and sea gulls. Very slow fading of lights to black, sound of bell buoys and sea gulls fading with the light.)*

END

In blackout actors get in place:
   MAO to top of U. C. platform.
   LONG-WINDED LADY—sits in L. deck chair.
   OLD WOMAN—sits on her suitcase inside of D. L. rail.
   MINISTER—stands at R. rail in plane of R. deck chair.

Quotations from
Chairman Mao Tse-Tung

SETTING: *The deck of an ocean liner.*
GENERAL LIGHTING COMMENTS: *We must be in bright daylight, that particular kind of brightness that is possible only in mid-ocean. When cyclorama fully lit—Mao as stage lights build descends* U. C. *platform steps and comes* D. C. *via between deck chairs. He removes 2d mask on stick and he bows.*

CHAIRMAN MAO. *(Chinese written in sounds.)* CHUNG-KWOR GU DAI MIN YUI YUO "YU-KUNG YEE SHIAN" DEE YI DWAUN GOO SHI. HWA DEE. *(He bows and starts again in English.)* There is an ancient Chinese fable called "The foolish old man who removed the mountains." It tells of an old man who lived in Northern China long, long ago and was known as the foolish old man of the north mountains. His house faced south and beyond his doorway stood the two great peaks, Taihand and Wangwu, obstructing the way. With great determination, he led his sons in digging up these mountains hoe in hand. Another greybeard, known as the wise old man, saw them and said derisively, "How silly of you to do this! It is quite impossible for you few to dig up those two huge mountains." The foolish old man replied, "When I die, my sons will carry on; when they die there will be my grandsons, and then their sons and grandsons, and so on to infinity. High as they are, the mountains cannot grow any higher and with every bit we dig, they will be that much lower. Why can't we clear them away?" Having refuted the wise old man's wrong view, he went on digging every day, unshaken in his conviction. God was moved by this, and he sent down two angels, who carried the mountains away on their backs. *(Mao crosses* D. R. *outside of rail and box.)* Today, two big mountains lie like a dead weight on the Chinese people. One is imperialism, the other is feudalism. The Chinese Communist party has long made up its mind to dig them up. We must persevere and work unceasingly, and we, too, will touch God's heart. Our God is none other than the masses of the Chinese people. If they stand up and dig together with us, why can't these two mountains be cleared away? *(Mao crosses* U. R. *outside of box.)*
LONG-WINDED LADY. Well, *(Minister turns.)* I daresay it's hard to compre-

hend *(Minister crosses* R. *chair, puts cup on floor and sits.)* . . . I
mean: *I* . . . at this remove . . . *I* find it hard to, well, not comprehend, but believe, or accept, if you will. So long ago! So much since.
But there it was: Splash!

OLD WOMAN. "Over the hill to the poor-house."

LONG-WINDED LADY. Well, not splash, exactly, more sound than that, more
of a . . . *(Little laugh.)* no, I can't do that—imitate it: for I only
imagine . . . what it must have sounded like to . . . an onlooker. An
overseer. Not to *me*, Lord knows! Being *in* it. Or doing it, rather. *(Mao
crosses inside rail* D.R.*)*

CHAIRMAN MAO. In drawing up plans, handling affairs or thinking over
problems, we must proceed from the fact that China has six hundred
million people, and we must never forget this fact. *(Mao crosses above*
U. C. *platform to* U. L. *outside of rail and box.)*

OLD WOMAN. By Will Carlton.

LONG-WINDED LADY. No. To an onlooker it would not have been splash,
but a sort of . . . different sound, and I try to imagine what it would
have been like—*sounded* like—had *I* not been . . . well, so involved, if
you know what I mean. And *I* was so *busy* . . . I didn't pay attention,
or, if I did . . . that part of it doesn't re . . . recall itself. Retain is
the, is what I started.

OLD WOMAN. "Over the Hill to the Poorhouse"—A poem by Will Carlton.

CHAIRMAN MAO. *(Crosses* D. L. *outside rail.)* Apart from their other charac-
teristics, the outstanding thing about China's six hundred million people is that they are "poor and blank." This may seem a bad thing, but in
reality it is a good thing. Poverty gives rise to the desire for change, the
desire for action and the desire for revolution. On a blank sheet of
paper free from any mark, the freshest and most beautiful characters
can be written, the freshest and most beautiful pictures can be painted.

LONG-WINDED LADY. And so high!

OLD WOMAN. *(She rises, crosses to* U. C. *platform.)*
Over the hill to the poor-house—I can't quite make it clear!
Over the hill to the poor-house—it seems so horrid queer!
Many a step I've taken a-toilin' to and fro,
But this is a sort of journey I never thought to go.
(Old Woman sits on suitcase.)

LONG-WINDED LADY. I'd never imagined it—naturally! It's not what one

266

would. The *echo* of a sound, or the remembering of a sound having happened. No; that's not right either. For *them*, for the theoretical . . . onwatcher. *(Pause.)* Plut! Yes!

CHAIRMAN MAO. Communism is at once a complete system of proletarian ideology and a new social system. It is different from any other ideological and social system, and is the most complete, progressive, revolutionary and rational system in human history. *(Mao crosses D. L. to proscenium.)* The communist ideological and social system alone is full of youth and vitality, sweeping the world with the momentum of an avalanche and the force of a thunderbolt.

LONG-WINDED LADY. Exactly: plut!

OLD WOMAN.

Over the hill to the poor-house I'm trudgin' my weary way—

I, a woman of seventy, and only a trifle gray—

I, who am smart an' chipper, for all the years I've told,

As many many another woman that's only half as old.

LONG-WINDED LADY. And then, with the wind, and the roar of the engines and the sea . . . maybe not even that, not even . . . plut! But, some slight sound, or . . . or the creation of one! The invention! What is that about consequence? Oh, *you* know! Everything has its consequence? Or, every action a reaction; something. But maybe nothing at all, no real sound, but the invention of one. I mean, if you see it happening . . . the, the thing . . . landing, and the spray, the sea parting, as it were . . . well, then . . . one makes a sound . . . in one's mind . . . to, to correspond to the sound one . . . didn't . . . hear. Yes?

CHAIRMAN MAO. *(Crosses D. L. outside rail.)* Imperialism will not last long because it always does evil things.

OLD WOMAN. Over the hill to the poor-house.

CHAIRMAN MAO. *(Crosses D. R. C.)* It persists in grooming and supporting reactionaries in all countries who are against the people; it has forcibly seized many colonies and semi-colonies and many military bases, and it threatens the peace with atomic war.

OLD WOMAN. By Will Carlton.

CHAIRMAN MAO. *(Crosses D. R. outside rail.)* Thus, forced by imperialism to do so, more than ninety per cent of the people of the world are rising or will rise up in struggle against it.

267

OLD WOMAN.

Over the hill to the poor-house, I'm trudgin' my weary way,

I, a woman of 70, and only a trifle gray.

CHAIRMAN MAO. Yet imperialism is still alive, still running amuck in Asia, Africa and Latin America. In the West, Imperialism is still oppressing the people at home. This situation must change.

OLD WOMAN.

I who am smart and chipper, for all the years I've told

As many another woman that's only half as old.

CHAIRMAN MAO. It is the task of the people of the whole world to put an end to the aggression and oppression perpetrated by imperialism, and chiefly by U. S. imperialism. *(Mao crosses* D. R. *rail end inside rail and box.)*

LONG-WINDED LADY. Yes. I think so.

CHAIRMAN MAO. Historically, all reactionary forces on the verge of extinction invariably conduct a last desperate struggle against the revolutionary forces, and some revolutionaries are apt to be deluded for a time by this phenomenon of outward strength but inner weakness, failing to grasp the essential fact that the enemy is nearing extinction while they themselves are approaching victory. *(Mao sits,* D. R. *on deck.)*

LONG-WINDED LADY. I remember once when I broke my finger, or my thumb, and I was very little, and they said, you've broken your thumb, look, you've broken your thumb, and there wasn't any pain . . . not *yet*, not for that first moment, just . . . just an absence of sensation—an interesting lack of anything.

OLD WOMAN. Over the hill to the poor-house.

LONG-WINDED LADY. When they said it again, look, you've broken your thumb, not only did I scream, as if some knife had ripped my leg down, from hip to ankle, all through the sinews layin̮ bare the bone . . . not only did I scream as only children can—adults do it differently: there's an animal protest there, a revenge, something . . . something other—not only did I scream, but I manufactured the pain. Right then! Before the hurt could have come through, I made it happen. *(Pause.)* Well; we do that.

OLD WOMAN.

What is the use of heapin' on me a pauper's shame?

Am I lazy or crazy? Am I blind or lame?

True, I am not so supple, nor yet so awful stout;

268

But charity ain't no favor, if one can live without.

LONG-WINDED LADY. Yes; we do that: we make it happen a little before it need. *(Pause.)* And so it might have been with someone watching—and maybe even to those who *were*. Who *were* watching. And there were, or I'd not be here. *(Pause.)* I daresay. *(Pause.)* The sound manufactured. Lord knows, if *I* had been among the . . . nonparticipators I should have done it, too; no doubt. Plup! Plut! Whichever. I'm sure *I* should have . . . if I'd seen it all the *way*, now. I mean, if I'd caught just the final instant, without time to relate the event to its environment—the thing happening to the thing happened *to* . . . then I doubt I would have. Nor would anyone . . . or most. *(Minister starts to sleep.)*

CHAIRMAN MAO. The imperialists and their running dogs, the Chinese reactionaries, will not resign themselves to defeat in this land of China.

OLD WOMAN.

What is the use of heapin' on me a pauper's shame?

Am I lazy or crazy? Am I blind or lame?

CHAIRMAN MAO. All this we must take fully into account.

LONG-WINDED LADY. *(Minister awakens.)* But just imagine what it must have been like . . . to be one of the . . . watchers! How . . . well, is marvelous the proper word, I wonder? Yes, I suspect. I mean, how often?! It's not too common an occurrence, to have it . . . plummet by! One is standing there, admiring, or faintly sick, or just plain throwing up, but how often is one *there. Ever!* Well, inveterates; yes; but for the casual crossers . . . not too often, and one would have to be exactly in place, at exactly the proper time, and alert! Very alert in . . . by nature, and able to relate what one sees to what is happening. Oh, I remember the time the taxi went berserk and killed those people!

CHAIRMAN MAO. Riding roughshod everywhere, U. S. imperialism has made itself the enemy of the people of the world *(Mao rises.)* and has increasingly isolated itself. Those who refuse to be enslaved will never be cowed by the atom bombs and hydrogen bombs in the hands of the U. S. imperialists. The raging tide of the people of the world against the U. S. aggressors is irresistible. Their struggle against U. S. imperialism and its lackeys will assuredly win still greater victories. *(Mao crosses u. r. inside rail and crosses r. outside of rail to r. of r. deck chair outside box.)*

LONG-WINDED LADY. Well, it didn't go berserk, of course, for it *is* a machine: a taxi. Nor did the driver . . . go berserk. Out of control, though! The driver lost and out of control it went! *Up* on the sidewalk, bowling them down like whatchamacallems, then crash!, into the store front, the splash of glass and then on fire. How many dead? Ten? Twelve? And I had just come out with the crullers.

OLD WOMAN.

I am willin' and anxious an' ready any day

To work for a decent livin', an' pay my honest way;

For I can earn my victuals, an' more too, I'll be bound,

If any body only is willin' to have me 'round.

(Old Woman eats spoon of apple sauce.)

LONG-WINDED LADY. The bag of crullers, and a smile on my face for everyone liked them so, and there it was! Careen . . . and dying . . . and all that glass. And I remember thinking: It's a movie! They're shooting some scenes right here on the street. *(Pause.)* They weren't, of course. It was real death, and real glass, and the fire, and the . . . people crying, and the crowds, and the smoke. Oh, it was real enough, but it took me time to know it. The mind does that.

CHAIRMAN MAO. *(Crosses D. R. outside of rail.)* If the U. S. monopoly capitalist groups persist in pushing their policies of aggression and war, the day is bound to come when they will be hanged by the people of the whole world. The same fate awaits the accomplices of the United States. *(Mao crosses to house box R. via D. R. aisle steps.)*

OLD WOMAN.

I am willin' and anxious an' ready any day

To work for a decent livin' an' pay my honest way,

For I can earn my victuals an' more, too, I'll be bound

If anybody only is willin' to have me 'round.

LONG-WINDED LADY. They're making a movie! What a nice conclusion, coming out with the crullers, still hot, with a separate little bag for the powdered sugar, of course it's a movie! One doesn't come out like that to carnage! Dead people and the wounded; glass all over and . . . confusion. One . . . concludes things—and if those things and what is really there don't . . . are not the *same* . . . well! . . . it would usually be better if it were so. The mind does that: it helps. *(Mao appears in R. house box seat area.)*

CHAIRMAN MAO. To achieve a lasting world peace, we must further develop our friendship and cooperation with the fraternal countries in the socialist camp and strengthen our solidarity with all peace-loving countries.

LONG-WINDED LADY. The mind does that.

CHAIRMAN MAO. We must endeavor to establish normal diplomatic relations, on the basis of mutual respect for territorial integrity and sovereignty and of equality and mutual benefit, with all countries willing to live together with us in peace.

LONG-WINDED LADY. It helps.

CHAIRMAN MAO. We must give active support to the national independence and liberation movement in Asia, Africa, and Latin America as well as to the peace movement and to just struggles in all the countries of the world.

VOICE. *(From "BOX")* Box.

LONG-WINDED LADY. *(Mao exits box R. Goes to L. aisle.)* So; if one happened to be there, by the rail, and not too discomfited, not in the sense of utterly defeated—though that would be more than enough—but in the sense of confused, or preoccupied, if one were not too preoccupied, and plummet! it went by! one, the mind, might be able to take it in, say: ah! there! there she goes!—or he; and manufacture the appropriate sound. But only then. And how many are expecting it!? Well, *I* am. *Now.* There isn't a rail I stand by, especially in full sun—my conditioning—that I'm not . . . already shuddering . . . *and* ready to manufacture the sound. *(Little laugh.)* Though not the sound *I* knew, for I was hardly thinking—a bit busy—but the sound I imagine someone else would have manufactured had *he* been there when I . . . WOOOOSSSH!! PLUT!! *(Little laugh.)*

VOICE. *(From "BOX.")* Box.

OLD WOMAN.

Once I was young an' han'some—I was, upon my soul—
Once my cheeks was roses, my eyes as black as coal;
And I can't remember, in them days, of hearin' people say,
For any reason, that I was in their way.

LONG-WINDED LADY. You never know until it's happened to you.

VOICE. *(From "BOX.")* Many arts; all craft now . . . and going further.

CHAIRMAN MAO. *(Appears at top, L. aisle steps.)* Our country and all the other socialist countries want peace; so do the peoples of all the countries of the world. The only ones who crave war and do not want peace are certain monopoly capitalist groups in a handful of imperialist countries which depend on aggression for their profits. *(Mao crosses behind* L. *chair through* L. *rail opening.)*

LONG-WINDED LADY. *Do* you.

VOICE. *(From* "BOX.") Box.

CHAIRMAN MAO. Who are our enemies? Who are our friends?

LONG-WINDED LADY. *Do* you.

CHAIRMAN MAO. Our enemies are all those in league with imperialism; *(Mao crosses* C.) our closest friends are the entire semiproletariat and petty bourgeoisie. *(Mao crosses above* R. *chair.)* As for the vacillating middle bourgeoisie, their right wing may become our enemy and their left wing may become our friend. *(Mao crosses* R. *outside rail to* R. *of* R. *chair via above* U. R. *rail ending.)*

LONG-WINDED LADY. Falling! My goodness. What was it when one was little? That when you fell when you were dreaming you always woke up before you landed, or else you wouldn't and you'd be dead. That was it, I think. And I never wondered why, I merely took it for . . . well, I *accepted* it. And, of course, I kept trying to dream of falling after I'd heard it . . . tried so hard! . . . and *couldn't,* naturally. Well, if we control the unconscious, we're either mad, or . . . dull-witted.

OLD WOMAN. Once I was young an' han'some . . . I was, upon my soul.

LONG-WINDED LADY. I think I dreamt of falling again, though, but after I'd stopped trying to, but I don't think I landed. Not like what I've been telling you, though that was more seaing than landing, you might say . . . if you like a pun. *(Minister gives a laugh.)* Once, though! Once, I dreamt of falling straight up . . . or out, all in reverse, like the projector running backwards, what they used to do, for fun, in the shorts. *(Some wonder.)* Falling . . . *up!*

CHAIRMAN MAO. In the final analysis, national struggle is a matter of class struggle. Among the whites in the United States it is only the reactionary ruling circles who oppress the black people.

LONG-WINDED LADY. Falling . . . *up!*

CHAIRMAN MAO. *(Crosses* D. R. *outside rail.)* They can in no way represent the workers, farmers, revolutionary intellectuals and other enlightened persons who comprise the overwhelming majority of the white people. *(Mao sits* D. R. *on raked stage at top of steps.)*

VOICE. *(From* "BOX.") Seven hundred million babies dead in half the time it takes, took, to knead the dough to make a proper loaf. Well, little wonder so many . . .

LONG-WINDED LADY. Not rising, you understand: a definite . . . falling, but . . . up!

OLD WOMAN.

'Tain't no use of boastin', or talkin' over free,

But many a house an' home was open then to me;

Many a han'some offer I had from likely men,

And nobody ever hinted that I was a burden then.

LONG-WINDED LADY. Did I call them crullers? Well, I should *not* have; for they were not even doughnuts, but the centers . . . hearts is what they called them: the center dough pinched out, or cut with a cutter and done like the rest, but solid, the size of a bantam egg, but round. Oh, they were good, and crisp, and all like air inside; hot, and you'd dip them in the confectioners' sugar. One could be quite a pig; everyone was; they were so good! You find them here and about still. Some, but not often.

OLD WOMAN. Over the hill to the poor-house.

CHAIRMAN MAO. All reactionaries are paper tigers. In appearance, the reactionaries are terrifying, but in reality they are not so powerful. From a long-term point of view, it is not the reactionaries but the people who are really powerful.

VOICE. *(From "BOX.")* Apathy, I think.

LONG-WINDED LADY. My husband used to say, don't leave her next to anything precipitous; there's bound to be a do; something will drop, or fall, her purse, her*self*. And, so, he had people be careful of me. Not that I'm fond of heights. I'm not unfriendly toward them—all that falling—but I have no . . . great affection. *(Little pause.)* Depths even less. *(Mao rises, crosses* D. R. C. *outside box.)*

OLD WOMAN. By Will Carlton.

CHAIRMAN MAO. I have said that all the reputedly powerful reactionaries are merely paper tigers. The reason is that they are divorced from the people. Look! *(Mao crosses* D. C.*)* Was not Hitler a paper tiger? Was Hitler not overthrown? *(Mao crosses* D. L. C.*)* I also said that the Czar of Russia, the emperor of China and Japanese imperialism were all paper tigers. As we know, they were all overthrown. *(Mao bows, crosses* D.L.*)*

LONG-WINDED LADY. All that falling.

CHAIRMAN MAO. U. S. imperialism has not yet been overthrown and it has the atom bomb. I believe it also will be overthrown. It, too, is a paper

273

tiger. *(Mao bows, crosses* U. L. *outside rail to around* U. L. *rail end to inside rail.)*

LONG-WINDED LADY. *(Looking at Life magazine.)* And it became something of a joke, I suppose . . . I suppose. Where is she? Watch her! Don't let her near the edge! She'll occasion a do!

OLD WOMAN.

And when to John I was married, sure he was good and smart,

But he and all the neighbors would own I done my part;

For life was all before me, an' I was young and strong,

And I worked the best that I could in tryin' to get along.

LONG-WINDED LADY. He was a small man—my husband, almost a miniature . . . not that I'm much of a giraffe. Small . . . and precise . . . and contained . . . quiet strength. The large emotions . . . *yes*, without them, what?—all there, and full size, full scope, but when they came, not a . . . spattering, but a single shaft, a careful aim. No waste, as intense as anyone, but precise. Some people said he was cold; or cruel. But he was merely accurate. Big people ooze, and scatter, and knock over things nearby. They give the impression—the illusion—of openness, of spaces through which things pass—excuses, bypassings. But small, and precise, and accurate don't . . . doesn't allow for that . . . for that *impression*. He wasn't cruel at all.

CHAIRMAN MAO. *(Crosses* D. L. *inside railing, sits* L. *deck platform corner.)* The socialist system will eventually replace the capitalist system; this is an objective law independent of man's will. However much the reactionaries try to hold back the wheel of history, sooner or later revolution will take place and will inevitably triumph.

OLD WOMAN.

Over the hill to the poor-house . . . I can't quite make it clear.

LONG-WINDED LADY. *Or* cold. Neat; accurate; precise. In everything. All our marriage. Except dying. Except that . . . dreadful death.

CHAIRMAN MAO. The imperialists and domestic reactionaries will certainly not take their defeat lying down and they will struggle to the last ditch. This is inevitable and beyond all doubt, and under no circumstances must we relax our vigilance.

LONG-WINDED LADY. That dreadful death—all that he was not: large, random, inaccurate—in the sense of offshoots from the major objective. A spattering cancer! Spread enough and you're bound to kill *something*. Don't aim! Engulf! Imprecision!

VOICE. *(From* "BOX.") When it was simple . . . *(Light, self-mocking laugh.)* Ah, well, yes, when it was simple.

OLD WOMAN.

And so we worked together: and life was hard, but gay,
With now and then a baby for to cheer us on our way!
Till we had half a dozen, an' all growed clean an' neat,
An' went to school like others, an' had enough to eat.

LONG-WINDED LADY. Don't let her near the edge!

CHAIRMAN MAO. *(Rises, crosses on deck to below* R. *chair.)* Make trouble, fail, make trouble again, fail again . . . till their doom; that is the logic of the imperialists and all reactionaries the world over in dealing with the people's cause, and they will never go against this logic. This is a Marxist law. *(Bows.)*

LONG-WINDED LADY. Don't let her near the edge.

CHAIRMAN MAO. *(Crosses* R. *of* L. *chair.)* When we say "imperialism is ferocious," we mean that its nature will never change, that the imperialists will never lay down their butcher knives, that they will never become Buddhas, till their doom. Fight, fail, fight again, fail again, fight again . . . till their victory; that is the logic of the people, and they too will never go against this logic. This is another Marxist law. *(Bows.)*

LONG-WINDED LADY. But I hadn't thought I *was*. Well, yes, of course I *was* . . . but guarded . . . well guarded. Or, so I *thought. (Mao crosses via above* L. *chair through* L. *rail opening, leans on rail outside box.)* It doesn't happen terribly often—falling . . . by indirection. *(Pause.)* Does it?

OLD WOMAN.

So we worked for the child'rn, and raised 'em every one;
Worked for 'em summer and winter, just as we ought to've done;
Only perhaps we humored 'em, which some good folks condemn,
But every couple's child'rn's a heap the best to them.

VOICE. *(From* "BOX.") Oh, shame!

LONG-WINDED LADY. Not death: I didn't mean death. I meant . . . falling off. *That* isn't done too often by indirection. *Is* it! Death! Well, my God, of course; yes. Almost always, 'less you take the notion of the collective . . . thing, which *must allow* for it, take it into account: I mean, if all the rest is part of a . . . predetermination, or something that has already happened—in principle—well, under *those* conditions *any* chaos becomes order. Any chaos at all.

VOICE. *(From "BOX.")* Oh, shame!

CHAIRMAN MAO. Everything reactionary is the same: BU DAR BU DOW. *(He bows.)* If you don't hit it, it won't fall.

VOICE. *(From "BOX.")* Oh, shame!

CHAIRMAN MAO. *(Crosses D. L. outside box.)* This is also like sweeping the floor; as a rule, where the broom does not reach, the dust will not vanish of itself. Nor will the enemy perish of himself. The aggressive forces of U. S. imperialism will not step down from the stage of history of their own accord.

VOICE. *(From "BOX.")* The *Pope* warned us; *he* said so. There are no possessions, he said: so long as there are some with nothing we have no right to anything.

LONG-WINDED LADY. And the thing about boats is . . . you're burned . . . always . . . sun . . . haze . . . mist . . . deep night . . . all the spectrum down. Something. Burning.

CHAIRMAN MAO. *(In Chinese only.)* SIOR YUO BY LIEH DOE LRU TSE, BU DAR BU DOW

LONG-WINDED LADY. I sat up one night—oh, *before* it happened, though it doesn't matter—I mean, on a deck chair, like this, well away from the . . . possibility, but I sat up, and the moon was small, as it always is, on the northern route, well out, and I *bathed* in the night, and perhaps my daughter came up from dancing, though I don't think so . . . dancing down there with a man, well, young enough to be her husband.

OLD WOMAN.

For life was all before me, an' I was young and strong

And I worked the best that I could in tryin' to get along.

LONG-WINDED LADY. Though not. Not her husband.

CHAIRMAN MAO. Classes struggle, some classes triumph, others are eliminated. Such is history, such is the history of civilization for thousands of years. To interpret history from this viewpoint is historical materialism; standing in opposition to this viewpoint is historical idealism.

LONG-WINDED LADY. Though not. Not her husband.

CHAIRMAN MAO. *(Crosses D. R. outside of box.)* No political party can possibly lead a great revolutionary movement to victory unless it possesses revolutionary theory and a knowledge of history and has a profound grasp of the practical movement. *(Mao crosses U. L. rail opening, still outside box and rail.)*

LONG-WINDED LADY. And what I mean is: the burn; sitting in the dim

276

moon, with not the sound of the orchestra, but the *possible* sound of it
—therefore, I suppose, the same—the daughter, *my* daughter, and me
up here, up *there*—this one? No.—And being burned! In that—what I
said—all that seasons, all lights, all . . . well, one never returns from a
voyage the same.

VOICE. *(From "BOX.")* It's the *little* things, the *small* cracks.

OLD WOMAN.

Strange how much we think of our blessed little ones!—
I'd have died for my daughters, I'd have died for my sons;
And God he made that rule of love; but when we're old and gray,
I've noticed it sometimes somehow fails to work the other way.

LONG-WINDED LADY. His scrotum was large, *(Minister reacts.)* and not only
for a small man, I think, as I remember back—and am I surmising my
comparisons here, or telling you something loose about my past?
(Shrugs.)

CHAIRMAN MAO. *(Crosses inside railing at* R. *rail opening.)* Classes struggle;
some classes triumph, others are eliminated.

LONG-WINDED LADY. What does it matter now, this late?—large, and not
of the loose type, but thick, and leather, marvelously creased and like a
neat, full sack. And his penis, too; *(Minister reacts.)* of a neat proportion; ample, but not of that size which moves us so in retrospect . . .
or is supposed to. Circumcised . . . well, no, not really, but trained
back, *to* it; trained; like everything; nothing surprising, but always there,
and ample. Do I shock you? *(Minister looks at Long-Winded Lady.)*

VOICE. *(From "BOX.")* And if you go back to a partita . . .

CHAIRMAN MAO. *(Crosses* D. R. *inside rail and box.)* Such is history.

LONG-WINDED LADY. Do I *shock* you? *(Minister feigns unshock.)*

CHAIRMAN MAO. The commanders and fighters of the entire Chinese people's Liberation Army absolutely must not relax in the least their will to
fight; *(Mao steps outside box.)* any thinking that relaxes the will to fight
and belittles the enemy is wrong.

LONG-WINDED LADY. That is the last I have in mind. My intention is only
to remember.

OLD WOMAN.

Strange how much we think of our blessed little ones.

CHAIRMAN MAO. *(Crosses* D. L. *outside Box.)* I hold that it is bad as far as
we are concerned if a person, a political party, an army or a school is not

attacked by the enemy, for in that case it would definitely mean that we have sunk to the level of the enemy.

LONG-WINDED LADY. That is the last I have in mind.

CHAIRMAN MAO. It is good if we are attacked by the enemy, since it proves that we have drawn a clear line of demarcation between the enemy and ourselves. *(Mao goes to* L. *house box via* L. *aisle steps.)*

LONG-WINDED LADY. And the only desperate conflict is between what we long to remember and what we need to forget. No; that is not what I meant at all. Or . . . well, yes it may *be,* it may be on the nose.

OLD WOMAN.

Strange, another thing: when our boys an' girls was grown,

And when, exceptin' Charley, they'd left us there alone;

When John he nearer an' nearer come, an' dearer seemed to be,

The Lord of Hosts he come one day an' took him away from me.

LONG-WINDED LADY. But, wouldn't you think a death would relate to a life? . . . if not resemble it, *benefit* from it? Be *taught?* In *some* way? *I* would think.

OLD WOMAN.

The Lord of Hosts He come one day an' took him away from me.

CHAIRMAN MAO. *(Appears in* L. *box.)* Whoever sides with the revolutionary people is a revolutionary. Whoever sides with imperialism, feudalism and bureaucrat-capitalism is a counter-revolutionary.

LONG-WINDED LADY. Be *taught?* In *some* way?

CHAIRMAN MAO. Whoever sides with the revolutionary people in words only but acts otherwise is a revolutionary in speech.

LONG-WINDED LADY. *I* would think.

CHAIRMAN MAO. Whoever sides with the revolutionary people in deed as well as in word is a revolutionary in the full sense.

VOICE. *(From* "BOX.") And if you go back to a partita . . . Ahhh, what when it makes you cry!?

LONG-WINDED LADY. Savage how it can come, but, *(Mao exits box and goes to* R. *aisle.)* even more the preparations for it. No, not *for* it, but the— *yes!* they *must* be preparations for it, unless we're a morbid species— that, over the duck one day—the cold duck, with the gherkins and the lemon slices, notched like a cog . . . and the potato salad, warm if you're lucky, somebody suddenly says to your husband, when were you first aware of death, and he's only forty! God!, and he looks, and he says, without even that flick, that instant of an eye to me, odd you should ask me and I'm not even . . . well, I'm thirty-nine, and I've begun though if you'd asked me two weeks ago, though you wouldn't have, and we saw you then—and it was true; we had; two weeks ago; two weeks *before*. Is it something that suddenly shows and happens at once? At one moment? When we are aware of it we *show* we are? My God!, he said; I hadn't thought of dying since I was twelve, and, then again, *what*, sixteen, *what*, when I wrote those sonnets, all on the boatman, ironic, though. No! And the other man said, no: death, not dying.

VOICE. *(From* "BOX.") And if you go back to a partita . . . ahhh, what when it makes you cry!? Not from the beauty of it, but from solely that you cry from loss . . . so precious.

OLD WOMAN.
Still I was bound to struggle, an' never to cringe or fall—
Still I worked for Charley, for Charley was now my all;
And Charley was pretty good to me, with scarce a word or frown,
Till at last he went a-courtin', and brought a wife from town.

LONG-WINDED LADY. And another man there—an older man—someone my family had known, some man we had at parties and once I'd called Uncle, though he wasn't, some man I think my sister had been seen to go around with . . . someone who was around, said, God, you're young! You think of death when you're knee-high to a knicker, and dying when your cock gets decent for the first or second time, and I mean *in* something, not the handy-pan, but when you think of *dead!* And . . . he was drunk, though . . . what!—well, my lovely husband looked at him with a kind of glass, and he was a host then, and he said, with a quiet and staid that I think is—well, what I have loved him for, or what is of the substance of what I have loved him for . . . Straight In The Eye! When I was young I thought of death; and then, when I was older—or what I suddenly seemed to be . . . dying . . . with a kind of long ng: Ngggggggg, *(Mao in* R. *aisle, freezes.)* with a look at me, as if he could go on . . . and by God!, he slapped away, and it was the first?, the only gesture I was . . . have, been . . . even . . . momentarily . . . DON'T TALK LIKE THAT!! *(Pause. Mao crosses up* R. *aisle steps onto raked stage.)* Slapped away with his eyes and said, I am suddenly dying, to which he added an it would seem, and while everybody tried to talk about death he wanted to talk about dying.

CHAIRMAN MAO. We should support whatever the enemy opposes and oppose whatever the enemy supports.

BOX AND QUOTATIONS FROM CHAIRMAN MAO TSE-TUNG

VOICE. *(From* "BOX.") When art begins to hurt . . . when art begins to hurt it's time to look around. Yes it is.

LONG-WINDED LADY. But, of course, my sister's . . . savior, or whatever you would have it, wouldn't not be still. *He* went *on!* Death!, he said. And then he would lapse . . . for nothing, that I could see, beyond the curious pleasure of lapsing . . . Death! Yes, my husband would say, or *said* . . . *said* this particular time—and Bishop Berkeley will be wrong, he added, and no one understood, which is hardly surprising—I am suddenly dying, and I want no nonsense about it! Death? You stop about death, finally, seriously, when you're on to *dying.* Oh, come on!, the other said; death is the whole thing. He drank, as . . . my sister did, too; she died. I think they got in bed together—took a bottle with them, made love perhaps. CRAP! He said—my husband said—which quieted the room some . . . and me, too. He never did that. Death is nothing; there . . . there *is* no death. There is only life and dying.

CHAIRMAN MAO. *(Steps inside box, crosses* C.) A revolution is not a dinner party, or writing an essay, or painting a picture, or doing embroidery; it cannot be so refined, so leisurely and gentle, so temperate, kind, courteous, restrained and magnanimous. A revolution *(Mao sits* C. *on deck platform.)* is an insurrection, an act of violence by which one class overthrows another.

VOICE. *(From* "BOX.") When art begins to hurt, it's time to look around. Yes it is.

LONG-WINDED LADY. And *I,* he said, *I*—thumping his chest with the flat of his hand, slow, four, five times—*I* . . . am *dying.*

CHAIRMAN MAO. *(Rises, crosses* D. L. *outside box.)* After the enemies with guns have been wiped out, there will still be enemies without guns; they are bound to struggle desperately against us, and we must never regard these enemies lightly. If we do not now raise and understand the problem in this way, we shall commit the gravest mistakes. *(Mao bows, crosses* U. L. *to* U. L. *rail opening, hand on rail—outside of box.)*

VOICE. *(From* "BOX.") Yes it is.

LONG-WINDED LADY. And I, he said, I am dying. And this was long before he did. That night he told me: I was not aware of it before. We were resting . . . *before* sex—which we would not have that night; on our sides, his chest and groin against my back and buttocks, his hand between my breasts, the sand of his chin nice against my neck. I always knew I would die—I'm not a fool, but I had no sense of time; I didn't

280

know it would be so soon. I turned; I cupped my hands around his lovely scrotum and our breaths were together. But, it won't be for so very *long.* Yes, he said; I know. Silence, then added; but always shorter.

OLD WOMAN.

And Charley was pretty good to me, with scarce a word or frown,
Till at last he went a-courtin', and brought a wife from town.

CHAIRMAN MAO. *(Crosses above* L. *chair with hands on each end of chair head rest.)* People all over the world are now discussing whether or not a third world war will break out. On this question, too, we must be mentally prepared and do some analysis. We stand firmly for peace and against war. But if the Imperialists insist on unleashing another war, we should not be afraid of it.

LONG-WINDED LADY. And I, he said, I am dying.

CHAIRMAN MAO. The 1st World War was followed by the birth of the Soviet Union with a population of 200 million. The 2nd World War was followed by the emergence of the Socialist camp with a combined population of 900 million. If the Imperialists insist on launching a third world war, the whole structure of Imperialism will utterly collapse.

LONG-WINDED LADY. But what about *me!* Think about *me! (Mao crosses* U. L. *via inside box and goes above* U. C. *platform to* U. R., *outside box.)*

OLD WOMAN.

She was somewhat dressy, an' hadn't a pleasant smile—
She was quite conceity, and carried a heap o' style;
But if ever I tried to be friends, I did with her, I know;
But she was hard and proud, an' I couldn't make it go.

LONG-WINDED LADY. *ME!* WHAT ABOUT ME! *(Pause.)* That may give the impression of selfishness, but that is not how I intended it, nor how it is . . . at all. *I* . . . am *left. (Helpless shrug.)* He isn't. I'll not touch his dying again. It was long, and coarse, and ugly, and cruel, and tested the man beyond his . . . beyond *anyone's* capacities. I dare you! I dare anyone! Don't scream! Don't hate! I dare anyone. *(Softer.)* All that can be done is turn into a beast; the dumb thing's agony is none the less, but it doesn't understand *why,* the agony. And maybe that's enough comfort: not to know why. *(Pause, wistful, sad.)* But *I* am *left. (Mao crosses inside rail to* D. R., *inside box.)*

VOICE. *(From* "BOX.") And the beauty of art is order.

CHAIRMAN MAO. We desire peace. However, if imperialism insists on fighting a war, we will have no alternative but to take the firm resolution to fight to the finish before going ahead with our construction. *(Mao steps outside of box.)* If you are afraid of war day in day out, what will you do if war eventually comes? *(Mao crosses* D. L.*)* I have said that the East Wind is prevailing over the West Wind and war will not break out, and now I have added these explanations about the situation in case war should break out. Both possibilities have thus been taken into account. *(Mao bows, crosses* U. L. *outside rail to inside box at* L. *rail opening.)*

OLD WOMAN.

She was somewhat dressy, an' hadn't a pleasant smile;
She was quite conceity, an' carried a heap o' style,
But if ever I tried to be friends, I did with her, I know.
But she was hard and proud an' I couldn't make it go.

LONG-WINDED LADY. Besides, his dying is all over; all gone, but his *death* stays. He said death was not a concern, but he meant his own, and for *him.* No, well, he was right: *he* only had his dying. I have both. *(Sad chuckle.)* Oh, what a treasurehouse! I can exclude his dying; I can *not* think about it, except the times I want it back—the times I want, for myself, something less general than . . . tristesse. Though that is usually enough. And what for my daughter—*mine,* now, you'll notice; no longer our; what box have I got for her? Oh . . . the ephemera: jewelry, clothes, chairs . . . and the money: enough. Nothing solid, except my dying, my death, those two, and the thought of her own. The former, though.

VOICE. *(From* "BOX.") Not what is familiar, necessarily, but order.

CHAIRMAN MAO. *(Crosses* L. *of* L. *chair.)* War is the highest form of struggle for resolving contradictions, when they have developed to a certain stage, between classes, nations, states, or political groups, and it has existed ever since the emergence of private property and of classes. *(Mao sits on deck platform,* L. *of* L. *chair.)*

LONG-WINDED LADY. *(A little stentorian, disapproving.)* Where were *you* those six last months, the time I did *not* need you, with my hands full of less each day; my arms. *(Sad, almost humorous truth.)* If you send them away to save them from it, you resent their going and *they* want what they've missed. Well . . . I see as much of you as I'd like, my dear. Not as much as either of us should want, but as much as we do. Odd.

VOICE. *(From* "BOX.") . . . . and the beauty of art is order—not what is familiar, necessarily, but order . . . on its own terms.

Quotations from Chairman Mao Tse-Tung

OLD WOMAN.
 She had an edication, an' that was good for her;
 But when she twitted me on mine, 'twas carryin' things too fur;
 An' I told her once, 'fore company (an' it almost made her sick),
 That I never swallowed a grammar, or 'et a 'rithmetic.
LONG-WINDED LADY. *(New subject.)* And there I was! Falling!
CHAIRMAN MAO. *(Rises, crosses up* L. *aisle steps through* U. L. *rail opening outside box.)* Revolutionary war is an antitoxin which not only eliminates the enemy's poison but also purges us of our own filth. *(Mao goes up* L. *aisle to* R. *house box.)*
VOICE. *(From* "BOX.")That is the thing about music. That is why we cannot listen any more. *(Pause.)* Because we cry.
LONG-WINDED LADY. We see each other less, she and I—my daughter—as I said, and most often on boats: something about the air; the burning. She was with me when I fell. Well: on *board.* When they . . . hauled me in—oh, what a spectacle *that* was!—there she was, looking on. Not near where I came in, exactly, but some way off: nearer where I'd done it; where it had been done. Red hair flying—not natural, a kind of purple to it, but stunning; quite stunning—cigarette; *always,* the French one. Nails the color of blood—artery blood, darker than the vein. The things one knows! Looking on, not quite a smile, not quite not. I looked up, dolphins resting on my belly, seaweed-twined, like what's-his-name, or hers . . . I'll bet all you'll say is Honestly, Mother! *(Slight pause.)* And when she came to my cabin, after the doctor, and the welcome brandy, and the sedative, the unnecessary sedative . . . there she stood for a moment, cigarette still on, in her mouth, I think. She looked for a moment. Honestly, Mother!, she said laughing a little in her throat, *at* it, humor *at* it. Honestly, Mother! And then off she went.
VOICE. *(From* "BOX.")That is why we cannot listen anymore.
OLD WOMAN.
 So 'twas only a few days before the thing was done—
 They was a family of themselves, and I another one;
 And a very little cottage one family will do,
 But I never have seen a house that was big enough for two.
VOICE. *(From* "BOX.")Because we cry.
LONG-WINDED LADY. Where is she now. This trip. Mexico. You'd better chain yourself to the chair, she said to me, later, the day after. You *will*

283

go on deck; put a long cord on yourself. It's not a usual occurrence, I told her; not even for me. No, but you're inventive, she said.

VOICE. *(From* "BOX.") Look! More birds! Another . . . sky of them.

CHAIRMAN MAO. *(Appears in* R. *house box.)* History shows that wars are divided into two kinds, just and unjust. We Communists oppose all unjust wars that impede progress, but we do not oppose progressive, just wars. Not only do we Communists not oppose just wars, we actively participate in them. All wars that are progressive are just, and all wars that impede progress are unjust. The way to oppose a war of this kind is to do everything possible to prevent it before it breaks out and, once it breaks out, to oppose war with war, to oppose unjust war with just war, whenever possible.

OLD WOMAN.
But I have never seen a house that was big enough for two.

LONG-WINDED LADY. *(Mao exits* R. *house box and goes to* L. *house box via mezzanine.)* Mexico; still; probably. I'm in Mexico, in case you care, she said. Four A.M. First words, no hello, Mother, or sorry to wake you up if you're sleeping, if you're not lying there, face all smeared, hair in your net, bed jacket still on, propped up, lights out wondering whether you're asleep or not. No; not that. Not even that. I'm in Mexico, in case you care.

VOICE. *(From* "BOX.") Look! More birds! Another . . . sky of them.

LONG-WINDED LADY. Oh. Well . . . how very nice. I'm in Mexico, in case you care. I'm with two boys. Sort of defiant. Oh? Well, how nice. Add 'em up and they're just my age; one's twenty and the other's not quite that. Still defiant. Well, that's . . . she lies a bit; she's forty-two. That's very *nice,* dear. They're both Mexican. She sounded almost ugly, over the phone, in the dark. Well . . . they're both uncircumcised, she said, and then waited. When this happens . . . when this happens, she will wait—not those very words, but something she hopes to affect me with, hurt me, shock, perhaps, make me feel less . . . well, I was going to say happy, but I am seldom that: not any more . . . make me feel less even. She'll wait, and I can hear her waiting, to see if I put the phone down. If I do *not,* after a certain time, of the silence, then she *will.* I put it down gently, when I do. She slams. This time, *I* put it down; gently. I've never known which makes her happier . . . if either does, though I suppose one must. Whether she is happier if she makes me do it, or if I pause too long, and she can. I would like to ask her, but it is not the sort of question one can ask a forty-two-year-old woman . . . daughter or no.

VOICE. *(From* "BOX.") It's only when you can't come back; when you get in some distant key; that when you say, the tonic!, the tonic! and they say, what is *that?* It's *then.*

OLD WOMAN.

An' I never could speak to suit her, never could please her eye,
An' it made me independent, an' then I didn't try;
But I was terribly staggered, an' felt it like a blow,
When Charley turned ag'in me, an' told me I could go.

LONG-WINDED LADY. I *do wish* sometimes . . . just in general, I mean . . . I *do wish* sometimes . . .

CHAIRMAN MAO. *(Appears in* L. *house box.)* Some people ridicule us as advocates of the "Omnipotence of war." Yes, we are advocates of the omnipotence of revolutionary war; that is good, not bad, it is Marxist.

LONG-WINDED LADY. Just in general, I mean . . . I *do wish* sometimes . . .

CHAIRMAN MAO. Experience in the class struggle in the era of imperialism teaches us that—LRU TSEE SHIH LEE SHIH CHUNG CHIENG KUNG. *(He bows.)* It is only by the power of the gun that the working class and the laboring masses can defeat the armed bourgeoisie and landlords; in this sense we may say that only with guns can the whole world be transformed.

LONG-WINDED LADY. I suppose that's why *(Mao exits* L. *house box and goes to aisle,* L.*)* I came this time . . . the Mexicans; the boys. Put an ocean between. It's not as far as a death, but . . . still.

OLD WOMAN. Over the Hill to the Poor-house, by Will Carlton.

LONG-WINDED LADY. I remember, I walked to the thing, the railing. To look over. Why, I don't *know:* water never changes, the Atlantic, *this* latitude. But if you've been sitting in a chair, that is what you *do:* you put down the Trollope or James or sometimes Hardy, throw off the rug, *(Long-Winded Lady rises.)* and, slightly unsteady from suddenly up from horizontal . . . *(Long-Winded Lady crosses to* D. L. *rail.)* you walk to the thing . . . the railing. It's that simple. You look for a bit, smell, sniff, really; you look down to make sure it's moving, and then you think shall you take a turn, and you usually do not; you go back to your rug and your book. Or *not* to your book, but to your *rug,* which you

285

pull up like covers and pretend to go to sleep. *(Long-Winded Lady to above L. chair.)* The one thing you do *not* do is fall off the ship!

VOICE. *(From "BOX.")* There! More! A thousand, and one below them, moving fast in the opposite way!

OLD WOMAN.

I went to live with Susan, but Susan's house was small,
And she was always a-hintin' how snug it was for us all;
And what with her husband's sisters, and what with child'rn three,
'Twas easy to discover that there wasn't room for me.

LONG-WINDED LADY. *Here's* a curious thing! Whenever I'm in an aeroplane—which I am not, often, for I like to choose my company: not that I'm a snob, heavens!, it's my daughter who will not see *me,* or, rather, not often. *(Long-Winded Lady crosses R. of L. chair and sits L. chair.)* Not that I am a snob, but I feel that travel in rooms is so much nicer: boats and trains, where one can get away and then out again; people are nicer when you come upon them around corners, or opening doors. But whenever I'm up there, closed in, strapped to my seat, with all the people around, and the double windows, those tiny windows, and the great heavy door, bolted from the outside, probably, even when I'm plumped down in an inside seat—or aisle, as they call them—*then!* It's then that I feel that I'm going to fall out. Fall right out of the aeroplane! I don't know how I could possibly do it—even through the most . . . reprehensible carelessness. I probably couldn't, even if I felt I had to. But I'm sure I will! Always! Though, naturally, I never do.

VOICE. *(From "BOX.")* What was it used to frighten me?

CHAIRMAN MAO. *(Crosses top of L. aisle steps to D. L. rail corner.)* Revolutions and revolutionary wars are inevitable in class society and without them, it is impossible to accomplish any leap in social development and to overthrow the reactionary ruling classes and therefore impossible for the people to win political power. *(Mao leans on rail outside box.)*

OLD WOMAN.

'Twas easy to discover that there wasn't room for me.

LONG-WINDED LADY. Coarse, and ugly, and long, and cruel. That dying. My lovely husband. *(Small pause.)* But I said I wouldn't dwell on that. *(Long-Winded Lady rises, crosses L. of L. chair.)*

OLD WOMAN.

An' then I went to Thomas, the oldest son I've got,
For Thomas's buildings'd cover the half of an acre lot;

But all the child'rn was on me—I couldn't stand their sauce—
And Thomas said I needn't think I was comin' there to boss.

LONG-WINDED LADY. Well! What can we say of an aging lady walks bright as you please from her rug and her Trollope or her James or sometimes her Hardy right up to the thing . . . the railing; *(Long-Winded Lady crosses* D. L. *rail, next to Mao.)* walks right up, puts her fingers, rings and all, right on the varnished wood, sniffs . . . that air!, feels the railing, hard as wood, knows it's there—it *is* there—and suddenly, as sudden and sure as what you've always known and never quite admitted to yourself, it is *not* there; there is no railing, no wood, no metal, no buoy-life-thing saying S.S. or H.M.S. whatever, no . . . nothing! Nothing at all! The fingers are claws, and the varnish they rubbed against is air? And suddenly one is . . . well, what would you expect?! One is suddenly leaning on one's imagination—which is poor support, let me tell you . . . at least in *my* case—leaning on that, which doesn't last for long, and over one goes! *(Minister starts to rise to help Long-Winded Lady.)*

VOICE. *(From* "BOX." *Mao crosses to* L. *of Long-Winded Lady, inside box.)* . . . a thousand miles from the sea. Land-locked, never been, and yet the sea sounds . . .

CHAIRMAN MAO. War, this monster of mutual slaughter among men, will be finally eliminated by the progress of human society, and in the not too distant future, too.

VOICE. *(From* "BOX.")* A thousand miles from the sea. Land-locked.

CHAIRMAN MAO. But there is only one way to eliminate it and that is to oppose war with war, *(Mao steps outside box to* D. R.) to oppose counter-revolutionary war with revolutionary war, to oppose national counter-revolutionary war with national revolutionary war, and to oppose counter-revolutionary class war with revolutionary class war.

VOICE. *(From* "BOX.")* Never been, and yet the sea sounds.

CHAIRMAN MAO. When human society advances to the point where classes and states are eliminated, there will be no more wars, counter-revolutionary or revolutionary, unjust or just. That will be the era of perpetual peace for mankind. *(Mao crosses* D. R. *rail end, outside of Box.)*

OLD WOMAN.
But all the child'rn was on me . . . I couldn't stand their sauce
And Thomas said I needn't think I was coming there to boss.

LONG-WINDED LADY. *(Minister rises, crosses* D. R. *end of* R. *chair.)* Over one goes, and it's a long way, let me tell you! No falling *up*, no, siree; or out! Straight down! As straight as anything! Plummet! Plut! Well, plummet for sure, plut conjectural. I wonder why I didn't kill myself. Exactly what my daughter said: I wonder why you didn't kill yourself. Though her reading was special. Had a note of derision to it.

OLD WOMAN.
An' then I wrote to Rebecca, my girl who lives out West,
And to Isaac, not far from her—some twenty miles at best;
And one of 'em said 'twas too warm there for any one so old,
And t'other had an opinion the climate was too cold.

VOICE. *(From "BOX.")* Well, we give up something for something.

LONG-WINDED LADY. I did *not* kill myself, as *I* see it, through a trick of the wind, or chance, or because I am bottom heavy. Straight down like a drop of shot! Except. Except, at the very end, a sort of curving, a kind of arc, which sent me gently into a rising wave, or throw-off from the boat, angling into it just properly, sliding in so that it felt like falling on leaves—the pile of autumn leaves we would make, or our brother would, and jump on, like a feather bed. A gust of wind must have done that. Well . . . something did.

CHAIRMAN MAO. *(Steps inside box, crosses* D. L. C.*)* "War is the continuation of politics." In this sense war is politics and war itself is a political action; since ancient times there has never been a war that did not have a political character. "War is the continuation of politics by other means."

VOICE. *(From "BOX.")* Something for something.

CHAIRMAN MAO. *(Sits* D. L. C. *deck platform.)* It can therefore be said that politics is war without bloodshed while war is politics with bloodshed.

VOICE. *(From "BOX.")* When art hurts. That is what to remember.

LONG-WINDED LADY. I try to recall if I recall the falling, *(Minister crosses below foot of* R. *chair.)* but I'm never sure, I think I do, and then I think I have not. It was so like being awake and asleep . . . at the same time. But I *do* recall being in the water. Heavens! What a sight! *I* must have been, too, but I mean what I *saw:* The sliding by of the ship, green foam in the mouth—kind of exciting—green foam as the wake went by. Lucky you missed the propellers, they said afterwards. Well, yes; lucky.

CHAIRMAN MAO. Without armed struggle neither the proletariat, nor the people, nor the Communist Party *(Mao rises, steps outside of box, crosses* D. L.*)* would have any standing at all in China and it would be

288

impossible for the revolution to triumph. *(Mao bows and crosses* U. L. *to above* U. C. *platform to* U. R., *still outside of Box, to* R. *of* R. *chair.)*

OLD WOMAN.

And one of 'em said 'twas too warm there for anyone so old
And t'other had an opinion the climate was too cold.

LONG-WINDED LADY. And sitting there! Sitting there in the water, bouncing around like a carton, screaming a little, not to call attention or anything like that, but because of the fright, and the surprise, and the cold, I suppose; and . . . well . . . because it was all sort of thrilling: watching the boat move off. My goodness, boats move fast! Something you don't notice till you're off one.

VOICE. *(From* "BOX.") Then the corruption is complete.

OLD WOMAN.

So they have shirked and slighted me, an' shifted me about—
So they have well-nigh soured me, an' wore my old heart out;
But still I've borne up pretty well, an' wasn't much put down,
Till Charley went to the poor-master, an' put me on the town.

LONG-WINDED LADY. *(Crosses to* L. *chair, sits. Minister crosses* L. *of* R. *chair.)* And then . . . and then horns, and tooting, and all sorts of commotion and people running around and pointing . . . *(Some disappointment.)* and then the boats out, the launches, and dragging me in and hauling me up—in front of all those people!—and then the brandy and the nurse and the sedative . . . and all the rest. *(Pause.)* I lost my cashmere sweater . . . and one shoe. *(Minister crosses to Long-Winded Lady, tucks blanket around her feet.)*

CHAIRMAN MAO. *(Crosses* D. R. *and takes two steps* L., *still outside box.)* We are advocates of the abolition of war; we do not want war; but war can only be abolished through war, and in order to get rid of the gun it is necessary to take up the gun.

LONG-WINDED LADY. You're a very lucky woman, I remember the chief purser saying to me, the next day; I was still groggy. You're a very lucky woman. Yes, I am, I said; yes; I am. *(Minister crosses above* R. *chair.)*

CHAIRMAN MAO. Every Communist must grasp the truth—LRU TSEE SHIH LEE SHIH CHUNG CHIENG KUNG LI CHAN TSEND CHIOU LIE DE. *(He bows.)* "Political power grows out of the barrel of a gun."

VOICE. *(From* "BOX.") Nothing belongs.

OLD WOMAN. *(Mao crosses* L. *inside of box to* U. L. *and sits* U. L. *rail.)*
But still I've borne up pretty well, an' wasn't much put down
'Till Charley went to the poor-master, an' put me on the town.

LONG-WINDED LADY. Then, of course, there were the questions. People don't fall off of ocean liners very often. No, I don't suppose they do. Broad daylight and all, people on deck. *(Minister crosses behind head piece of* R. *chair.)* No; no; I don't imagine so. Do you think you slipped? Surely not! Dry as paint. Have you . . . do you cross often? Oh, heavens, yes! I've done it for years. Have you . . . has this sort of thing ever happened before? What do you take me for!? I'm lucky I'm back from this one, I suppose. Then—gratuitously, and a little peevish, I'm afraid—and I shall cross many times more! And I have—many times, and it's not happened again. Well, do you . . . do you think maybe you were—wincing some here: them; not me—you were helped? Helped? What do you mean? Well . . . aided. What do you mean *pushed?* Bedside nod. Yes. A laugh from me; a young girl laugh: hand to my throat, head back. Pushed! Good gracious, no! I had been *reading.* What were you reading—which struck me as beside the point and rather touching. Trollope, I said, which wasn't true, for that had been the day before, but I said it anyway. *(Some wonder.)* They didn't know who Trollope was. Well, *there's* a life for you!

OLD WOMAN.
Over the hill to the poor-house— *(She rises, takes suitcase, purse and coat, crosses* D. L. *inside rail.)* my child'rn dear, good-by!
Many a night I've watched you when only God was nigh;
And God'll judge between us; but I will al'ays pray
That you shall never suffer the half I do today.
(Old Woman sits on suitcase D. L., *inside rail.)*

VOICE. *(From "BOX.")* Look; more of them; a black net . . . skimming. *(Pause.)* And just one . . . moving beneath . . . in the opposite way.

LONG-WINDED LADY. Isn't that *some*thing? You lead a whole life; you write books, or you do not; you strive to do good, and succeed, sometimes, amongst the bad—the bad never through design, but through error, or chance, or lack of a chemical somewhere, in the head, or cowardice, maybe—you raise a family and live with people, see them *through* it; you write books, or you do not, and you say your name is Trollope . . . or whatever it may be, no matter what, you say your name . . . and they have . . . never . . . heard of it. That *is* a life for you.

VOICE. *(From "BOX." Minister crosses rail R. of R. chair.)* Milk.

CHAIRMAN MAO. *(Crosses onto U. C. platform.)* People of the world, unite and defeat the U. S. aggressors and all their running dog! People of the world, be courageous, dare to fight, defy difficulties and advance wave upon wave. Then the whole world will belong to the people. Monsters of all kinds shall be destroyed.

OLD WOMAN. Over the Hill to the Poorhouse, by Will Carlton.

VOICE. *(From "BOX.")* Milk.

LONG-WINDED LADY. Is there any chance, do you think. . . . Hm? . . . I say, is there any chance, do you think, well, I don't know how to put it . . . do you think . . . do you think you may have done it on purpose? Some silence. I look at them, my gray eyes gently wide, misting a little in the edges, all innocence and hurt: *true* innocence; *true* hurt. That I may have done it on purpose? Yes; thrown yourself off. *(Some bewilderment and hurt.)* . . . Me?

VOICE. *(From "BOX.")* If only they had told us . . . clearly.

CHAIRMAN MAO. People of the world, unite and defeat the U. S. aggressors and all their running dogs.

VOICE. *(From "BOX.")* If only they had told us.

CHAIRMAN MAO. LRU TSEE SHIH LEE SHIH CHUNG CHIENG KUNG LI CHAN TSEND CHIOU LIE DE.

LONG-WINDED LADY. Well; yes; I'm sorry. Thrown myself off? A clearing of the throat. Yes. Tried to kill yourself. *(A sad little half-laugh.)* Good heavens, no; *I* have nothing to die for.

(Actors in same positions as opening.)

VOICE. *(From "BOX." Coda reprise.)* If only they had *told* us! Clearly! When it was clear that we were not only corrupt—for there is nothing that is not, or little—but corrupt to the selfishness, to the corruption that we should die to keep it . . . go under rather than . . . *(Three second silence. Sigh.)* When art begins to hurt . . . when art begins to hurt it's time to look around. Yes it is *(Three second silence.)* Yes it is. *(Three second silence.)* So much . . . flies. A billion birds at once, black net skimming the ocean . . . *(Two second silence.)* When the beauty of it reminds us of *loss*. Instead of the attainable. When it tells us what we cannot have . . . well, then . . . it no longer relates . . . *does* it. That is the thing about music. That is why we cannot listen any more. *(Pause.)* Because we cry. *(Five second silence.)* What was it used to frighten me? Bell buoys and sea gulls; the *sound* of them, at night, in

291

a fog, when I was very young. *(A little laugh.)* Before I had ever seen them, before I had heard them. *(Some wonder.)* But I knew what they *were* . . . a thousand miles from the sea. Land-locked, never been, and yet the sea sounds . . . *(Three second silence.)* But it *couldn't* have been fog, not the sea-fog. Not way back *there.* It was the memory of it, to be seen and proved later. The memory of what we have not known. *(Three second silence.)* And even that can happen here, I guess. But unprovable. Ahhhhh. That makes the difference, does it *not.* Nothing can seep here except the memory of what I'll not prove. *(Two second silence. Sigh.)* Well, we give up something for something. *(Three second silence.)* When art hurts. That is what to remember. *(Two second silence.)* What to look for. Then the corruption . . . *(Three second silence.)* Then the corruption is complete. *(Five second silence. The sound of bell buoys and sea gulls begins, faintly, growing, but never very loud.)* Nothing belongs. *(Three second silence. Great sadness.)* Look; more of them; a black net . . . skimming. *(Pause.)* And just one . . . moving beneath . . . in the opposite way. *(Three second silence. Very sad, supplicating.)* Box. *(Silence, except for the sound of bell buoys and sea gulls. Slow fading sound of bell buoys and sea gulls. The light fades in silence.)*

END

Monologue of the Long-Winded Lady

Well, I daresay it's hard to comprehend . . . I mean, *I* . . . at this remove . . . *I* find it hard to, well, not comprehend, but believe, or accept, if you will. So long ago! So much since. But there it was: splash!

Well, not splash exactly, more sound than that, more of a . . . *(Little laugh.)* no, I can't do that—imitate it; for I only *imagine* . . . what it must have sounded like to . . . an onlooker. An overseer. Not to *me*, Lord knows! Being *in* it. Or *doing* it, rather.

No. To an onlooker it would not have been splash, but a sort of . . . different sound, and I try to imagine what it would have been like—*sounded* like—had *I* not been . . . well, so involved, if you know what I mean. And *I* was so *busy* . . . I didn't pay attention, or, if I *did* . . . that part of it doesn't re . . . recall itself. Retain is the, is what I started.

And so high!

I'd never imagined it—naturally! It's not what one *would*. The *echo* of a sound, or the remembering of a sound having happened. No; that's not right, either. For *them*, for the theoretical . . . onwatcher. *(Pause.)* Plut! Yes!

Exactly: Plut!

And then, with the wind, and the roar of the engines and the sea . . . maybe not even that, not even . . . plut! But, some slight sound, or . . . or the creation of one! The invention! What is that about consequence? Oh, *you* know! Everything has its consequence? Or, every action a reaction; something. But maybe nothing at all, no real sound, but the invention of one. I mean, if you see it happening . . . the, the thing . . . landing, and the spray, the sea parting, as it were . . . well, then . . . one makes a sound . . . in one's mind . . . to, to correspond to the sound one . . . didn't . . . hear. Yes?

Yes. I think so.

I remember once when I broke my finger, or my thumb, and I was very little, and they said, you've broken your thumb, look, you've broken your thumb, and there wasn't any pain—not *yet*, not for that first moment, just . . . just an absence of sensation—an interesting lack of anything . . . when they said it again, look, you've broken your thumb, not only did I scream, as if some knife had ripped my leg down, from hip to ankle, all through the sinews laying bare the bone . . . not only did I scream as only children can—adults do it differently: there's an animal protest there, a revenge, something . . . something other—not only did I scream, but I manufactured the pain. Right then! Before the hurt could have come through, I made it happen. Well; we do that.

Yes; we do that: we make it happen a little before it need. *(Pause.)* And so it might have been with someone watching—and maybe even to those who *were*. Who *were* watching. And there were, or I'd not be here. *(Pause.)* I daresay. *(Pause.)* The sound manufactured. Lord knows, if *I* had been among the . . . nonparticipators I should have done it, too; no doubt. Plup! Plut! Whichever. I'm sure I should have . . . if I'd seen it all the *way* now. I mean, if I'd caught just the final instant, without time to relate the event to its environment—the thing happening to the thing happened *to* . . . then I doubt I would have. Nor would anyone . . . or most.

But just imagine what it must have been like . . . to be one of the . . . watchers! How . . . well, is marvelous the proper word, I wonder? Yes, I suspect. I mean, how often? It's not too common an occurrence, to have it . . . plummet by! One is standing there, admiring, or faintly sick, or just plain throwing up, but how often is one *there*. *Ever!* Well, inveterates; yes; but for the casual crosser . . . not too often, and one would have to be exactly in place, at exactly the proper time, and alert! Very alert in . . . by nature, and able to relate what one sees to what is happening. Oh, I remember the time the taxi went berserk and killed those people!

Well, it didn't go berserk, of course, for it *is* a machine: a taxi. Nor did the driver . . . go berserk. Out of control, though! The driver lost, and out of control it went! *Up* on the sidewalk, bowling them down like whatchamacallems, then crash! into the store front, the splash of glass and then on fire. How many dead? Ten? Twelve? And I had just come out with the crullers.

The bag of crullers, and a smile on my face for everyone liked them so, and there it was! Careen . . . and dying . . . and all that glass. And I remember thinking: it's a movie! They're shooting some scenes right here in the street. *(Pause.)* They weren't, of course. It was real death, and real glass, and the fire, and the . . . people crying, and the crowds, and the smoke. Oh, it was real enough, but it took me time to know it. The mind does that.

They're making a movie! What a nice conclusion, coming out with the crullers, still hot, with a separate little bag for the powdered sugar, of course it's a movie! One doesn't come out like that to carnage! Dead

people and the wounded; glass all over and . . . confusion. One . . .
concludes things—and if those things and what is really there don't . . .
are not the *same* . . . well! . . . it would usually be better if it were so.
The mind does that: it helps.

The mind does that.

So; if one happened to be there, by the rail, and not too discomfited,
not in the sense of utterly defeated—though that would be more than
enough—but in the sense of confused, or preoccupied, if one were not too
preoccupied, and plummet! it went by! one, the mind, might be able to
take it in, say: ah! there! there she goes!—or he; and manufacture the
appropriate sound. But only then. And how many are expecting it!? Well,
I am. *Now.* There isn't a rail I stand by, especially in full sun—my conditioning—that I'm not . . . already shuddering . . . *and* ready to manufacture the sound. *(Little laugh.)* Though not the sound *I* knew, for I was
hardly thinking—a bit busy—but the sound I imagine someone else would
have manufactured had *he* been there when I . . . WOOOOSSSSH!
PLUT! *(Little laugh.)*

You never know until it's happened to you.

Do you.

Do you.

Falling! My goodness. What was it when one was little? That when you
fell when you were dreaming you always woke up before you landed, or
else you wouldn't and you'd be dead. That was it, I think. And I never
wondered why, I merely took it for . . . well, I *accepted* it. And, of
course, I kept trying to dream of falling after I'd heard it . . . tried so
hard! . . . and *couldn't,* naturally. Well, if we control the unconscious,
we're either mad, or . . . dull-witted.

I think I dreamt of falling again, though, but after I'd stopped trying to,
but I don't think I landed. Not like what I've been telling you, though
that was more seaing than landing, you might say . . . if you like a pun.
Once, though! Once I dreamt of falling straight up . . . or out, all in
reverse, like the projector running backwards, what they used to do, for
fun, in the shorts. *(Some wonder.)* Falling . . . *up!*

Not rising, you understand: a definite . . . falling, but . . . up!

Did I call them crullers? Well, I should *not* have; for they were not even
doughnuts, but the centers . . . hearts is what they called them: the
center dough pinched out, or cut with a cutter and done like the rest, but
solid, the size of a bantam egg, but round. Oh, they were good, and crisp,

and all like air inside; hot, and you'd dip them in the confectioners' sugar. One could be quite a pig; everyone was; they were so good! You find them here and about still. Some, but not often.

My husband used to say, don't leave her next to anything precipitous; there's bound to be a do; something will drop, or fall, her purse, her*self*. And, so, he had people be careful of me. Not that I'm fond of heights. I'm not unfriendly toward them—all that falling—but I have no . . . great affection. *(Little pause.)* Depths even less.

All that falling.

And it became something of a joke, I suppose . . . I suppose. Where is she? Watch her! Don't let her near the edge! She'll occasion a do!

He was a small man, almost a miniature—not that I'm much of a giraffe. Small . . . and precise . . . and contained . . . quiet strength. The large emotions . . . *yes*, without them, what?—all there, and full size, full scope, but when they came, not a . . . a spattering, but a single shaft, a careful aim. No waste; as intense as anyone, but precise. Some people said he was cold; or cruel. But he was merely accurate. Big people ooze, and scatter, and knock over things nearby. They give the impression —the illusion—of openness, of spaces through which things pass—excuses, by-passings. But small, and precise, and accurate don't . . . doesn't allow for that . . . for that *impression*. He wasn't cruel at all.

Or cold. Neat; accurate; precise. In everything. All our marriage. Except dying. Except that . . . dreadful death.

That dreadful death—all that he was not: large, random, inaccurate—in the sense of offshoots from the major objective. A spattering cancer! Spread enough and you're bound to kill *some*thing. Don't aim! Engulf! Imprecision!

Don't let her near the edge!

Don't let her near the edge.

But I hadn't thought I *was*. Well, yes, of course I *was* . . . but guarded . . . well guarded. Or, so I *thought*. It doesn't happen terribly often . . . by indirection. *(Pause.)* Does it?

Not death: I didn't mean death. I meant . . . falling off. *That* isn't done too often by indirection. Is it? Death! Well, my God, of course; yes. Almost always, 'less you take the notion of the collective . . . thing, which *must allow* for it, take it into account: I mean, if all the rest is part of a . . . predetermination, or something that has already happened—in principle . . . well, under *those* conditions *any* chaos becomes order. Any chaos at all.

And the thing about boats is . . . you're burned . . . always . . . sun . . . haze . . . mist . . . deep night . . . all the spectrum down. Something. Burning.

I sat up one night—oh, *before* it happened, though it doesn't matter—I mean, on a deck chair, like this, well away from the . . . possibility, but I sat up, and the moon was small, as it always is, on the northern route, well out, and I *bathed* in the night, and perhaps my daughter came up from dancing, though I don't think so . . . dancing down there with a man, well, young enough to be her husband.

Though not. Not her husband.

Though not. Not her husband.

And what I mean is: the burn; sitting in the dim moon, with not the sound of the orchestra but the *possible* sound of it—therefore, I suppose, the same—the daughter, *my* daughter, and me up here, up *there*—*this* one? No.—and being burned: In that—what I said—that all seasons, all lights, all . . . well, one never returns from a voyage the same.

His scrotum was large, and not only for a small man, I think, as I remember back—and am I surmising my comparisons here, or telling you something loose about my past?

(Shrugs.) What does it matter now, this late?—large, and not of the loose type, but thick, and leather, marvelously creased and like a neat, full sack. And his penis, too; of a neat proportion; ample, but not of that proportion which moves us so in retrospect . . . or is supposed to. Circumcised . . . well, no, not really, but trained back, *to* it; trained; like everything; nothing surprising, but always there, and ample. Do I *shock* you?

Do I *shock* you?

That is the last I have in mind. My intention is only to remember.

That is the last I have in mind.

And the only desperate conflict is between what we long to remember and what we need to forget. No: that is not what I meant at all. Or . . . well, yes it may *be:* it may be on the nose.

But, wouldn't you think a death would relate to a life? . . . if not resemble it, *benefit* from it? Be *taught?* In *some* way? I would think.

Be *taught?* In *some* way?

I would think.

Savage how it can come, but, even more the preparations for it. No, not *for* it, but the—*yes!* They *must* be preparations for it, unless we're a morbid species—that, over the duck one day—the cold duck, with the gherkins and the lemon slices, notched like a cog . . . and the potato salad, warm if you're lucky, somebody suddenly says to your husband, when were you first aware of death, and he's only forty! God! and he looks, and he says, without even that flick, that instant of an eye to me, odd you should ask me and I'm not even . . . well, I'm thirty-nine, and I've be-gun though if you'd asked me two weeks ago, though you wouldn't have, and we saw you then—and it was true; we had; two weeks ago; two weeks *before.* Is it something that suddenly shows and happens at once? At one moment? When we are *aware* of it we *show* we are? My God!, he said; I hadn't thought of dying since I was twelve, and, then again, *what,* sixteen, *what,* when I wrote those sonnets, all on the boatman, ironic, though. No! And the other one said, no: death, not dying.

And another man there—an older man—someone my family had known, some man we had at parties and once I'd called Uncle, though he wasn't, some man I think my sister had been seen to go around with . . . someone who was around, said, God, you're young! You think of death when you're knee-high to a knicker, and dying when your cock gets decent for the first or second time, and I mean *in* something, not the handy-pan, but when you think of *dead!* And—he was drunk, though . . . what!— well, my lovely husband looked at him with a kind of glass, and he was a host then, and he said, with a quiet and staid that I think is—well, what I have loved him for, or what is of the substance of what I have loved him for . . . Straight In The Eye! When I was young I thought of death; and then, when I was older—or what I suddenly seem to be . . . dying . . . with a kind of long ng: nggggg, with a look at me, as if could he go on . . . and by God!, he slapped away, and it was the first?, the only gesture I was . . . have, been . . . even . . . momentarily . . . DON'T TALK LIKE THAT! *(Pause.)* Slapped away with his eyes and said, I am suddenly dying, to which he added an it would seem, and while everybody tried to talk about death he wanted to talk about dying.

But, of course, my sister's . . . savior, or whatever you would have it, wouldn't not be still. *He* went *on!* Death!, he said. And then he would lapse . . . for nothing, that I could see, beyond the curious pleasure of lapsing . . . Death! Yes, my husband would say, or *said* . . . *said* this particular time . . . and Bishop Berkeley will be wrong, he added, and no one understood, which is hardly surprising . . . I am suddenly dying, and I want no nonsense about it! Death? You stop about death, finally, seriously, when you're on to *dying.* Oh, come on!, the other said; death is the whole thing. He drank, as . . . my sister did, too; she died. I think they got in bed together—took a bottle with them, made love perhaps. Crap! He said—my husband said—which quieted the room some . . . and me, too. He never did that. Death is nothing; there . . . there *is* no death. There is only life and dying.

And *I,* he said, *I*—thumping his chest with the flat of his hand, slow, four, five times—*I* . . . am *dying.*

And I, he said, I am dying. And this was long before he did. That night he told me: I was not aware of it before. We were resting . . . *before* sex —which we would not have that night; on our sides, his chest and groin against my back and buttocks, his hand between my breasts, the sand of his chin nice against my neck. I always knew I would die—I'm not a fool, but I had no sense of time; I didn't know it would be so soon. I turned; I cupped my hand around his lovely scrotum and our breaths were together. But, it won't be for so very *long.* Yes; he said; I know. Silence, then added; but always shorter.

And I, he said, I am dying.

But what about *me!* Think about *me!*

ME! WHAT ABOUT ME! *(Pause.)* That may give the appearance of selfishness, but that is not how I intended it, nor how it is . . . at all. *I* . . . am *left. (Helpless shrug.)* He isn't. I'll not touch his dying again. It was long, and coarse, and ugly, and cruel, and tested the man beyond his . . . beyond *anyone's* capacities. I dare you! I dare anyone! Don't scream! Don't hate! I dare anyone. *(Softer.)* All that can be done is turn into a beast; the dumb thing's agony is none the less, but it doesn't understand *why,* the agony. And maybe that's enough comfort: not to know why. *(Pause, wistful, sad.)* But *I* am *left.*

Besides, his dying is all over; all gone, but his *death* stays. He said death was not a concern, but he meant his own, and for *him.* No, well, he was right: *he* only had his dying. I have both. *(Sad chuckle.)* Oh, what a treasurehouse! I can exclude his dying; I can *not* think about it, except the times I want it back—the times I want, for myself, something less general than . . . tristesse. Though that is usually enough. And what for my daughter—*mine,* now, you'll notice; no longer ours; what box have I got for her? Oh . . . the ephemera: jewelry, clothes, chairs . . . and the money: enough. Nothing solid, except my dying, my death, those two, and the thought of her own. The former, though.

(A little stentorian, disapproving.) Where were *you* those six last months, the time I did *not* need you, with my hands full of less each day; my arms. *(Sad, almost humorous truth.)* If you send them away to save them from it, you resent their going and they want what they've missed. Well . . . I see as much of you as I'd like, my dear. Not as much as either of us should want, but as much as we do. Odd.

(New subject.) And there I was! Falling!

We see each other less, she and I—my daughter—as I said, and most often on boats: something about the air; the burning. She was with me when I fell. Well, on *board.* When they . . . hauled me in—oh, what a spectacle *that* was!—there she was, looking on. Not near where I came in, exactly, but some way off: nearer where I'd done it; where it had been done. Red hair flying—not natural, a kind of purple to it, but stunning; quite stunning—cigarette; *always,* the French one. Nails the color of blood—artery blood, darker than the vein. The things one knows! Looking on, not quite a smile, not quite not. I looked up, dolphins resting on my belly, seaweed-twined, like what's-his-name, or hers . . . I bet all you'll say is Honestly, Mother! *(Slight pause.)* And when she came to my cabin, after the doctor, and the welcome brandy, and the sedative, the unnecessary sedative . . . there she stood for a moment, cigarette still on, in her mouth, I think. She looked for a moment. Honestly, Mother!, she said, laughing a little in her throat, *at* it, humor *at* it. Honestly, Mother! And then off she went.

Where is she now. This trip. Mexico. You'd better chain yourself to the chair, she said to me, later, the day after. You *will* go on deck; put a long cord on yourself. It's not a usual occurrence, I told her; not even for me. No, but you're inventive, she said.

Mexico; still, probably. I'm in Mexico, in case you care, she said. Four A.M. First words, no hello, Mother, or, sorry to wake you up if you're sleeping, if you're not lying there, face all smeared, hair in your net, bed jacket still on, propped up, lights out, wondering whether you're asleep or not. No; not that. Not even that. I'm in Mexico, in case you care.

Oh. Well . . . how very nice. I'm with two boys. Sort of defiant. Oh? Well, how nice. Add 'em up and they're just my age; one's twenty and the other's not quite that. Still defiant. Well, that's . . . she lies a bit: she's forty-two. That's very *nice,* dear. They're both Mexican. She sounded

almost ugly, over the phone, in the dark. Well . . . they're both uncircumcised, she said, and then waited. When this happens . . . when this
happens, she will wait—not those very words, but something she hopes to
affect me with, hurt me, shock, perhaps, make me feel less . . . well, I
was going to say happy, but I am seldom that: not any more . . . make
me feel less even. She'll wait, and I can hear her waiting, to see if I put the
phone down. If I do *not*, after a certain time, of the silence, then she *will*.
I put it down gently, when I do. She slams. This time, *I* put it down;
gently. I've never known which makes her happier—if either does, though
I suppose one must. Whether she is happier if she makes me do it, or if I
pause too long, and she can. I would like to ask her, but it is not the sort of
question one can ask a forty-two-year-old woman . . . daughter or no.

I *do wish* sometimes . . . just in general, I mean . . . I *do wish* sometimes . . .

Just in general, I mean . . . I *do wish* sometimes . . .

I suppose that's why I came this time . . . the Mexicans; the boys. Put
an ocean between. It's not as far as a death, but . . . still.

I remember, I walked to the thing . . . the railing. To look over. Why,
I don't *know:* water never changes, the Atlantic, *this* latitude. But if
you've been sitting in a chair, that is what you *do:* you put down the
Trollope or James or sometimes Hardy, throw off the rug, and, slightly
unsteady from suddenly up from horizontal . . . you walk to the thing
. . . the railing. It's that simple. You look for a bit, smell, sniff, really; you
look down to make sure it's moving, and then you think shall you take a
turn, and you usually do not; you go back to your rug and your book. Or
not to your book, but to your *rug*, which you pull up like covers and
pretend to go to sleep. The one thing you do *not* do is fall off the ship!

Here's a curious thing! Whenever I'm in an aeroplane—which I am
not, often, for I like to choose my company: not that I am a snob, heavens!, it's my daughter who will not see *me*, or, rather, not often. Not that I
am a snob, but I feel that travel in rooms is so much nicer: boats and
trains, where one can get away and then out again; people are nicer when
you come upon them around corners, or opening doors. But whenever I'm
up there, closed in, strapped to my seat, with all the people around, and
the double windows, those tiny windows, and the great heavy door, bolted
from the outside probably, even when I'm plumped down in an inside seat
—or aisle, as they call them—*then!* It's then that I feel that I'm going to
fall out. Fall right out of the aeroplane! I don't know how I could possibly

do it—even through the most . . . reprehensible carelessness. I probably couldn't, even if I felt I had to. But I'm sure I will! Always! Though, naturally, I never do.

Coarse, and ugly, and long, and cruel. That dying. My lovely husband. *(Small pause.)* But I said I wouldn't dwell on that.

Well! What can we say of an aging lady walks bright as you please from her rug and her Trollope or her James or sometimes her Hardy right up to the thing . . . the railing; walks right up, puts her fingers, rings and all, right on the varnished wood, sniffs . . . that air! feels the railing, hard as wood, knows it's there—it *is* there—and suddenly, as sudden and sure as what you've always known and never quite admitted to yourself, it is *not* there; there is no railing, no wood, no metal, no buoy-life-thing saying S.S. or H.M.S. whatever, no . . . nothing! Nothing at all! The fingers are claws, and the varnish they rubbed against is air? And suddenly one is . . . well, what would you expect!? One is suddenly leaning on one's imagination—which is poor support, let me tell you . . . at least in *my* case—leaning on that, which doesn't last for long, and over one goes!

Over one goes, and it's a long way, let me tell you! No falling *up*, No, siree; or out! Straight down; as straight as anything. Plummet! Plut! Well, plummet for sure, plut conjectural. I wonder why I didn't kill myself. Exactly what my daughter said: I wonder why you didn't kill yourself. Though her reading was special. Had a note of derision to it.

I did *not* kill myself, as *I* see it, through a trick of the wind, or chance, or because I am bottom heavy. Straight down like a drop of shot! Except. Except, at the very end, a sort of curving, a kind of arc, which sent me gently into a rising wave, or throw-off from the boat, angling into it just properly, sliding in so that it felt like falling on leaves—the pile of autumn leaves we would make, or our brothers would, and jump on, like a feather bed. A gust of wind must have done that. Well, something did.

I try to recall if I recall the falling, but I'm never sure. I think I do, and then I think I have not. It was so like being awake and asleep . . . at the same time. But I *do* recall being in the water. Heavens! What a sight! *I* must have been, too, but I mean what I *saw*: the sliding by of the ship, green foam in the mouth—kind of exciting—green foam as the wake went by. Lucky you missed the propellers, they said afterwards. Well, yes; lucky.

And sitting there! Sitting there in the water, bouncing around like a carton, screaming a little, not to call attention or anything like that, but because of the fright, and the surprise, and the cold, I suppose; and . . .

well . . . because it was all sort of thrilling: watching the boat move off. My goodness, boats move fast! Something you don't notice 'til you're off one.

And then . . . and then horns, and tooting, and all sorts of commotion and people running around and pointing . . . *(Some disappointment.)* and then the boats out, the launches, and dragging me in and hauling me up—in front of all those people!—and then the brandy and the nurse and the sedative . . . and all the rest. *(Pause.)* I lost my cashmere sweater . . . and one shoe.

You're a very lucky woman, I remember the chief purser saying to me, the next day; I was still groggy. You're a very lucky woman. Yes, I am, I said; yes; I am.

Then, of course, there were the questions. People don't fall off of ocean liners very often. No, I don't suppose they do. Broad daylight and all, people on deck. No; no; I don't imagine so. Do you think you slipped? Surely not! Dry as paint. Have you . . . do you cross often? Oh, heavens, yes! I've done it for years. Have you . . . has this sort of thing ever happened before? What do you take me for!? I'm lucky I'm back from this one, I suppose. Then—gratuitously, and a little peevish, I'm afraid—and I shall cross many times more! And I have—many times, and it's not happened again. Well, do you . . . do yu think maybe you were—wincing some here: them; not me—you were helped? Helped? What do you mean? Well . . . aided. Do you mean *pushed?* Bedside nod. Yes. A laugh from me; a young girl laugh: hand to my throat, head back. Pushed! Good gracious, no! I had been *reading.* What were you reading—which struck me as beside the point and rather touching. Trollope, I said, which wasn't true, for that had been the day before, but I said it anyway. *(Some wonder.)* They didn't know who Trollope was. Well, *there's* a life for you!

Isn't that *some*thing? You lead a whole life; you write books, or you do not; you strive to do good, and succeed, sometimes, amongst the bad—the bad never once through design, but through error, or chance, or lack of a chemical somewhere, in the head, or cowardice, maybe—you raise a family and live with people, see them *through* it; you write books, or you do not, and you say your name is Trollope . . . or whatever it may be, no matter what, you say your name . . . and they have . . . never . . . heard of it. That *is* a life for you.

Is there any chance, do you think. . . . Hm? . . . I say, is there any chance, do you think, well, I don't know how to put it . . . do you think

. . . do you think you may have done it on purpose? Some silence. I look at them, my gray eyes gently wide, misting a little in the edges, all innocence and hurt: *true* innocence; *true* hurt. That I may have done it on purpose? Yes; thrown yourself off. *(Some bewilderment and hurt.)* . . . Me?

Well; yes; I'm sorry. Thrown myself off? A clearing of the throat. Yes. Tried to kill yourself. *(A sad little half-laugh.)* Good heavens, no; *I* have nothing to die for.

ALL OVER

A Play (1971)

For
Bernard and Rebecca Reis

FIRST PERFORMANCE
March 27, 1971, Martin Beck Theater, New York City

JESSICA TANDY *as* THE WIFE
MADELEINE SHERWOOD *as* THE DAUGHTER
COLLEEN DEWHURST *as* THE MISTRESS
NEIL FITZGERALD *as* THE DOCTOR
JAMES RAY *as* THE SON
GEORGE VOSKOVEC *as* THE BEST FRIEND
BETTY FIELD *as* THE NURSE
JOHN GERSTAD, CHARLES KINDL, *and* ALLEN WILLIAMS
as TWO PHOTOGRAPHERS AND A REPORTER

The Characters:

THE WIFE: *71; small-boned, not heavy. Dresses well, if conservatively; gray-haired, probably.*

THE MISTRESS: *61; auburn or dark blond hair; a great beauty fading some; more voluptuous than* THE WIFE, *maybe a bit taller; given to soft, pastel clothes.*

THE SON: *52; a heavy-set man, soft features; dark hair, business clothes.*

THE DAUGHTER: *45; angular; once attractive, now a little ravaged; doesn't care much about how she dresses.*

THE BEST FRIEND: *73; an erect, good-looking gray-haired man, thin to middling; well dressed, well groomed.*

THE DOCTOR: *86; a tiny, shrunken white-haired man; needn't be tiny, but it would be nice.*

THE NURSE: *65; a large woman, gray-streaked blond hair; wears a nurse's uniform.*

TWO PHOTOGRAPHERS AND A REPORTER; *no matter; middle-aged, or whoever understudies the male principals.*

ONE IDEA OF A SET: *A paneled bed-sitting room. The bed—a huge, canopied four-poster on a raised platform to the rear. Back there, an armoire, perhaps a bureau, a hospital stand for instruments and medicines, a hospital screen hiding the occupant of the bed. In the sitting-room part, a huge fireplace in the stage-right wall, and a door leading to a bathroom upstage of it. In the stage-left wall, a door leading to the hall. The room is solid and elegant, a man's room. The furniture, all of which is good and comfortable, is most probably English. Several chairs, a sofa, side tables, lamps. A tapestry, eighteenth-century family portraits. An Oriental carpet.*

TIME: *The present.*

ACT ONE

THE DOCTOR *at the bed with the patient;* THE NURSE *at the foot of the bed. The others about, the three women probably sitting,* THE SON *and* THE BEST FRIEND *maybe not.*

Unless otherwise indicated, the characters will speak in a conversational tone, without urgency, more languorously than not. But there will be no whispering; the languor is not boredom, but waiting. The fireplace has an ebbing fire in it; the room is warm.

THE WIFE *(Gazing at the fire).* Is he dead?

THE DAUGHTER *(A gentle admonishment: not a rebuke).* Oh, mother.

THE MISTRESS. I wish you wouldn't say that: is he dead?

THE WIFE *(Too polite; small smile).* I'm sorry.

THE MISTRESS. It's not your curiosity I mind; it is a wifely right, and I know it's not impatience. It's the *form.* We talked about it once, I remember—he and I did—though not how it came up; I don't remember that, but let me see. He put down his fork, one lunch, at *my* house . . . what had we been talking about? Maeterlinck and that plagiarism business, I seem to recall, and we had done with that and we were examining our salads, when all at once he said to me, "I wish people wouldn't say that other people 'are dead.' " I asked him why, as much as anything to know what had turned him to it, and he pointed out that the verb to be was not, to his mind, appropriate to a state of . . . non-being. That one cannot . . . *be* dead. He said his objection was a quirk —that the grammarians would scoff—but that one could be dying, or have died . . . but could not . . . be . . . dead.

THE WIFE *(Quiet amusement).* Maeterlinck?

THE MISTRESS *(Lightly).* Oh, well; that was just one day. I'm sorry for having taken issue.

THE WIFE *(Gazing into the fire again).* No matter. Let me rephrase it, then.

(Raises her head, inclines it slightly toward THE DOCTOR*)*

Has he . . . died?

THE DOCTOR *(Pause).* Not yet.

THE WIFE *(Pressing a small point).* Will he die *soon?*

THE SON *(Faint distaste).* Please, mother.

THE WIFE *(Tiny laugh).* I would like to know. Merely that.

THE DOCTOR. Relatively.

309

THE WIFE. To?

THE DOCTOR. To the time it has taken him so far.

THE DAUGHTER. Then what was the urgency?

THE DOCTOR. Hunch.

THE BEST FRIEND *(More curiosity than reproach)*. Don't you *want* to be here?

THE DAUGHTER *(Considering it for the first time)*. Well . . . I don't *know*.

(THE MISTRESS *laughs gently*)

THE BEST FRIEND. It's not required that you *do* know. It *is* more or less required that you *be* . . . I think: here. Family. Isn't it one of our customs? That if a man has not outlived his wife and children—will not outlive them . . . they gather?

THE WIFE *(To* THE BEST FRIEND*)*. And his closest friend, as well.

(THE BEST FRIEND *bows slightly, cocks his head.* THE WIFE *indicates* THE MISTRESS)

And don't forget *her*.

THE BEST FRIEND *(Matter-of-fact, but friendly)*. And his . . . very special friend, too.

THE MISTRESS *(Smiles)*. Thank you.

THE BEST FRIEND. And we do it—custom—wanted, or not. We wait until we cannot be asked—unless there is something written, or said, refusing it—and we . . . gather, often even *if* we are refused.

THE WIFE. And is that *so?* In your lawyerish way . . .

THE BEST FRIEND. No; we have not been refused.

THE WIFE *(To* THE DOCTOR*)*. A hunch. *Nothing* more . . . technical than that? More medical? Your hunch it will be *soon?* Your intuition if you were a woman, or are doctors graced with that?

(To her DAUGHTER; *somewhat chiding)*

We've not *come* any distance. Is it just we're in the room with him—not at the hotel, or downstairs?

THE DAUGHTER. I suppose. And that we lived here once.

THE WIFE *(To* THE DAUGHTER*)*. That was another century.

(To THE DOCTOR*)*

Hunch.

THE DOCTOR *(To* THE WIFE*)*. I can't give it to you to the minute. Did I predict when she would be born?

(Refers to THE DAUGHTER*)*

The hour—the day, for that matter? Or him?
(Refers to THE SON*)*

THE MISTRESS *(Back to the point).* Though you have *reason.*

THE DOCTOR. Yes.

(Pause)

THE WIFE *(A little as though she were speaking to a backward child).* And
what *is* it?

THE NURSE *(Fact more than reproach).* You should let him die in the
hospital.

THE DAUGHTER. Yes!

THE WIFE *(Quietly indigant).* Hooked up?

THE NURSE *(Shrugs).* Whatever.

THE MISTRESS *(Soft-smiling; shaking her head; faintly ironic).* Yes, of course
we should have.

(To THE WIFE*)*

Can you imagine it?

THE WIFE. Tubes; wires. All those machines, leading to and from? A central gadget?

(To them all, generally)

That's what he had become, with all those tubes and wires: one more
machine.

(To THE MISTRESS*)*

Back me up.

THE MISTRESS. Oh, far more than *that.*

THE WIFE. A city seen from the air? The rail lines and the roads? Or, an
octopus: the body of the beast, the tentacles electrical controls, record-
ers, modulators, breath and heart and brain waves, and the tubes!, in
either arm and in the nostrils. Where had he gone!? In all that . . .
equipment. I thought for a moment *he* was keeping *it* . . . function-
ing. Tubes and wires.

THE NURSE. They help to keep time, to answer your questions easier.

(Shakes her head)

That's all.

THE MISTRESS. The questions are very simple now. A stopwatch should do
it, a finger on the wrist . . .

THE DAUGHTER *(Fairly arch).* We are led to understand . . .

THE MISTRESS *(No nonsense).* He said . . . here.

THE DAUGHTER *(None too pleasant).* We have your word for it.

THE WIFE *(Shrugs)*. We have her word for *every*thing.

THE MISTRESS *(Not rising to it)*. He *said* . . . *here*. When it becomes hopeless . . . no, is that what he said? Pointless! When it becomes pointless, he said . . . have me brought back here. I want a wood fire, and a ceiling I have memorized, the knowledge of what I could walk about in, *were* I to. I want to leave from some place . . . I have known.

(Changed tone; to THE DAUGHTER*)*

You have my *word* for it; yes, you have only my word . . . for so very much . . . if he loved you, for example . . . any more.

(To them all; triste)

You *all* have my word, and that is all. I translate for you, as best I can; I tell you what I remember, or think I remember, and I lie sometimes, and give you what he would have said . . . *had* he: thought to . . . or bothered.

THE DAUGHTER *(Dogged, but not forceful)*. That will not do.

THE SON *(Quiet)*. Please?

THE DAUGHTER *(Scoffing)*. You!

THE WIFE. When I came there, to the hospital—the last time, before the . . . removal here—I said . . .

(Turns to THE MISTRESS*)*

you were not there, were shopping, or resting, I think . . .

(Turns back generally)

looking at him, all wired up, I stood at the foot of the bed—small talk all gone, years ago—I shook my head, and I clucked, I'm afraid—tsk-tsk-tsk-tsk—for he opened his eyes a little, baleful, as I suppose my gaze must have seemed to him, though it was merely . . . objective. This won't do at all, I said. Wouldn't you rather be somewhere else? Do you want to be here? He kept his eyes half open for a moment or so, then closed them, and nodded his head, very slowly. Well, which?, I said, for I realized I'd asked two questions, and a nod could mean either yes or no. Which is it?, I said; do you want to be here? Slow shake of the head. You *would* rather be somewhere else. Eyes opened and closed, twice, in what I know—from eons—to be impatience; then . . . nodding. Well, naturally, I said, in my bright business tone, of course you don't want to be here. Do you want to go home? No reply at all, the eyes burning at me. Your own home, I mean, not mine certainly. Or hers. Perhaps you want to go there. Shall I arrange something? Eyes still on me, no movement. Do you want *her* to arrange it? Still the eyes, still no movement. Has it been arranged? Has she arranged it already? The eyes lightened; I could swear there was a smile in them. She *has*. Well; good. If it is done, splendid. All I care is whether it is *done*. I no longer feel possessive, have not for . . . and the eyes went out—stayed open, went out, as they had . . . oh . . . so often; so far back.

(To THE MISTRESS*)*

That is one of those things . . .

THE DAUGHTER *(Possessive, in a very female way)*. MOTHER!

THE WIFE. Do not . . . *deflect* me.

THE DAUGHTER *(More a whine, but protective)*. MOTHER.

THE WIFE *(As cool as possible)*. Yes?

(Pause)

Out. Stayed open, went out.

THE MISTRESS. Ah, well; that happened often.

THE WIFE *(Quiet, almost innocent interest)*. Yes?

THE MISTRESS. Ah; well, yes.

THE WIFE. Odd I don't remember it. The opening and closing . . . of course, the . . . impatience, but . . . out.

THE MISTRESS *(Gently)*. Ah, well; perhaps you should have noticed. It must have happened.

THE WIFE *(A small smile)*. Well, yes, perhaps I should have. Doubtless it did.

THE MISTRESS. It was always—for me . . .

THE DAUGHTER. Was? The past tense? Why not *is?*

THE MISTRESS *(Not rising to it; calm)*. He has not, for some time. You *were* a little girl. Are you still?

*(*THE DAUGHTER *turns away)*

THE WIFE *(A little laugh)*. Semantics from a C minus?

THE SON *(Softly)*. Leave her alone.

THE WIFE *(Not harsh)*. Was it not? At school? A C minus, if that? *You* were little better.

THE MISTRESS. It was always—for me—an indication that . . . .

THE DOCTOR *(No urgency)*. Nurse.

(Some reaction from them all; not panic, but a turning of heads; a quickening)

THE WIFE *(A little breathless)*. Something?

313

THE DOCTOR *(Looks up at them; a slight smile; some surprise)*. Oh . . . oh, *no*. Just . . . business.

' *(Slight pause)*

THE MISTRESS *(Not pressing; continuing)*. . . . an indication that . . . some small fraction had gone out of him, some . . . faint shift from total engagement. Or, if not that, a warning of it: impending.

THE WIFE *(A smile)*. Ah. Then I *do* know it . . . the sense of it, and probably from what you describe, without knowing I was aware of it.

THE BEST FRIEND. *I* have been aware of it.

THE WIFE *(Referring to her husband)*. In *him?*

THE BEST FRIEND. No. In myself.

THE WIFE *(Mildly mocking)*. You *have?*

THE BEST FRIEND *(Smiles)*. Yes; I have.

THE WIFE *(Smiling, herself)*. How extraordinary.

(Thinks about it)

When?

THE BEST FRIEND *(To THE WIFE)*. In relation to my wife, when I was wavering on the divorce, during that time you and I were—how do they put it?—comforting one another; that secret time I fear that everyone knew of.

THE MISTRESS. *He* never knew of it. *I* did. I didn't tell him.

THE WIFE *(Sad; smiling)*. Well, there wasn't very much to tell.

THE BEST FRIEND. No; but some; briefly. It was after I decided not to get the divorce, that year . . . until I committed her. Each thing, each . . . incident—uprooting all the roses, her hands so torn, so . . . killing the doves and finches . . . setting fire to her hair . . . all . . . all those times, those things I knew were pathetic and not wanton, I watched myself withdraw, step back and close down some portion of . . .

THE MISTRESS. Ah, but that's not the same.

THE WIFE *(Not unkindly; objectively)*. No, not at all; she was *insane* . . . your wife.

THE MISTRESS. And that is not what we meant at all.

THE WIFE. No, not at all.

THE BEST FRIEND. It is what you were talking about.

THE MISTRESS *(Laughs a little; sadly)*. No. It's when it happens calmly and in full command: the tiniest betrayal—nothing so calamitous as a lie held on to in the face of fact, or so niggling as a fantasy during the act of love, but in between—and it can be anything, or nearly nothing, except that it moves you back into yourself a little, the knowledge that all your sharing has been . . .

THE WIFE. . . . arbitrary . . .

THE MISTRESS. . . . . willfull, and that nothing has been inevitable . . . or even necessary. When the eyes close down; go out.

THE SON *(Intense)*. My father is dying!

THE WIFE *(After a tiny pause)*. Yes. He is.

THE DOCTOR. If you want to go back downstairs, any of you . . .

THE DAUGHTER. . . . to the photographers? The people from the papers? I put my foot on the staircase and they're all around me: Has it happened yet? *Is* he? May we go up now? Eager. Soft voices but very eager.

THE WIFE *(Soothing)*. Well, they have their families . . . their wives, their mistresses.

THE DAUGHTER *(Generally)*. Thank you: I'll stay up here; I'll sit it out.

THE WIFE *(With a wrinkling of her nose)*. Neat.

THE DAUGHTER *(Slightly incredulous)*. Did you say neat?

THE MISTRESS. Yes; she did.

THE DAUGHTER *(To her mother)*. Because I said sit it out?

THE WIFE *(Without expression; waiting)*. Um-humm.

THE DAUGHTER *(Startlingly shrill)*. WELL, WHAT ARE YOU DOING!?

THE WIFE *(Looks up at her, smiles vaguely, speaks softly)*. I am waiting out a marriage of fifty years. I am waiting for my *hus*band to *die*. I am thinking of the little girl I was when he came to me. I am thinking of . . . do you want me to stop? . . . almost everything I can except the two of you—you and your . . . unprepossessing brother—

(Light, to THE SON*)*

Do forgive me.

(Back)

I am sitting it out. *I* . . . am sitting it out.

(To THE DAUGHTER*)*

And *you* are?

THE DAUGHTER. Enjoying it less than you.

THE MISTRESS *(To* THE DAUGHTER; *a quiet discovery; as if for the first time, almost)*. You are not a very kind woman.

THE WIFE *(Passing it off)*. She has been raised at her mother's knee.

THE DAUGHTER *(To* THE MISTRESS*)*. And am I suddenly *your* daughter?

THE MISTRESS. Oh; my stars! No!

THE DAUGHTER. Well, you have assumed so much . . .

THE WIFE *(Announcement of a subject).* The little girl I was when he came to me.

THE MISTRESS. So much?

(To THE WIFE*)*

Interesting: it's only the mother who can ever really know whose child it is. Well, the husband knows his wife is *having* the baby . . .

THE WIFE *(Laughs gaily).* He took me aside one day—before you and he had made your liaison; they were grown, though—and, rather in the guilty way of "Did I *really* back the car through the *whole* tulip bed?", asked me, his eyes self-consciously focusing just off somewhere . . . "*Did* I make these children? Was it *our* doing: the two of us alone?" I laughed, with some joy, for while we *were* winding down we were doing it with talk and presence: the silences and the goings off were later; the titans were still engaged; and I said, "Oh, yes, my darling; yes, we did; they are our very own."

(She chuckles quietly.

Brief pause; THE DAUGHTER *rises, almost languidly, walks over to where* THE WIFE *is sitting, slaps her across the face, evenly, without evident emotion, returns to where she is sitting.*

After a pause; to THE MISTRESS; *small smile)*

Excuse me.

(She rises, just as languidly, walks over to where THE DAUGHTER *is sitting, slaps her across the face, evenly, without evident emotion, returns to where she is sitting. After a noncommittal sigh at* THE DAUGHTER, *who is glaring straight ahead, over her shoulder, to* THE DOCTOR*)*

And what do you think now?

THE DOCTOR *(Patient smile).* Are you back at my intuition again? My hunch? Your funny names for all the years I've watched you come and go? Both your parents, both of his. My sixty years of practice.

(Indicates THE NURSE*)*

The forty years she's come here with me to sit up nights with you all?

THE WIFE. Yes.

THE MISTRESS *(Some wonder).* Sixty years of *something.*

THE WIFE *(Still to* THE DOCTOR*).* Even on the chance of frightening the horses, or being taken as heartless—which I am *not*—are you holding him back, or are you seeing him through to it?

(THE DAUGHTER *stiffens, turns on her heel, moves to the door, opens it, exits, slams it after her*)

THE DOCTOR *(Watching this before he answers)*. I've stopped the intravenous feeding. We're letting him . . . starve, if you will. He's breathing very slowly now . . . like sleep. His heart is . . . *(Shrugs)*
. . . well, weak . . . bored is close to it. He's bleeding . . . internally. Shall I go on?

THE WIFE *(No expression)*. Please do.

THE DOCTOR. If you'd like to come and look . . . he seems to have diminished every time I turn my head away and come back. There'll be precious little left for the worms.

THE MISTRESS. The flames.

THE WIFE *(Having heard something on the wind)*. Oh? Yes?

THE MISTRESS. He will be burned. "And you are not to snatch my heart from the flames," he said, "for it is not a tasty organ."

THE WIFE *(Schoolmarmish)*. Per*haps*. Per*haps* he will be burned.

THE BEST FRIEND *(Quite serious; really!)*. Surely he didn't suggest an outdoor event . . . a funeral pyre!
(He is stopped by a concert of THE WIFE *and* THE MISTRESS *in rather cold, knowing, helpless laughter)*

THE SON *(Finally)*. Don't you . . . *have* something? Some papers?

THE WIFE *(Rather helpless in quiet, terrible laughter)*. You *must!*

THE SON *(Doubtless the most intense in his life)*. You MUST!

THE MISTRESS. Yes!

THE BEST FRIEND *(After an embarrassed pause)*. There . . . *are* . . . papers . . . envelopes I've not opened, on instruction; there may be

THE MISTRESS *(Adamant; cool)*. It was a verbal . . . envelope.

THE BEST FRIEND. I will go by what is *down*.

THE WIFE *(Half sardonic, half leaning)*. Of *course* he will.

THE MISTRESS *(Cold; a diamond hardness, yet womanly)*. Oh, Christ; you people! You will go by what I tell you; finally; as I have told you.

THE WIFE *(Almost as if improvising; bright)*. No! We will go with what *is*, with what resides. Goodness, if a man desires to go up in flames, let him put it down—on a tablet! Or shall we go over and shake him . . . wake him to the final glory before the final glory, and have two women at him, with a best friend overhead, and make him make his *mind* up!

"My darling, we merely want to know! Is it flame or worm? Your mistress tells me you prefer the flame, while I, your merely wife of fifty years, the mother of your doubted children—true, oh, true, my darling —wants you to the worms. Do tell us. Yes? Open your awful lips for a moment, or do your eyes: open and close them, put them on and out; let us . . . finally . . . misunderstand."

(THE MISTRESS *smiles, slowly applauds. Five sounds; seven; always an odd number. Brief pause following the applause, during which* THE WIFE *nods her head gently toward* THE MISTRESS)

THE DOCTOR *(To himself, but not sotto voce).* Death is such an old disease. *(Realizes he is being listened to; speaks to* THE WIFE *and* THE MISTRESS, *laughs a little)*

That being so, it must be a comfort having someone as old as I am by the bed: familiar with it, knowing it so well.

THE MISTRESS. Well, let me discomfort you. I was *not* pleased to have you. Get a younger man, I said to him . . .

THE WIFE. Be kind.

THE BEST FRIEND. There are customs . . .

THE DOCTOR *(Not hurt; not angry; shrugs).* And you had them . . . the surgeons, the consultants, younger—well, not brash, but I doubt you'd have wanted that . . .

THE WIFE. . . . some bouncy intern with a scalpel in one hand, a racquet under his arm . . .

THE MISTRESS *(Mildly annoyed).* Don't be ridiculous.

THE DOCTOR *(Chuckles).* I'm rather like a priest: you have me for the limits, for birth and dying, *and* for the minor cuts and scratches in between. If that nagging cough keeps nagging, now it's not *me* opens up the throat or the chest; not *me. I* send you on to *other* men . . . and very quickly. I am the most . . . general of practitioners.

THE MISTRESS. I'm sorry.

THE DOCTOR. 'Course, if you think some younger man would do better here, have him back on his feet and at the fireplace, clinking the ice in a bourbon, looking better than ever . . .

THE MISTRESS *(Wants no more of it).* No! I *said* I am sorry. Just . . . railing against it.

(Gently)

I *am* sorry.

THE BEST FRIEND *(To* THE MISTRESS, *really; but, to* THE DOCTOR, *and to the*

others). The custom of the house. And it *has* been, for so long. "You
end up with what you start out with."

THE WIFE *(Quiet, choked laughter).* Oh; God! "The little girl I was when
he came to me."

THE MISTRESS *(After a pause).* The house? The custom of which house?

THE BEST FRIEND *(Dogged, not unpleasant).* Of wherever he is: the house
he carries on his back, or in his head.

THE MISTRESS *(Mildly assertive; slightly bewildered).* Well . . . I thought
I knew it *all:* having been so . . . having participated so fully.

THE WIFE *(To* THE BEST FRIEND). Is it written on one of your lovely things?
. . . your pieces of paper? That we end up with what we start out
with? Or that *he* does?

THE BEST FRIEND *(Quiet smile).* No.

THE WIFE. I thought not, for Dr. Dey, who brought him into this world
. . . into all this, went down with that boat, ship, rather—the iceberg
one, or was it the German sub; the iceberg, I think.

THE SON. Titanic.

THE WIFE. Thank you.

THE NURSE. Dey did not go down with a ship.

THE WIFE and THE BEST FRIEND *(Slightly overlapping, almost simultaneously).* He did *not?*

THE NURSE *(To* THE DOCTOR). May I? . . .

(THE DOCTOR *nods)*

. . . Dey went down with what we all go down with, and one *day,* you
will forgive the pun, he realized the burning far too up in the chest, and
the sense of the kidneys saying they can not go on, and the sudden
knowledge that it has all gone on . . . from what central, possibly
stoppable place—like eating that last, unwanted shard, that salad,
breathing that air from the top of . . . where?—that one thing we are
born to discover and never find.

(Pause)

He locused in on his killer, and he looked on it, and he said, "I will not
have you."

(Pause)

And so he booked on the Titanic, of *course.*

THE SON *(Abstracted).* Well . . . that is what I thought.

THE MISTRESS *(Sensing something).* Of course.

THE NURSE *(Lighter).* Or something like it. I mean, if the cancer's on you

and you're a doctor to boot and know the chances *and* the pain, well
. . . what do you do save book on a boat you think's going to run into
an iceberg and sink.

THE SON *(Frowning)*. Oh. Then he did *not* go down on the Titanic.

THE NURSE. No; he went to Maine, to his lodge, and fished . . . for about
a week. Then he killed himself.

THE WIFE. And the story of the ship . . .

THE NURSE. . . . was a fiction, invented by his wife and agreed to by his
mistress, by the happy coincidence that the Titanic *did* go down when
he did. Oh, nobody *believed* it, you understand; the obituaries were
candid; but it became a euphemism and was eventually accepted.

THE WIFE. Poor woman.

THE MISTRESS. Poor *women*.

THE WIFE. Who was his mistress? I didn't know he had one.

THE NURSE *(Casual)*. *I* was.

THE WIFE. My gracious; you're . . . *old, aren't* you.

THE NURSE. Yes; very.

THE WIFE *(After the slightest pause)*. It never occurred to me before.
You've always been such a . . . presence. I don't believe a single word
you've told us.

THE NURSE *(Shrugs)*. *I* don't care.

(Returns to her place by the bed.)

(Pause)

THE DOCTOR. You see . . .

THE MISTRESS *(Quite annoyed)*. You *always* say that!

THE WIFE *(Not sure, but interested)*. *Does* he?

THE DOCTOR. You see, I did my tithe all at once, in the prisons, when I was
young. After my internship; I went to help.

THE WIFE. *We* never knew that.

THE MISTRESS. No.

THE DOCTOR. No?

(Shrugs, chuckles)

It was a while ago: it was before our minds had moved to the New
Testament, or our reading of it. Men would die, then—for their killings
—soon, if . . . well, perhaps not decently, but what passed for decently if burning a man alive survived the test . . . we were all Old
Testament Jews, and we still are, two hundred million of us, save the
children, for we believe what we no longer practice . . . *if: if* the jus-

tice was merciful, for that is what sets us medicine men apart from jurors: we are not in a hurry. But, I was with them; stayed with them; helped them have what they wanted for the last time. I would be with them, and they were alone in the death cells, no access to each other, and the buggery was over, had it ever begun, the buggery and the rest; and there were some, in the final weeks, who had abandoned sex, masturbation, to God, or fear, or some enveloping withdrawal, but not all; some . . . some made love to themselves in a frenzy—indeed, I treated more than one who was bleeding from it, from so much—and several confided to me that their masturbation image was their executioner . . . some fancy of how he looked.

THE WIFE *(Remembering an announcement)*. The little girl I was when he came to me.

THE DOCTOR. You see:

THE WIFE *(Laughing a little)*. You see? No one cares.

THE DOCTOR. I . . . am eighty-six . . . which, I was informed by my grandson, or perhaps my great-nephew—I confuse them, not the two, but the . . .

(Confiding)

well, they look alike, and have what I confess I think of as wigs, though I know they are not . . .

(Some, though not fruity, longing here)

. . . long, lovely . . . turning down and underneath at the shoulders . . . blond and grail-like hair . . . but they said . . . or one of them did . . .

(Not loud, but emphasized)

. . . "Eighty-six! Man, that means going out!" Well, of course, I knew what they meant, but I was coy with it—and I asked them why—what does that make me? "Eighty-six and out." Does that make me . . . and suddenly I knew! I knew I wanted to lie in the long blond hair, put my lips there in the back of the neck, with the blond hair over me . . .

THE SON *(Great urgency)*. I don't *follow* you!

THE DOCTOR. I was completing what I had begun before: how we become enraptured by it . . .

(Small smile)

. . . by the source of our closing down. You see: I suddenly loved my executioners . . . well, figurative; and in the way of . . . nestling up against them, huddling close—for we do seek warmth, affection even, from those who tell us we are going to die, or when.

THE MISTRESS *(After a pause). I* believe in the killing; *some* of it; for *some* of them.

THE WIFE. Of *course.* Give us a theory and we'll do it in.

THE BEST FRIEND *(Quiet distaste).* You *can't* believe in it.

THE WIFE. See . . . your own wife.

THE BEST FRIEND *(Gut betrayal, but soft-keyed).* You *can't* do that. There was no killing there.

THE WIFE. Just . . . divorce. It wasn't *us* that did her in—our . . . late summer . . . arrangement: there had been others. *Our* . . . mercy to each other, by the lake, the city . . . *that* didn't take a wild woman who could still bake bread and give a party half the time and send her spinning back into the animal brain; no, my dear; fucking—as it is called in public by everyone these days—is not what got at her; yours and mine, I mean. Divorce: leave *alone:* So don't tell *me* you don't believe in murder. You *do. I* do.

(Indicates THE MISTRESS)

She does, and admits it.

THE SON *(Without moving).* I WANT TO TALK TO HIM!

THE BEST FRIEND *(To* THE WIFE, *quiet; intense).* You said she was insane. You *all* said it.

THE WIFE *(Rather dreamy).* Did I? Well, perhaps I meant she was *going.*
(Enigmatic smile)

Perhaps we all did.

(To THE SON)

Then talk to him. You can preface every remark by saying "for the first and last time." And you'll get no argument—there's *that.* I'd not *do* it, though.

(Dry)

You'd start to cry; you've little enough emotion in you: I'd save it.

THE SON *(To his mother; frustration; controlled rage).* He's *dying!*

THE WIFE *(Sad; comforting; explaining).* I *know.*

THE BEST FRIEND *(Quiet; more or less to himself).* It was progressive. I *asked* them. The violence was transitional.

(To THE WIFE)

I saw her not two months ago.

THE MISTRESS *(Seeing that* THE WIFE *is preoccupied). Did* you!

Act One

THE BEST FRIEND. I had been to the club, and was getting in my car; another pulled up alongside and someone said—coolly, I think—"Well; I declare." It was a voice I knew, and I turned my head and it was her sister behind the wheel, with another woman in the death seat beside her, as it is called. "I *do* declare," she said—definitely cool—and I perceived it in an instant, before I looked, that my wife was in the back, my ex-wife, and the woman in the front was from the hospital: no uniform, but an attendant of some sort. "Look who we have here!" That was the way she talked, the smile set, the eyes madder than my wife's could ever be—a sane woman, though. The attendant was smoking, I remember that. Of course I looked, and indeed she *was* there, in the back, catercorner, a fur rug half backdrop, half cocoon, and how small she was in it! "Look who's here," her sister said, this time addressing *her*, her head turned to catch both our expressions. The windows were down and I put my hands on the sill—if that *is* what car doors have—and bent down some. "Hello," I said, "how are you?", realizing as I said it that if she laughed in my face, or screamed, or went for me I would not have been surprised. She smiled, though, and stroked the fur beside her cheek with the back of her hand. Her voice was calm, and extremely . . . rested. "It's fine in here," she said, "how is it out there?" I didn't reply: I was so aware of her eyes on me, and her sister's, and the attendant not turned, but looking straight ahead, and smoking. She went on: "Oh, it would be so nice to say to you, 'Come closer, so I can whisper something to you.' That way I could put my hand to the back of your head and say very softly, 'Help me'; either that or rub my lips against your ear, the way you like, and then *grab* you with my teeth, and hold on as you pulled away, blood, and ripping." It was so . . . objective, and without rancor, I didn't move at all; the attendant did, I remember; she turned. "I can't do that, though," my wife said—sadly, I think. "Do you know why?" "No, I don't know why." "Because," she said, "when I look at your ear I see the rump and the tail of a mouse coming out from it; he must be chewing very deeply." I didn't move; my fingers stayed where they were. It could be I was trying to fashion some reply, but there *is* none to that. Her sister gunned the motor then; having seen me when she parked, she must have thought to keep it idling. "Nice to see you," she said to me, the same grim smile, mad eyes, and she backed out, curving, shifted, and moved off. And what I retain of their leaving, most of all, above the mouse, my wife, my*self,*

323

for that matter, is the sound of her sister's bracelet clanking against the steering wheel—a massive gold chain with a disc suspended from it, a large thin disc, with her first name, in facsimile, scrawled across one face of it; that; clanking as she shifted.

(Pause)

THE WIFE *(Having listened to almost all the story).* Then I'm sorry.

THE BEST FRIEND *(Quietly; a little weary).* It's all right.

(Pause)

THE SON. It's not true, you know: there's more emotion in me than you think.

THE WIFE *(Gentle, placating).* Well, I hope so.

(Pause; to THE MISTRESS*)*

You're very silent.

THE MISTRESS. I was *wondering* about that: why I *was.* I'd *noticed* it and was rather puzzled. It's not my *way.*

THE WIFE *(Agreeing).* No.

THE MISTRESS. Outsider, I guess.

THE WIFE *(Friendly).* Oh, stop!

THE MISTRESS. No; really; yes. In this context. Listening to you was a capping on it, I suppose: *God;* that was effective as you did it, and I dare say you *needed* it. Maybe that's how we keep the nineteenth century going for ourselves: pretend it exists, and . . . well . . . outsider.

THE WIFE *(Objective curiosity, but friendly).* What will you *do?*

THE MISTRESS *(Thinks about that for a while).* I don't *know.* I really don't. Give me a schedule. Who runs to the coverlet first? And who throws her arms where, and where, and where does it matter? Who grabs the shoulders, to shake the death out of them, and who collapses at the knees?

THE WIFE *(Not sure, herself).* You don't *know.*

THE MISTRESS *(Laughs, so sadly).* Oh, God, the little girl you were when he came to you.

THE WIFE *(Sad truth).* Yes!

THE MISTRESS *(Sad truth).* I don't *know.*

*(*THE DAUGHTER *enters; her swift opening of the door jars them all to quiet attention; she chuckles a little, unpleasantly, at their reaction, and moves to the fireplace without a word; she rests her hands on the mantel, and stares into the fire)*

Ultimately, an outsider. I was *thinking* about that, and I concluded it
was ritual that made it so.

(Looking about; almost amused)

This is . . . ritual, is it not?

(Normal tone)

Twenty years without it, except an awkwardness at Christmas, perhaps.

(To THE WIFE*)*

I remember one December in particular, when it was in the papers you
were suing for divorce. Glad you didn't, I think; it would have forced
him to marry me . . . or not. Move off.

(Generally)

He missed you all then. Oh, he always *has* . . . mildly, but *that* Christmas—we were at the lodge; it was the next year we took to the islands,
to avoid the season as much as anything, though it *was* good for his
back, the sun—that one in particular, we sat before the great fire, with
all the snow and the pines, and I knew he missed . . . well: family.

(Small laugh)

He missed the ritual, I think.

(Not unkindly)

I doubt you were very good with Christmas, though; hardly . . . proto-
typical: wassail, and chestnuts.

THE SON *(Slightly triste)*. Once. Chestnuts.

THE WIFE *(To* THE MISTRESS*; a smile)*. You *are* right.

THE MISTRESS. In front of the fire; Christmas Eve. We *had* been holding
hands, but were *not;* not at that moment, and did he sigh? Perhaps; but
there was a great . . . all of a sudden, a . . . slack, and I caught his
profile as he stared into the fire, that . . . marvelous granite, and it was
as if he had . . . deflated, just perceptibly. I took his hand, and he
turned to me and smiled: came back. I said, "You should spend it with
them; every *year.*" He said he thought not, and it was not for *my* sake.

THE DAUGHTER *(Still staring into the fire; she intones the word, spreads it)*.
Drone. Drone!

THE MISTRESS *(Looks up at* THE DAUGHTER*'s back, pauses a moment, looks
out at nothing; continues)*. It *is* the ritual, you see, that gives me the
sense. The first few times I wouldn't go to his doctorates, until he *made*
me do it, and the banquets when he *spoke!* Naturally, I've never
thought of myself as a secret—for I am not a tart, and I would never
have been good at it—but the rituals remind me of what I believe is

called my . . . status. To be something so fully, and yet . . . well, no
matter.

(A quick, bright laugh; the next directed to THE WIFE*)*

I wonder: if I had been *you*—the little girl you were when he came to
you—would you have come along, as I did? Would *you* have come to
take *my* place?

THE DAUGHTER *(As* THE WIFE *is about to speak; turns, but stays at the
fireplace).* They're all down there! The cameramen, the television crews,
the reporters. They gave me a container of coffee.

THE WIFE. Well, why aren't they being *looked* after? Didn't you tell them
in the kitchen to see what was needed, and . . .

THE DAUGHTER. The ones *outside:* the crews with their trucks and lights.
They gave me the coffee.

(Laughs, but it is not pleasant)

It's like a *fungus.* The TV people are on the stoop, with all their equipment on the sidewalk, and you and your tubes and wires! Like a fungus:
all of those outside, and the photographers have assumed the entrance
hall, like a stag line—nobody sits!, and the newspapermen have taken
the library, for that is where the Scotch is.

THE WIFE *(To* THE BEST FRIEND*).* Go down and *do* something!

THE DAUGHTER *(It is clear she's enjoying it, in a sad way).* Don't bother!
It's all been set. Touch it and you'll have it on the landing. Leave it.

(Looks toward her father's bed; overplayed)

Who *is* this man?

THE WIFE *(Trailing off).* Well, I suppose . . .

THE DAUGHTER. I forgot to mention the police.

THE WIFE *(Mild anxiety).* The police!

THE DAUGHTER *(Very much "on").* For the people. Well, there aren't many
there now, people, twenty-five, maybe—the kind of crowd you'd get for
a horse with sunstroke, if it were summer. The TV has brought them
out, the trucks and the tubes. They're lounging, nothing better to do,
and if it weren't night and a weekend, I doubt they'd linger. I mean,
God, we don't have the President in here, or anything.

THE SON *(Quiet, but dismayed).* Don't talk like that.

THE WIFE *(To* THE BEST FRIEND*). Shouldn't* you go down?

THE BEST FRIEND *(Shakes his head).* No; it's a public event; *will* be.

THE NURSE. That's the final test of fame, isn't it, the degree of it: which is
newsworthy, the act of dying itself, or merely the death.

Act One

THE MISTRESS *(Aghast)*. MERELY!

THE NURSE *(Almost a reproach)*. I wasn't speaking for me, or you. *Them.*
The public; whether it's enough for them to read about it in the papers
without a kind of anger at having missed the dying, too. They were
cheated with the Kennedys, both of them, *and* with King. It happened
so fast; all people could figure for themselves was they'd been clubbed
in the face by history. Even poor Bobby; he took the longest, but
everybody knew he was dead before he died. Christ, that loathsome
doctor on the tube kept telling us.

(Imitation of a person despised)

"There's no chance at *all* as I see it; the hemorrhaging, the bullet where
it is. No chance. No chance." Jesus, you couldn't even *hope*. It was a
disgusting night; it made me want to be young, and a man, and violent
and unreasoning—rage so that it meant something. Pope John was the
last one the public could share in—two weeks of the vilest agony, and
conscious to the very end, unsedated, because it was something his God
wanted him to experience. I don't know, maybe a bullet *is* better. In
spite of everything.

THE WIFE. Perhaps.

THE MISTRESS *(Quiet sadness)*. What a sad and shabby time we live in.

THE WIFE. Yes.

THE DAUGHTER *(Begins to laugh; incredulous, cruel)*. You . . . hypocrites!

THE WIFE. Oh?

THE DAUGHTER. You pious hypocrites!

(Mocking)

The sad and shabby time we live in. "Yes." You dare to sit there and
shake your heads like that?

(To THE WIFE*)*

To hell with you with your . . . affair with him, though that's not bad
for sad and shabby, *is* it.

(Points to THE MISTRESS*)*

But what about *her!*

THE WIFE *(Curious)*. What *about* her?

THE MISTRESS *(She, too)*. Yes; what *about* me?

THE DAUGHTER. Mistress is a pretty generous term for what it's all about,
isn't it? So is *kept*. Isn't that *another* euphemism? And how much do
you think she's gotten from him? Half a million? A million?

THE MISTRESS. There are things you do *not* know, little girl.

327

THE WIFE *(Steel)*. You live with a man who will not divorce his wife, who has become a drunkard because of him, and who is doubtless supplied with her liquor gratis from *his liquor* store—a business which is, I take it, the height of his ambition—who has taken more money from you than I like to think about, who has broken one rib that I know of, and blackened your eyes, and has *dared* . . . *dared* to come to me and suggest I intercede with your father . . .

THE DAUGHTER *(Furious)*. ALL RIGHT!

THE WIFE. . . . in a political matter which *stank* of the Mafia . . .

THE DAUGHTER *(A scream)*. ALL RIGHT!

THE WIFE *(A change of tone to loss)*. You know a lot about sad and shabby; you know far too much to turn the phrase on others, especially on those who do *not* make a point of doing what they will or must as badly as possible. That is probably what I have come to love you so little for— that *you* love yourself so little. Don't ever tell *me* how to make a life, or *anyone* who does things out of love, or even affection.

(Pause)

You were beautiful, you know. You really were. Once.

(THE DAUGHTER *opens her mouth as if to respond; thinks otherwise; moves away. Silence as they think on this)*

THE MISTRESS *(Some delight; really to bring them all back)*. My parents are both still alive—I suddenly remember. They are neither . . . particularly *limber*, they keep to themselves more than not, and my father's eyesight is such that when he dares to drive at all it is down the center line of the road. Oh, it makes the other drivers cautious. She's learned that snapping at him does no good at all, and the one time she put her hand on the wheel, thinking—she told me later—that his drift to the left was becoming more pronounced than ever, he resisted her, and the result was weaving, and horns, and a ditch, or shoulder, whichever it is, and a good deal of heavy breathing.

THE BEST FRIEND. Why doesn't *she* drive?

THE MISTRESS *(Smiles a little)*. No; she could learn, but I imagine she'd rather sit there with him and see things his way.

THE DAUGHTER *(Dry)*. Why doesn't she walk, or take a taxi, or just not go?

THE MISTRESS *(Knows she is being mocked, but prefers to teach rather than hit back)*. Oh; she loves him, you see.

(Laughs again)

My *grand*father died only last year.

THE DAUGHTER *(Spat out).* Oh, *stop* it!

THE MISTRESS *(Controlled). Please* stop telling me to stop it.
(Generally)
He was a hundred and three, my mother's father, and he was not at all like those centenarians you're always reading about: full head of snow-white hair, out chopping wood all the time when they weren't burying their fourth wife or doing something worthy in the Amazon; not a bit of it. He was a wispy little man, whom none of us liked very much—not even my mother, who would be a saint one day, were it not for Luther; a tiny man, with the face of a starving child, and blond hair of the type that white does not become, and very little of that, and bones, it would appear, of the finest porcelain, for he fell, when he was seventy-two, and did to his pelvis what you would do to a teapot were you to drop it on a flagstone floor.

THE DOCTOR *(Factual; nothing else).* The bones dry out.

THE MISTRESS. Indeed they must, for he took to his bed—or was taken there—and remained in it for thirty-one years. He wanted to be read to a lot.

THE WIFE *(She tries to get the two words out sensibly, but breaks up during it into a helpless laughter; she covers her mouth, and her eyes dart from person to person; the words are:).* Poor man!
(Finally she quiets herself, but a glance at her daughter staring at her with distaste sends her into another outburst; this one she controls rather more easily)

THE MISTRESS *(After the second outburst has quieted; very serious).* Shh, now. As I said, he wanted to be read to a lot.
(THE WIFE *smothers giggles occasionally during this*)
This was not easy for his family and fast-diminishing set of friends, for he was hard of hearing and one had to shout;
(She holds her right index finger up)
plus; plus, everyone knew he had the eyesight of a turkey buzzard.
(THE BEST FRIEND *starts to giggle a bit, too, now*)

THE DAUGHTER. Stop it!

THE MISTRESS. So, finally, of course, one had to start hiring people.

THE DAUGHTER *(As* THE WIFE *laughs).* Stop it!

THE WIFE *(She can no longer control her hysteria).* A turkey buzzard!?
(Her newest explosion of laughter is enough to set THE SON *off as well, and, to a lesser degree,* THE DOCTOR *and* THE NURSE)*

THE DAUGHTER. Stop it!

THE WIFE. It's not *true, is* it!

THE MISTRESS *(As she breaks up, herself)*. No; not a word of it!

(Note: While this laughter should have the look, to those who have watched it, and the feel, to those who have experienced it, of the self-generating laughter possible under marijuana, we should be aware that it is, in truth, produced by extreme tension, fatigue, ultimate sadness and existentialist awareness: in other words . . . the reason we always react that way. Further note: The ones who have laughed least freely should stop most precipitously, though THE SON *might keep his mirth awhile longer than most.* THE WIFE *and* THE MISTRESS *have an arm around one another)*

THE DAUGHTER *(She has been saying, "Stop it, stop it; stop it, you fucking bitches!" all through the ultimate laughter, mostly to* THE WIFE *and* THE MISTRESS, *but at* THE SON, THE NURSE, THE BEST FRIEND *and* THE DOCTOR *as well. Clearly, she has meant it for them all, for, as they stop, not without a whoop or two at her from time to time, her volume stays constant, so that, finally, hers is the voice we hear, and hers only)*. Stop it; stop it; stop it, you bitches, you filthy . . . you filth who allow it . . . you . . . you . . .

(Stop)

THE WIFE *(She is the one who stops first, becomes fixed on* THE DAUGHTER*)*. You! *You* stop it!

THE DAUGHTER. You bitches! You fucking . . .

(Stops; realizes)

THE WIFE *(A quiet, post-hysterical smile)*. Why don't you go home to your *own* filth? You . . . you . . . issue!

(Sits back, eyes her coldly)

THE DAUGHTER *(Rage only, now)*. Your morality is . . . it's incredible; it really is; it's a model for the world. You're smug, and excluding. You're incredible! All of you!

THE WIFE *(Calm; seemingly detached)*. Well, since you've nothing else to do, why don't you run downstairs and tell the waiting press about . . . *our* morality? And while you're at it . . . tell them about your own as well.

THE DAUGHTER *(So intense she can barely get it through her teeth)*. This woman has come and taken . . . my . . . *father!*

THE WIFE *(After a pause; not sad; a little weary; empty, perhaps).* Yes. My *hus*band. Remember?

(Sighs)

And that makes all the difference. Perhaps your fancy man has people who care for him, who worry after him; they are not my concern. They may be *yours*, but I doubt it. *I . . . care;* about what happens *here.* This woman loves my husband—as *I* do—and she has made him happy; as *I* have. She is good, and decent, and she is not moved by envy and self-loathing . . .

THE DAUGHTER *(Close to rage again).* . . . like some people?!! . . .

THE WIFE. . . . Indeed. Like *some* people.

THE DAUGHTER *(A stuck record).* Like *you!?* Like *you!?* Like *you!?*

THE WIFE *(Shuts her eyes for a moment, as if to shut out the sound).* Somewhere, in the rubble you've made of your life so far, you must have an instinct tells you why she's part of us. No? She *loves* us. And we love *her.*

THE DAUGHTER *(A rough, deep voice).* Do *you* love *me?*

(Pause; her tone becomes fiercer)

Does *anyone* love me?

THE WIFE *(A bright little half-caught laugh escapes her; her tone instantly becomes serious).* Do *you* love anyone?

(A silence. THE DAUGHTER *stands for a moment, swaying, quivering just perceptibly; then she turns on her heel, opens the door and slams it behind her)*

THE BEST FRIEND *(As* THE WIFE *sighs, reaches for* THE MISTRESS' *hand).* Will she? Will she go down and tell the waiting press?

THE WIFE *(True curiosity).* I don't *know.* I don't think she would; but I don't *know.*

(Laughs as she did before)

I laughed before, because it was so unlikely. I had an aunt, a moody lady, but with cause. She died when she was twenty-six—died in the heart, that is, or whatever portion of the brain controls the spirit; she went on, all the appearances, was snuffed out, finally, at sixty-two, in a car crash, all done up in jodhpurs and a derby, yellow scarf with the foxhead stickpin, driving in the vintage car, the old silver touring car, the convertible with the window between the front and back seats, back from the stable, from jumping, curved, bashed straight into the bread truck, Parkerhouse rolls and blood, her twenty-six-year heart emptying out of her sixty-two-year body, on the foxhead pin and the metal and the gasoline, and all the cardboard boxes sprawled on the country road. *(Slight pause)*

"Does anyone love me?" she asked, once, back when I was nine, or ten. There were several of us in the room, but they were used to it. "Do *you* love anyone?" I asked her back. Slap! Then tears—hers *and* mine; mine not from the pain but the . . . effrontery; hers . . . both; effrontery *and* pain.

THE MISTRESS *(After a short silence)*. Hmmmm. Yes.

(The door bursts open, and THE DAUGHTER *catapults into the room, leaving the door wide)*

THE DAUGHTER. *YOU* tell them!

*(*TWO PHOTOGRAPHERS *and* A REPORTER *enter tentatively; in the moment it takes for the people assembled to react, they have moved a step or two in. Then the room moves into action.* THE DOCTOR *and* THE NURSE *stay where they are, but transfixed;* THE SON *rises from his chair;* THE BEST FRIEND *takes a step or two forward;* THE WIFE *and* THE MISTRESS *rise, poised)*

THE BEST FRIEND. Get back downstairs; you can't come . . .

(But it is THE WIFE *and* THE MISTRESS *who move)*

THE WIFE *(A beast's voice, really)*. Get . . . out . . . of . . . here!

(The two women attack, fall upon the intruders with fists and feet, and there is an animal fury within them which magnifies their strength. The struggle is brief, but intense; one of the cameramen has his camera knocked to the floor, where he leaves it as the three men retreat. THE WIFE *forces the door shut, turns, leans against it.* THE DAUGHTER *has her back to the audience, with* THE WIFE *and* THE MISTRESS *to either side of her, facing her. No words; heavy breathing; almost a tableau. Finally; it is an animal's sound; rage, pain)*

AARRRGGGHHH.

(Two seconds silence)

CURTAIN

ACT TWO

The scene: the same as before, fifteen minutes later. THE DOCTOR *and* THE
NURSE *are at the bed, half asleep on their feet, or perhaps* THE DOCTOR *has
fallen asleep on a chair near the bed.* THE BEST FRIEND *is by the fireplace,
gazing into it;* THE WIFE *is dozing in a chair;* THE MISTRESS *is in a chair
near the fireplace;* THE DAUGHTER *is in a chair somewhat removed from the
others, facing front;* THE SON *is massaging her shoulders.*
*It seems very late: the exhaustion has overwhelmed them; even awake they
seem to be in a dream state. What one says is not picked up at once by
another.*

THE SON *(Gently).* You shouldn't have done that. You know you shouldn't.
THE DAUGHTER *(Really not anxious to talk about it).* I know I shouldn't.
  Gentler.
THE SON. No matter how you feel.
THE DAUGHTER. I *know.* I *said* I *know.*
THE SON. If they'd gotten in . . . .
THE DAUGHTER. Not with our sentries; you'd need an army for that.
THE SON. No matter *how* you feel.
THE DAUGHTER *(Languid).* I feel . . . well, how you must have felt when
  you were young, at school, and you'd fail, or be dismissed, to make some
  point you didn't know quite what. Like that.
  (Quite without emotion)
  I feel like a child, rebellious, misunderstood and known oh, so very well;
  sated and . . . empty. I'm *on* to myself; there's no mistake there. I'm
  all the things you think of me, every one of you, and I'm also many
  more.
  (An afterthought)
  I wonder why they didn't kill me, the two of them.
THE SON. There's enough death going here.
THE DAUGHTER. Oh, I don't know. God knows, I can probably go my own
  way now, without a word or a look from any of you. Non grata *has* its
  compensations. Go my own way. What a relief.
  (Ironic)
  Back to that "degradation" of mine. Imagine her!, degrading a family as
  famous as this, up by its own boot straps—well, the only one of it who
  mattered, anyway—all the responsibility to itself, the Puritan moral
  soul. How does it go?: "Since we have become what we are, then the

333

double edge is on us; we cannot back down, for we are no longer private, and the world has its eye on us." Christ, you'd think we were only nominally mortal, *he* at any rate; he's the only one who matters, and *he's* mortal enough, is going to prove to be. And the eye of the world! Eyes are attached to the brain, I believe, and the monster is sluggish nowadays, all confused and retreating, surly but withdrawn. *Folk* heroes, maybe, but not *his* type, too much up *here.* If you can't take it in all at once—relate to it, dear God—grant it its due, but don't dwell on it. The dust bin; anachronism. Well, I'll be glad when he's gone—no, no, not for the horrid reasons, not for all of your mistakes about me, but simply that the tintype can be thrown away, the sturdy group, and I can be what I choose to be with only half of the disapproval, no longer the public. *You* won't get in the press because you're someone's son, unless you get arrested for something serious, *or* newsworthy. Nor will I. I'll have my man—such as he is and such as I want him for—and only mother will really mind. We'll see each other less, all of us, and finally not at all, I'd imagine—except on . . . occasions. Whatever we disdain will be our own affair. You can, too, probably, very soon . . . when all *this* is finished.

THE SON. Do *what.*

THE DAUGHTER. Resign . . . You'll be rich enough, or do you want to go on with it, even when he's gone? Isn't it pointless for you there? Aren't you useless?

THE SON *(Wry little laugh).* Probably. I don't like it very much; I don't feel *part* of it, though it's a way of getting through from ten to six, and avoiding all I know I'd be doing if I didn't have it . . .
(Smiles a bit)
those demons of mine.

THE DAUGHTER *(Laughs a little).* Ah, those demons. You're no different.
(Turns toward THE BEST FRIEND*)*
Will you keep him on—
(Mildly mocking)
at the *firm*—after . . . all this is finished, and you've no more obligation to our father, or did you make a bond to keep it up forever?

THE BEST FRIEND *(Quietly).* There's no bond; your brother isn't with me as a charity.
(To THE SON*)*
You don't think that, do you? You fill your position nicely and you're

nicely paid for doing it. If you choose to leave, of course, nothing will falter, nor, for that matter, will I feel any . . . particular loss, but we know that about each other, don't we. But no one's waiting to throw you down. That's your sister's manner.

(To THE DAUGHTER*)*

Don't ask me to talk about it now.

THE SON *(To* THE BEST FRIEND; *very simple).* I didn't know that you didn't care for me. I suppose I always assumed . . . well, that we were all a form of family, and . . .

(Shrugs)

THE DAUGHTER *(Sad advice).* Don't assume.

THE SON. Well; no matter.

THE BEST FRIEND *(A little impatient).* Did I say I didn't *care* for you? I thought I said I'd feel no loss if you were gone. I'm pretty much out of loss.

(He turns back to the fire)

THE SON. Sorry; that *is* what you said.

(To THE DAUGHTER*)*

Enough? More?

THE DAUGHTER. The base of the neck, and slowly, very slowly. Uh hunh.

(Sensuous, as he massages her neck)

They were animals, and I had a moment of . . . absolutely thrilling dread, very much as when I read of the Chinese, and how they are adept at keeping a man alive and conscious, *conscious,* for hours, while they strip the skin from his body. They tie him to a pole.

THE SON. What for?

THE DAUGHTER. So he won't wander off, I'd imagine. I'm not your usual masochist, in spite of what *she* thinks. I mean, a broken rib really *hurts,* and everybody over twelve knows what a black eye on a lady *means.* I don't fancy any of that, but I do care an awful lot about the guilt I can produce in those that do the hurting.

(Suddenly a little girl)

Mother?

THE SON. She's sleeping.

THE DAUGHTER *(Turns to* THE MISTRESS*). You're* not.

THE MISTRESS *(Coming back).* Hm?

THE DAUGHTER. *You're* not, *are* you. Sleeping.

THE MISTRESS *(Not hostile; still half away).* No. I'm far too exhausted.

THE DAUGHTER *(To* THE SON; *plaintive).* Wake mother up.

THE BEST FRIEND *(Sotto voce).* Let her sleep, for God's sake!

THE MISTRESS *(Voice low; cool).* Do you want to start in again? Do you have some new pleasure for us?

THE DAUGHTER *(Heavy sigh).* I want to tell her that I'm sorry.

THE MISTRESS. I dare say she knows that; has, for years.

THE DAUGHTER. Still . . .

THE MISTRESS. Nobody's a fool here.

THE DAUGHTER *(Mildly biting).* You were never a mother.

THE MISTRESS *(Smiles).* No, nor have you been, but you've been a woman.

THE DAUGHTER *(Ironic).* And the old instinct's always there, right?

THE MISTRESS. Right.

THE DAUGHTER. But you have been a wife, haven't you, twice as I remember, not to count your adventures in mistresshood. How many men have you gone through, hunh? No divorces, you; just bury them.

THE MISTRESS *(Calm, but intent).* Listen to me, young lady, there are things you have no idea of, matters might cross your mind were you not so . . . self-possessed. You lash out—which can be a virtue, I dare say, stridency aside, if it's used to protect and not just as a revenge . . .

THE DAUGHTER *(To cut it off).* O.K. O.K.

THE MISTRESS. . . . but you're careless, not only with facts, but of yourself. What words will you ever have left if you use them all to kill? What words will you summon up when the day *comes,* as it may, poor you, when you suddenly discover that you've been in love—oh, for a week, say, and not known it, not having been familiar with the symptoms, being such an amateur? Love with mercy, I mean, the kind you can't hold back as a reward, or use as any sort of weapon. What vocabulary will you have for that? Perhaps you'll be mute; many are—the self-conscious—in a foreign land, with only the phrases the guidebook gives them, or maybe it will be dreamlike for you—nightmarish—lockjawed, throat constricted, knowing that whatever word you use, whatever phrase you might say will come out, not as you mean it then, but as you have meant before, that "I love you; I need you," no matter how joyously meant, will be the snarl of a wounded and wounding animal. You'd better go back to grade school.

THE DAUGHTER *(Contempt and self-disgust).* Oh, I'm far too old for that, aren't I?

THE MISTRESS *(Shrugs).* Perhaps you are. It would serve you right.

THE DAUGHTER. There's ignorance enough in you, too, you know. You've not been that much in touch—except with *him,* and he's hardly one to keep you up to date.

THE MISTRESS. So true. But—and I *do* hate to say it, I really do—unless you're some kind of unique, I've seen your type before.

THE DAUGHTER *(Quietly).* Fuck yourself.

(To THE SON*)*

You've stopped.

THE SON *(Not starting again).* Yes. My fingers ache.

THE DAUGHTER *(Quietly, without emotion).* You never were much good at anything.

THE MISTRESS *(To* THE BEST FRIEND; *mock ingenuous).* How am I supposed to do that, I wonder?

THE BEST FRIEND *(Dry, weary).* It's usually said to men, but even there it's a figure of speech.

(He shakes his head, turns back to the fire)

Don't involve me; please.

*(*THE DOCTOR *has moved toward them; he stands for a moment)*

THE DOCTOR *(Quietly).* That's very interesting; it *is.*

THE SON *(Soft, but frightened).* What is?

THE DOCTOR. His heart stopped beating . . . for three beats. Then it started again.

THE DAUGHTER *(To* THE SON; *anxious).* Wake mother!

THE DOCTOR *(With a gesture).* No; no; it *began* again.

THE DAUGHTER. Maybe you were asleep: you're old enough.

THE DOCTOR. Surely, but I wasn't. Fall asleep with the stethoscope to his chest, dream of stop and go? Wake immediately, jolted back by the content? No. His heart stopped beating . . . for three beats. Then it started again. Nothing less than that. I thought I'd report it.

(He starts to turn back; re-turns)

It's interesting when it happens, but it's nothing to write home about. Just thought I'd report it, that's all.

THE MISTRESS. What does it signify? It must, something.

THE DOCTOR *(Thinks, shrugs).* Weakening. What did you mean, something conscious like fighting it off?

THE MISTRESS *(Wistful).* Maybe.

THE DOCTOR *(Gentle; a smile).* Nooooo. You're better than that.

(He moves back whence he came)

337

THE DAUGHTER. They tell you more on television.

(THE MISTRESS *laughs a little*)

They do!

THE MISTRESS. In a way.

THE SON *(Sober)*. Just think: it could have been finished then.

(Quickly)

I don't mean anything but the wonder of it.

THE MISTRESS *(Dry)*. Why, don't you believe in suffering?

THE DAUGHTER. Does he know he is? Suffering?

THE MISTRESS. I didn't mean him.

(Refers first to THE DAUGHTER, *then* THE SON)

I meant you . . . and you. I *do*: believe in suffering.

THE DAUGHTER *(Quiet scorn)*. What *are* you, a fundamentalist, one of those "God designed it so it must be right" persons, down deep beneath the silvery surface?

THE SON. She didn't mean that.

THE DAUGHTER *(Ibid.)*. How would *you* know? You're not much good at anything.

THE SON *(To* THE MISTRESS). *Did* you? *Mean* that?

THE MISTRESS. I meant at least two things, as I usually do.

(To THE DAUGHTER)

No divorces, I just bury them? Well, what would you have me do? I know, you meant it as a way of speaking; you were trying to be unkind, but keep it in mind should your lover be rid of his wife, marry you, and die. You've been a woman, but you haven't been a wife. It isn't very nice, you know, to get it all at once—for both my deaths were sudden: heart attack, and car.

(Sighs, almost begins to laugh)

Well, maybe it's better than . . .

(Indicates the room with a general gesture)

this. It's all done at once, and you're empty; you go from that to grief without the intervening pain. You can't suffer with a man because he's dead; his dying, yes. The only horror in participating is . . .

(Thinks better of it)

. . . well, another time.

(Pause; shift of tone)

Look here! You accused me before of being—what is that old-fashioned word?—a gold digger, of having insinuated myself into . . .

THE DAUGHTER. I said you *probably!*

THE MISTRESS. Yes, of course, but you're imprecise and I know what you meant. That I am expecting something less than I have received from your father—money, in other words, a portion of what you are expecting for having permitted yourselves to be born.

(Turns to THE BEST FRIEND, *takes his hand; he still stares into the fire)*

May I engage you?

*(*THE BEST FRIEND *shakes his head, leaves his hand where it is; she removes hers)*

No? All right.

(Back to THE DAUGHTER*)*

You will see, in good time.

(Laughs)

I remember a family once, two children, both well into their fifties, with a dying mother, eighty-something. These children—and there is no allegory here; read yourselves in if you want, but I hope not—these elderly children didn't like each other very much; the daughter had married perhaps not wisely for her second time—penniless, much younger than she, rather fruity to the eye and ear, but perhaps more of a man than most, you never know—but the reasons went further back, the dislike, to some genesis I came upon them too late for, and in the last months of their mother's life they did battle for a percentage of her will, for her estate. But fifty-fifty wouldn't do, and it would shift from that to sixty-forty—seventy-thirty once, I'm told! The mother, you see, had loved them both, and either one who came to her would tilt the balance. But she ended it exactly where she'd started it—half to each—and all that had happened was damage. The daughter was the one at fault, or more grievously, for she had been spoiled in a way that sons are seldom. But all of this is to tell you that I'm not an intruder in the dollar sense. I've more than enough—I was born with it. Don't you people ever take the trouble to scout? And I told your father I wanted nothing beyond his company . . . *and* love. He agreed with me, you'll be distressed to know, said *you needed* it. So. I am not your platinum blonde with the chewing gum and the sequined dress.

THE DAUGHTER *(After a pause).* I'm supposed to like you now, I take it, fall into your arms and cry a little and choke out words like sorry and forgive. Well, you've got the wrong lady.

THE MISTRESS *(Light)*. *I* wouldn't expect it, and I really don't much care. I've more important things.

(Less light)

He taught me a sense of values, you know, beyond what I'd thought was adequate. Cold, I suppose, but right on the button. Took a little while, but I guess I knew I'd go through this someday; so I learned. And you know something else? I'll be there at the funeral, ashes if I have my way —if *he* has *his*—either way. It's one . . . ritual I'll not defer for.

THE DAUGHTER. You wouldn't dare!

THE MISTRESS. You don't know me, child.

THE DAUGHTER. I won't *have* it.

THE SON *(Gently)*. Be calm.

THE MISTRESS *(Laughs a little)*. It's not a mind gone mad with power, or a dip into impropriety, or the need to reopen a wound—for the wound *is* closed, you know, your mother knows; *you* do, too; you're railing because you never saw it open; *you* can't even find a scar; you don't know where it *was;* that *must* be infuriating—none of those things, but simply that I'll not be put down by sham, and I'll *be* there, dressed in my gray and white, a friend of the family. There'll be none of your Italian melodrama, with all the buzz as to who is that stranger off to one side, that woman in black whom nobody knows, wailing louder than the widow and the family put together. None of that. I have always known my place, and I shall know it then. Don't wake her. Let her sleep.

THE DAUGHTER *(As THE NURSE approaches, tapping a cigarette)*. You're right: I *am* an amateur.

THE NURSE. May I join you?

(Nobody replies; she eases into a chair, clearly exhausted. She lights her cigarette, inhales, exhales with a great, slow breath)

Sensible shoes help, but when you're well up into the 'teens, like me, there's nothing for it but this, sometimes.

THE MISTRESS *(Looking away)*. Any change?

THE NURSE. No; none. Well, of course, some. Procession, but nothing, really.

(Looks at THE SON)

You're much too fat; heavy, rather.

THE SON *(Matter-of-fact)*. I'm sedentary.

THE NURSE. Eat less; do isometrics. You won't last out your fifties.

THE SON *(Quiet; an echo of something)*. Maybe not?

THE NURSE. Well, I'm not skin and bones, myself, but it's different for a woman: our hearts are better. Eat fish and raw vegetables and fruit; avoid everything you like.

(An afterthought)

Except sex; have a lot of that: fish, raw vegetables, fruit and sex.

THE SON *(Embarrassed)*. Th-thank you.

THE NURSE. Eggs, red flesh, milk-cheese-butter, nuts, most starches 'cept potatoes and rice . . . all bad for you; ignore them. Two whiskies before dinner, a glass of good burgundy *with* it, and sex before you go to sleep. That'll do the trick, keep you going.

THE SON. For?

THE NURSE *(Rather surprised at his question)*. Until it's proper time for you to die. No point in rushing it.

THE DAUGHTER *(Eyes upward, head rolling from side to side; through her teeth)*. Death; death; death; death; death . . .

THE NURSE *(Taking a drag on her cigarette)*. Death, yes; well, it gets us where we live, doesn't it.

(A sound startles them. It comes from THE WIFE; it is a sharp, exhaled "Ha-ah." The first one comes while she is still asleep in her chair. She bolts upright and awake. She does it again: "Ha-ah")

THE WIFE *(Fully awake, but still a trifle bewildered)*. I was *asleep*. I *was* asleep. I was dreaming, and I dreamt I was asleep, and it wakened me. Have—have I . . . is every—every . . .

THE NURSE. It's all right; go back to sleep.

THE WIFE. No, I mustn't; I can't.

(She rises, a little unsteady, and begins to move toward THE DOCTOR) Is everything all right, is . . .

THE DOCTOR. Everything is all right. Really.

(THE WIFE moves toward the grouping, sees THE DAUGHTER, pauses, eyes her with cold loathing, moves to THE MISTRESS and THE BEST FRIEND, puts a hand absently on THE MISTRESS' shoulder, looks at THE BEST FRIEND's back, then at THE NURSE)

THE WIFE *(To THE NURSE; no reproach)*. Shouldn't you be back there?

THE NURSE *(Smiles)*. If I should be, I would be.

THE WIFE. Yes; I'm sorry.

(Generally; to no one, really)

I was dreaming of so many things, odd and . . . well, that I was shopping, for a kind of thread, a brand that isn't manufactured any more, and I knew it, but I thought that they might have some in the back. I couldn't remember the name of the maker, and of course that didn't help. They showed me several that were very much like it, one in particular that I almost settled on, but didn't. They tried to be helpful; it was what they used to call a dry goods store, and it was called that, and I remember a specific . . . not smell, but scent the place had, one that I only remember from being little, so I was clearly in the past, and when they couldn't help, I asked if I could go in the back, the stock. They smiled and said of course, and so I went through a muslin curtain, into the stock, and it was not at all what I'd expected—shelves of cardboard boxes, bales of twine, bolts of fabric, some of the boxes with labels, some with buttons pasted to the end, telling what was there— none of it; it was all canned fruit, and vegetables, peas and carrots and string beans and waxed beans, and bottles of chili sauce and catsup, and canned meats, and everything else I'd not expected and was not a help to me. So I walked back through the muslin and into the living room my family'd had when I was twelve or so, a year before we moved. It was the room my aunt had slapped me in, and I sensed that I was asleep, and it woke me.

THE SON (*Moves toward a door beside the fireplace, upstage*). Excuse me.

THE MISTRESS (*Wistful*). Dreams.

THE WIFE (*A little sad*). Yes.

(THE SON *closes the door behind him*. THE WIFE *turns to* THE BEST FRIEND)

Are you all right?

THE BEST FRIEND (*Straightens up, turns, finally, sighs*). I suppose. Trying to shut it all out helps. I felt a rush of outrage—back awhile—not over what *she* brought on,

(*Indicating* THE DAUGHTER)

or my wife's sister, or *myself*, for that matter, or

(*Indicates generally*)

. . . all this, but very generally, as if my brain was going to vomit, and I thought that if I was very still—as I was when I was a child, and felt I was about to be sick over something—it would go away. Well, no, not go away, but . . . recede.

(*Smiles, sadly*)

It has, I think; some.

THE DAUGHTER (*Shy, tentative*). Mother?

THE WIFE *(Tiniest pause, to indicate she has heard; speaks to* THE BEST FRIEND*)* I upset you, then. I'm sorry; what I said wasn't kind. You *do* understand it as well as the next.

THE DAUGHTER *(Still pleading quietly, but with an edge to it).* Mo-ther.

THE WIFE *(As before).* And *excluding* you was never my intention, for any cruel reason, that is. Oh, I may have wanted to join the two of us together
(Indicates THE MISTRESS*)*
as close as we were but had not admitted, or discussed, certainly, for we have so much to learn from each other . . .

THE DAUGHTER *(A growl of frustration and growing anger).* Mooootherrrr!

THE BEST FRIEND. You'd better answer her: she'll go downstairs again.

THE WIFE *(Calm, smiling a little).* No; she's done that once and won't succeed with it again, for no reason other than you wouldn't let her out the door . . . would you.
(Pause, as THE BEST FRIEND *winces, smiles sadly)*
Besides, it wouldn't be shocking any more, merely tiresome; she'd be pounding her fists on the wind.

THE DAUGHTER *(Bolt upright in her chair, hands grasping the arms, neck tendons tight; a howl).* MOOOOTHERRRRR!!

THE MISTRESS *(After a pause; gently).* Do answer her.

THE WIFE *(Pats* THE MISTRESS *gently on the shoulder; looks at* THE DAUGHTER*; speaks wistfully, eyes always on her).* I may never speak to her again. I'm not certain now—I have other things on my mind—but there's a good chance of it: I seldom speak to strangers, and if one should try to be familiar at a time of crisis, or sorrow, I'd be enraged.
(Talks to THE MISTRESS *now)*
Well, I suppose were I to stumble on the way to the gravesite and one—she—were to take my elbow to keep me from falling, I might say thank you, looking straight ahead. Unlikely, though, isn't it . . . stumbling.
(Small smile; quietly triumphant)
No; I don't think I shall speak to her again.
*(*THE DAUGHTER *rises;* THE WIFE *and* THE MISTRESS *watch.* THE DAUGHTER *seems drained and very tired; she stands for a moment, then slowly moves to the upstage chair or sofa recently abandoned by* THE WIFE*; she throws herself down on it, turns over on her back, puts one arm over her eyes, is still. Softly)*
So much for that.

343

ALL OVER

(Directly to THE MISTRESS' *back-of-the-head)*

You notice I *did* say gravesite, and I am not speaking of an urn of ashes.

THE MISTRESS *(Small smile).* I know; I heard you.

THE WIFE *(Almost apologetic).* I *will* do battle with you there, no matter what you tell me, no matter what an envelope may say, I will have my way. Not a question of faith, or a repugnance; merely an act of will.

THE MISTRESS *(Gently).* Well, I won't argue it with you now.

(THE SON *emerges, closes the door, leans against it, pressed flat, his head up, his eyes toward the ceiling. He is wracked by sobbing, and there is a crumpled handkerchief in his hand)*

THE SON *(Barely able to get it out, for the sobs).* It's all . . . still there . . . all . . . just as it . . . was.

(Quite suddenly he manages to control himself. This effect is not comic. It is clear an immense effort of will has taken place. His voice is not quite steady, falters once or twice, but he is under control)

I'm sorry; I'm being quite preposterous; I'm sorry. It's just that . . . it's all still there, just as I remember it, not from when I may have seen it last—when? twenty years?—but as it was when I was a child: the enormous sink; the strop; the paneling; the pier glass; the six showerheads and the mosaic tile; and . . . the . . . the white milk-glass bottles with the silver tops, the witch hazel and cologne, the gilt lettering rubbed nearly off; and . . .

(Softer; sadder)

. . . the ivory brushes, and the comb.

(Shakes his head rapidly, clearing it; full control)

Sorry; I'm sorry.

(Pause)

THE WIFE *(Sighs, nods several times).* It would take *you, wouldn't* it. Choose anything, any of the honors, the idea of a face in your mind, something from when he took you somewhere once, or came halfway round the world when you were burning up and the doctors had no way of knowing what it was, then, in those times, sat by your bed the four days till it began to slacken, *then* slept.

(Her anger, her contempt, really rising)

No! Not any of it! Give us you, and you find a BATHROOM . . . *MOVING?*

(Pause. Softer, a kind defeat)

Well . . . I can't expect you to be the son of your father and *be* much: it's too great a *burden;* but to be so little is . . .
(Dismisses him with a gesture, paces a little)
You've neither of you had children, thank God, children that I've *known* of.
(Harsh)
I hope you never marry . . . *either* of you!
(Softer, if no gentler)
Let the line end where it is . . . at its zenith.

THE SON *(A rasped voice).* Mother! Be kind!

THE WIFE *(To* THE MISTRESS; *rather fast, almost singsong).* We made them both; remember how I told you that he asked me that? If it were true? And how I laughed, and said, oh, yes? Remember?
*(*THE MISTRESS *nods, without looking at her)*

THE SON *(Moves toward the stage-left door, stops by* THE DAUGHTER; *speaks to her).* I'm going across the hall, to the solarium.
*(*THE WIFE *turns to notice this exchange)*

THE DAUGHTER *(Without moving).* All right.

THE SON. So you'll know where I am.

THE DAUGHTER. All right.

THE SON. In case.

THE DAUGHTER. All right.

THE WIFE *(As* THE SON *reaches the door to the hallway; mocking, but without vigor).* Aren't you up to it?

THE SON *(Mildly; matter-of-fact).* Not up to you, mother; never was.
(He exits)

THE WIFE *(At something of a loss).* Well.
(Pause)
Well.
(Pause)
Indeed.
*(*THE DAUGHTER *speaks next; while she does,* THE WIFE *moves about, listening, looking at* THE DAUGHTER *occasionally, but generally at furniture, the floor, whatever)*

THE DAUGHTER *(Never once removing her arm from across her eyes).* Dear God, why can't you leave him alone? Why couldn't you let him be, this *once.* Everyone's the target of something, something unexpected and maybe even stupid. You can shore yourself up beautifully, guns on every

degree of the compass, a perfect surround, but when the sky falls in or the earth gives way beneath your feet . . . so what? It's all untended, and what's it guarding? Those movies—remember them?—way back, India, usually, or in the west, the forts against the savages: the rescue party finally got there, and there was the bastion, guns pricking out from every window and turret, the white caps of the soldiers, the flag of the regiment blowing, but something was wrong; the Max Steiner music had stopped and the only sound was the blowing of the sand; and then the head of the rescue party would shoot off his pistol as a signal to those inside, and wait; still, just the blowing of the sand, and no Max Steiner music; they'd approach, go in, and there it all was, just as all of us except the rescue party knew it would be—every last soldier dead, propped up into position as some kind of grisly joke by the Tughees, or the Sioux, or whatever it was. Why couldn't you have just left him alone? He's spent his grown life getting set against everything, fobbing it all off, covering his shit as best he can, and so what if the sight of one unexpected, ludicrous thing collapses it all? So *what!* It's proof, isn't it? Isn't it proof he's not as . . . little as you said he was? It is, you know.
(Slight pause)
You make me as sick as I make you.
(Pause. THE WIFE *looks at* THE DAUGHTER *for a little, opens her mouth as if to speak, doesn't, looks back at* THE DOCTOR, *who seems to be dozing, turns to* THE NURSE*)*
THE WIFE *(To* THE NURSE*)*. You . . .
(Has to clear her throat)
. . . you'd better go back, I think; he may have fallen asleep.
THE NURSE *(Swivels in her chair, looks back)*. Doubt it; it's a trick he has, allows patients think he isn't watching.
THE WIFE *(Abrupt)*. Don't be ridiculous!
THE NURSE *(Calm)*. Don't be *rude*.
THE WIFE *(Sincerely)*. I'm sorry.
THE DOCTOR *(From where he is, without raising his head)*. If I *am* dozing— which *is* possible, though I don't think I've slept in over forty years—if I *am*, then I imagine my intuition would snap me back, if anything needed doing, wouldn't you think? My famous intuition?
THE WIFE *(Sings it back to him)*. Sor-ry.
(To THE MISTRESS; *wryly)*
That's all I seem to say. Shall I apologize to you for anything?

THE MISTRESS *(Smiles, shakes her head)*. No thank you.

THE WIFE. I may—just automatically—so pay no attention.

THE MISTRESS *(Stretches)*. You *could* answer my question, though.

THE WIFE. Have I forgotten it?

THE MISTRESS. Probably. I was wondering, musing: If I had been *you*—the little girl you were when he came to you—would you have come along as I did? Would *you* have come to take *my* place?

THE WIFE *(Smiles as she thinks about it)*. Hmmmmmm. No; I don't think so. We function so differently. I function as a wife, and you—don't misunderstand me—you do not. Married twice, yes, you were, but I doubt your husbands took a mistress, for you were *that*, too. And no man who has a mistress for his wife will take a wife as mistress.

(THE MISTRESS *laughs, softly, gaily)*

We're different kinds; whether I had children or not, I would always be a wife and mother, a symbol of stability rather than refuge. Both your husbands were married before they met you, no?

THE MISTRESS. Um; yes.

THE WIFE *(Light)*. Perhaps you're evil.

THE MISTRESS. No, I don't think so; I never scheme; I have never sought a man out, said, I think I will have this one. Oh, *is* he married? I see; well, no matter, that will fall like a discarded skin. I am not like that at all. I have cared for only three men—my own two husbands . . . and yours. My, how shocking that sounds. Well, three men and one boy. That was back, very far, fifteen and sixteen. God!, we were in love: innocent, virgins, both of us, and I doubt that either of us had ever told a lie. We met by chance at a lawn party on a Sunday afternoon, and had got ourselves in bed by dusk. You may not call that love, but it was. We were not embarrassed children, awkward and puppy-rutting. No; fifteen and sixteen, and never been before, but our sex was a strong and practiced and assisting . . . "known" thing between us, from the very start. Fumbling, tears, guilt? No, not a bit of it. He was the most . . . beautiful person I have ever seen: a face I will not try to describe, a lithe, smooth swimmer's body, and a penis I could not dismiss from my mind when I was not with him—I am not one of your ladies who pretends these things are of no account. We were a man and woman . . . an uncorrupted man and woman, and we made love all the summer, every day, wherever, whenever.

347

(Pause)

And then it stopped. *We* stopped.

THE DAUGHTER *(After a moment; same pose)*. What happened? Something tragic? Did he die, or become a priest?

THE MISTRESS *(Ignoring her tone; remembering)*. No, nothing like it. We had to go back to school.

THE DAUGHTER *(Snorts)*. Christ!

THE MISTRESS. We had to go back to *school*. Could anything be simpler?

THE DAUGHTER *(Raising herself half-up on her elbows; mildly unpleasant tone)*. No burning correspondence, love and fidelity sworn to eternity? Surely a weeping farewell, holding hands, staring at the ceiling, swearing your passion until Christmas holidays.

THE MISTRESS *(Still calm)*. No, not that at all. We made love, our last day together, kissed, rather as a brother and *sister* might, and said: "Goodbye; I love you." "Goodbye; I love you."

THE DAUGHTER. A couple of horny kids, that's all.

THE MISTRESS *(Smiles a little)*. No, I think you're wrong there. Oh, we were *that*, certainly, but I also think we were very wise. "Leave it; don't touch it again." I told you; it was very simple: we had to go back to school; we were *children*.

THE DAUGHTER *(Reciting the end of a fairy tale)*. And you never saw him again.

THE MISTRESS. True. He was from across the country, had been visiting that summer.

THE WIFE *(Very nice)*. What became of him?

THE MISTRESS *(Waves it away)*. Oh . . . things, things I've read about from time to time; nothing.

THE DAUGHTER. Oh, come on! What became of him!?

THE MISTRESS *(Irritated, but by the questioner, not the question)*. Whatever you like! He died and became a priest! *What* do *you* care?

THE DAUGHTER. I don't

THE MISTRESS. Then shut it up.

(THE DAUGHTER sinks back to her previous position)

THE WIFE *(After a pause)*. Four men, then.

THE MISTRESS. Hm? Oh; well, yes; yes, I suppose he *was* a man. Four men, then. Not too bad, I guess; spread out, not all bunched together.

THE WIFE. Yes.

(Slowly; something of a self-revelation)

I have loved only . . . once.

THE MISTRESS *(Nods, smiles; kindly)*. Yes.

THE BEST FRIEND *(Swings around)*. What if there *is* no paper? What if all the envelopes are business, and don't say a thing about it? What if there *are* no instructions?

THE WIFE *(Dry, but sad)*. Then it is in the hands of the wife . . . is it not?

THE BEST FRIEND. Yes, certainly, but . . . still.

THE WIFE *(On her guard)*. Still?

THE BEST FRIEND *(Pained)*. After a time, it . . . after a time the prerogative becomes *only* legal.

THE WIFE. *Only*, and *legal?* Those two words *next* to each other? From you?

THE BEST FRIEND *(Helpless)*. *I* can't stop you.

THE WIFE. Why would you want to, and why are we playing "what if"? He's a thorough man, knows as much law as you, or certainly *some* things. I am not a speculator.

THE BEST FRIEND. Those envelopes are not from yesterday.

THE WIFE. I dare say not. How *old* were you when you became aware of death?

THE BEST FRIEND. Well . . . what it meant, you mean.

(Smiles, remembering)

The age we all become philosophers—fifteen?

THE WIFE *(Mildly impatient; mildly amused)*. No, no, when you were aware of it for yourself, when you knew you were at the top of the roller-coaster ride, when you knew half of it was probably over and you were on your *way* to it.

THE BEST FRIEND. Oh.

(Pause)

Thirty-eight?

THE WIFE. Did you make a will then?

THE BEST FRIEND *(A rueful smile)*. Yes.

THE WIFE. Instructions in it?

THE BEST FRIEND *(Curiously angry)*. Yes! But not about that! Not about what was to be *done* with me. Maybe that's something women think about more.

THE WIFE *(Surprised, and grudging a point)*. May-*be*.

THE BEST FRIEND *(He, too).* And maybe it's something I never thought to *think* about.

THE WIFE. Do I sound absolutely *tribal?* Am I wearing feathers and mud, and *are* my earlobes halfway to my shoulders? I wonder! My rationale has been perfectly simple: you may lose your husband while he is alive, but when he is not, then he is yours again.

THE DAUGHTER *(Same position).* He still *is.*

(THE WIFE *opens her mouth to reply, stops herself)*

THE BEST FRIEND. What.

THE DAUGHTER. Alive.

THE BEST FRIEND *(Controlling his anger).* We *know* that.

THE DAUGHTER. Wondered; that's all.

THE MISTRESS *(Gently).* Let's not talk about it any more. We're misunderstood.

THE BEST FRIEND. It's just that . . . well, never mind.

THE WIFE *(Nicely).* That you're his best friend in the world, and you care about what happens to him?

THE BEST FRIEND *(Glum).* Something like that.

THE WIFE. Well, there are a number of his best friends here, and we all seem quite concerned. That we differ is incidental.

THE BEST FRIEND. Hardly. I warn you: if there *is* no paper, and I doubt there is, and you persist in having your way, I'll take it to court.

THE WIFE *(Steady).* That will take a long time.

THE BEST FRIEND. No doubt.

THE WIFE. Well.

(Pause)

It was pleasant having you as my lawyer.

THE BEST FRIEND. Don't be like that.

THE WIFE *(Furious).* Don't *be* like that!? Don't *be* like that!? We are talking of *my* husband. Surely you've not forgotten. You were a guest in our house—in the days when we *had* a house together. We entertained you. Here! You and your wife spent Christmas with us; many times! Who remembered to bring you your cigars from Havana whenever we were there? Who went shopping with you to surprise your wife, to help you make sure it was right and not the folly you husbands make of so many things? Me! *Wife!* Remember!?

(THE BEST FRIEND *goes to her where she sits, kneels beside her, takes her hands, puts them to his lips)*

I think I shall cry.

THE BEST FRIEND. No, now.

THE WIFE *(Wrenches her hands free, looks away; weary).* Do what you want with him; cast him in bronze if you like. I won't do battle with you: I like you both too much.

THE MISTRESS. I told you what he wants, that's all, or what he wanted when he told me. Let's not fall out over the future.

THE BEST FRIEND *(Gentle).* If I retract, will you hire me back again?

THE WIFE. You were never fired; what would I do without you? Rhetoric.

THE DAUGHTER *(Same position).* Join hands; kiss; sing.

THE WIFE *(Rather light tone, to* THE BEST FRIEND*).* What *is* it if you kill your daughter? It's matricide if *she* kills *you,* and infanticide if you do her in when she's a tot, but what if she's all grown up and beginning to wrinkle? Justifiable homicide, I suppose.

*(*THE NURSE *half emerges from behind the screen)*

THE NURSE. Doctor!?

(He joins her, and they are only partially visible. THE WIFE *stays where she is, grips the arms of her chair, closes her eyes.* THE MISTRESS *rises, stays put.* THE BEST FRIEND *moves toward the bed.* THE DAUGHTER *rises, stays where she is)*

THE NURSE *(Reappearing).* Stay back; it's nothing for you.

(She goes back to the bed. THE MISTRESS *sits again;* THE BEST FRIEND *goes into a chair.* THE DAUGHTER *returns to her sofa)*

THE DAUGHTER *(She pounds her hands on the sofa, more or less in time to her words; her voice is thick, and strained and angry. She must speak with her teeth clenched).* Our Father, who art in heaven; hallowed be thy name; thy kingdom come, thy will be done on earth as it is in heaven; give us this day!

(They are all silent. THE NURSE *reappears; her uniform is spotted with blood, as if someone had thrown some at her with a paint brush. There is blood on her hands, too)*

THE NURSE. It's all right; it's a hemorrhage, but it's all right.

THE WIFE *(Eyes still closed).* Are you certain!

THE NURSE *(Forceful, to quiet them).* It's all right!

(She returns to the bed)

THE MISTRESS *(To* THE WIFE, *after a pause).* Tell me about something; talk to me about anything—anything!

THE WIFE *(Struggling for a subject).* We . . . uh . . . the . . . the garden, yes, the garden we had, when we had our house in the country, outside of Paris. We were in France for nearly three years. Did you . . . did he tell you that?

THE MISTRESS. Yes; was it lovely?

THE WIFE. He couldn't, he couldn't have taken you there. It was lovely; it burned down; they wrote us.

THE MISTRESS. What a pity.

THE WIFE. Yes; it was lovely.

(She struggles to get through it)

It wasn't just a garden; it was a world . . . of . . . floration. Is that a word? No matter. It was a world of what it was. One didn't walk out into a garden—in the sense of when they say to you: "Come see what we've done." None of any of that. Of *course*. It had been planned, by careful minds—a woman *and* a man, I think, for it was that kind, or several; generations—and it resembled nothing so much as an environment.

(Head back, loud, to THE DOCTOR *and* THE NURSE*)*

IS ANYONE TELLING ME THE TRUTH?

THE NURSE *(Reappearing briefly)*. Yes.

(Goes back)

THE WIFE *(Quietly)*. Thank you.

THE MISTRESS. The garden.

THE WIFE. Yes.

(Pause, while she regathers)

The . . . the house, itself, was centuries old, rather Norman on the outside, wood laid into plaster, but not boxy in the Norman manner, small, but rambling; stone floors; huge, simple mantels, great timbers in the ceilings, a kitchen the size of a drawing room—*you* know. And all about it, clinging to it, spreading in every way, a tamed wilderness of garden. No, not tamed; planned, a planned wilderness. Such profusion, and all the birds and butterflies from miles around were privy to it. *And* the bees. One could walk out and make bouquets Redon would have envied.

(Pause)

I don't think I want to talk about it any more.

(THE DOCTOR *appears, finishing drying his hands with a towel. He comes forward)*

THE DOCTOR. Close, but all right; there's no predicting those. May I join you?

(He sits with THE WIFE *and* THE MISTRESS*)*

That's better. I suddenly feel quite old . . .

(Chuckles)

. . . which could pass for a laugh, couldn't it?

THE MISTRESS. Are you going to retire, one day?

THE DOCTOR. Couldn't, now; I'm way past retirement age. I should have done it fifteen years ago. Besides, what would I do?

THE WIFE *(Not looking at* THE DOCTOR*)*. Did it . . . hasten it?

THE DOCTOR *(Pause)*. Sure. What else would you expect? Every breath diminishes; each heartbeat is taking a chance.

THE MISTRESS *(An attempt to change the subject)*. I've never understood how you doctors stay so well in the midst of it all—the contagions. You must rattle from the pills and be a mass of pricks.

THE DOCTOR. Oh, it's easier now; used to be a day, though. Still, it's interesting. In Europe, in the time of the black plague—and I *read* about it, don't be thinking fresh—when eighty percent of a town would go, wiped out in a week, the doctors, such as they were, would lose only half. There wasn't much a doctor could do, in those days, against the bubonic—and especially the pneumonic—but saddling up and running wouldn't have helped, postponed, maybe, so they stayed, tried to get the buboes to break, nailed some houses shut with all the living inside if there was a case, and preceded the priests by a day or two in their rounds. The priests had the same break as the doctors, the same percentages. Might *mean* something; probably not.

(Pause)

Want some more history?

THE WIFE *(Shakes her head, smiles a little)*. No.

THE MISTRESS *(Ibid.)*. Not really.

THE DOCTOR *(Rises, with an effort)*. I'll go back, then. If you do, let me know; I'm up on it.

(Starts back, passes THE DAUGHTER, *recumbent)*

Got a headache, or something?

(Moves on)

THE DAUGHTER *(Rises, swiftly; under her breath)*. Christ!

(Generally)

I'll be in the solarium, too.

ALL OVER

(She exits, slamming the door after her. Some silence)

THE WIFE *(To* THE MISTRESS, *gently)*. What *will* you do?

THE MISTRESS *(Smiles sadly)*. I don't *know*. I've *thought* about it, of course, and nothing seems much good. I'm not a drinker, and I'm far too old for drugs. I've thought of taking a very long trip, of going places I've not been before—*we've* not been—but there's quite a lot against that, too. Do I want to forget, or do I want to remember? If the choice comes down to masochism or cowardice, then maybe best do nothing. Though, I must do *something*. The sad thing is, I've seen so many of them, the ones who are suddenly without their men, going back to places they have known together, sitting on terraces and looking about. They give the impression of wanting to be recognized, as if the crowd in Cannes that year had all the people from the time before and someone would come and say hello. They overdress, which is something they never would have done before: at three in the afternoon they're wearing frocks, and evening jewelry, and their make-up is for the dim of the cocktail lounge, and not the sun. I'm not talking of the women who fall apart. No, I mean the straight ladies who are mildly startled by everything, as if something they could not quite place were not quite right. Well, it is all the things they have come there to not admit—that the present is not the past, that they must order for themselves, and trust no one. And the groups are even worse, those three or four who make the trips together, those coveys of bewildered widows, talking about their husbands as if they'd gone to a stag, or were at the club. There's a coarsening in that, a lack of respect for oneself, ultimately. I *shall* go away; I *know* that; but it won't be to places unfamiliar, either. There are different kinds of pain, and being once more where one has been, and shared, *must* be easier than being where one *cannot* ever . . . I think what I shall do is go to where I've been, *we've* been, but I shall do it out of focus, for indeed it will be. I'll go to Deauville in October, with only the Normandie open, and take long, wrapped-up walks along the beach in the cold and gray. I'll spend a week in Copenhagen when the Tivoli's closed. And I'll have my Christmas in Venice, where I'm told it usually snows. Or maybe I'll just go to Berlin and stare at the wall. We were there when they put it up. There's so much one can do. And so little.

(Long pause; finally, with tristesse)

What will *you* do?

THE WIFE *(Pause)*. It's very different. I've been practicing widowhood for so many years that I don't know what effect the fact will have on me. Maybe none. I've settled in to a life which is comfortable, interesting, and useful, and I contemplate no change. You never know, though. It may be I have told myself . . . all lies and I am no more prepared for what will happen—when? tonight? tomorrow morning?—than I would be were he to shake off the coma, rise up from his bed, put his arms about me, ask my forgiveness for all the years, and take me back. I can't predict. I know I want to feel something. I'm waiting to, and I have no idea what I'm storing up. You make a lot of adjustments over the years, if only to avoid being eaten away. Anger, resentment, loss, self-pity— *and* self-loathing—loneliness. You can't live with all that in the consciousness very long, so, you put it under, *or* it gets well, and you're never sure which. Worst might be if there's nothing there any more, if everything has been accepted. I'm not a stoic by nature, by any means —I would have killed for my children, back when I cared for them, and he could please and hurt me in ways so subtle and complex I was always more amazed at *how* it had happened than I was by *what*. I remember once: we were in London, for a conference, and, naturally, he was very busy.

(Pause)

No; I don't want to talk about *that*, either. Something *must* be stirring: it's the second time I've balked.

THE MISTRESS *(Nicely)*. *You* won't mind.

THE WIFE. Well, I won't know till it's too late, will I?

(Turns to THE BEST FRIEND*)*

You're going to ask me to marry you, *aren't* you.

THE BEST FRIEND *(From where he sits)*. Certainly.

THE WIFE *(Smiles)*. And I shall *refuse*, shall I *not*.

THE BEST FRIEND. Certainly; I'm no bargain.

THE WIFE. Besides; fifty years married to one man, I wouldn't be settling on three or four with another—or even ten, if you outwit all the actuaries. And besides—though listen to how it sounds from someone *my* age, *my* condition—I am devoted to you, sir, but I am not in love with you. Fill my mouth with mould for having said it, but I love my husband.

THE MISTRESS *(Smiles, nicely)*. Of course you do.

THE BEST FRIEND *(As if nothing else had entered his mind and he is not disputing it)*. Of course you do.

355

THE WIFE *(A bit put off by their acquiescence)*. Yes. Well.

(Shakes her head, slowly, sadly)

Oh, God; the little girl.

(Does she move about? Perhaps)

Eighteen . . .

(To THE MISTRESS*)*

and none of yours, no summer lovemaking; no thought to it, or anything like it; alas.

(Pause, gathers herself again)

Some would-be beaux, but, like myself, tongue-tied and very much their ages. They would come to call, drink lemonade with my mother there, an aunt or so, an uncle; they would take me walking, play croquet, to a dance. I didn't fancy any of them.

THE MISTRESS *(Smiles)*. No; you were waiting.

THE WIFE *(Shakes her head, laughs)*. Of course! For Prince Charming!

(THE MISTRESS *chuckles.* THE WIFE *shrugs)*

And then—of course—he came *along*, done with the university, missing the war in France, twenty-four, already started on his fortune—just begun, but straight ahead, and clear. We met at my rich uncle's house, where he had come to discuss a proposition, and he made me feel twelve again, or younger, and . . . comfortable, as if he were an older brother, though . . . different; very different. I had never felt threatened, by boys, but he was a man, and I felt secure.

THE MISTRESS. Did you fall in love at once?

THE WIFE. Hm?

(Thinks about it)

I don't *know;* I knew that I would marry him, that he would ask me, and it seemed very . . . right. I felt calm. Is that an emotion? I suppose it is.

THE MISTRESS. Very much.

THE WIFE *(Sighs heavily)*. And two years after that we were married; and thirty years later . . . he met *you*. Quick history. Ah, well.

(A quickening)

Perhaps if I had been . . .

(Realizes)

No; I don't suppose so.

(A silence)

356

THE DOCTOR *(Emerging from where the bed has hidden him; to* THE BEST
FRIEND*).* Where are the others?

THE BEST FRIEND *(Rising).* In the solarium.

THE DOCTOR *(Level).* You'd best have them come in.

THE WIFE *(Pathetic; lost).* No-o!

THE BEST FRIEND *(Moving toward the door; to* THE DOCTOR*).* I'll get them.

THE WIFE *(Ibid.).* Not yet!

THE BEST FRIEND *(Misunderstanding).* They should *be* here.

THE WIFE *(Ibid.).* I don't mean them!

THE BEST FRIEND *(Hard to breathe).* I'll get them.

(He exits)

THE WIFE *(Turning back to* THE DOCTOR*; as before; pathetic, lost).* Not yet!

THE MISTRESS *(Takes* THE WIFE*'s hand).* Shhhhhhhhh; be a rock.

THE WIFE *(Resentful).* Why!

THE MISTRESS. They need you to.

THE WIFE *(Almost sneering).* Not you?

THE MISTRESS *(Matter-of-fact).* I'll manage. It would help, though.

THE WIFE *(Takes her hand away; hard).* You be; *you* be the rock. I've *been*
one, for all the years; steady. It's profitless!

THE MISTRESS. Then, just a little longer.

THE WIFE *(Almost snarling).* You be; *you've* usurped!

(Pause; finally; still hard)

I'm sorry!

THE MISTRESS. That's not fair.

THE WIFE *(Still hard).* Why? Because I no longer had what you up and
took?

THE MISTRESS *(Her tone hard, too).* Something like that.

THE WIFE *(A sudden, hard admitting, the tone strong, but with loss). I*
don't love *you.*

*(*THE MISTRESS *nods, looks away)*

I don't love *anyone.*

(Pause)

Any more.

(The door opens; THE DAUGHTER *enters, followed by* THE SON*, followed by* THE BEST FRIEND*.* THE BEST FRIEND *moves wearily, the other
two shy, as if they were afraid that by making a sound or touching
anything the world would shatter.* THE BEST FRIEND *quietly closes the
door behind him; the other two move a few paces, stand there.*

357

On her feet, now; to THE DAUGHTER, *same tone as before)*

I don't love *you,*

(To THE SON)

and I don't love *you.*

THE BEST FRIEND *(Quietly).* Don't do that.

THE WIFE *(Quieter, but merciless).* And you know I don't love *you.*

(An enraged shout which has her quivering)

I LOVE MY HUSBAND!!

(THE NURSE *has moved forward;* THE DAUGHTER *moves to her, buries herself in* THE NURSE'*s arms.* THE SON *falls into a chair, covers his face with his hands, sobs. To* THE SON)

STOP IT!!

(THE SON *abruptly ceases his sobbing, doesn't move)*

THE MISTRESS *(Steady). You* stop it.

(Silence; THE BEST FRIEND *moves to the fireplace;* THE MISTRESS *and* THE WIFE *are both seated;* THE SON *stays where he is;* THE DAUGHTER *returns to the sofa;* THE DOCTOR *is by the bed;* THE NURSE *stands behind the sofa and to one side, eyes steady, ready to assist or prevent. Nobody moves from these positions, save* THE DOCTOR, *from now until the end of the play)*

THE WIFE *(Calm, now, almost toneless. A slow speech, broken with long pauses).* All we've done . . . is think about ourselves.

(Pause)

There's no help for the dying. I suppose. Oh my; the burden.

(Pause)

What will become of *me* . . . and *me* . . . and *me.*

(Pause)

Well, we're the ones have got to go on.

(Pause)

Selfless love? *I* don't think so; we love to *be* loved, and when it's taken away . . . then why *not* rage . . . or pule.

(Pause)

All we've *done* is think about ourselves. Ultimately.

(A long silence. Then THE WIFE *begins to cry. She does not move, her head high, eyes forward, hands gripping the arms of her chair. First it is only tears, but then the sounds in the throat begin. It is controlled weeping, but barely controlled)*

THE DAUGHTER *(After a bit; not loud, but bitter and accusatory).* Why are you crying!

THE WIFE *(It explodes from her, finally, all that has been pent up for thirty years. It is loud, broken by sobs and gulps of air; it is self-pitying and self-loathing; pain, and relief).* Because . . . I'm . . . unhappy.

(Pause)

Because . . . I'm . . . unhappy.

(Pause)

BECAUSE . . . I'M . . . UNHAPPY!

(A silence, as she regains control. Then she says it once more, almost conversational, but empty, flat)

Because I'm unhappy.

(A long silence. No one moves, save THE DOCTOR, *who finally removes the stethoscope from* THE PATIENT's *chest, then from his ears. He stands, pauses for a moment, then walks a few steps forward, stops)*

THE DOCTOR *(Gently).* All over.

(No one moves)

END

SEASCAPE

A Play (1975)

For
Ella Winter
and
Donald Ogden Stewart
with love

FIRST PERFORMANCE: January 26, 1975
New York City, Sam S. Shubert Theatre

DEBORAH KERR *as* NANCY
BARRY NELSON *as* CHARLIE
FRANK LANGELLA *as* LESLIE
MAUREEN ANDERMAN *as* SARAH

Directed by EDWARD ALBEE

CHARACTERS

NANCY
CHARLIE
LESLIE
SARAH

ACT ONE

The curtain rises. NANCY *and* CHARLIE *on a sand dune. Bright sun. They are dressed informally. There is a blanket and a picnic basket. Lunch is done;* NANCY *is finishing putting things away. There is a pause and then a jet plane is heard from stage right to stage left—growing, becoming deafeningly loud, diminishing.*

NANCY. Such noise they make.

CHARLIE. They'll crash into the dunes one day. I don't know what good they do.

NANCY *(Looks toward the ocean; sighs)*. Still . . . Oh, Charlie, it's so nice! Can't we stay here forever? Please!

CHARLIE. Unh-unh.

NANCY. That is not why. That is merely no.

CHARLIE. Because.

NANCY. Nor is that.

CHARLIE. Because . . . because you don't really mean it.

NANCY. I do!

CHARLIE. Here?

NANCY *(Expansive)*. Yes!

CHARLIE. Right here on the beach. Build a . . . a tent, or a lean-to.

NANCY *(Laughs gaily)*. No, silly, not this very spot! But *here*, by the shore.

CHARLIE. You wouldn't like it.

NANCY. I would! I'd love it here! I'd love it right where we are, for that matter.

CHARLIE. Not after a while you wouldn't.

NANCY. Yes, I *would*. I love the water, and I love the air, and the sand and the dunes and the beach grass, and the sunshine on all of it and the white clouds way off, and the sunsets and the noise the shells make in the waves and, oh, I love every bit of it, Charlie.

CHARLIE. You wouldn't. Not after a while.

NANCY. Why wouldn't I? I don't even mind the flies and the little . . . sand fleas, I guess they are.

CHARLIE. It gets cold.

NANCY. When?

CHARLIE. In the winter. In the fall even. In spring.

NANCY *(Laughs)*. Well, I don't mean this one, literally . . . not all the

365

time. I mean go from beach to beach . . . live by the water. Seaside nomads, that's what we'd be.

CHARLIE *(Curiously hurt feelings).* For Christ's sake, Nancy!

NANCY. I mean it! Lord above! There's nothing binding us; you *hate* the city . . .

CHARLIE. No.

NANCY *(Undaunted).* It would be so lovely. Think of all the beaches we could see.

CHARLIE. No, now . . .

NANCY. Southern California, and the Gulf, and Florida . . . and up to Maine, and what's-her-name's—Martha's—Vineyard, and all those places that the fancy people go: the Riviera and that beach in Rio de Janeiro, what is that?

CHARLIE. The Copacabana.

NANCY. Yes, and Pago Pago, and . . . Hawaii! Think, Charlie! We could go around the world and never leave the beach, just move from one hot sand strip to another: all the birds and fish and seaside flowers, and all the wondrous people that we'd meet. Oh, say you'd like to do it, Charlie.

CHARLIE. No.

NANCY. Just *say* you'd like to.

CHARLIE. If I did you'd say I meant it; you'd hold me to it.

NANCY *(Transparent).* No I wouldn't. Besides, you have to be pushed into everything.

CHARLIE. Um-hum. But I'm not going to be pushed into . . . into *this*— this new business.

NANCY *(Private rapture).* One great seashore after another; pounding waves and quiet coves; white sand, and red—and black, somewhere, I remember reading; palms, and pine trees, cliffs and reefs, and miles of jungle, sand dunes . . .

CHARLIE. No.

NANCY. . . . and all the people! Every . . . language . . . every . . . race.

CHARLIE. Unh-unh.

NANCY. Of course, I'd never push you.

CHARLIE. You? Never!

NANCY *(Gay).* Well, maybe a hint here; hint there.

CHARLIE. Don't even do that, hunh?

NANCY. That's all it takes: figure out what you'd really like—what you
want without knowing it, what would secretly please you, put it in your
mind, then make all the plans. *You* do it; *you* like it.

CHARLIE *(Final)*. Nancy, I don't want to travel from beach to beach, cliff
to sand dune, see the races, count the flies. Anything. I don't want to
do . . . anything.

NANCY *(Testy)*. I see. Well.

CHARLIE. I'm happy . . . doing . . . nothing.

NANCY *(Makes to gather some of their things)*. Well then, we'd best get
started. Up! Let's get back!

CHARLIE *(Not moving)*. I just . . . want . . . to . . . do . . . nothing.

NANCY *(Gathering)*. Well, you're certainly not going to do that.

(Takes something from him, a pillow, perhaps)

Hurry now; let's get things together.

CHARLIE *(Aware)*. What . . . Nancy, what on earth are you . . .

NANCY *(Busy)*. We are *not* going to be around forever, Charlie, and you
may *not* do nothing. If you don't want to do what *I* want to do—which
doesn't matter—then we will do what *you* want to do, but we will not
do nothing. We will do *something*. So, tell me what it is you want to do
and . . .

CHARLIE. I *said*. Now give me back my . . .

NANCY. You said, "I just want to do nothing; I'm happy doing nothing."
Yes? But is that what we've . . . come all this way for?

(Some wonder and chiding)

Had the children? Spent all this time together? All the sharing? For
nothing? To lie back down in the crib again? The same at the end as at
the beginning? Sleep? Pacifier? Milk? Incomprehensible once more?

(Pause)

Sleep?

(Pause)

Sleep, Charlie? Back to sleep?

CHARLIE. Well, we've earned a little . . .

NANCY. . . . rest.

(Nods, sort of bitterly)

We've earned a little rest. Well, why don't we act like the old folks, why
don't we sell off, and take one bag apiece and go to California, or in the
desert where they have the farms—the retirement farms, the old folks'
cities? Why don't we settle in to waiting, like . . . like the camels that

we saw in Egypt—groan down on all fours, sigh, and eat the grass, or whatever it is. Why don't we go and wait the judgment with our peers? Take our teeth out, throw away our corset, give in to the palsy, let our mind go dim, play lotto and canasta with the widows and the widowers, eat cereal . . .

(CHARLIE *sighs heavily, exasperatedly*)

Yes! Sigh! Go on! But once you get there, once you *do* that, there's no returning, that purgatory *before* purgatory. No thank you, sir! I haven't come this long way.

CHARLIE *(Chuckles a little, resigned)*. What do you want to do, Nancy?

NANCY. Nor have you! Not this long way to let loose. All the wisdom—by accident, by accident, some of it—all the wisdom and the . . . unfettering. My God, Charlie: See Everything Twice!

CHARLIE *(Settling back)*. What do you want to do?

NANCY. You are *not* going to live forever, to coin a phrase. Nor am I, I suppose, come to think of it, though it would be nice. Nor do I imagine we'll have the satisfaction of doing it together—head-on with a bus, or into a mountain with a jet, or buried in a snowslide, if we ever *get* to the Alps. No. I suppose I'll do the tag without you. Selfish, aren't you—right to the end.

CHARLIE *(Feeling for her hand, taking it)*. What do you want to do?

NANCY *(Wistful)*. If you get badly sick I'll poison myself.

(Waits for reaction, gets none)

And you?

CHARLIE *(Yawning)*. Yes; if you get badly sick I'll poison *my*self, too.

NANCY. Yes, but then if I *did* take poison, you'd get well again, and there I'd be, laid out, all for a false alarm. I think the only thing to do is to *do* something.

CHARLIE *(Nice)*. What would you like to do?

NANCY *(Far away)*. Hm?

CHARLIE. Move from one sand strip to another? Live by the sea from now on?

NANCY *(Great wistfulness)*. Well, we have nothing holding us, except together; chattel? Does chattel mean what I think it does? We *have* nothing we *need* have. We could do it; I would so like to.

CHARLIE *(Smiles)*. All right.

NANCY *(Sad little laugh)*. You're humoring me; it *is* something I want, though; maybe only the principle.

(Larger laugh)

I suspect our children would have us put away if we announced it as a plan—beachcombing, leaf huts. Even if we did it in hotels they'd have a case—for our *reasons.*

CHARLIE. Mmmmmmm.

NANCY. Let's merely have it for today . . . and tomorrow, and . . . who knows: continue the temporary and it becomes forever.

CHARLIE *(Relaxed; content).* All right.

(The sound of the jet plane from stage right to stage left—growing, becoming deafeningly loud, diminishing)

NANCY. Such noise they make!

CHARLIE. They'll crash into the dunes one day; I don't know what good they do.

NANCY *(After a pause).* Still . . . Ahhh; breathe the sea air.

(Tiny pause; suddenly remembers)

Didn't you tell me? When you were a little boy you wanted to live in the sea?

CHARLIE. Under.

NANCY *(Delighted).* Yes! Under the water—in it. That all your friends pined to have wings? Icarus? Soar?

CHARLIE. But not too near the sun; and real wings, not pasted on.

NANCY. Yes, but you wanted to go under. Gills, too?

CHARLIE. As I remember. A regular fish, I mean fishlike—arms and legs and everything, but able to go under, live down in the coral and the ferns, come home for lunch and bed and stories, of course, but down in the green, the purple, and big enough not to be eaten if I stayed close in. Oh yes; I *did* want that.

NANCY *(Considers it, with some wonder).* Be a fish.

(Lightly)

No, that's not among what *I* wanted—when *I* was little, not that I remember. I wanted to be a pony once, I think, but not for very long. I wanted to be a *woman.* I wanted to grow up to be *that,* and all it had with it.

(Notices something below her in the distance, upstage. Offhand)

There are some people down there; I thought we were alone. In the water; some people, I think.

(Back)

And, I suppose I *have* become that.

CHARLIE *(Smiling)*. You have.

NANCY. In any event, the appearances of it: husband, children—precarious, those, for a while, but nicely settled now—to all appearances—and the grandchildren . . . here, and on the way. The top of the pyramid! Us two, the children, and all of theirs.

(Mildly puzzled)

Isn't it odd that you can build a pyramid from the top down? Isn't that difficult? The engineering?

CHARLIE. There wasn't anyone before us?

NANCY *(Laughs lightly)*. Well, yes, but everybody builds his own, starts fresh, starts up in the air, builds the base around him. Such levitation! Our own have started *theirs*.

CHARLIE. It's all one.

NANCY *(Sort of sad about it)*. Yes.

(Bright again)

Or maybe it's the most . . . difficult, the most . . . breathtaking of all: the whole thing balanced on one point; a reversed *pyramid*, always in danger of toppling over when people don't behave themselves.

CHARLIE *(Chuckling)*. All right.

NANCY *(Above it)*. You have no interest in imagery. None.

CHARLIE *(Defiance; rue)*. Well, I used to.

NANCY. The man who married a dumb wife; not you! Was that Molière? Beaumarchais?

CHARLIE. Anatole France.

NANCY. Was it?

CHARLIE *(Continuing from before)*. I used to go way down; at our summer place; a protected cove. The breakers would come in with a storm, or a high wind, but not usually. I used to go way down, and try to stay. I remember before that, when I was tiny, I would go in the swimming pool, at the shallow end, let out my breath and sit on the bottom; when you let out your breath—all of it—you sink, gently, and you can sit on the bottom until your lungs need air. I would do that—I was so young —sit there, gaze about. Great trouble for my parents. "Good God, go get Charlie; he's gone and sunk again." "Will you look at that child? Put him in the water and he drops like a stone." I could swim perfectly well, as easy as walking, and around the same time, but I used to love to sink. And when I was older, we were by the sea. Twelve; yes, or thirteen. I used to lie on the warm boulders, strip off . . .

(Quiet, sad amusement)

. . . learn about my body; no one saw me; twelve or thirteen. And I would go into the water, take two stones, as large as I could manage, swim out a bit, tread, look up one final time at the sky . . . relax . . . begin to go down. Oh, twenty feet, fifteen, soft landing without a sound, the white sand clouding up where your feet touch, and all around you ferns . . . and lichen. You can stay down there so long! You can build it up, and last . . . so long, enough for the sand to settle and the fish come back. And they do—come back—all sizes, some slowly, eyeing past; some streak, and you think for a moment they're larger than they are, sharks, maybe, but they never are, and one stops being an intruder, finally—just one more object come to the bottom, or living thing, part of the undulation and the silence. It was very good.

NANCY. Did the fish talk to you? I mean, did they come up and stay close, and look at you, and maybe nibble at your toes?

CHARLIE *(Very shy)*. Some of them.

NANCY *(Enthusiastic)*. Why don't you go and do it! Yes!

CHARLIE *(Age)*. Oh, no, now, Nancy, I couldn't.

NANCY. Yes! Yes, you could! Go do it again; you'd love it!

CHARLIE. Oh, no, now, I . . .

NANCY. Go down to the edge; go in! Pick up some stones . . .

CHARLIE. There're no coves; it's all open beach.

NANCY. Oh, you'll find a cove; go on! Be young again; my God, Charlie, be young!

CHARLIE. No; besides, someone'd see me; they'd think I was drowning.

NANCY. Who's to see you?! Look, there's no one in the . . . no, those . . . people, they've come out, the ones were in the water, they're . . . well, they're lying on the beach, to sun; they're prone. Go on down; I'll watch you from here.

CHARLIE *(Firm, through embarrassment)*. No! I said no!

NANCY *(Undaunted; still happy)*. Well, I'll come with you; I'll stand by the edge, and if anyone comes by and says, "Look, there's a man drowning!" I'll laugh and say, "La! It's my husband, and he's gone down with two stones to sit on the bottom for a while."

CHARLIE. No!

NANCY. The white sand clouding, and the ferns and the lichen. Oh, do it, Charlie!

CHARLIE. I wouldn't like it any more.

NANCY *(Wheedling, taunting)*. Awwww, how long since you've done it?!

CHARLIE *(Mumbles)*. Too long.

NANCY. What?

CHARLIE *(Embarrassed; shy)*. Not since I was seventeen?

NANCY *(This time pretending not to hear)*. What?

CHARLIE *(Rather savage; phlegm in the throat)*. Too long.

(Small pause)

Far too long?

(Silence)

NANCY *(Very gentle; not even urging)*. Would it be so very hard now? Wouldn't you be able to? Gently? In some sheltered place, not very deep? Go down? Not long, just enough to . . . reconfirm.

CHARLIE *(Flat)*. I'd rather remember.

NANCY. If *I* were a man—What a silly thing to say.

CHARLIE. Yes. It is.

NANCY. Still, if I were . . . I don't think I'd let the chance go by; not if I had it.

CHARLIE *(Quietly)*. Let it go.

NANCY. Not if *I* had it. There isn't that much. Sex goes . . . diminishes; well, it becomes a holiday and rather special, and not like eating, or going to sleep. But that's nice, too—that it becomes special—

(Laughs gaily)

Do you know, I had a week when I thought of divorcing you?

CHARLIE *(Quite surprised, vulnerable; shakes his head)*. No.

NANCY. Yes. You were having your thing, your melancholia—poor darling —and there I was, brisk and thirty, still pert, learning the moles on your back instead of your chest hairs.

CHARLIE *(Relieved, if sad)*. Ah. Then.

NANCY *(Nods)*. Um-hum. Then. Rereading Proust, if I have it right. Propped up in bed, all pink and ribbons, smelling good, not all those creams and looking ten years married as I might have, and who would have blamed me, but fresh, and damned attractive, if I have to say it for myself; propped up in bed, literate, sweet-smelling, getting familiar with your back. One, two, three moles, and then a pair of them, twins, flat black ones . . .

CHARLIE *(Recalling)*. *That* time.

NANCY *(Nods)*. . . . ummmm. The ones I said should go—*still* think they should—not that it matters: they haven't done anything. It was at

Act One

the . . . center of your thing, your seven-month decline; it was *then* that I thought of divorcing you. The deeper your inertia went, the more *I* felt alive. Good wife, patient, see him through it, whatever it is, wonder if it isn't something *you* haven't done, or have; write home for some advice, but oh, so busy, with the children and the house. Stay neat; don't pry; weather it. But right in the center, three and a half months in, it occurred to me that there was nothing wrong, save perhaps another woman.

CHARLIE *(Surprised; hurt).* Oh, Nancy.

NANCY. Well, one has a mind, and it goes about its business. If one is happy, *and* content, it doesn't mean that everyone else is; never assume that. Maybe he's found a girl; not even looking, necessarily; maybe he turned a corner one afternoon and there was a girl, not prettier even, maybe a little plain, but unencumbered, or lonely, or lost. That's the way it starts, as often as not. No sudden passion over champagne glasses at the fancy ball, or seeing the puppy love again, never like that except for fiction, but something . . . different, maybe even a little . . . less: the relief of that; simpler, not quite so nice, how much nicer, for a little.

CHARLIE. *Nothing* like that.

NANCY *(Laughs a little).* Well, *I* know.

CHARLIE. Nothing at *all.*

NANCY. Yes, but the *mind.* And what bothered me was not what *you* might be doing—oh, well, certainly; *bothered,* yes—not entirely what you might be doing, but that, all of a sudden, *I* had not. *Ever.* Had not even thought of it. A child at thirty, I suppose. Without that time I would have gone through my entire life and never thought of another man, another pair of arms, harsh cheek, hard buttocks, pleasure, never at all. *(Considers that)*
Well, I might have, and maybe this was better. All at once I thought: it was over between us—not our life together, that would go on, and we would be like a minister and his sister—the . . . active part of our life, the rough-and-tumble in the sheets or in the grass when we took our picnics, that all of that had stopped between us, or would become cursory, and I wouldn't have asked why, nor would you have said, or if I *had*—asked why—you would have said some lie, or truth, would have made it worse, and I thought back to before I married you, and the boys I would have done it with, if I had been that type, the firm-fleshed boys I would have taken in my arms had it occurred to me. And I began to

373

think of them, Proust running on, pink and ribbons, looking at your back, and your back would turn and it would be Johnny Smythe or the Devlin boy, or one of the others, and he would smile, reach out a hand, undo my ribbons, draw me close, ease on. Oh, that was a troubling time.

CHARLIE *(Sad remembrance).* You were never one for the boys, were you?

NANCY *(She, too).* No.

(Pause)

But I thought: well, if he can turn his back on me like this—nice, isn't it, when the real and the figurative come together—*I* can turn, too—if not my back, then . . . back. I can have me a divorce, I thought, become eighteen again.

(Sudden thought)

You know, I think that's why our women want divorces, as often as not —to be eighteen again, no matter how old they are; and daring. To do it differently, and still for the first time.

(Sighs)

But it was only a week I thought about that. It went away. You came back . . . eventually.

CHARLIE *(A statement of fact that is really a question).* You never thought I went to anyone else.

NANCY. She said to me—wise woman— "Daughter, if it lasts, if you and he come back together, it'll be at a price or two. If it lasts there'll be accommodation, wandering; if he doesn't do it in the flesh, he'll think about it; one night, in the dark, if you listen hard enough, you'll hear him think the name of another woman, kiss *her,* touch *her* breasts as he has his hand and mouth on you. *Then* you'll know something about loneliness, my daughter; yessiree; you'll be halfway there, halfway to compassion."

CHARLIE *(After a pause; shy).* The other half?

NANCY. Hm?

(Matter-of-fact)

Knowing how lonely *he* is . . . substituting . . . using a person, a body, and wishing it was someone else—almost anyone. *That* void. *Le petit mort,* the French call the moment of climax? And that lovely writer? Who talks of the sadness after love? After intimate intercourse, I think he says? But what of *during?* What of the loneliness and death

then? During. They don't talk of that: the sad fantasies; the substitutions. The thoughts we have.
(Tiny pause)
One has.
CHARLIE *(Softly, with a timid smile).* I've never been with another woman.
NANCY *(A little laugh).* Well, *I* know.
CHARLIE *(Laughs ruefully).* I think one time, when you and I were making love—when we were nearly there, I remember I pretended it was a week or so before, one surprising time we'd had, something we'd hit upon by accident, or decided to do finally; I pretended it was the time before, and it was quite good that way.
NANCY *(Some wonder).* You pretended I was me.
CHARLIE *(Apology).* Well . . . yes.
NANCY *(Laughs delightedly; thinks).* Well; perhaps I was.
(Pause)
So much goes, Charlie; we shouldn't give up until we have to.
(Gentle)
Why don't you go down; why don't you find a cove?
CHARLIE *(Smiles; shakes his head).* No.
NANCY. It's something *I've* never done; you could teach me. You could take my hand; we could have two big stones, and we could go down together.
CHARLIE *(Not a complaint; an evasion).* I haven't got my suit.
NANCY. Go bare! You're quite presentable.
CHARLIE. Nancy!
(Mildly put off, and a little pleased)
NANCY *(Almost shy).* *I* wouldn't mind. I'd like to see you, pink against the blue, watch the water on you.
CHARLIE. Tomorrow.
NANCY. Bare?
CHARLIE. We'll see.
NANCY *(Shrugs).* I'm used to that: we'll see, and then put off until it's forgotten.
(Peers)
I wonder where they've gone.
CHARLIE *(Not interested).* Who?
NANCY. Those people; well, those that were down there.
CHARLIE. Gone in.

NANCY. The water? Again?

CHARLIE. No. Home.

NANCY. Well, I don't think so. I thought maybe they were coming up to us.

CHARLIE. Why?

NANCY. They . . . looked to be. I mean, I thought . . . well, no matter.

CHARLIE. Who were they?

NANCY. You know my eyes. I thought they were climbing, coming up to see us.

CHARLIE. If we don't know them?

NANCY. *Some* people are adventurous.

CHARLIE. Mmmmm.

NANCY. I wonder where they've gone.

CHARLIE. Don't spy!

NANCY *(Looking down)*. I'm not; I just want to . . . Lord, why couldn't my ears be going instead? I think I see them halfway up the dune. I think I can make them out; resting, or maybe sunning, on an angle for the sun.

CHARLIE. A lot of good *you'd* be under water.

NANCY *(Considers what she has seen)*. Rather odd.

(Dismisses it)

Well, that's why you'll have to take me if I'm going to go down; you wouldn't want to lose me in the fernery, and all. An eddy, or whatever that is the tide does underneath, might sweep me into a cave, or a culvert, and I wouldn't know *what* to do. No, you'll have to take me.

CHARLIE. You'd probably panic . . . if I took you under.

(Thinks about it)

No; you wouldn't; you'd do worse, most likely: start drowning and not let on.

(They both laugh)

You're a good wife.

NANCY *(Offhand)*. You've been a good husband . . . more or less.

CHARLIE *(Not aggressive)*. Damned right.

NANCY. *And* you courted me the way I wanted.

CHARLIE. Yes.

NANCY. *And* you gave me the children I wanted, as many, and when.

CHARLIE. Yes.

NANCY. *And* you've provided a sturdy shoulder and a comfortable life. No?

376

CHARLIE. *Yes.*

NANCY. And I've not a complaint in my head, have I?

CHARLIE. No.

NANCY *(Slightly bitter)*. Well, we'll wrap you in the flag when you're gone, and do taps.

(A fair silence)

CHARLIE *(Soft; embarrassed)*. We'd better . . . gather up; . . . We should go back now.

NANCY *(Nudges him on the shoulder)*. Ohhhhhhhh . . .

(CHARLIE *shakes his head, keeping his eyes averted.*)

NANCY. Ohhhhhhhhh . . .

CHARLIE. I don't want to stay here any more. You've hurt my feelings, damn it!

NANCY *(Sorry)*. Ohhh, Charlie.

CHARLIE *(Trying to understand)*. You're not cruel by nature; it's not your way. Why do you *do* this? Even so rarely; *why?*

NANCY *(As if it explained everything)*. I was being *pet*ulant.

CHARLIE *(More or less to himself, but not sotto voce)*. I *have* been a good husband to you; I *did* court you like a gentleman; I *have* been a good lover . . .

NANCY *(Light)*. Well, of course I have no one to compare you with.

CHARLIE *(Preoccupied; right on)*. . . . you *have* been comfortable, and my shoulder *has* been there.

NANCY *(Gaily)*. I *know;* I *know.*

CHARLIE. You've had a good *life.*

NANCY. Don't *say* that!

CHARLIE. And you'll not pack it up in a piece of cloth and put it away.

NANCY. No! Not if *you* won't! Besides, it was hyperbole.

CHARLIE *(Slightly testy)*. *I* knew that. Not if *I* won't, eh? Not if I won't what?

NANCY. Pack it up in a piece of cloth and put it away. When's the last time you were stung by a bee, Charlie? Was it that time in Maine . . . or Delaware? When your cheek swelled up, and you kept saying, "Mud! Get me some mud!" And there wasn't any mud that *I* could see, and you said, "Well, *make* some."

CHARLIE. Delaware.

NANCY. After all the years of making you things, my mind couldn't focus on how to make *mud.* What *is* the recipe for *that*, I said to myself . . .

What sort of *pan* do I use, for one; water, yes, but water and . . . what? Earth, naturally, but what *kind* and . . . oh, I felt so foolish.

CHARLIE *(Softer)*. It was Delaware.

NANCY. *So* foolish.

CHARLIE *(Mildly reproachful)*. The whole cheek swelled up; the eyes was half closed.

NANCY *(Pedagogic)*. Well, that's what a bee sting does, Charlie. And that's what brings on the petulance—mine; it's just like a bee sting, and I remember, though it's been years.

CHARLIE *(To reassure himself)*. Crazy as a loon.

NANCY. No; not at all. You asked me about the petulance—why it comes on me, even rarely. Well, it's like the sting of a bee: something you say, or do; or don't say, or don't do. And it brings the petulance on me— that I like it, but it's a healthy sign, shows I'm still nicely alive.

CHARLIE *(Not too friendly)*. Like when? Like what?

NANCY. What brings it on, and when?

CHARLIE *(Impatient)*. Yes!

NANCY. Well, so many things.

CHARLIE. Give me *one*.

NANCY. No; I'll give you several.

CHARLIE. All *right*.

NANCY. "You've had a good life."

(Pause)

CHARLIE *(Curiously angry)*. *All* right. *Go* on.

NANCY. Do you know what I'm *say*ing?

CHARLIE. You're throwing it up to me; you're telling me I've had a . . .

NANCY. No-no-no! I'm saying what you *said*, what you told *me*. You told me, you said to me, "You've had a good life." I wasn't talking about *you*, though you *have*. I was saying what you said to me.

CHARLIE *(Annoyed)*. Well, you have! You *have* had!

NANCY *(She, too)*. Yes! Have *had!* What *about* that!

CHARLIE. What about it!

NANCY. *Am* not *having*.

(Waits for reaction; gets none)

Am not *having?* Am not *having* a good life?

CHARLIE. Well, of *course!*

NANCY. Then why say had? Why put it that way?

CHARLIE. It's a way of speaking!

NANCY. No! It's a way of thinking! *I* know the language, and I know *you*. You're not careless with it, or didn't used to be. Why *not* go to those places in the desert and let our heads deflate, if it's all in the past? Why not just *do* that?

CHARLIE. It was a way of speaking.

NANCY. Dear God, we're *here*. We've served our time, Charlie, and there's nothing telling us do *that*, or any conditional; not any more. Well, there's the arthritis in my wrist, of course, and the eyes have known a better season, and there's always the cancer or a heart attack to think about if we're bored, but besides all these things . . . what is there?

CHARLIE *(Somewhat triste)*. You're at it again.

NANCY. I am! Words are lies; they *can* be, and you *use* them, but I know what's in your gut. I *told* you, didn't I?

CHARLIE *(Passing it off)*. Sure, sure.

NANCY *(Mimicking)*. Sure, sure. Well, they are, and you do. What *have* we got left?

CHARLIE. What! You mean besides the house, the kids, *their* kids, friends, all that? What?!

NANCY. Two things!

CHARLIE. Yeah?

NANCY. Ourselves and some time. Charlie—the pyramid's building by itself; the earth's spinning in its own fashion without any push from us; we've done all we ought to—and isn't it splendid we've enjoyed so much of it.

CHARLIE *(Mild irony)*. We're pretty splendid people.

NANCY. Damned right we are, and now we've got each other and some time, and all *you* want to do is become a vegetable.

CHARLIE. Fair, as usual.

NANCY *(Shrugs)*. All right: a lump.

CHARLIE. We've earned . . .

NANCY *(Nods)*. . . . a little rest. My God, you say that twice a day, and sometimes in between.

(Mutters)

We've earned a little *life*, if you ask *me*.

(Pause)

Ask me.

CHARLIE *(Some rue)*. No; you'd tell me.

NANCY *(Bold and recriminating).* Sure! Course I would! When else are we going to get it?

CHARLIE *(Quite serious; quite bewildered).* What's to be gained? And what would we really get? Some . . . illusion, I suppose; some smoke. There'd be the same sounds in the dark—or similar ones; we'd have to sleep and wonder if we'd waken, either way. It's six of one, except we'll do it on familiar ground, if *I* have *my* way. I'm not up to the glaciers and the crags, and I don't think you'd be . . . once you got out there.

NANCY *(Grudging).* I do admit, you make it sound scary—first time away to camp, sleeping out, the hoot owls and the goblins. Oh, that's scary. Are you telling me you're all caved in, Charlie?

CHARLIE *(Pause; considers the fact).* Maybe.

NANCY *(Pause while she ponders this).* All closed down? Then . . . what's the difference? You make it ugly enough, either way. The glaciers and the crags? At least we've never *tried that.*

CHARLIE *(Trying to justify, but without much enthusiasm).* There's comfort in settling in.

NANCY *(Pause).* Small.

CHARLIE *(Pause, final).* Some.

(A silence)

(LESLIE *appears, upper half of trunk pops up upstage, from behind the dune. Neither* CHARLIE *nor* NANCY *sees him.* LESLIE *looks at the two of them, pops back down out of sight)*

NANCY *(To bring them back to life again).* Well. I've got to do some postcards tonight; tell all the folks where we are.

CHARLIE. Yes?

NANCY. . . . what a time we're having. I've got a list . . . somewhere. It wouldn't be nice not to. They do it for us, and it's such fun getting them.

CHARLIE. Um-hum.

NANCY. You do some, too?

CHARLIE. You do them for both of us.

NANCY *(Mildly disappointed).* Oh.

(Pause)

All right.

CHARLIE *(Not very interested).* What do you want to do, then?

NANCY *(While* NANCY *speaks,* LESLIE *and* SARAH *come up on the dune,*

380

behind CHARLIE *and* NANCY, *but some distance away. They crawl up; then they squat down on their tails.* NANCY *stretches).*

Oh, I don't know. Do you want to have your nap? Cover your face if you do, though; put something on it. *Or* . . . we could go on back. *Or* . . . we *could* do a stroll down the beach. If you won't go in, we'll find some pretty shells . . . *I* will.

CHARLIE *(Small smile).* What a wealth.

NANCY *(Fairly cheerful).* Well . . . we make the best of it.

(CHARLIE *senses something behind him. He turns his head, sees* LESLIE *and* SARAH. *His mouth falls open; he is stock-still for a moment; then, slowly getting on all fours, he begins, very cautiously, to back away.* NANCY *sees what* CHARLIE *is doing, is momentarily puzzled. Then she looks behind her. She sees* LESLIE *and* SARAH)

NANCY *(Straightening her back abruptly).* My goodness!

CHARLIE *(On all fours; ready to flee).* Ohmygod.

NANCY *(Great wonder).* Charlie!

CHARLIE *(Eyes steady on* LESLIE AND SARAH). Oh my loving God.

NANCY *(Enthusiasm).* Charlie! What *are* they?!

CHARLIE. Nancy, get back here!

NANCY. But, Charlie . . .

CHARLIE *(Deep in his throat; trying to whisper).* Get back here!

(NANCY *backs away until she and* CHARLIE *are together.)*

NOTE: CHARLIE *and* NANCY *are now toward stage right,* LESLIE *and* SARAH *toward stage left. They will not hear each other speak until indicated.*

(Whispering)

Get a stick!

NANCY *(Interest and wonder).* Charlie, what are they?

CHARLIE *(Urgent).* Get me a stick!

NANCY. A what?

CHARLIE *(Louder).* A stick!

NANCY *(Looking about; uncertain).* Well . . . what *sort* of stick, Charlie?

CHARLIE. A stick! A wooden *stick!*

NANCY *(Begins to crawl stage right).* Well, of course a wooden stick, Charlie; what other kinds of sticks *are* there, for heaven's sake? But what sort of stick?

CHARLIE *(Never taking his eyes off* LESLIE *and* SARAH). A big one! A big stick!

NANCY *(None too happy about it)*. Well . . . I'll *look*. Driftwood, I suppose . . .

CHARLIE. Well, of course a *wooden* stick, Charlie; what other kinds of
sticks . . .

(LESLIE *moves a little, maybe raises an arm*)

GET ME A GUN!

NANCY *(Astonished)*. A *gun*, Charlie! Where on earth would anyone find a
gun up here.

CHARLIE *(Shrill)*. Get me a stick!

NANCY *(Cross)*. All right!

CHARLIE (SARAH *moves toward* LESLIE; CHARLIE *stiffens, gasps*). Hurry!

NANCY. I'm looking!

CHARLIE *(A bleak fact, to himself as much as anything)*. They're going to
come at us, Nancy . . .

(An afterthought)

. . . and we're arguing.

NANCY *(Waving a smallish stick; thin, crooked, eighteen inches, maybe)*. I
found one, Charlie; Charlie, I found one!

CHARLIE *(Not taking his gaze off* LESLIE *and* SARAH; *between his teeth)*.
Well, bring it here.

NANCY *(Crawling to* CHARLIE *with the stick between her teeth)*. It's the best
I could do under the circumstances. There was a big trunk or something . . .

CHARLIE *(His hand out)*. Give it to me!

NANCY. Here!

(Gives the stick to CHARLIE, *who, without looking at it, raises it in his
right hand)*

Charlie! They're magnificent!

CHARLIE *(Realizes what he is brandishing, looks at it with distaste and
loss)*. What's *this?*

NANCY. It's your stick.

CHARLIE *(Almost crying)*. Oh my God.

NANCY *(Eyes on* LESLIE *and* SARAH). Charlie, I think they're absolutely
beautiful. What *are* they?

CHARLIE. What am I supposed to *do* with it?!

NANCY. You *asked* for it, Charlie; you said you wanted it.

CHARLIE *(Snorts: ironic-pathetic)*. Go down fighting, eh?

(LESLIE *clears his throat; it is a large sound, rather like a growl or a bark. Instinctively,* CHARLIE *gathers* NANCY *to him, all the while trying to brandish his stick)*

NANCY *(Not at all sure of herself).* Fight, Charlie? Fight? Are they going to hurt us?

CHARLIE *(Laughing at the absurdity).* Oh, God!

NANCY *(More vigor).* Well, at least we'll be together.

(LESLIE *clears his throat again, same sound;* CHARLIE *and* NANCY *react a little, tense.* LESLIE *takes a step forward, stops, bends over and picks up a large stick, four feet long and stout; he brandishes it and clears his throat again)*

Now, *that's* an impressive stick.

CHARLIE *(Shakes his stick at her).* Yeah; thanks.

NANCY *(Some pique).* Well, thank *you* very much. If I'd known I was supposed to go over there and crawl around under their flippers, or pads, or whatever they have . . .

CHARLIE *(Final words; some haste).* I love you, Nancy.

NANCY *(The tiniest pause; a trifle begrudging).* Well . . . I love *you,* too.

(LESLIE *slowly, so slowly, raises his stick above him in a gesture of such strength that should he smite the earth it would tremble. He holds the stick thus, without moving)*

CHARLIE. Well, I certainly hope so: here they come.

(LESLIE *and* SARAH *slowly begin to move toward* CHARLIE *and* NANCY. *Suddenly the sound of the jet plane again, lower and louder this time.* LESLIE *and* SARAH *react as animals would; frozen for an instant, tense seeking of the danger, poised, every muscle taut, and then the two of them, at the same instant and with identical movement—paws clawing at the sand, bellies hugging the earth—they race back over the dune toward the water.*

CHARLIE *and* NANCY *are as if struck dumb; they stare, open-mouthed, at the now-vacated dune)*

NANCY *(Finally, with great awe).* Charlie!

(Infinite wonder)

What have we *seen?!*

CHARLIE. The glaciers and the crags, Nancy. You'll never be closer.

NANCY. All at *once!* There they *were,* Charlie!

CHARLIE. It was the liver paste. That explains everything.

NANCY *(Tolerant smile).* Yes; certainly.

CHARLIE. I'm sure it was the liver paste. I knew it. When you were packing the lunch this morning, I said what is that? And you said it's liver paste, for sandwiches; what's the matter, don't you like liver paste any more? And I said what do we need *that* for? For sandwiches, you said. And I said yes, but what do we *need* it for?

NANCY. But, Charlie . . .

CHARLIE. You've got a roasted chicken there, and peaches, and a brie, and bread and wine, what do we need the sandwiches for, the liver paste?

NANCY. You might want them, I said.

CHARLIE. But, with all the rest.

NANCY. Besides, I asked you what would happen if you picked up the roasted chicken and dropped it in the sand. What would you do—rinse it off with the wine? Then I'd have to make iced tea, too. Miles up on the dunes, no fresh water anywhere? Bring a thermos of iced tea, too, in case you dropped the chicken in the sand?

CHARLIE. *When* have I dropped a chicken in the sand? *When* have I done that?

NANCY *(Mildly piqued).* I wasn't suggesting it was a thing you *did;* I wasn't pointing to a history of it; I said you *might.* But, Charlie . . . at a time like *this* . . . they may come back.

CHARLIE. Liver paste doesn't keep; I *told* you that: goes bad in a minute, with the heat and all.

NANCY. Wrapped up in silver foil.

CHARLIE. Aluminum.

NANCY. . . . whatever; wrapped up and perfectly safe, it keeps.

CHARLIE. It goes bad in a minute, which is what it did: the liver paste clearly went bad. It went bad in the sun and it poisoned us.

NANCY *(Sees* SARAH *in the distance, or thinks she does).* Pardon?

CHARLIE *(Dogmatic; glum).* It went bad, as I said it would: the liver paste, for all your wrapping up. It went bad, and it poisoned us; *that's* what happened!

NANCY. *Poisoned* us?!

(Disbelieving, and distracted)

And *then* what happened?

CHARLIE *(Looks at her as if she's simple-minded).* Why . . . we *died,* of course.

NANCY. We died?

CHARLIE. We ate the liver paste and we died. That drowsy feeling . . . the sun . . . and the wine . . . none of it: all those night thoughts of what it would be like, the sudden scalding in the center of the chest, or wasting away; milk in the eyes, voices from the other room; none of it. Chew your warm sandwich, wash it down, lie back, and let the poison have its way . . .

(LESLIE and SARAH reappear over the dune; formidable, upright. NANCY begins laughing)

. . . talk—*think* you're talking—and all the while the cells are curling up, disconnecting . . . Nancy, don't do that! . . . it all goes dim . . . Don't laugh at me! . . . and then you're dead.

(Between her bursts of laughter)

How can you *do* that?

(LESLIE and SARAH move toward CHARLIE and NANCY, cautiously and intimidatingly; NANCY sees them, points, and her laughter changes its quality)

How can you laugh when you're dead, Nancy? Now, don't *do* that!

NANCY. We may be dead already, Charlie, but I think we're going to die again. Here they come!

CHARLIE. Oh my *dear* God!

(LESLIE and SARAH approach, but stop a fair distance away from CHARLIE and NANCY; they are on their guard)

NANCY *(After a pause).* Charlie, there's only one thing for it. Watch me now; watch me carefully.

CHARLIE. Nancy . . .

(She smiles broadly; with her feet facing LESLIE and SARAH, she slowly rolls over on her back, her legs drawn up, her hands by her face, fingers curved, like paws. She holds this position, smiling broadly)

NANCY. Do *this,* Charlie! For God's sake, do *this!*

CHARLIE *(Confused).* Nancy . . .

NANCY. It's called "submission," Charlie! I've seen it in the books. I've read how the animals do it. Do it, Charlie! Roll over! Please!

(CHARLIE hesitates a moment, looks at LESLIE and SARAH)

Do it, Charlie!

(Slowly, CHARLIE smiles broadly at LESLIE and SARAH, assumes NANCY's position)

CHARLIE *(Finally).* All right.

NANCY. Now, Charlie, smile! And mean it!

CURTAIN

ACT TWO

The curtain rises. The set: the same as the end of ACT ONE. CHARLIE, NANCY, LESLIE, *and* SARAH *as they were. All are stock-still for a moment.*

LESLIE *(Turns his head toward* SARAH). Well, Sarah, what do you think?
SARAH *(Shakes her head).* I don't know, Leslie.
LESLIE. What do you think they're doing?
SARAH. Well, it *looks* like some sort of a submission pose, but you never know; it might be a trick.
LESLIE. I'll take a look.
SARAH. Well, be very careful.
LESLIE *(A weary sigh).* Yes, Sarah.
  (LESLIE *starts moving over to where* CHARLIE *and* NANCY *lie in their submission postures)*
CHARLIE. Oh my God, one of them's coming.
NANCY. Stay very still.
CHARLIE. What if one of them touches me?
NANCY. Smile.
CHARLIE. I'll scream.
NANCY. No, don't do *that.*
CHARLIE *(Whispers out of the side of his mouth).* It's coming! It's coming!
NANCY. Well . . . hold on, and don't panic. If we had a tail, this'd be the perfect time to wag it.
  (LESLIE *is very close)*
CHARLIE. Oh, God.
  (LESLIE *stops, leans forward toward* CHARLIE, *and sniffs him several times. Then he straightens up and pokes* CHARLIE *in the ribs with his footpaw.* CHARLIE *makes an involuntary sound but holds his position and keeps smiling.* LESLIE *looks at* NANCY, *sniffs her a little, and pokes her, too. She holds her position and wags her hands a little.* LESLIE *surveys them both, then turns and ambles back to* SARAH)
SARAH. Well?
LESLIE. Well . . . they don't look very . . . formidable—in the sense of prepossessing. Not young. They've got their teeth bared, but they don't look as though they're going to bite. Their hide is funny—feels soft.
SARAH. How do they smell?
LESLIE. Strange.
SARAH. Well, I should suppose *so.*

386

LESLIE *(Not too sure)*. I guess it's *safe*.

SARAH. Are you *sure?*

LESLIE *(Laughs a little)*. No; of course not.
(*Scratches his head*)

NANCY *(Sotto voce)*. What are they doing?

CHARLIE. It poked me; one of them poked me; I thought it was all over.

NANCY *(Not to be left out)*. Well, it poked *me*, too.

CHARLIE. It *sniffed* at *me*.

NANCY. Yes. Keep where you are, Charlie; don't move. It sniffed at *me*, too.

CHARLIE. Did you smell it?

NANCY. Yes; fishy. And beautiful!

CHARLIE. Terrifying!

NANCY *(Agreeing)*. Yes; beautiful.

LESLIE. Well, I suppose I'd better go over and . . .
(*Sort of shrugs*)

SARAH *(Immediately)*. I'll come with you.

LESLIE. No; you stay here.

SARAH *(Determined)*. I *said* I'll come *with* you.

LESLIE *(Weary)*. Yes, Sarah.

SARAH. There's no telling what kind of trouble you'll get yourself into.

LESLIE. Yes, Sarah.

SARAH. If you're going to take *that* attitude, we might as well . . .

LESLIE *(Rather abrupt)*. All *right*, Sarah!

SARAH *(Feminine, submissive)*. All right, Leslie.

CHARLIE. What's happening?

NANCY. I think they're having a discussion.

LESLIE. Are you ready?

SARAH *(Sweet)*. Yes, dear.

LESLIE. All right?
(SARAH *nods*)
All right.
(*They slowly advance toward* CHARLIE *and* NANCY)

CHARLIE. Here they come!

NANCY. We're making history, Charlie!

CHARLIE *(Snorts; fear and trembling)*. The sound of one hand clapping, hunh?

(LESLIE *and* SARAH *are before them.* LESLIE *raises paw to strike* CHAR-LIE)

SARAH. Don't hurt them.

(LESLIE *gives* SARAH *a disapproving look, pokes* CHARLIE)

CHARLIE. OW!

NANCY *(Chiding)*. Charlie! Please!

CHARLIE. It poked me!

LESLIE *(To* CHARLIE *and* NANCY; *clears his throat)*. Pardon me.

CHARLIE *(To* NANCY). What am I supposed to do if it pokes me?

LESLIE *(Louder)*. Pardon me.

NANCY *(Indicating* LESLIE). Speak to it, Charlie; answer it.

CHARLIE. Hm?

NANCY. *Speak* to it, Charlie!

CHARLIE. "Don't just lie there," you mean?

NANCY. I guess.

(Sits up and waves at SARAH, *tentatively)*

Hello.

SARAH *(To* NANCY). Hello.

(To LESLIE)

It said hello. Did you hear it?

LESLIE *(His attention still on* CHARLIE). Um-hum.

NANCY. Go on, Charlie.

SARAH. Speak to the other one.

LESLIE. I've spoken to it twice; maybe it's deaf.

NANCY. Go on.

CHARLIE. No; then I'd have to accept it.

SARAH. Maybe it's shy—or frightened. Try once again.

LESLIE *(Sighs)*. All right.

(Prods CHARLIE; *says, rather too loudly and distinctly)*

Pardon me!

NANCY *(Stage whisper)*. Go on, Charlie.

CHARLIE *(Pause; then, very direct)*. Hello.

(Turns to NANCY)

All right?

(Back to LESLIE)

Hello!

(Brief silence)

388

SARAH *(Overlapping with* NANCY's *following).* There! You see, Leslie, every-thing's going to be . . .

NANCY. Good for you, Charlie! Now, that wasn't so . . .
(A raised paw and a growl from LESLIE *silences them both in mid-sentence)*

LESLIE *(Moves a step toward* CHARLIE, *eyes him).* Are you unfriendly?
(SARAH *and* NANCY *look to* CHARLIE. CHARLIE *lowers his legs and comes up on one elbow)*

CHARLIE. Well . . .

NANCY. Tell him, Charlie!

CHARLIE *(To* NANCY, *through clenched teeth).* I'm thinking of what to say.
(To LESLIE)
Unfriendly? Well, no, not by nature. I'm certainly on my guard, though.

LESLIE. Yes, well, so are we.

SARAH. Indeed we are!

CHARLIE. I mean, if you're going to kill us and eat us . . . then we're unfriendly: we'll . . . resist.

LESLIE *(Looks to* SARAH *for confirmation).* Well, I certainly don't think we were planning to do *that. Were* we?

SARAH *(None too sure).* Well . . . no; at least, I don't *think* so.

NANCY. Of *course* you weren't! The very idea! Charlie, let's introduce ourselves.

LESLIE. After all, you're rather large . . . and quite unusual.
(Afterthought)
Were you thinking of eating *us?*

NANCY *(Almost laughs).* Good heavens, no!

SARAH. Well, we don't know your habits.

NANCY. I'm Nancy, and this is Charlie.

CHARLIE. How do. We don't know *your* habits, either. It'd be perfectly normal to assume you ate whatever . . . you ran into . . . you know, whatever you ran into.

LESLIE *(Cool).* No; I don't know.

SARAH *(To* NANCY). I'm Sarah.

NANCY. Hello, Sarah.

CHARLIE *(Somewhat on the defensive).* It's perfectly simple: we don't eat . . . we're not cannibals.

LESLIE. What is this?

CHARLIE. Hm? We do eat other flesh . . . you know, cow, and pigs, and chickens, and all . . .

LESLIE *(To* SARAH, *very confused).* What are *they?*

(SARAH *shrugs)*

CHARLIE. I guess you could put it down as a rule that we don't eat anything that . . . well, anything that *talks;* you know, English, and . . .

NANCY *(To* CHARLIE). Parrots talk; some people eat parrots.

CHARLIE. Parrots don't *talk;* parrots *imitate.* Who eats parrots?

NANCY. In the Amazon; I'm sure people eat parrots there; they're very poor, and . . .

LESLIE. What are you *saying?!*

CHARLIE *(Frustrated).* I'm trying to tell you . . . we don't eat our own kind.

SARAH *(After a brief pause; flat).* Oh.

LESLIE *(Rather offended).* Well, we don't eat our own kind, either. Most of us. Some.

NANCY *(Cheerful).* Well. You see?

LESLIE *(Dubious).* Well . . .

(To make the point)

You see . . . you're *not* our kind, so you can understand the apprehension.

NANCY. Besides, we cook everything.

SARAH. Pardon?

NANCY. We cook everything. Well, most things; *you* know . . . no, you don't, do you?

SARAH. This is Leslie.

NANCY *(Extending her hand).* How do you do, Leslie?

LESLIE *(Regards her gesture).* What is that?

NANCY. Oh; we . . . well, we shake hands . . . flippers, uh . . . Charlie?

CHARLIE. When we meet we . . . take each other's hands, or whatever, and we . . . touch.

SARAH *(Pleased).* Oh, that's *nice.*

LESLIE *(Not convinced).* What for?

SARAH *(Chiding).* Oh, Leslie!

LESLIE *(To* SARAH, *a bit piqued).* I want to know what *for.*

CHARLIE. Well, it *used* to be, since most people are right-handed, it used to be to prove nobody had a weapon, to prove they were friendly.

LESLIE *(After a bit)*. We're ambidextrous.

CHARLIE *(Rather miffed)*. Well, that's *nice* for you. Very nice.

NANCY. And some people used to hold on to their sex parts, didn't you tell me that, Charlie? That in olden times people used to hold on to their sex parts when they said hello . . . their own?

CHARLIE. I don't think I told you quite that. Each other's, maybe.

NANCY. Well, no matter.

 To LESLIE)

 Let's greet each other properly, all right?

 (Extends her hand again)

 I give you my hand, and you give me your . . . what *is* that? What is that called?

LESLIE. What?

NANCY *(Indicating LESLIE's right arm)*. That there.

LESLIE. It's called a leg, of course.

NANCY. Oh. Well, we call this an arm.

LESLIE. You have four arms, I see.

CHARLIE. No; she has two arms.

 (Tiny pause)

 And two legs.

SARAH *(Moves closer to examine NANCY with LESLIE)*. And which are the legs?

NANCY. These here. And these are the arms.

LESLIE *(A little on his guard)*. Why do you differentiate?

NANCY. Why do we differentiate, Charlie?

CHARLIE *(Quietly hysterical)*. Because they're the ones with the hands on the ends of them.

NANCY *(To LESLIE)*. Yes.

SARAH *(As LESLIE glances suspiciously at CHARLIE)*. Go on, Leslie; do what Nancy wants you to.

 (To NANCY)

 What is it called?

NANCY. Shaking hands.

CHARLIE. Or legs.

LESLIE *(Glowers at CHARLIE)*. Quiet.

CHARLIE *(Quickly)*. Yes, sir.

LESLIE *(To NANCY)*. Now; what is it you want to do?

NANCY. Well . . .

(A glance at CHARLIE, *both reassuring and imploring)*

. . . you give me your . . . that leg there, that one, and I'll give you my . . . leg, or arm, or whatever, and we'll come together by our fingers . . . these are your fingers . . .

LESLIE. Toes.

NANCY. Oh, all right; toes.

(Shakes hands with LESLIE)

And we come together like this, and we do this.

(They continue a slow, broad handshake)

LESLIE. Yes?

NANCY. And now we let go.

(They do)

There! You see?

LESLIE *(Somewhat puzzled about it)*. Well, that's certainly an unusual thing to want to do.

SARAH. Let *me!* I want to!

*(*SARAH *shakes hands with* NANCY, *seems happy about doing it)*

Oh, my; that's very interesting.

(To LESLIE)

Why haven't *we* ever done anything like that?

LESLIE *(Shrugs)*. Damned if *I* know.

SARAH *(To* LESLIE, *referring to* CHARLIE). You do it with *him,* now.

*(*CHARLIE *smiles tentatively, holds his hand out a little;* LESLIE *moves over to him)*

LESLIE. Are you *sure* you're friendly?

CHARLIE *(Nervous, but serious)*. I *told* you: you'll never meet a more peaceful man. Though of course if I thought you were going to *go* at me, or Nancy here, I'd probably defend myself . . . I mean, I *would.*

LESLIE. The danger, as *I* see it, is if one of us panics.

*(*CHARLIE *gives a hollow laugh)*

I think I'd like to know what frightens you.

*(*CHARLIE *laughs again)*

Please?

NANCY *(Nicely)*. Tell him, Charlie.

SARAH. Please?

CHARLIE *(A pause, while the nature of his questioner sinks in)*. What frightens me? Oh . . . deep space? Mortality? Nancy . . . not being with me?

(Chuckles ruefully)

Great . . . green . . . creatures coming up from the sea.

LESLIE. Well, that's it, you see: what we don't *know*. Great green creatures, and all, indeed! You're pretty odd yourselves, though you've probably never looked at it that way.

CHARLIE. Probably not.

LESLIE. You're not the sort of thing we run into every day.

CHARLIE. Well, *no* . . .

LESLIE *(Points at* CHARLIE). What's all *that?*

CHARLIE *(Looks at himself)*. What?

LESLIE *(Touches* CHARLIE's *shirt; says it with some distaste)*. All *that.*

CHARLIE. This? My shirt.

("Naturally" implicit)

LESLIE. What *is* it?

NANCY. Clothes; they're called clothes; we put them on; we . . . well, we cover our skins with them.

LESLIE. What for?

NANCY. Well . . . to keep warm; to look pretty; to be decent.

LESLIE. What is *that?*

NANCY. Which?

LESLIE. Decent.

NANCY. Oh. Well . . . uh, not to expose our sexual parts. My breasts, for example.

(Touches them)

CHARLIE. Say "mammaries."

NANCY. What?

SARAH *(Fascinated)*. What *are* they?

NANCY. Well, they . . . no, you don't seem to have them, do you? They're . . . secondary sex organs.

(Realizes it's hopeless as she says it)

No? well . . .

(Beckons SARAH, *begins to unbutton her blouse)*

Come here, Sarah.

CHARLIE. Nancy!

NANCY. It's all *right*, Charlie. Come look, Sarah.

SARAH *(Puts one paw on* NANCY's *blouse, peers in)*. My gracious! Leslie, come see!

CHARLIE. Now just a minute!

NANCY *(Laughs).* Charlie! Don't be silly!

LESLIE *(To* CHARLIE; *ingenuous).* What's the matter?

CHARLIE. I don't want you looking at my wife's breasts, that's all.

LESLIE. I don't even know what they are.

NANCY *(Buoyant).* Of course not! Are you *jealous,* Charlie?

CHARLIE. Of course not! How could I be jealous of . . .

(Indicates LESLIE *with some distaste)*

. . . how *could* I be?

NANCY *(Agreeing with him).* No.

CHARLIE *(Reassuring himself).* I'm *not.*

SARAH *(No overtones).* I think Leslie *should* see them.

NANCY. Yes.

LESLIE *(To* CHARLIE; *shrugs).* It's up to *you;* I mean, if they're something you *hide,* then maybe they're embarrassing, or sad, and I shouldn't *want* to see them, and . . .

CHARLIE *(More flustered than angry).* They're not embarrassing; *or* sad; They're lovely! Some women . . . some women Nancy's age, they're . . . some women . . .

(To NANCY, *almost spontaneously bursting into tears)*

I *love* your breasts.

NANCY *(Gentle).* Yes; *yes. Thank* you.

(More expansive)

I'm not an exhibitionist, dear, as you very well know . . .

CHARLIE. . . . except that time you answered the door stark naked . . .

NANCY *(An old story).* We'll not discuss that now.

(To LESLIE *and* SARAH*)*

It was nothing.

CHARLIE *(By rote).* So *she* says.

NANCY *(To the others).* It was nothing. Really.

(To CHARLIE*)*

What I was trying to say, Charlie, was—and prefacing it with that I'm not an exhibitionist, as you very well know—that if someone . . .

CHARLIE *(To* NANCY*).* Stark naked.

NANCY. . . . has *not* . . . has gone through life and *not* seen a woman's breasts . . . why, it's like Sarah never having seen . . . the sky. Think of the wonder of *that,* and think of the wonder of the other.

CHARLIE *(Rather hurt).* One of the wonders, hunh?

NANCY. I didn't *mean* it that way!

(Shakes her head; buttons up)

Well . . . no matter.

LESLIE *(Shrugs)*. It's up to you.

SARAH. They're really very interesting, Leslie; I'm sorry you didn't see them.

LESLIE. Well, another time, maybe.

SARAH *(Delighted and excited)*. I suddenly remember something! Leslie, do you remember when we went way north, and it was very cold, and the scenery changed, and we came to the edge of a deep ravine, and all at once we heard those strange and terrible sounds . . .

LESLIE *(Disturbed at the memory)*. Yes; I remember.

SARAH. Oh, it was a frightening set of sounds, echoing . . . all around us; and then we saw them . . . swimming by.

LESLIE. Enormous . . .

SARAH. Huge! Huge creatures; ten of them, maybe more. I'd never seen the size. They were of great girth.

CHARLIE. They were whales; I'm sure they were whales.

LESLIE. Is *that* what they were?

SARAH. We observed them, though, and they had young with them; young! And it was most interesting: the young would attach themselves to what I assume was the female—the mother—would attach themselves to devices that I *think* were very much like those of *yours;* resemble them.

NANCY. Of course! To the mammaries! Oh, Sarah, those *were* whales, for whales are mammals and they feed their young.

SARAH. Do you remember, Leslie?

LESLIE *(Nods)*. Yes, I think I do.

(To NANCY*)*

And you have those? That's what *you* have?

NANCY. Yes; well . . . very much like them . . . in principle.

LESLIE. My gracious.

CHARLIE *(To clear the air; brisk)*. Do you, uh . . . do *you* have any children? Any young?

SARAH *(Laughs gaily)*. Well, of course I have! Hundreds!

CHARLIE. Hundreds!

SARAH. Certainly; I'm laying eggs all the time.

CHARLIE *(A pause)*. You . . . lay eggs.

SARAH. Certainly! Right and left.

(A pause)

NANCY. Well.

LESLIE *(Eyes narrowed)*. You, uh . . . you *don't* lay eggs, hunh?

CHARLIE *(Incredulous)*. No; of course not!

LESLIE *(Exploding)*. There! You see?! What did I tell you?! They don't even lay eggs!

NANCY *(Trying to save the situation)*. How many . . . uh . . . eggs have you laid, Sarah?

SARAH *(Thinks about it for a bit)*. Seven thousand?

NANCY *(Admonishing)*. Oh! Sarah!

SARAH. No?

NANCY. Well, I dare say! Yes! But, really!

SARAH. I'm sorry?

NANCY. No! Never that!

CHARLIE *(To* LESLIE, *with some awe)*. Seven thousand! Really?

LESLIE *(Gruff; the usual husband)*. Well, *I* don't know. I mean . . .

NANCY. What do you *do* with them, Sarah? How do you take *care* of them?

SARAH. Well . . . they just . . . float away.

NANCY *(Chiding)*. Oh, Sarah!

SARAH. Some get eaten—by folk passing by, which is a blessing, really, or we'd be inundated—some fall to the bottom, some catch on growing things; there's a disposition.

NANCY. Still!

SARAH. Why? What do *you* do with them?

NANCY *(Looks at her nails briefly)*. It's different with us, Sarah. In the birthing, I mean; I don't know about . . . well, how you go about it!

SARAH *(Shy)*. Well . . . we couple.

LESLIE. Shhh!

NANCY. Yes; I thought. And so do we.

SARAH *(Relieved)*. Oh; good. And then—in a few weeks—

NANCY. Oh, it takes a lot longer for us, Sarah: nine months.

SARAH. Nine months! Leslie!

LESLIE. Wow!

SARAH. Nine months.

NANCY. And then the young are born. *Is* born . . . usually.

SARAH. Hm?

NANCY. *Is.* We usually have one, Sarah. One at a time. Oh, two, occasionally; rarely three or more.

SARAH *(Commiserating).* Oh, Nancy!

LESLIE *(To* CHARLIE*).* If you have only one or two, what if they're washed away, or eaten? I mean, how do you . . . perpetuate?

NANCY *(Gay laugh).* That never happens. We keep them with us . . . till they're all grown up and ready for the world.

SARAH. How long is that?

CHARLIE. Eighteen . . . twenty years.

LESLIE. You're not serious!

NANCY. Oh, we *are!*

LESLIE. You *can't* be.

CHARLIE *(Defensive).* Why not?!

LESLIE. Well . . . I mean . . . *think* about it.

CHARLIE *(Does).* Well . . . it *is* a long time, I suppose, but there's no other way for it.

NANCY. Just as you let them float away, or get caught on things; there's no other way for it.

SARAH. How many have you birthed?

NANCY. Three.

SARAH *(Still with the wonder of that).* Only three.

NANCY. Of course, there's *another* reason we keep them with us.

SARAH. Oh? What is that?

NANCY *(Puzzled at her question).* Well . . . we *love* them.

(Pause)

LESLIE. Pardon?

CHARLIE. We *love* them.

LESLIE. Explain.

CHARLIE. What?

LESLIE. What you said.

CHARLIE. We said we love them.

LESLIE. Yes; explain.

CHARLIE *(Incredulous).* What love means?!

NANCY *(To* SARAH*).* Love? Love is one of the emotions.

(They look at her, waiting)

One of the *emotions,* Sarah.

SARAH *(After a tiny pause).* But, what *are* they?!

NANCY *(Becoming impatient)*. Well, you *must* have them. You *must* have emotions.

LESLIE *(Quite impatient)*. We may, or we may not, but we'll never know unless you define your terms. Honestly, the imprecision! You're so thoughtless!

CHARLIE *(Miffed)*. Well, we're sorry!

LESLIE. You have to make allowances!

CHARLIE. All *right!!*

LESLIE. Just . . . thoughtless.

CHARLIE. All *right!*

SARAH. *Help* us, Nancy.

NANCY *(To* SARAH *and* LESLIE*)*. Fear. Hatred. Apprehension. Loss. Love.
(Pause)
Nothing?
(A bedtime story)
We keep them with us because they need us to; and we feel possessive toward them, and grateful, and proud . . .

CHARLIE *(Ironic)*. And lots of *other* words describing emotions. You can't *do* that, Nancy; it doesn't help.

NANCY *(Annoyed)*. Then *you* do it! And when we get back home, I'm packing up and taking a good long trip. *Alone.* I've been married to you far too smoothly for far too long.

CHARLIE *(To* LESLIE*)*. That's an example of emotion: frustration, anger . . .

NANCY *(To herself)*. I'm too *old* to have an affair.
(Pause)
No, I'm not.
(Pause)
Yes, I am.

CHARLIE *(Chuckling)*. Oh, come on, Nancy.
(To LESLIE *and* SARAH*)*
Maybe *I* can do it. How did you two get together? How'd ya meet?

LESLIE. Well, I was just going along, one day, minding my own business . . .

SARAH. Oh, Leslie!
(To CHARLIE*)*
I was reaching my maturity, and so, naturally, a lot of males were paying attention to me—milling around—you know, preening and snapping at

each other and generally showing off, and I noticed one was hanging around a little distance away, not joining in with the others . . .

LESLIE. That was me.

SARAH. . . . and I didn't pay too much attention to him, because I thought he was probably sickly or something, and besides, there were so many others, and it was time to start coupling . . .

LESLIE. *You* noticed me.

SARAH. . . . when, all of a sudden! There he was, right in the middle of them, snapping away, really fighting, driving all the others off. It was quite a rumpus.

LESLIE *(An aside, to* CHARLIE*).* They didn't *amount* to much.

SARAH *(Shrugs).* And so . . . all the others drifted away . . . and there he was.

LESLIE. They didn't *drift* away: I drove them away.

SARAH. Well, I suppose that's true.

(Bright)

Show them your scar, Leslie!

(To CHARLIE *and* NANCY*)*

Leslie has a marvelous scar!

LESLIE *(Proud).* Oh . . . some other time.

SARAH. And there he *was* . . . and there *I* was . . . and here we *are*.

CHARLIE. Well, yes! That proves my point!

LESLIE. What?

CHARLIE *(Pause).* About *love*.

(Pause)

He *loved* you.

SARAH. Yes?

CHARLIE. Well, *yes*. He drove the others away so he could have *you*. He wanted *you*.

SARAH *(As if what* CHARLIE *has said proves nothing).* Ye-es?

CHARLIE. Well . . . it's so *clear*. Nancy, isn't it clear?

NANCY. I don't *know*. Don't talk to me; you're a terrible person.

CHARLIE *(Under his breath).* Oh, for God's sake! Leslie! *Why* did you want Sarah?

LESLIE. Well, as I told you: I was just going along one day, minding my own business, and there was this great commotion, with all the others around her, and so I decided *I* wanted her.

399

CHARLIE *(Losing, but game)*. Didn't you think she was . . . pretty—or whatever?

LESLIE. I couldn't really see, with all the others hovering. She *smelled* all right.

CHARLIE. Have you ever, you know, coupled with anyone else since you met Sarah?

NANCY. Charlie!

LESLIE *(Pause; too defensive)*. Why should I?

CHARLIE *(Smiles)*. Just asking.
   (Patient)
Is that your *nature?* Not to go around coupling whenever you feel like it, whatever female strikes your fancy?

SARAH *(Fascinated)*. *Very* interesting.

LESLIE *(To shut her up)*. It is *not!*
   (To CHARLIE)
I've coupled in my time.

CHARLIE. Since you met Sarah?

LESLIE. I'm not going to *answer* that.

SARAH *(Hurt)*. You *have?*

CHARLIE. No; he means he hasn't. And he's embarrassed by it. What about you, Sarah? Have you been with anyone since Leslie?

LESLIE. Of *course* she hasn't!

NANCY. What an *awful* question to ask Sarah! You should be *ashamed* of yourself!

CHARLIE. It's not an awful question at all.

NANCY. It *is!* It's dreadful! Of course she hasn't.

CHARLIE *(Annoyed)*. What *standards* are you using? How would *you* know?

NANCY *(Up on her high horse)*. I just know.

CHARLIE. Things might be different, you know . . .
   (Gestures vaguely around)
   . . . down . . . *there*. I don't think it's dreadful at *all*.

SARAH *(To* NANCY *and* CHARLIE). The truth of the matter is: no, I haven't.

LESLIE. What are you getting at?!

CHARLIE. It's hard to explain!

LESLIE. Apparently.

CHARLIE. Especially to someone who has no grasp of conceptual matters, who hasn't heard of half the words in the English language, who lives on the bottom of the sea and has green scales!

LESLIE. Look, buddy . . . !

SARAH. Leslie . . .   NANCY. Now you two boys just . . .

CHARLIE *(Half to himself)*. Might as well be talking to a fish.

LESLIE *(Really angry; starts toward* CHARLIE*)*. That does it!

NANCY. Charlie! Look out! Sarah, stop him!

SARAH *(Stamps her paw)*. Leslie! You be nice!

LESLIE *(To* SARAH*)*. He called me a fish!

SARAH. He did not!

NANCY. No he didn't; not quite. He said he might as well.

LESLIE. Same thing.

CHARLIE *(A glint in his eye)*. Oh? What's the matter with fish?

NANCY *(Sotto voce)*. Calm down, Charlie . . .

CHARLIE *(Persisting)*. What's the matter with fish, hunh?

SARAH. Be good, Leslie . . .

LESLIE *(On his high horse—so to speak)*. We just don't think very highly of fish, that's all.

CHARLIE *(Seeing a triumph somewhere)*. Oh? You don't like fish, hunh?

NANCY. Now, *both* of you!

CHARLIE. What's the matter with fish all of a sudden?

LESLIE *(Real middle class, but not awful)*. For one thing, there're too many of them; they're all over the place . . . racing around, darting in front of you, *picking* at everything . . . moving in, taking over where you live . . . and they're stupid!

SARAH *(Shy)*. Not all of them; porpoises aren't stupid.

LESLIE *(Still wound up)*. All right! Except for porpoises . . . they're stupid!

(Thinks about it some more)

And they're dirty!

CHARLIE *(Mouth opens in amazement and delight)*. You're . . . you're prejudiced! Nancy, he's . . . You're a bigot!

(Laughs)

You're a goddamn bigot!

LESLIE *(Dangerous)*. Yeah? What's that?

NANCY. Be careful, Charlie.

LESLIE *(Not amused)*. What *is* that?

CHARLIE. What? A bigot?

LESLIE. I don't know. Is that what you said?

SEASCAPE

CHARLIE *(Right on with it)*. A bigot is somebody who thinks he's better than somebody else because they're different.

LESLIE *(Brief pause; anger defused)*. Oh; well, then; that's all right. I'm not what you said. It's *not* because they're different: it's because they're stupid and they're dirty and they're all over the place!

CHARLIE *(Parody of studying and accepting)*. Oh. Well. That's all right, then.

NANCY *(Wincing some)*. Careful, Charlie.

LESLIE *(Absorbed with his own words)*. Being different is . . . interesting; there's nothing implicitly inferior or superior about it. *Great* difference, of course, produces natural caution; and if the differences are too extreme . . . well, then, reality tends to fade away.

NANCY *(An aside; to CHARLIE)*. And so much for conceptual matters.

CHARLIE *(Dismissing it with bravado)*. Oooooooh, he probably read it somewhere.

SARAH *(Looks at the sky, and about her, expansively)*. My! It *is* quite something out here, isn't it? You can see! So very far!

(She sees birds with some consternation)

What are those?

(LESLIE sees them. Tenses. Does an intake of breath)

NANCY *(looking up)*. Birds. Those are birds, Sarah.

(LESLIE in reaction to the birds starts moving up the dune)

SARAH. Leslie! Leslie!

(LESLIE continues to move to top of the dune; growling)

NANCY. What's he doing?

SARAH. He's . . .

(Shrugs)

. . . well, he does it everywhere we go, so why not up here? He checks things out, makes sure a way is open for us . . .

CHARLIE. It's called instinct.

SARAH *(Polite, but not terribly interested)*. Oh? *Is* it.

CHARLIE *(Nods; quite happy)*. Instinct.

SARAH. Well, this isn't the sort of situation we run into every day, *and* . . . creatures do tend to be devious; you don't know what's going to happen from one minute to the next . . .

NANCY. Certainly, certainly. Will he be all right? I mean . . .

SARAH. Oh, certainly. He's kind and he's a good mate, and when he tells

402

me what we're going to do, I find I can live with it quite nicely. And you?

NANCY. Uh . . . well, we manage rather like that I guess.

SARAH *(Rapt)*. Oh, my goodness; *see* them up there! How they *go!*

CHARLIE. Seagulls.

SARAH. Sea . . . gulls.

(Still absorbed)

The wonder of it! What holds them up?

CHARLIE *(Shy, but helpful)*. Aerodynamics.

SARAH *(Still enraptured)*. Indeed.

NANCY. Tsk.

CHARLIE *(Feelings hurt)*. Well, it *is.*

SARAH *(To him)*. Oh, I wasn't *doubting* it.

(Attention back to the birds)

See them swim!

CHARLIE *(More sure of himself now)*. Fly, they fly; birds fly.

SARAH *(Watching the birds)*. The rays are rather like that: swimming about; what do you call it—flying. Funny creatures; shy, really; don't give that impression, though; stand-offish, rather curt.

NANCY. Rays. Yes; well, we know them.

SARAH *(Pleased)*. Do you!

CHARLIE. Nancy means we've *seen* them; photographs.

SARAH. What is *that?*

CHARLIE. Photographs? It's a . . . no, I'd better not try.

SARAH *(Coquettish)*. Something I shouldn't know? Something you could tell Leslie but not me?

NANCY *(Laughs)*. Heavens, no!

SARAH. I mean, I *am* a married woman.

CHARLIE *(Surprised)*. Do you *do* that? I mean, do you . . . . ? I don't know what I mean.

NANCY. Charlie! Just think what we can tell our children and our grand-children: that we were here when Sarah saw it all!

CHARLIE. Sure! And if you think they'd have us put away for all that other —for living on the beach . . .

NANCY *(Nodding along)*. . . . "from beach to beach, seaside no-mads . . ."

CHARLIE. . . . yes, then *what* do you *think* they'd *say* about *this!*

(Mimics her)

403

"Charlie and I were sitting around, you see, when all at once, lo and behold, these two great green lizards . . ." How do you think they'd take to *that*?! Put it in one of your postcards, Nancy, and mail it out.

NANCY. Ohhhhh, Charlie! You give me the pip, you know that?

SARAH *(Calling to* LESLIE). Leslie, Leslie.

LESLIE (LESLIE *cautiously starts down the dune).* Are you all right?

SARAH. Oh, Leslie, I've had an absolutely fascinating time. Leslie . . .

(Points to the sky)

. . . up there.

LESLIE. What *are* they?

SARAH *(Bubbling with it).* They're called *birds*, and they don't swim, they fly, and they stay up by something called aerodynamics . . .

LESLIE. What is *that?*

SARAH *(Rushing on).* I'm sure I don't know, and *I* said they looked like rays, and *they* said they knew rays through something called photographs, though they wouldn't tell me what that *was*, and Charlie gives Nancy the pip.

LESLIE. There, I was right! You can't trust somebody like that! How can you trust somebody like that? You can't trust somebody like that!

NANCY *(With a desperate attempt to save the situation).* Well, what does it matter? We're all *dead*.

SARAH. Dead? Who's dead?

NANCY. *We* are.

SARAH *(Disbelief).* No.

NANCY. According to Charlie here.

CHARLIE *(Without humor).* It's not to be joked about.

SARAH. *All* of us?

NANCY *(Chuckles).* Well, I'm not certain about that; he and I, apparently. It all has to do with liver paste. The fatal sandwich.

CHARLIE. Explain it right! Leave it alone if you're not going to give it the dignity it deserves.

NANCY *(To* LESLIE *and* SARAH; *a trifle patronizing).* I mean, we *have* to be dead, because Charlie has decided that the wonders do not occur; that what we have not known does not exist; that what we cannot fathom cannot be; that the miracles, if you will, are bedtime stories; he has taken the leap of faith, from agnostic to atheist; the world is flat; the sun and the planets revolve about it, and don't row out too far or you'll fall off.

CHARLIE *(Sad; embarrassed)*. I couldn't live with you again; I'm glad it doesn't matter.

NANCY *(To* CHARLIE; *nicely)*. Oh, Charlie.

LESLIE *(To* CHARLIE, *not believing any of it)*. When did you die?

CHARLIE. Pardon?

SARAH *(To* NANCY; *whispering)*. He's not dead.

NANCY *(To* SARAH*)*. I know.

LESLIE. Did we frighten you to death, or was it before we met you?

CHARLIE. Oh, *before* we met you; after lunch.

LESLIE. Then I take it *we* don't *exist*.

CHARLIE *(Apologetic)*. Probably not; I'm sorry.

LESLIE *(To* NANCY*)*. That's quite a mind he's got there.

NANCY *(Grudgingly defending* CHARLIE*)*. Well . . . he thinks things through.

(Very cheerful)

As for *me*, I couldn't care less: I'm having far too interesting a time.

SARAH. Oh, I'm so glad!

LESLIE *(Puzzled)*. I *think* I exist.

CHARLIE *(Shrugs)*. Well, *that's* all that matters; it's the same thing.

NANCY *(To* SARAH; *considerable enthusiasm)*. Oh, a voice from the dead.

LESLIE *(To* CHARLIE*)*. You mean it's all an illusion?

CHARLIE. Could be.

LESLIE. The whole thing? Existence?

CHARLIE. Um-hum!

LESLIE *(Sitting down with* CHARLIE*)*. I don't believe *that* at *all*.

CHARLIE. Well, it isn't *my* theory.

LESLIE. Whose theory *is* it, then?

CHARLIE *(Angry)*. What?!

LESLIE. Whose theory *is* it? Don't you yell at me.

CHARLIE. I am not *yelling* at you!

LESLIE. *Yes*, you are! You *did!*

CHARLIE. Well, then, I'm sorry.

LESLIE. Whose *theory* is it?

CHARLIE *(Weary)*. Descartes.

LESLIE *(Annoyed)*. What is *that?*

CHARLIE. What?

LESLIE. What you *said*.

CHARLIE *(Barely in control).* DESCARTES!! DESCARTES!! I THINK: THEREFORE I AM!!
(Pause)
COGITO! ERGO! SUM! I THINK: THEREFORE I AM!!
(Pause. Pleading)
Now you're going to ask me what *think* means.

NANCY *(Comforting, moving to him, genuine).* No, he's *not;* he wouldn't *do* that.

CHARLIE. I haven't got it *in* me.

NANCY. It's all right.

LESLIE *(To SARAH). I* know what think means.

SARAH. Of course you do!

LESLIE *(Agreeing).* Well!

CHARLIE. I couldn't take it.

NANCY. It's not going to happen.

CHARLIE. It's more than I could . . . Death is release, if you've lived all right, and *I* have.
(NANCY hugs him, but he goes on)
As well as most, easily; when it comes time, and I put down my fork on the plate, line it up with the knife, take a last sip of wine, or water, touch my lips and fold the napkin, push back the chair . . .

NANCY *(Shakes him by the shoulders, looks him in the eye).* Charlie!
(Kisses him on the mouth, her tongue entering, for quite a little; he is passive, then slowly responds, taking comfort, and sharing; they come apart, finally; he shrugs, chuckles timidly, smiles, chucks her under the chin)

CHARLIE *(Shy).* Well.

NANCY. It is all *right;* and you're alive. It's all right and, if it isn't . . . well, it will just have to do. No matter what.

CHARLIE *(Irony).* This will have to do.

NANCY. Yes, this will have to do.

SARAH. Is he all right?

NANCY. Well . . . he's been through life, you see and . . . yes, I suppose he's all right.
(The sound of the jet plane again from stage left to stage right, growing, becoming deafeningly loud, diminishing.
CHARLIE *and* NANCY *follow its course;* LESLIE *and* SARAH *are terrified; they rush half out of sight over the dune)*

406

NANCY *(In the silence following the plane).* Such *noise* they make.

CHARLIE. They'll crash into the dunes one day; I don't know what good they do.

NANCY *(Seeing* LESLIE *and* SARAH, *pointing to them).* Oh, Charlie! Look! Look at them!

CHARLIE. Hm? What?

(Sees them)

Oh!

NANCY. Oh, Charlie; they're frightened. They're so frightened!

CHARLIE *(Awe).* They are.

LESLIE *(From where he is; calling).* What *was* that?!

NANCY *(Calling; a light tone).* It was an aeroplane.

LESLIE. Well, what *is* it?!

CHARLIE. It's a machine that . . . it's a method of . . .

LESLIE. What?

CHARLIE *(Shouting).* It's a machine that . . . it's a method of . . .

(LESLIE *and* SARAH *begin to move back, paw in paw, glancing back at the plane as they move)*

It's a . . . it's like a bird, except that we make them—we put them together, and we get inside them, and that's how we fly . . . sort of.

SARAH *(Some awe).* It's terrifying!

NANCY. Well, you get used to it.

LESLIE *(To* CHARLIE; *to get it straight).* You . . . fly.

CHARLIE. Yes. Well, some do. *I* have. Yes! *I* fly. We do all sorts of things up here.

LESLIE. I'll bet you do.

CHARLIE. Sure; give us a machine and there isn't anywhere we won't go. Why, we even have a machine that will . . . go down there; under water.

LESLIE *(Brow furrowed).* Then . . . you've *been*—what do you call it: under water?

CHARLIE. Well, not in one of the machines, no. And nowhere near as deep as . . .

NANCY. Charlie *used* to go under—near the shore, of course; not very deep.

CHARLIE. Oh, God . . . years ago.

NANCY. Yes, and Charlie has missed it. He was telling me how much he used to love to go down under, settle on the bottom, wait for the fish to come . . .

CHARLIE *(Embarrassed; indicating* LESLIE *and* SARAH*)*. It was a *long* time ago.

(To NANCY*)*

Nancy, not now! Please!

LESLIE *(Very interested). Really.*

CHARLIE. It didn't *amount* to much.

NANCY. Oh, it *did;* it *did* amount, and to a great deal.

CHARLIE *(Embarrassed and angry).* Lay off, Nancy!

NANCY *(Turns on* CHARLIE, *impatient and angry).* It used to make you *happy,* and you used to be *proud* of what made you happy!

CHARLIE. LEAVE OFF!!

(Subsides)

Just . . . leave off.

(A silence. Now, to LESLIE *and* SARAH; *quietly)*

It was just a game; it was enough for a twelve-year-old, maybe, but it wasn't . . . finding out, you know; it wasn't *real.* It wasn't enough for a memory.

(Pause; shakes his head)

CHARLIE *(Barely controlled rage; to* LESLIE*).* Why did you come up here in the first place?

LESLIE *(Too matter-of-fact).* I don't know.

CHARLIE *(Thunder).* COME! ON!

LESLIE. I don't know!

(To SARAH; *too offhand)*

Do I know?

SARAH *(Yes and no).* Well . . .

LESLIE *(Final).* I don't know.

SARAH. We had a sense of not belonging any more.

LESLIE. Don't, Sarah.

SARAH. I should, Leslie. It was a growing thing, nothing abrupt, nor that anything was different, for that matter.

LESLIE *(Helpless).* Don't go on, Sarah.

SARAH. . . . in the sense of having changed; but . . . *we* had changed . . .

(Looks about her)

. . . all of a sudden, everything . . . down there . . . was terribly

408

. . . interesting, I suppose; but what did it have to do with *us* any more?

LESLIE. Don't, Sarah.

SARAH. And it wasn't . . . comfortable any more. I mean, after all, you make your nest, and accept a whole . . . array . . . of things . . . and . . . we didn't feel we *belonged* there any more. And . . . what were we going to do?!

CHARLIE *(After a little; shy)*. And that's why you came up.

LESLIE *(Nods, glumly)*. We talked about it.

SARAH. Yes. We did, for a long time. Considered the pros and the cons. Making do down there or trying something else. But what?

CHARLIE. And so you came up.

LESLIE. Is that what we did? Is that what we were doing? I don't know.

CHARLIE *(He has hardly been listening; speaks to himself more than to anyone else)*. All that time; the eons.

LESLIE. Hm?

NANCY. What was that, Charlie?

CHARLIE. The eons. How long is an eon?

NANCY *(Encouraging him)*. A very long time.

CHARLIE. A hundred million years? Ten times that? Well, a distance certainly. What do they call it . . . the primordial soup? the glop? That heartbreaking second when it all got together, the sugars and the acids and the ultraviolets, and the next thing you knew there were tangerines and string quartets.

LESLIE. What are *they?*

CHARLIE *(Smiles, a little sadly, shrugs)*. It doesn't matter. But somewhere in all that time, halfway, probably, halfway between the aminos and the treble clef—

(Directed to SARAH *and* LESLIE*)*

listen to this—there was a time when we *all* were down there, crawling around, and swimming and carrying on—remember how we read about it, Nancy . . .

NANCY. Yes . . . crawling around, and swimming . . . rather like it is now, but very different.

CHARLIE. Yes; very.

(To LESLIE *and* SARAH*)*

Are you interested in any of this?

SARAH *(Genuine, and pert)*. Oh! Fascinated!

CHARLIE. And you understand it; I mean, you follow it.

LESLIE *(Hurt, if not quite sure of himself)*. Of *course* we follow it.

SARAH *(Wavering a little)*. Of . . . of course.

NANCY. Of *course* they do.

LESLIE *(A kind of bluff)*. "Rather like it is now, but very different" . . . *(Shrugs)* Whatever that means.

CHARLIE *(Enthusiastic didacticism)*. It means that once upon a time you and I lived down there.

LESLIE. Oh, come on!

CHARLIE. Well, no, not literally, and *not* you and me, for that matter, but what we became.

LESLIE *(Feigning enthusiastic belief)*. Um-hum; um-hum.

SARAH. When were we all down there?

CHARLIE. Oh, a long time ago.

NANCY. Once upon a time, Sarah.

SARAH *(After a pause)*. Yes?

NANCY *(Laughs, realizing she is supposed to continue)*. Oh my goodness. I feel silly.

CHARLIE. Why? All you're going to do is explain evolution to a couple of lizards.

NANCY *(Rising above it)*. Once upon a time, Sarah, a long, long time ago, long before you were born—even before Charlie here was born . . .

CHARLIE *(Feigning great boredom)*. Veeeerrry funny.

NANCY. Nothing was like it is at all today. There were fish, but they didn't look like any fish you've ever seen.

SARAH. My goodness!

LESLIE. What happened to them?

NANCY *(Trying to find it exactly)*. Well . . . they were dissatisfied, is what they were. So, they grew, or diminished, or . . . or sprouted things— tails, spots, fins, feathers.

SARAH. It sounds extremely busy.

NANCY. Well, it *was*. Of course, it didn't happen all at once.

SARAH *(Looks to LESLIE)*. Oh?

NANCY *(A pleased laugh)*. Oh, *heavens* no. Small changes; adding up. Like . . . well, there probably was a time when Leslie didn't have a tail.

SARAH *(Laughs)*. Oh, really!

LESLIE *(Quite dry)*. I've always had a tail.

NANCY *(Bright).* Oh, no; there was a time, way back, you didn't. Before you needed it you didn't have one.

LESLIE *(Through his teeth).* I have *always* had a *tail.*

SARAH. Leslie's very proud of his tail, Nancy . . .

CHARLIE. You like your tail, do you?

LESLIE *(Grim; gathers his tail in front of him).* I have *always* had a *tail.*

SARAH. Of course you have, Leslie; it's a lovely tail.

LESLIE *(Hugging his tail in front of him, anxiety on his face).* I have. I've always had one.

NANCY *(Trying again).* Well, of course you have, and so did your father before you, and his, too, I have no doubt, and so on back, but maybe they had a smaller tail than you, or a larger.

LESLIE. Smaller!

SARAH. Leslie's extremely proud of his tail; it's very large and sturdy and . . .

NANCY. Well, I'm sure; yes.

LESLIE *(Eyeing CHARLIE). You* don't have a tail.

CHARLIE *(Rather proud).* No, I don't.

LESLIE. What happened to it?

CHARLIE. It fell off. Mutate or perish. Let your tail drop off, change your spots, or maybe just your point of view. The dinosaurs knew a thing or two, but that was about it . . . great, enormous creatures, big as a diesel engine—

(To LESLIE*)*

whatever that may be—leviathans! . . . with a brain the size of a lichee nut; couldn't cope; couldn't figure it all out; went down.

LESLIE *(Quite disgusted).* What are you talking about?

CHARLIE. Just running on, and trying to make a point. And do you know what happened once? Kind of the crowning moment of it all for me? It was when some . . . slimy creature poked his head out of the muck, looked around, and decided to spend some time up here . . . Came up into the air and decided to stay? And as time went on, he split apart and evolved and became tigers and gazelles and porcupines and Nancy here . . .

LESLIE *(Annoyed).* I don't believe a word of this!

CHARLIE. Oh, you'd better, for he went back under, too; part of what he became didn't fancy it up on land, and went back down there, and

411

turned into porpoises and sharks, and manta rays, and whales . . . and you.

LESLIE. Come off it!

CHARLIE. It's called flux. And it's always going on; right now, to all of us.

SARAH *(Shy)*. Is it . . . is it for the better?

CHARLIE. Is it for the *better?* I don't *know*. Progress is a set of assumptions. It's very beautiful down there. It's all still, and the fish float by. It's very beautiful.

LESLIE. Don't get taken in.

CHARLIE. What are you going to tell me about? Slaughter and pointlessness? Come on *up* here. *Stay*. The optimists say you mustn't look just yet, that it's all going to work out fine, no matter *what* you've heard. The pessimists, on the other hand . . .

NANCY. It *is*. It all *is*.

CHARLIE *(Slightly mocking)*. Why?!

NANCY. Because I couldn't bear to think of it otherwise, that's why. I'm not one of these people says that I'm better than a . . . a rabbit; just that I'm more interesting: I use tools, I make art . . .

(Turning introspective)

. . . and I'm aware of my own mortality.

(Pause)

Very.

(Pouting; very much like a little girl)

All rabbits do is eat carrots.

SARAH *(To* CHARLIE; *after a little pause; sotto voce)*. What are carrots?

CHARLIE *(Shrugs it off; not interested)*. Oh . . . something you eat. They make noise.

LESLIE *(Curiously bitter)*. And tools; and art; and mortality? Do you eat *them?* And do *they* make a noise?

CHARLIE *(Staring hard at* LESLIE*)*. They make a noise.

NANCY *(She, too)*. What is it, Leslie?

LESLIE *(Intense and angry)*. What *are* these things?!

NANCY. Tools; art; mortality?

CHARLIE. They're what separate *us* from the brute beast.

NANCY *(Very quiet)*. No, Charlie; don't.

LESLIE *(Quiet, cold, and formal)*. You'll have to forgive me, but what is brute beast?

NANCY. Charlie; no!

CHARLIE *(Defiant)*. Brute beast?

LESLIE *(Grim)*. *I* don't like the sound of it.

CHARLIE *(Stares right at him)*. Brute beast? It's not even aware it's *alive*, much less that it's going to die!

LESLIE *(Pause; then, as if to memorize the words)*. Brute. Beast. Yes?

CHARLIE. Right on.

(Pause)

LESLIE *(Suddenly aware of all eyes on him)*. Stop it! Stop it! What are you looking at? Why don't you mind your own business?

NANCY. What more do you want?

CHARLIE *(Intense)*. I don't *know* what more I want.

(To LESLIE *and* SARAH*)*

I don't know what I want for *you*. I don't know what I feel toward you; it's either love or loathing. Take your pick; they're both emotions. And you're finding out about them, aren't you? About emotions? Well, I want you to know about *all* of it; I'm impatient for you. I want you to experience the whole thing! The full sweep! Maybe I envy you . . . down *there*, free from it all; down there with the *beasts?*

(A pause)

What would you do, Sarah? . . . if Leslie went away . . . for a long time . . . what would you do then?

SARAH. If he didn't tell me where he was going?

CHARLIE. If he'd gone!

(Under his breath)

For God's sake.

(Back)

If he'd taken off, and you hadn't seen him for the *longest* time.

SARAH. I'd go look for him.

LESLIE *(Suspicious)*. What are you *after?*

CHARLIE *(To* SARAH; *ignoring* LESLIE*)*. You'd go look for him; fine. But what if you knew he was never coming back?

*(*SARAH *does a sharp intake of breath)*

What about that?

NANCY. You're heartless, Charlie; you're relentless and without heart.

CHARLIE *(Eyes narrowing)*. What would you do, Sarah?

(A pause, then she begins to sob)

SARAH. I'd . . . I'd . . .

CHARLIE. You'd cry; you'd cry your eyes out.

413

SARAH. I'd . . . cry; I'd . . . I'd cry! I'd . . . I'd cry my eyes out! Oh
. . . Leslie!

LESLIE *(Trying to comfort* SARAH*)*. It's all right, Sarah!

SARAH. I want to go back; I don't want to stay here any more.
(Wailing)
I want to go *back!*
(Trying to break away)
I want to go *back!*

NANCY *(Moves to* SARAH, *to comfort her)*. Oh, now, Sarah! Please!

SARAH. Oh, Nancy!
(Bursts into new sobbing)
I want to go back!

NANCY. Sarah!

CHARLIE. I'm sorry; I'm . . . I'm sorry.

LESLIE. Hey! Mister!
(Hit)
You've made her cry; she's never done anything like that.
(Hit)
You made her cry!
(Hit)

CHARLIE. I'm sorry, I . . . stop that!
I'm sorry; I . . .
(Hit)
. . . stop that!

LESLIE. You made her cry!
(Hit)

CHARLIE. STOP IT!

LESLIE. I ought to tear you apart!

CHARLIE. Oh my god!
(LESLIE *begins to choke* CHARLIE, *standing behind* CHARLIE, *his arm
around* CHARLIE's *throat. It has the look of slow, massive inevitability,
not fight and panic)*

NANCY. Charlie!
(SARAH *and* NANCY *rush to stop it)*

SARAH. Leslie! Stop it!

CHARLIE. Stop . . . it . . .

LESLIE *(Straining with the effort)*. You . . . made . . . her . . . cry
. . . mister.

NANCY. Stop! Please!

SARAH. Leslie!

CHARLIE *(Choking)*. Help . . . me . . .

  (LESLIE *suddenly lets go;* CHARLIE *sinks to the sand)*

LESLIE. Don't you talk to me about brute beast.

SARAH *(To* LESLIE*)*. *See* to him.

LESLIE *(Cold)*. Are you all right?

CHARLIE. Yes; yes, I am.

  (Pause)

LESLIE *(Attempts a quiet half joke)*. It's . . . rather dangerous . . . up here.

CHARLIE *(Looks him in the eye)*. Everywhere.

LESLIE. Well. I think we'll go back down now.

NANCY *(Hand out; a quiet, intense supplication)*. No!

LESLIE. Oh, yes. I think we must.

NANCY. No! You mustn't!

SARAH *(As a comfort)*. Leslie says we must.

  (LESLIE *puts his paw out)*

NANCY. No!

  (CHARLIE *takes it)*

LESLIE. This *is* how we do it, isn't it?

SARAH *(Watching; tentative)*. Such a wonderful thing to want to do.

LESLIE *(Tight; formal)*. Thank you very much.

NANCY. No!

CHARLIE *(Eyes averted)*. You're welcome.

NANCY. NO!

LESLIE *(Sighs)*. Well.

  (LESLIE *and* SARAH *start moving up to the upstage dune to exit)*

NANCY *(In place)*. Please?

  (NANCY *moves to follow them)*

SARAH. It's all right; it's all right.

NANCY. You'll have to come back . . . sooner or later. You don't have any choice. Don't you know that? You'll have to come back up.

LESLIE *(Sad smile)*. Do we?

NANCY. Yes!

LESLIE. *Do* we have to?

NANCY. Yes!

LESLIE. Do we *have* to?

415

NANCY *(Timid).* We could *help* you. Please?

LESLIE *(Anger and doubt).* How?

CHARLIE *(Sad, shy). Take* you by the hand? You've got to *do* it—sooner or later.

NANCY *(Shy).* We *could* help you.

(LESLIE *pauses; descends a step down the dune; crouches; stares at them)*

LESLIE *(Straight).* All right. Begin.

CURTAIN

THE MAN
WHO HAD
THREE ARMS

(A Play 1982)

For
Robert Drivas
(1936–1896)

CHARACTERS

MAN
WOMAN
HIMSELF

ACT ONE

If there is a curtain, the MAN *and the* WOMAN *are discovered sitting On-stage,* SHE *Stage Right,* HE *Stage Left. If there is no curtain, then let the* TWO *of them saunter On a few minutes before the play is to begin—talk to each other, examine notes, whatever. When it is time for the play to begin —this determined by the* MAN, *when* HE *sees the audience mostly in place —the* MAN *rises, glances Off, both Left and Right, gets his signal, glances at the audience, moves to the podium.*
House lights still on.

MAN *(Clears his throat).* I, uh . . . I believe we can begin now. Are we all assembled? Is . . .
(Glances at those still arriving)
. . . is everyone in his . . . or her . . . ? Perhaps if we waited a few moments more?
(Turns to the WOMAN, *smiles;* SHE *smiles helpfully back)*
Do . . . do take your seats now, if you would be so good. We really should get underway; should we not.
WOMAN. *(Whispers at him across the stage).* He's getting very impatient.
MAN. Hm? Oh; yes; well.
(More forceful)
Come now, ladies and gentlemen, let's . . . uh, get our act together, as I think I heard my nephew say the other day.
(Jocular)
All right. Are we ready now? Yes? Fine.
(House lights down)
Then let us begin.
(Takes out index cards, reads from them, and none too well)
It is my pleasure—my *singular* pleasure, sorry—to welcome you here tonight.
(Note: or "this afternoon" as the situation demands)
To welcome you to our presentation, the two hundred and thirty-first lecture in our series "Man on Man." There is nothing sexist in that, you understand—man on man, woman on woman . . . person on *person* we might think of calling it if we were not two hundred and thirty lectures into . . .
(Mumbling)
into a series entitled "Man on Man."

WOMAN. They can't hear you!!

MAN. What?

WOMAN. They can't hear you!!

MAN *(Louder)*. A series entitled "Man on Man"! Is that better?

WOMAN. Yes.

MAN. Good. Seven times a year for thirty-three years we have gathered here and become participants in the exploration of ourselves in the company, in the *focus* of those illustrious, gifted, intelligent beings whom we have invited here to enlighten us on the subject of . . . well, of ourselves. And what a list!! . . . Albert Einstein, Paul Tillich, Norman Thomas, Herbert Hoover, Robert Frost and Dylan Thomas, and on and on. And I mention only the dead, you notice—the no-longer-with-us-in-person. What an illustrious list! What a grand march of minds across the . . . something of our something.

(Consults his notes carefully)

I sat on my good glasses yesterday, looking for them. I wonder where my good glasses are, I said to myself, sitting to puzzle it out. Sit; crunch. Too late!

(Indicates the glasses HE has with him)

These are a power or two less than . . . What a march of minds . . .

(Reads)

across the . . . carbon of our receptive intellects.

(Renewed energy)

We have been taken to areas we dared only dimly imagine, into creativity and creation itself. We are the most fortunate of mortals!

WOMAN *(An embarrassed giggle)*. Really!

MAN. Hm? We are *not?* We are *not* the most fortunate of mortals?

(Considers it)

Well, no: the Christ's disciples, Leonardo's assistants, Jefferson's dinner guests, et cetera, et cetera.

WOMAN. *(Sotto voce; corner of mouth)*. Get on with it!

(Broad smile to the audience)

MAN. It is my . . . pleasure, my goodness . . . to introduce you to a lady who, to most of you, needs, as they say, no introduction.

(To himself)

Then why do I introduce her? Why don't I just point in her direction, bow, back off? Why am I here at all? Is all illusion? Do I exist?

WOMAN. Get *on* with it!

MAN. . . . who needs no introduction, our . . . distinguished and be-
loved Madame President.
(Applause; HE *bows to the audience, to* MADAME PRESIDENT, *and
backs to his seat as* SHE *approaches the podium)*
WOMAN *(A gracious bow to the audience, while the applause dies).* Thank
you, thank you, thank you, thank you, dear friends.
(Turns to the MAN, *peremptory)*
And thank you, dear friend, for your good words, for your . . .
MAN *(Half rising).* . . . oh, my dear, think nothing of it; my pleasure, my
goodness, my . . .
WOMAN *(Loud, to stop him).* . . . for your good words!
(Tight smile; to the audience again)
Dear friends. I have one or two announcements to make before we
proceed with "the matter at hand"?—if you will forgive my levity?
(No one seems to recognize her levity)
Matter at hand?
MAN *(Chuckles).* Oh, very good, very good!
WOMAN *(Slightly miffed).* One or two announcements.
(Sour acknowledgment of MAN)
Thank you, my dear.
(To the audience)
One or two announcements. You may recall that for tonight's [or
today's] meeting, we have had scheduled for the longest time—two
years now, I believe—the noted zoologist, Dr. Henry Speedthrift Tomlinson, prize winner—No*bel* Prize winner, to name but one of his big
guns!—author, professor, lecturer and whatever else you may care to
mention.
Well . . . the other week we wrote Dr. Tomlinson's lecture bureau, since
—as is the way of these things—they had been tardy in returning a
signed contract, and since we wanted to fête the good doctor as is our
wont, and make him as comfortable as a person could want, as is our
wont as well. Imagine our surprise—astonishment!—and dismay, then,
when we received the following terse, I thought, and not altogether
understanding letter from the Doctor's lecture bureau.
*(*SHE *reads)*
"Dear Madame President: We received your letter of [two weeks prior
to whatever date it presently is] with . . .
(Hurries over it)

astonishment and dismay. Doctor Tomlinson passed away somewhat over a year ago, the precise date being unascertainable since the Doctor's body, he having fallen into an Andean crevasse . . ." . . . which I take to be a crevasse in the Andes . . . "having fallen into an Andean crevasse was not recovered until such time as it was in a state of advanced decomposition." Why do they want to tell me these things!? ". . . decomposition and, indeed, was identifiable only from dental records, and by a locket which contained two photographs, one of the late Doctor himself, and the other of . . .

(Disbelief)

. . . a large pig."

MAN. A large what?

WOMAN. Pig! Pig!

MAN. A large pig?

WOMAN *(Reads again)*. "You can understand, therefore, why Doctor Tomlinson will not be addressing your group on the evening of [whatever it is]." Yes, well, indeed we can.

(Reads again)

"We're certain he would have enjoyed being with you, and we are puzzled only by how the Doctor's demise could have escaped your attention, given, as it was, such worldwide coverage."

(Shrugs)

I suppose, these days, if one turns one's back for a moment . . .

(Snaps her fingers)

. . . the . . . the letter—and *not* an entirely understanding one, as I am sure you will agree by now, went on, concluded by offering us, in Doctor Tomlinson's place, a number of other lecturers in their . . . stable, I suppose it could be called, among whom, it being such an abrupt and confusing state of affairs, we chose yet another Doctor, Doctor Abraham Fischman, the internationally famous plastic surgeon, practicing in Mexico, to address us on the topic "Face to Face."

MAN *(A private grief)*. Oh my, oh my, oh my my my!

WOMAN. "Face to Face." Well, and the world is a very strange place. We received a telephone call yesterday morning from the lecture bureau, to say that Dr. Fischman had been arrested in Tijuana and that he would not be with us today either. However, they have, at a moment's notice, and at considerable savings to us, I may add, provided us with tonight's speaker, in anticipation of whom I'm sure your heads are buzzing. One other item first, however: the matter of the poisoned quiche Lorraine and our lawsuit against the Tante Marie Quiche and Cheesecake Company. All of you who are not our newest members will remember that terrible July Fourth, our picnic in the park; our festive tables and our near fatal quiche. Some six hundred of us were felled, were we not! Diarrhea! Vomiting! Wracking headaches! Dehydration! Spasms! It was awful! It was really *awful!* You will recall that we brought suit against Tante Marie even as she—they—had declared bankruptcy and dissolved in spite of the counterclaim that we ourselves were negligent— some nonsense about lack of refrigeration, sitting in the hot sun, et cetera. Well, the case *has* been settled, and we have recovered damages to a sum which al*most*, but not quite covers our legal costs. It has not been one's most reassuring dip into the jurisprudential mire. There is a rainbow of sorts however; the Tante Marie Quiche and Cheescake Company people have resurfaced as a new corporate entity, known as the Frère Jacques Cheesecake and Quiche Company, Limited, and they have offered to cater our next picnic at what they refer to as "wholesale, or near." We have taken this offer under advisement, at least as far as the *cheese*cake end of it is concerned, and we will let you know what we think.

We are taking under similar advisement the suggestion of the Men's Committee that a good old-fashioned Fourth of July calls for hot dogs, potato salad, beer and apple pie, nothing more and nothing less, as the memo came . . . uh, *up* to us. I warn you gentlemen, though, that potato salad can have a life of its own, a crawly one, at that, left out too long.

(Laughs)

Well, we will solve it all and let you know in sufficient time.

(A deep breath)

Now, what we have all been waiting for, the appearance of our guest speaker. Dear friends, we *have* been fortunate over the years, being witness, as we have, to those who have made our history and shaped our culture, men and women whose accomplishments have wreaked their order on our havoc.

MAN. Oh! What a very nice phrase!

WOMAN *(Genuinely pleased)*. Thank you, *thank* you!

(To her notes again)

425

. . . their order on our havoc and identified our reality by creating it for us.

MAN. Even better!

(Begins applauding)

My goodness!

WOMAN *(Trying to cover)*. Our guest today . . .

(Louder)

Our guest today, for whom you have been waiting with breath as bated as mine, certainly needs no introduction. His . . . truly miraculous story has been reported in *every* newspaper around the world; he has appeared before august medical bodies, before crowned heads; how famous can you be!? Well, ladies and gentlemen, if you are a man who has —has *had*—three arms, you become pretty famous, indeed!! And a movie of his life entitled *Now You See It, Now You Don't* is scheduled for production in the near future. And so, dear friends, without any further ado, we are proud to welcome into our midst, to hear what he has to tell us, the illustrious, the world-famous . . .

(HIMSELF *appears Onstage, bowing, before* SHE *can say his name*)

HIMSELF. Thank you; thank you. Thank you very much. What a pleasure it is to be here. A lovely city. Are you all natives? Any tourists? Yes?

(Reacts to one)

Where are you from? Oh? That's nice.

(To another)

What about you? Really? How about that!

(Generally)

How about a big hand for [whatever]!? So.

I was in Chicago last week, doing my thing—big barn of a place, and they had this legend carved into the proscenium: "You yourselves must set flame to the faggots which you have brought." Who says Chicago isn't a tough town?

Look at your eager little faces. Waiting for revelation, are you? On the subject which has brought you here this [evening? afternoon?] out of what? curiosity? wonder? morbidity?

(Turns to WOMAN*)*

I thank you for the introduction, truly I do. Be careful when you go on a talk show, though: the dumb ones use a club, and the bright ones have a knife. Trust no one, never turn your back, and stay out of alleys. And as for ptomaine if you really want to do it right, lay some boiled shrimp out in the sun; that'll do it. Cut your membership right in half.

WOMAN *(Slightly hysterical)*. Thank you, we'll keep it in mind.

MAN. Oh, now, no, that would be terrible!

WOMAN *(To the* MAN*)*. Hush!

MAN *(To the* WOMAN, *sotto voce)*. It would! It would be terrible!

HIMSELF *(Looking across the front row)*. Where is she? Where is she, I wonder; the lady, the girl, usually, who sits there in the front row, almost *always,* wherever, whenever I speak—not the *same* girl, woman, you understand, but of a certain type: plain, more than a little over-weight, smock top, jeans, sandals, dirty toenails—sits there in the front row, and, as I lecture, *try* to lecture, try to fill you in, so to speak, make you understand, sits there and runs her tongue around her open mouth, like this,

(Demonstrates)

hand in her crotch, likely as not, bitten fingers, lascivious, obscene, does it over and over, all through my lecture, my expiation, my sad, sad tale, unnerves me, bores me, finally wearies me with her longing. Well, I wonder where she is? I don't see her; perhaps you put her type away here. Maybe you have asylums full of them, sitting in their rooms or in the recreation area . . . sitting there in their smock tops, dirty toe-nails, opening and closing their mouths,

(Demonstrates)

tonguing their perimeters; maybe you've put them all away; maybe you don't "put up with that sort of thing" here. Maybe you have them committed. Good for you! I am committed—hah!—I am committed, usually, on these lecture tours, to a press conference, a "small" dinner beforehand—and, afterwards, to an "informal reception" at which I am pressed to consume undrinkable rosé wine and eat something called cheese food, at which I am slapped on the back and generally touched . . . slap, slap, thump, thump.

(Laughter)

The press conferences I have gotten used to—well, in the way we become used to din, to callousness, or the thought of dying. Your press here is no different from the average, I suppose—some brighter, some not, one sow; the questions—wherever I go—are of such a pattern I'd do as well to hand out prepared answers: "Yes, it *was* quite a surprise growing a third arm; well, yes, children would stare sometimes; did I

feel like a martyr? Well, I suppose so; do I miss having a third arm? Yes and no." *Do* I miss it? Well, does one miss oneself? Think about it. Well! These small dinners [lunches, whatever] preceding my lecture—no longer demonstration!
(Laughter)
Thank you, thank you very much; every bit . . . these "small" meals, by which is meant, of course, not that the meals them*selves* are small—tiny carrots, mini-cutlets, string beanettes, et cetera . . .
(Laughter)
Thank you, thank you very much . . . not that the meals are small, nor that the people attending them are small—a congress of dwarfs, a confederacy of midgets.
(Laughter)
Thank you, thank you very much . . . but simply that the *group* is to be limited in number, so as not to exhaust the speaker before the speak —the speech. A manageable group: in other words, anywhere from six to a hundred and fifty.
(Chuckles sadly)
How we live; how we live.
(Imitates a hostess)
"Well, we *did* try to keep it small, but so many people wanted to have a little quiet time with you," my hostess shrieks above the din, the callousness, the forks against the plates, hoots and banter. The average menu at these "small meals" consists of thawed shrimp, overcooked green beans and chicken in musilage; iceberg lettuce!—those who grow it should be horsewhipped!—iceberg lettuce with a choice of dreadful dressings, filled with sugar and sodium something-or-other; and for dessert—far more often than chance would accommodate—a lemonish chiffon of the density of flown hope.
(Some laughter)
Thank you, oh, thank you. That is your average menu. The quenelle, the quail, the walnut oil and the cheese, the perfect berries happen now and again—enough, perhaps, to mourn the death of God.
Once or twice these small gatherings have *been small!* have been civilized and civilizing events, joys of exquisite cuisine, top wines and ravishing exchange. Everything *may* be on its way downhill, may even be giving that destination a new depth, but all is not that way: there are oases. But one of the rules of an oasis would seem to be that the surrounding

desert stretches beyond conjecture; otherwise, one would be yawning, saying, "God! yet another oasis! Will they never stop?!" But the way of the world does *not* give us an excess of oases: Beethoven quartets, Mantegna paintings and other waterholes; the phrase "too much of a good thing" is meaningless; it can never happen, therefore cannot be proved. No?

At your average meal the one thing they did not discuss—mention, breathe!—was my arm, back when I had three of them. Maybe it was nothing more than it was not considered fit conversation for the table. War, divorce, money, death, greed, deception, yes—but . . . not an arm.

They would look at me, these people; I would look at *them*. I would unfocus my eyes, finally, stare off into the middle distance—humiliated by my specialness. I hadn't split the atom; I hadn't written fifteen string quartets, or saved the country from itself. I'd grown a fucking third arm! Where's the talent in that?

I used to make little jokes now and again, to try to ease the tension . . . when the food was good, that is . . . "Let not your right hand know what your left hand know what your . . . and so forth." It would get a laugh—peas rolling off forks, butter knives clattering, and so forth. If the meal was *awful*, and it, *I*, was feeling especially awful—hung over, trouble with old number three and its mind of its own, whatever—I would become provocative: stretch and eat at the same time; pass the salt, pepper and bread simultaneously. Produced shrieks, faintings once or twice, a vomiting here and there. Not nice, I suppose, but think about it—what would you have done?

(So reasonable)

And so it was with me—has been. I have seen both, the blinding flash guns, the idiotic, truly idiotic adulation of the vacant . . . *and* the middle distance. Ask me to tell you about the middle distance. Perhaps I will . . . and then again . . .

Signing autographs was interesting. It was! Really, it was! I am, by nature, left handed, which, on occasion, allowed me to sign two autographs at once . . . and, at times, it did not. I never knew, for example, from one day to the next—whether I would be doubled to the right or to the left. "How can this be?" you ask, scoffing laugh, wise eyes turned to your neighbor; "How can this be!? The fellow's putting us on." Well, I wish I could demonstrate it to you. If I could, of course, I'd probably not *be* here—certainly not at *this* price! I have photos, though, which I will be happy to show you, assuming the equipment is working?

(This last to the WOMAN)

WOMAN *(Model calm).* Well, I certainly assume so.

MAN. I tested it myself yesterday.

HIMSELF. Good!

(Out)

Happy? I have photos, as I said, slides, to be precise, which I will show you, assuming the equipment *is* working, has not taken it into its mechanical little head to break down.

(To the MAN)

MAN *(Amused).* Oh, I say!

SLIDE: *3 Pornographic slides in succession.*

WOMAN. Gilbert! Gilbert! When the cat's away the mice will play.

HIMSELF. And so much for the informal receptions.

(Off, to WOMAN, *more or less)*

There is one following this, I believe?

(Out)

I'm sure there is. We'll get to mix.

Three arms he had, did he? Well, let's see 'em!

(Change of tone)

All in good time. You want the climax at the beginning, a life of detumescence? All right! All right! Jesus!

(Shows his right arm)

Here's one.

(Shows his left arm)

Here's another. I'm sorry. What can I do? What can I say? You're a little late. But we've got to lead up to these things. Really, edge up, regular green beret stuff. Don't worry! I'll show it all to you—all the treasures. I have a tale will tear your heart out . . . so to speak. After we are done here, as you move into the lobby, you will find a table, a long one, with photographs, groups of photographs, booklets, a clinical case study, the coffee table volume, as well as my autobiography—illustrated, naturally! All for sale, all rare, all well worth the small price. And if you see me there, I beg you, please be gentle. I am not a freak. I am an average gentleman—easily injured . . . crushed! I am nothing more—*or* less—than a quiet man who, at one time, for a little, was possessed of . . . an extra arm. I no longer am. Please don't stare at

me when we meet as if I were obscene, or deformed. I do not, I no
longer bear arms. There is no appendage lurking underneath my jacket:
it's gone. I waved it goodbye and it waved back. Gone.
(Chuckles to himself)
I was asked once—recently—if I thought it would return, and, if it
would, would that make me happy.
(Afterthought)
Again. This assumes that the first visitation *did* make me happy, that I
am less happy now, and *was*, before. I don't know; I really don't know. I
have never thought it was man's lot—his right—to be "happy." To be
conscious, yes—the pain of consciousness—to be aware of passing
through it, that what little repose, less delight and least ecstasy we were
granted was a blessing.

I was not . . . *un*happy be*fore* it; certainly it changed my life and
therefore all my definitions. I *am* unhappy now, though possibly for
reasons having less to do with *it* than with *me;* were it to . . . return?
Would that make me happy again? Probably not.

Well, Perhaps I'd best tell you how it all happened—stop skirting, or,
more accurately, cuffing the issue. The meal [dinner, whichever] by the
way, the one today, on a graph of one to ten was . . .
(Very expansive)
. . . well, what did you think!? Way up there. At least a three! No, I'm
only kidding.
(To the WOMAN*)*
Really, kidding.
(Out)
Seven! Eight! It was a smallish group today [or, tonight], nice ladies and
gentlemen, and a minister—one of the more . . . relaxed denomina-
tions.
(Note: The MAN *and the* WOMAN *will unobtrusively prepare for the
roles* THEY *will momentarily assume;* SHE *may have to do nothing save
remove or put on a scarf;* HE *should get a cigarette, a drink, and reverse
his collar. No rush. Harsh chuckle)*
Hanh! I remember *one* time, *one* meal, back when I still had three
arms, where I was seated across from a Catholic priest, ginned up to his
elbows, cloth ashed and spotted; he smoked constantly, and his little
fingers were all yellow; thin, ridged nails. Are you many Catholic here?
Well, he shamed you! There are some who do. His hair was white, and

431

streaked with a yellow identical to his finger stain. He had one eye did not *exactly* pay attention to the other; most of the time it *related*, if not precisely, but, on occasion, it would develop a will of its own and range about . . . as if it had had a private sight and was straining to be off after it. "You are an accident of nature," he hissed at me, the priest, the priest hissed at me over the split pea soup. He had been eyeing me—so to speak—at the "stand-up," the cocktail hour, but he had kept his distance. "That's our father so-and-so," my hostess said to me in her brightest voice when she saw his baleful eye on me. "He is of the old school."

WOMAN. That's our father so-and-so; he's of the old school.

(Has SHE *risen? I'm not sure)*

HIMSELF. I *sort* of knew what she meant: driven into it—the cloth— driven into it by tradition, fourth son of an ignorant and impoverished family, promised at the deathbed of a grandmother, sex terrors, caned, starved, frozen in the seminary, dreams of glory . . . for a while. "I can make red."

MAN *(Wistful)*. I can make red.

HIMSELF. I can make red. God, do they all dream of it—becoming Cardinals. Pope even? The sin of pride not necessarily preceding the fall, the fall coming on by itself, no great height to topple from, merely that there *is* a hierarchy, and some are in at the top, and others . . . are not —who your ward captain is, so to speak. I find it hard to believe—well, there you are!—I find it hard to believe that there's any of them hasn't shuddered, reddened, if only once, with the thought of the glory, of the red and the amethyst, the paradox—most high, most low—has not, only once, squared the shoulders, stuck out Adam's apple, gulped and offered, "If debasement can be glory, then the highest can also be my martyrdom: the faith of paradox, the paradox of faith."

MAN. If debasement can be glory, then the highest can also be my . . .

HIMSELF *(Cutting in)*. . . . or some such gibberish! But it fades; the awareness comes, that low is all, that endless, hopeless drudge and grind and scuff and tatter is the end, is the service . . . is the "way." We all come to it—in one way or another. There is not a life, not one—name it if you can!—not a life hasn't seen futility at the end, up ahead, like a highway turning into sand. No matter how rich the life, filled, *filled* with joy, and "great doings," the sense comes that there is nothing

except the doing of it, and it fills the mouth with mold, as good old
Melville had it.

(Out)

Man A. Man A keeps his eyes closed so as not to see too much, to know
too much; man B closes his after he has seen it all, closes with sadness,
loathing and relief; and man C—is there a man C?—never blinks, keeps
his eyes wide open, staring into the blinding dark.

There were—still are, probably!—holy men in India gaze into the sun
from rise to set, never blinking. They have gone blind, of course, years
back, the eyes burned out by the glory, but every day they sit, blind eyes
staring at the burning, making the slowest of arcs as the earth moves,
the sun moves. Man C. Man C is the happiest of men: he has seen the
futility; it destroys him; he worships it. His is the only certainty—no
hope; merely . . . adoration.

MAN *(Coming up behind* HIMSELF, *clergy garb. Hissed).* You are an accident of nature.

HIMSELF. "You are an accident of nature," he hissed at me: the priest; the
priest hissed at me, over the split pea soup.

MAN. I've been watching you.

HIMSELF. "I've been watching you." Over the split pea soup.

(An aside; out, though)

There were saltines for the split pea soup, two to a cellophane package.
Is it cellophane any longer? I wonder. Two to a package, cellophane—
or whatever—with a red strip for opening. The crackers were not man-
datory; God! the soup was like a porridge, or a yellow paste, and the
crackers, probably served as a thickener in some dim, gone time, now
would . . . sit on the stuff when you crumbled them into it—*onto* it.
Sit there. Well, one could push them down *into* the glue, lose them *into*
it with the round spoon, and there they would stay, little oases of dough
in the doughy goo.

MAN *(As before).* Your are an accident of nature.

HIMSELF. And he looked at me, across the shrieking board, cigarette and
gin in one hand, cracker crumble in the other, declined his head a trifle,
shot one eye off toward our hostess, kept the other focused on my nose.
"There is no redemption, then," I said.

(To the MAN)

There is no redemption, then?

(Out)

433

THE MAN WHO HAD THREE ARMS

We freaks, you know. We've got to be careful.

WOMAN (SUGAR LADY). Ohhhh!

(Giggles)

You men.

HIMSELF. "If you would die," he drawled.

MAN *(As* PRIEST *still).* If you would die—*were* to—then you would have *been* an accident of nature, but no longer, softened, straightened by the great bosom. All is forgiven . . . ultimately.

HIMSELF *(Out).* If I would only die. One of the comforts, I suppose: in the hospital bed, inventing new definitions of pain, or crumbled over the dinner table, breathless, wrenched with impossible stabbings, one could die; one could die, and in the meanwhile ponder this: it's all a test; God loves you; hi there, Job; love ya, baby; it's all a test. "I love you. Do you love me?" It's a spoiled child, or a lunatic—all the old hat stuff.

Any faith supposes cessation is an answer, well . . .

(Leaves it unfinished. Grudging)

Well, for everything there is a reason, for every pro a con and such like; everything transforms: pain into cessation, consciousness into faith. All of this comforts me less than . . .

MAN *(Still as* PRIEST). How can you eat at the table with other people!?

HIMSELF *(To the* MAN). I would be happy *not* to eat with you. You fill me with revulsion, a state impenetrable by pity, and I fear for my soul, deed I do, but there it is in my contract; I have no choice. It says it so clearly —not only will you present yourself at the place of assembly, or some other place determined by the sponsor, no later than one hour before the time of your revealing, but you shall, as well, break both bread and your heart either before or after the whatever, at the discretion of the whomever.

(Out)

"Revulsion," I said, right at him, "a state impenetrable by pity, and I fear for my soul." And it was amazing!

(Note: the MAN *demonstrates what is described)*

He raised his ginned and cigaretted hand in a blessing or a warding off and spread his lips with a bubbling hiss, which chilled the room, the table, at any rate, and would have the soup, were *it* not already on its own way there, did not live a life of its own, a condition I all at once envied—oh, to be soup! "Father X is a man of the old cloth," my hostess reminded me.

WOMAN (SUGAR LADY). He really is: a man of the old cloth.

(To HIMSELF; *tentative)*

Would you like some wine?

HIMSELF *(To her).* Of course, my dear; whatever you think goes best with the soup.

(Out)

I drove my spoon toward the greeny thing and, lo! a crust, or armor, had formed on its surface, and the spoon rebounded, would not penetrate. I suppose if I'd given it a good shove, but I hadn't the heart. White, I think, my dear. The staring eye bulged. "You have no soul, sir."

MAN. You have no soul, sir.

HIMSELF *(Out).* Well, this *was* something to think about: you have no soul, sir. I was suddenly filled with a childish pride—not to possess a soul! I was, you see, to his way of viewing the world, all at once in a class with kangaroos and Negroes—unusual to the point of bizarre, therefore beneath, therefore soulless. It was ludicrous, of course, and laughter could have fallen from the mouth . . . like vomit, but it was, at the same time, and in some deeper context, freeing. All the weight was suddenly lifted from me, the guilt, the fear . . . *and* the hope. No more hope; neither salvation nor damnation. I was to one side of . . . everything. I was free to be what I had always been. It was liberating to the point of hallucination.

(To the MAN/PRIEST*)*

If only I had asked you sooner!

WOMAN *(As* SUGAR LADY; *to herself).* You're not eating your soup.

HIMSELF *(To her).* I attempted it, Madame. It wanted no part of me.

WOMAN. Would you like another cup?

HIMSELF *(To her).* I would rather develop a second nose.

MAN *(As* PRIEST*).* Wouldn't surprise me a bit. Once it's out of hand . . .

HIMSELF. . . . so to speak . . .

MAN *(Ibid).* . . . . once it begins, there's no telling: it's like the heresies.

HIMSELF *(Out).* And this in the midst of all the reforms, this . . . throwback after John twenty-three and J.P.2.

(To the MAN*)*

Eternal vigilance being the price of the cloth?

MAN *(Wintry smile). On* the button.

*(*MAN *and* WOMAN *exit)*

HIMSELF *(To the* MAN*).* Right!

THE MAN WHO HAD THREE ARMS

(Out)
I tell you these things—I share parts of my past with you—so you will have some sense of how it was back when—back when I was a freak. But I think I'd better tell you HOW IT ALL BEGAN! How *I* all began, to be precise.
(Off)
Are the slides ready? Are the slides ready? Hm? Yes? No? Yes? Good!

WOMAN. Yes!

HIMSELF *(Out)*. The slides are ready. This Is My Life. I was born some [however old the actor playing HIMSELF is] years ago in a town no more than eighteen hundred miles from here, a town like any other town.
(Waits; nothing happens)
Start the fucking slides, will you!?
(Slide show commences.
Note on slides: whenever the text says SLIDE, *the appropriate slide is shown.*

SLIDE: *A town like any other town)*
A town like any other town. Trees.

(SLIDE)
Houses.

(SLIDE)
Banks.

(SLIDE *of one)*
A bibliothèque.

(SLIDE)
Four drunks.

(SLIDE)
One gay.

(SLIDE; *normal face)*
One hideously lonely gay.

(SLIDE: *same, crying)*
Seven voluptuaries.

(SLIDE)
And a drum and fife corps.

(SLIDE: *famous painting of revolutionary corps)*
It was a town like any other town, except . . . except that on [actor's birthdate] in a house on Prune Street,

(SLIDE)

436

the corner of Prune and Hoover, there was born to my parents . . . me.

(SLIDE: *newborn baby*)

Me . . . a healthy, bouncing baby boy. Not bouncing, actually, literally, not literally bouncing, but healthy and a baby and a boy. I wonder why they say that— "She had a baby." What were they expecting—a sixteen-year-old? An oven mitt?

I grew rapidly and without incident.

(SLIDE: *a three-year-old boy.* HIMSELF *looks at it*)

Photo of me as a three-year-old boy.

(SLIDE: *a three-year-old black boy.* HIMSELF *looks at it*)

Photo of me as *another* three-year-old child?

(Note: if a black actor plays HIMSELF, *reverse the previous)*

HIMSELF. I hated neither of my parents—that, I think, is more a city habit —and it was only later, much later, that I discovered I had loved them more than I think they had loved me. It's not the sort of thing, though, you can go up and ask them.

(MAN *and* WOMAN BOTH *enter)*

WOMAN. Hello, son.

HIMSELF. Hello, Ma.

WOMAN. Dad? Look who's here.

MAN. Hm? Well, my golly, look who's here.

HIMSELF. I have a question I have to ask you both.

MAN *(To the* WOMAN). A what?

WOMAN. A question! A question! He wants to ask us a question.

MAN *(Sort of surprised).* Well, of course! Why not!

(To HIMSELF)

Shoot!

HIMSELF. It's about love.

MAN *(To the* WOMAN). About what?

WOMAN. Love! Love!

MAN. Well, of course! Why not?

HIMSELF. I know you love me, have loved me, but I think in general I have loved you more.

MAN *(To the* WOMAN). What does he say?

WOMAN. That we love him; he knows we've loved him.

MAN. Well, of course! Why not?

HIMSELF *(To the* WOMAN). That's not what I said.

437

MAN *(To the* WOMAN*)*. What's that?

WOMAN. He thinks perhaps we have loved one another unequally.

HIMSELF *(to the* WOMAN*)*. That is not what I said; that is not precisely what I said. I said, I think in general I have loved you more than you have loved me.

WOMAN *(Smiles)*. It will do.

MAN *(To the* WOMAN*)*. What?

WOMAN *(To the* MAN*)*. Nothing.

HIMSELF *(Out; the* OTHER TWO *still standing)*. You see? You can't ask them. The shortest distance between two generations is *not* a straight answer. Well . . . what does it matter—they're dead.

MAN *(To the* WOMAN*)*. What? What was that?

WOMAN *(To the* MAN*)*. We died.

MAN *(To* HIMSELF*)*. Well, of course! Why not?

(MAN *and* WOMAN *re-sit)*

HIMSELF *(To* MAN *and* WOMAN*)*. Thank you both.

(Out)

In any event, I grew; I went to school, I pubed, I developed simultaneous crushes on the Nabokovian girl-child two seats up from me in English class,

(SLIDE: *a nymphet*)

Aha! There is the girl; pretty thing; I have no idea what happened to her.

(SLIDE: *the boy*)

and the captain of the swimming team, a superbly handsome brute of a boy, now senator and, some say, on his way to the Oval Office. He's certainly less handsome now, though no less brutish. I imagine he'll make it.

(SLIDE: *both the boy and the girl*)

This bi of mine, this crush on both sexes, led to nothing, in the sense that while I was possessed by both of them . . . I possessed neither.

(SLIDE *off*)

I settled finally—and naturally, for me—on a heterosexual quest, the usual progression: self-abuse, self-abuse with fantasy, simple dates, complex dates, light petting, heavy petting, "all the way," love and longing, broken hearts and aching nuts, the whole thing. I'm afraid I don't have slides of this.

I graduated high school.

MAN *(Calling)*. Congratulations, son!

HIMSELF. . . . and went off to college.

WOMAN *(Calling)*. Stay warm!

HIMSELF. . . . off, I say, away from the farm,

(SLIDE: *city)*

so to speak, and up to the city—first city on the way to others, larger, more distant, more . . . complex. It is a progression devoutly to be wished, or some such thing.

(SLIDE *out)*

I was bright, ambitious, more than a little curious about the world around me, and, soon enough, cosmopolite.

(To the wings)

Do we have a photo marked "cosmopolite"?

(Pause)

No? No matter.

(Out)

Take it on faith, why don't you—soon enough, cosmopolite. You can't go home again, they tell you, by which they mean you cannot become yourself as a child again—until the final senility, and then only in manner. Nor does it matter.

I became a city boy. I graduated from the U.

(SLIDE: *huge graduating class)*

That's me, seventeen rows from the front, forty-third in from the left.

(SLIDE *off)*

My parents came to it, *for* it; I was an only child—two would-be sisters died at birth. I have no photos of them. God! who would have photos of dead newborns!? What do you want!?

My parents came to it,

(SLIDE: *parents)*

came to the city, wondered at it, were polite about its . . . excesses, its dirt, its . . . diversity, by which *they* meant Chinks, Jews and Spics and all that. Forgive them; they were good people. Agee-ans. "One was my Mother who was good to me; one was my Father who was good to me." James Agee. Remember it? No? Ah, well.

Good folk, but not city; they watched me graduate, smiled, swelled, were truly, *truly* proud—neither had been beyond tenth grade—truly proud, and anxious to be home. They kissed me, hugged me, went to the station, got on the train, went home . . . died. I have compressed time a little—for the sake of narrative.

(SLIDE: *side-by-side gravestones*)

And there they are.

MAN. Well, of course! Why not!?

(SLIDE *off*)

HIMSELF *(Out)*. And on I went—bright, *very* bright, and shrewd, and . . . dare I say it? talented, *in*to advertising, *up* the ladder. I had my own accounts in *no* time.

(Curiously offhand)

Oh. I married along the way, on one of the rungs.

(SLIDE: *his wife; she must look quite like the* WOMAN; *perhaps the photo is of the* WOMAN *at an earlier age*)

There she is: a pretty, old-fashioned girl.

Will you laugh that we had not been to bed until our wedding? Some of you won't; some of you must have gone the same route—

(Some contempt)

the same old-fashioned "think of it as a gift, a sort of wedding present" manner, the old "who would want a girl who gives it away?" routine. Routine? Unfair! Unfair!

(SLIDE *out*)

Just because your city sluts are pros at twelve doesn't mean the corn and wheat fields don't produce a . . . slower carnality. Everything in its own good time—God's good time; society's good time.

(A confidence)

Look, fucking yourself cross-eyed is a mound of fun, and no mistake about it. Even when *I* was a pup, out in puppyland, there were those girls who took a lineup of the local boys easy as beaten biscuits. We had names for 'em: round heels, easy, everybody's, *any*body's, Saturday night special, et cetera, et cetera. And we *liked* those girls; they were nice, friendly, laughing, with an easy manner and a gentle, willing way in the sack. But it's *true:* we didn't marry them. We married the other ones, and those lovely acquiescent girls fanned out across the land, found husbands—most of them—whom they made happier than chance would have it.

My wife and I had a good and happy life . . . . .

(SLIDE: *another photo of wife*)

for a while. We were congenial and compatible, and she was a helpmeet in every way. We moved into a lovely house,

(SLIDE *of it*)

and we had our children early,

(SLIDE: *husband, wife, three kids—two boys, one girl*)

so as to get it underway, *out* of the way, and build . . . *build.* My career was a straight line *up,* my prospects were unlimited, and with my wife at my side, the toddlers toddling at my knees, there was nothing but joy and accomplishment and security and predictability—the swift ascent, the long, rich crest, the planned deceleration: easy life and easy cease. And then.

(SLIDE *out.*

Pause)

And then it happened, the event which changed my life forever, created me, destroyed me, raised me up . . . and brought me here.

(Tiny pause)

To you. To your stares, your awful receptions, your terrible food, your . . .

(Catches himself)

No; that's not fair: today's meal was nice. Really it was.

WOMAN. Well, we're glad.

HIMSELF. I don't like my salad first, but I am in a minority these days, this land. Appetizer, soup, fish, flesh, salad, cheese, dessert, fruit and nuts. That *used* to be the way of the world. God! I was somewhere in the ["your" if played in the Midwest] Midwest once when they served coffee as soon as we sat down to table—and they drank it! my hosts and hostesses, smiling and sipping while all *I* wanted was another gin, which, come to think of it . . . ?

(To the WOMAN)

Is it possible to get a . . . ?

WOMAN *(As herself again).* I beg your pardon?

HIMSELF. I said: is it possible to have a glass of gin brought up here?

WOMAN *(Appalled, if mildly).* A glass of gin!? Up here!?

HIMSELF. I feel the need for a nip; I am nip-needy.

WOMAN *(Self-conscious).* Just . . . go about your business.

MAN *(To the* WOMAN). I could . . . go . . . if you think . . . ?

WOMAN. Certainly not!

HIMSELF. Oh, please!

441

WOMAN. Sir! You are addressing us!

HIMSELF *(Louder; tense)*. Well, why can't I do it with a glass of gin in my hand?!! If priests do it, why, oh why can't I? It isn't as if I asked for a bottle, for Christ's sake!

MAN *(Rising)*. I'll just steal off . . .

(Begins to do so)

I'll just . . . you know: steal off.

WOMAN *(To them BOTH)*. I don't approve!

MAN *(To HIMSELF)*. I'll be right back; we'll see what we can do. You stay right where you are.

(Exits)

HIMSELF *(To the exiting MAN)*. You are a very helpful old man.

WOMAN. I really don't approve.

HIMSELF *(To her)*. It's not very much to ask!

(Out)

It's not very much to ask. It's not as if I asked for a fucking bottle!

(So reasonable)

Every once in a while a man needs a little nip—and no jokes, please! One can go along quite nicely, sometimes for hours, ginless, joyless, fully in control, and then one needs a nip of gin.

WOMAN. It's unprofessional.

HIMSELF *(To her; and out)*. Balderdash! Show me a contract specifies the speaker can't have a gin if he wants it—needs it—*wants* it. Besides the lecture circuit is strewn with drunks and secret junkies, pill poppers, winos. Take a look at your famous some day: take a look at your big stars —How many do you think've hit fifty-plus intact? Hunh!? Take a look around you.

(Calmer)

Today's meal was nice, the placement of the salad aside.

WOMAN *(Ice)*. We're sorry.

HIMSELF *(To the WOMAN; brutal)*. THEN LEARN FROM IT, LADY!!

(Control regained; out)

Sometimes, one doesn't get to eat at all. Today I did; today was fine.

WOMAN *(Cool)*. Thank you.

HIMSELF. You're welcome.

(Out)

I wasn't too happy about the press, if truth is of any interest.

WOMAN. Oh?

HIMSELF *(To her).* Only one.
> *(Out)*
> The rest was your usual, but there was this one came to the press conference all prepared, not homework-wise, but . . . opinioned. The article was already written; all she wanted was my assent, my agreement to the dismemberment. "You do admit, don't you, that taking money the way you do, for a deformation—a former deformation, at that—blah blah blah." Where's my gin!? I want my gin!! Shit like that; you know them; you know those . . . journal*istes:* they would have been party members in the thirties; they write with spite and polish; they crucify and vilify and get all runny in the name of "good hard journalism." They tend to be prettier now than they used to be: fewer hairy upper lips, less hippiness; manicured for a change, less lesbo, but still killers.
> *(Smiles)*
> She's sitting there among you; she's smiling at me, killer smile; she loves the recognition; she hates me for it. She won't be shamed into decency; it'll just move her a little further into shrewd slaughter.
> *(Waves)*
> Hello, dear! Look at her! Purring away. Wave back, why don't you? Reveal your sources, so to speak. No? Cunt!

WOMAN *(Outraged).* Please!

HIMSELF *(To her; curt).* Sorry.
> *(Out)*
> Give me an old-fashioned journalist any time: some drama critic fired from the sports department, say; some borderline psychotic from the foreign desk; some crusty editor doesn't give a shit and does his job, just does his job.
> *(Points out generally)*
> Protect us all from *that.*
> *(Waves)*
> Hello, dear! Be sure to put something in about the gin; attribute everything to that: "The arm fell off because of the gin," or something like that.
> *(More general now)*
> The arm did *not* . . . fall off. Thud! My goodness, look at that! There's an arm lying there amid the sawdust; poor thing, fell off because of the gin, most likely. Speaking of which . . .

(Off)

Any luck? Any gin?

WOMAN. I'm going to phone your agent!

HIMSELF. Good. Maybe she'll talk to you.

(Back)

I should have it put in my contract: let there be gin. I suppose that might . . . diminish my engagements? Make wary the sponsors, warier the already wary? And Christ knows we can't afford diminishment at this . . . blunt point in time, to use the awful phrase. We are diminished already—diminish-ed—our major attraction, you might say, gone as it came. And how long can we plow the furrow of what was? They used to pay me twenty-five thousand dollars an hour. Twenty-five . . . thousand . . . dollars . . . an *hour*—merely to wave it a little, do a few tricks . . . back when I was a freak!

(A confidence)

The fee for a former freak is somewhat less, I dare say you'll believe me when I tell you. I have been had for as little as half a grand. And a tottle of gin, or two.

(Off)

Any luck, old man?

(Shrugs)

The rest of the press was . . . fine: they wondered the usual and I replied the same. *Plus* the lesser usuals—the wife, the kids, do I miss them, the special tailoring, the Pope. You know . . . the usual. "Why are we to believe you met the Pope?" the cunt asked.

(The WOMAN *is uneasy at that word.*

An aside, to the WOMAN*)*

Sorry.

(Back)

—the cunt asked in the midst of all the pleasantries. "Because I have a photo of it, you painted whore," I lisped between my smiling teeth. "And besides," I went on, all oily, "and besides, why would the Pope lie about it?"

Well, that got a laugh from the presslet—score one for *me*—save the killer didn't even blirk. She merely decided *not* to write that one down —might show humanity, or wit, or something: wouldn't do; wouldn't fit.

(Curious pleading)

444

I have so much to tell you, so, so much to share. Such wonders . . . such wonder. I will take you with me on such a ride. I do a splendid show for my crust of bread; you'll not be sorry you invited me. It's just . . . I must have a glass of gin.

WOMAN. We're trying.

HIMSELF. Well, it's not good enough; I think you'd better have an intermission.

WOMAN. We hadn't planned on an intermission.

HIMSELF. Well, then, sit there and cross your eyes for fifteen minutes or so. *I'm* going to have an intermission—a gin, and a pee, and a quiet cry —two sobs and a gulp and a freshet of tears in a corner somewhere. *(Out)*

If you come upon me, my back to you, my shoulders shaking with my sobbing, please leave me be; don't . . . touch me, comfortingly, gently, on the golden spot; don't offer solace. Just . . . leave me be and let me sob it out.

(Looks at his watch)

I'll see you, then, at [fifteen minutes from whatever time it is].

(HE *starts Off, bowing)*

Thank you, thank you, thank you all.

(Exits)

WOMAN *(Making the best of a bad thing)*. I . . . I take it we're about to have an intermission.

(Walks Off)

END OF ACT ONE

ACT TWO

*Stage bare of actors; set as at end of Act I. Toward the end of the audience
return, let* HIMSELF *appear in the auditorium, manically urging the audience to its seats.*

HIMSELF. All right, now! Come on! Back to your seats! Don't dawdle!
   Come on, show on the road! You've paid your money; I've paid my
   time. Let's get it together! Come on, now! Hurryhurryhurry! Show's
   about to begin! Up we go!
   (HE *jumps on the stage, sees no one else there; calls Off*)
   Let's get a move on out there!
   (Out)
   Back to your seats! No talking; shuffle on, gather round, stir the çaul-
   dron, make a wish!
   (The WOMAN *comes On, with as much dignity as* SHE *can manage)*
WOMAN. Are we . . . you would like to begin now? Rebegin?
HIMSELF. Where's your friend . . . the geezer?
MAN *(Rushing—for him—On, fixing his fly)*. Oh my, oh my, oh my!
HIMSELF *(Loud slapping together of hands)*. O.K.! Here we are!
   (To the WOMAN*)*
   Any more announcements? Lies? Evasions? Would-be jokes? De-
   nouncements?
WOMAN *(Sitting; great composure)*. Nothing, thank you.
HIMSELF *(Mimicking)*. Nothing, thank you.
   (To the MAN*)*
   And you?
MAN *(Not quite with it)*. Hm? Pardon?
HIMSELF. Anything from you? Any . . . redundancies?
MAN. I'm not sure I . . .
HIMSELF. Did you have a nice intermission?
MAN. Well . . . *yes*, come to think of it; very nice, indeed. I ran into a
   couple I hadn't seen in . . . oh, years: fifteen, perhaps.
HIMSELF. Isn't that nice.
   (Out)
   Isn't that nice?
MAN. I had seen them last in Muncie, I think.
   [Unless we are there; if we are: Cincinnati]
WOMAN. *Do* get on with it.

446

MAN *(Taking this as encouragement. Out, as well as to them)*. Randall and Beatrice Endicott—she a Springfield Endicott, he a Munician, *both* with the same last name: like marrying one's cousin, I suppose . . . in a way.

(Realizing)

WOMAN. *May* we get on with it?

MAN. Nice people, the Endicotts—philosophers, the both.

(A nod out)

Nice people.

WOMAN *(To* HIMSELF*)*. Please?

HIMSELF *(Gracious, having had his fun)*. Of course!

(Out, with considerable energy)

Well; here we are, all refreshed—freshened—ready for revelation, resolution, come what may. *I* enjoyed the interval—intermission. You *did* leave me alone, most of you. I thank you for that. Couple of sneers, two or three blue-hairs shaking their heads; what's-her-name, the actress. One autograph: ten-year-old boy, hideous glasses, likewise suit, teeth like a rabbit. Patted him between the ears. Oh! and our Lady of the Lake came up to me—the lady I was telling you about, the journalist, the journal*iste?* Came right up to me, the baggage! right into the anteroom I'd slid into after the rabbit. "You're good," she said, "you're really good." There was a loathing to it, a condemnation that I dare be articulate, coherent. "You're really good." "So are you," I said. "You've got balls."

The energy of the hatred here, the mutual rage and revulsion was such that, had we fucked, we would have shaken the earth with our cries and thumps and snarls and curses: a crashing around of Gods—chewed nipples, bleeding streaks along the back. Had we fucked . . . Oh, Jesus! what issue! *But* . . . but the only issue was the issue of me, the . . . dismemberment of me. "You've got balls!" I said. And I crashed my hand into her crotch like a goosing twelve-year-old. "Get your hands off me," she said. "Get your filthy hands off me." I withdrew my hand: it had hit rock. "If you'll excuse me," she said, ice, shoving past me. She *is* an impressive lady.

MAN *(Chuckling)*. You didn't *really* do that.

HIMSELF *(To the* MAN*)*. Well my goodness. I certainly hope I didn't. I'd worry about myself if I had.

MAN *(To the* WOMAN*)*. He didn't really *do* that.

447

WOMAN *(Generally)*. Well, I certainly hope *not.*

HIMSELF *(Out)*. I didn't really do that? All right.

(Calls)

You can forget it, puddin' pie; it never really happened!

(To them ALL; *to himself)*

I am *trying* to be nice; I have *promised* myself I will be nice—and perhaps if I knew what the term *meant*, then perhaps I would be, *could* be. So!

(Tiny pause)

So, all in all, it was an interesting intermission: I was physically abusive to a lady, and contemptuously dismissive of a sincere and well-intentioned boy child. Par for the course.

(A confidence)

I find it hard sometimes to distinguish between my self-disgust and my disgust with others, and I worry about that; I really do, truly do. I mean, I'm a nice person or at least I used to be. It occurs to me: look here, old man, you *really* ought to be able to distinguish between self-disgust and your disgust with others. Give it a good try! Don't mix 'em up like that. I mean, you have no trouble with pity—you can tell self-pity from the Christlike a mile away—well, a hundred yards.

WOMAN. *Talk* about yourself.

HIMSELF *(to the* WOMAN*)*. I thought I was.

(Out)

I thought I was!

(To the WOMAN *again)*

Did you talk to my agent?

WOMAN. They weren't in.

HIMSELF *(Both to her and out)*. Out scouting up new clients, probably. They have me, two sisters used to be on radio, a defrocked Satanist, three defectors from the EPA, an overweight diet expert, the plastic butcher of your next meeting. And, of course, the late, lamented Doctor What's-his-name.

MAN. Plastic butcher.

WOMAN *(Hard)*. Get on with it!

HIMSELF *(To* WOMAN; *saluting)*. Yes, Sir!

(Out)

So. I had my cry, too. Remember my cry. Who remembers my cry? My promised cry?

Promise them circuses, eh?

(To someone in the front)

Do you remember what I said? Before we broke? Remember I said that if you came upon me sobbing in a corner, not to disturb? That it was a way I had and not to worry? Do you remember?

(Note: If the person says "yes," say: "You do!" If the person says "no," say: "You don't!" If person fails to respond, wing it, choosing what you like)

Splendid; it's those of you pay attention cheers me up in the low times. I had my sob, my cry, my cryette. It was in the anteroom after Miss fourth estate and I had had our set-to, our little chat. I sat on a settee, the edge of it, a spongy thing covered in . . . purple plastic sheen—a kind of iridescence—the sort of sofa gives one second thoughts about the West. I sat there; I put my hands to my dry eyes, to rub them: These lights . . . they strain. I put my dry hands to rub my dry eyes and they came away wet—as if the hands were a signal to the eyes, their coming to them a sign to flood. I discovered I was crying, and therefore I made the *sounds* of crying, the sobs, the gasps, and I let it grow into a full and theoretically satisfying cry. It occurred to me, though, in the middle of it, the cry, that I didn't know *why, why* I was crying. There was so much to choose from! . . . such a wealth of the ludicrous, the painful, the emptying, that I would never know. And I let *that* become the source: thoughts about the source became the source. Isn't that wonderful?—so much to weep over one cannot be sure which one has chosen. Who says we're not a healthy land!

(Pause; claps hands together once, loud)

O.K.!! On we go!

MAN *(Startled)*. What!? What!?

HIMSELF. On with the story! The saga of the man who had three arms! Where was I? Had I brought you up to "the moment"?—the moment that changed my life forever?

(Fast)

Ma? Pa? Education? Job? Wifey?

Right! O.K.! "And then it happened."

This is what you *came* for, isn't it!?

O.K.? O.K.?

O.K. And then it happened.

One Saturday morning, nearer to noon than not, after a good hot A.M.

449

time post breakfast with my wife—that being second preference only to five P.M.—I had gone to shower. I had shampooed my hair—a thing I did first—and was finishing with my body. I had done my groin—that always first—my armpits, my chest, my legs, my backside and my lower back, and I was ending as I always did—no longer do; I no longer shower; I tub—finishing with my upper back, that awkward area between the shoulder blades. I had my soapy cloth, and I was doing away with a sort of lackadaisical diligence when I felt a . . . a kind of bump —a bump*ette*, to be more exact—between my blades; not a pimple, not a boil, but a . . . small bump; not a mole, nothing on the surface, but a kind of rising under the skin.

I have no photos of this, of course. It was not until later—much later— that the photos started. If you have expected a visual progression of it from the very first, then you will be sadly disappointed—perhaps even to the point of bitterness, in which case . . . tough!

Aha! I said to myself, and what is *this?* What is this bump?

(WOMAN *rises, moves Center; appropriate action for the following*)

My wife had come into the bathroom, her eyes dreamy with post-coital mist, her negligee agape.

(To WOMAN*)*

Sweetie?

WOMAN. Mmmmm?

HIMSELF. Will you feel this thing on my back?

WOMAN. What thing?

HIMSELF. Come see; right . . . there, between my shoulder blades.

WOMAN *(Peers)*. It's a bump. It's a little bump. Will you be long?

HIMSELF. What does it look like?

WOMAN *(Peers again)*. It looks like a bump.

HIMSELF. Is it . . . red, or anything?

WOMAN. No, quite a normal little bump. Will you be long?

HIMSELF. No, I'm done.

(Out)

And that was that . . . for a little while. I felt it the next day—my bump—following another post-coital shower—it being Sunday—and while it was still there, since there was no pain, apparently no inflamation, I let it go. Well, look: one never lets things "go," entirely. I mean, one is always conscious of something like that, but one becomes *used* to it, if you know what I mean. I had determined that if there were pain, or growth, or redness, or a sudden, instinctive cancer-panic I would hotfoot it down to the doctor—otherwise, not. Let nature take its course—create, cure.

WOMAN. How's your bump?

HIMSELF. . . . my wife said to me another time, maybe a week after I'd first made her conscious of it.

WOMAN. How's your bump? Is it still there?

HIMSELF *(To the* WOMAN*)*. I haven't paid any attention to it. Why don't you have a look?

(Out)

This was a weekday, eight in the A.M. She looked, looked a bit longer than casual.

WOMAN. Hm!

HIMSELF *(To the* WOMAN*)*. What! What!?

WOMAN. HM!!

HIMSELF *(To the* WOMAN*)*. For Christ's sake, woman! What *is* it!?

WOMAN *(Calm; curious)*. I don't exactly know. Why don't you pop down to the doctor?

HIMSELF *(Out)*. I leaned against the sink to support myself. I looked in the mirror and I was gray.

(To the WOMAN; *doomed tone)*

What is it, sweetie!?

(Out)

She chuckled, and her tone was almost amused.

WOMAN *(Chuckle)*. Well, if I didn't know better, I'd say you were growing a little . . . fern, or something.

HIMSELF *(To the* WOMAN*)*. A fern!

WOMAN. Well, that's certainly what it looks like. Do you want a mirror?

HIMSELF *(Out)*. And she brought over the mirror she uses for the back of her hair, and she positioned it so as I could see the area of my back where whatever was there was . . . well, *there*. I couldn't make any-thing *out* . . . clearly. I can't see anything, I said.

WOMAN. Well, it's not very large, you know, about the size of my thumbnail.

HIMSELF *(To the* WOMAN; *mildly hysterical)*. It's a *plant!?*

WOMAN *(Calm)*. A fern. Or . . . fernlike. Is that better? I'd trot on down to the doctor if I were you, see if you're becoming a vegetable.

HIMSELF *(Out)*. Count on her for calm, for making light, for the even keel,

451

the sense of proportion: good girl! I *called* my doctor, *our* doctor, the family . . . what? physician? I told him I had something funny growing on my back and, in effect, what did he intend to do about it. What he intended to do about it he said, was send me to a specialist, a man dealt with plants and things growing out of people's backs—according to their wives. Didn't *he* want to see me? No, whatever for? Of course: whatever for?

(Shrugs)

He made the appointment for me, for a week or so later, and I went. I took the day off, which wasn't any problem since I was a full partner now, right *up* there—I was a big boy—or plant, or whatever.

(In this next section—several visits to the specialist—separation is determined by HIMSELF *standing and bending over.*

The MAN *rises, becomes the* SPECIALIST; *the* WOMAN *rises, becomes the* NURSE, *unobtrusively passing the prop table as* THEY *come Up. Out)*

The specialist was a dignified gentleman of innumerable years who had trained in Paris and Peking—and I had no reason to doubt him—and had treated among others, he said, Noël Coward, Chou En-lai, one of the Marx Brothers—I forget which, a minor one—the Queen of the Netherlands and, I assumed, Thomas Burpee and the Jolly Green Giant.

MAN *(Jolly)*. So, you have a growth you want me to look at, eh?

HIMSELF *(To the* MAN). Yes, apparently I have.

MAN. Well, let's have a look, shall we?

(Note: Does HIMSELF *merely bend over a little as the* DOCTOR *examines him each time, or does* HE *bend over the prop table, say? To be decided)*

Mmmmmmmmmm . . . goodness!

HIMSELF *(Apprehension)*. Yes?

MAN *(To the* WOMAN). Come here and look.

HIMSELF. What is it!?

WOMAN *(Peering)*. My goodness!

HIMSELF. What *is* it!!?

MAN. Well, I don't rightly know quite yet.

HIMSELF. Take it off!

MAN. What's your hurry? I don't even know what it *is*.

HIMSELF. Is it . . . is it a plant?

452

WOMAN *(Laughs).* A what!?

MAN. A what!? A plant!?

HIMSELF. A fern; my wife says it's a fern.

MAN *(Trying to be serious).* Well, I don't think it's a fern, if that's what you're afraid of. People don't . . . grow ferns.

(Second thought)

Well, we *do*, actually, but not from our backs—in *pots*, usually . . .

HIMSELF. I don't understand you people.

(Out)

Nor did I think I wanted to. The relief of knowing a plant was not protruding from me was less than I would have hoped.

MAN *(So reassuring).* All that is growing from you . . . is *you.* Now, I will see you in a week.

HIMSELF *(Out).* And once a week I returned. On my second visit . . .

MAN. Very interesting. Really very interesting.

(To the WOMAN*)*

Come see.

WOMAN *(Peering).* Oh, indeed it is.

HIMSELF *(To the* MAN*).* What!? What is!?

MAN. It seems to be growing just a bit.

HIMSELF. Take it off!!

MAN *(Reassuring).* No, no, we'll let it go a little. Come see me in a week.

HIMSELF *(Out).* He affixed a bandage—a loose one, so as not to disturb the little fellow, as he put it—which made it difficult for my wife to have a look at it, and reduced me to sponge baths and bent-over hair washings. At the end of the fifth week—during which time my attention at the office was less than it might have been—I was determined both to have a look at whatever it was and have it lopped—done away with, excised . . . removed.

(To the MAN*)*

I want it removed!

MAN. What? You want what removed?

HIMSELF *(Gesturing futilely).* This . . . whatever it is. I want it *off!*

MAN *(Sighs).* I think we'd better have a little talk.

HIMSELF *(Out).* This was it! It *was* cancer, one of those swiftly growing ones, lymph nodes already involved, dead in three weeks. Why me!? Why me!? And we sat down, the three of us, all of us on the examination table, sitting on the edge of it. A crossing of legs.

(To the MAN*)*

How long have I got?

MAN. Before what?

HIMSELF *(Little boy lost)*. Before I die?

MAN *(As the* WOMAN *giggles)*. Who knows? Twenty-five years if your heart's good; ten seconds if you get in front of the wrong taxi.

HIMSELF. You mean it's not a cancer!

MAN. Goodness, no! It's not a cancer at all.

HIMSELF *(To the* MAN*)*. Well . . . if it's not a cancer . . . what *is* it?

MAN. I have been in practice a very long time.

HIMSELF *(To the* MAN*)*. I know.

MAN. I studied in Paris and Peking.

HIMSELF. I know; I know.

MAN. Noël Coward was a patient of mine.

HIMSELF. I know; you told me.

MAN. And in all my years . . .

HIMSELF *(Out; an aside)*. He was a man took forever.

(To them BOTH*)*

WHAT IS IT!!??

(Out)

I mean . . . Jesus!

MAN. My dear fellow, what is happening is that . . . well, is that you are growing a third arm.

HIMSELF *(A beat)*. I beg your pardon.

MAN. A third arm; you are growing a third arm.

HIMSELF *(Rage; hysteria)*. A THIRD ARM!!!???

(Pause. Out; great calm)

This comes as no surprise to *you*, of course; you've been way ahead all along; you knew about it; I did not. Place yourself in *my* position.

(To a lady in balcony)

For example, Madam, say one afternoon you awoke from a nap, went to your dressing table to . . . to powder your breasts, say, and, lo, there was something between them—a mound, a tiny lump of something. You would panic, would you not? The dread cancer? And what if it grew and grew and your doctor would not remove it—seemed spellbound by the thing? And what if one day it all fell into place, so to speak, developed its own nipple and nimbus—aureole, rather—and it was explained to you—the obvious and inconceivable—that you were growing a third breast, nicely rising between Gertrude and Gloria, or whatever your husband called them; that it seemed a perfectly normal, healthy breast, and that with any luck it would probably stop growing when it attained the size of the others. How would you feel about that . . . eh?

(To a man in the audience)

Or you, sir. What if one day, fumbling into your fly at the urinal, whipping it out to take a pee, you noticed a kind of . . . well, a kind of little lump, or something, right next to it? Oh, shit! A social disease. Some new strain of something brought over from the Orient, resistant to all known medicine! What the fuck am I going to tell the wife!? And it grows, and it grows, *and* the specialist seems fascinated by it, and finally he lets you in on the joyous news you've grown another dick—no bigger than the other one, alas, but there it is.

I ask you . . .

(Out)

I ask you all—wouldn't you be just a . . . tiny bit surprised? Here you have passed your lives in relative content and dignity, with no more falling off of honor or dream or whatever than usual; you have settled into an acceptable pattern—individuality within conformity—and . . . all . . . of . . . a . . . sudden . . . you've become a *freak!* Place yourself in my position: not now . . . *then!*

(To MAN*)*

A THIRD ARM!!!!????

MAN *(Matter-of-fact)*. Yes, a third arm.

HIMSELF *(Faintly hysterical)*. Whose *is* it?

MAN. Why . . . yours, of course.

HIMSELF. This sort of thing doesn't happen!

MAN. Just because it is emerging . . . a little late . . .

HIMSELF. A little *late!!*

WOMAN. Better late than never.

HIMSELF. I . . .

(To WOMAN*)*

You render me speechless.

(Out)

So, there I was—bearing arms, armed for anything, all those puns I had to put up with later . . . when it all came out, so to speak. But now, here I was, newly armed and up in arms about it.

455

(Gestures for laughter; gets some canned)

What to do.

Well, indeed, what to do? I had an obligation to it, I was told, and to society. What did they think I was going to do . . . go on tour with it!? God!!

My wife had to be told, of course, and right away.

(WOMAN *rises, becomes* WIFE.

To WOMAN)

I think we'd better have a little talk.

WOMAN *(Cheerful)*. O.K.

HIMSELF. A . . . a serious talk.

WOMAN. O.K.

HIMSELF. You'd better sit down.

WOMAN. What is it . . . you've been cheating on me?

HIMSELF. No.

WOMAN. *I've* been cheating on *you?*

HIMSELF. No, of course not.

WOMAN *(Relieved)*. What then?

HIMSELF *(Out)*. And so I told her, and she took it rather well—a little disbelief, a little revulsion, a little . . . panic, but . . . all in all, rather well.

(To WOMAN)

I think you'd better have a look at it.

WOMAN *(Quiet disbelief)*. Look at it? You want me to *look* at it?

HIMSELF *(Out)*. And so she had her first real look at the little fellow.

(WOMAN *examines* HIMSELF's *bent back)*

WOMAN *(Finally)*. It's kind of cute. Once you get over wanting to throw up it's kind of cute.

HIMSELF. Help me!

WOMAN. I'll try.

HIMSELF. What am I going to do?

WOMAN. Are you waving at me?

HIMSELF. I beg your pardon?

WOMAN. It's waving, I think. Are you waving it at me?

(Giggle)

HIMSELF *(Out)*. And it was here that I had my first sense of the complexity of it all. No, I was *not* waving, but *it was*. It was a baby arm at the moment, and moved spasmodically, as from the impulses of a baby

456

brain. It would come under my control eventually, do my bidding, but never entirely; it retained—right to the very end—a . . . mind of its own.

WOMAN. I'm going to touch it; I'm going to tickle its little palm. *(Does so)*

HIMSELF *(To the* WOMAN*)*. That tickles! *(Out)*

And I felt its tiny fingers close on my wife's great tickling finger, and I was aware of sensation.

WOMAN. That *is* cute. Let go; thank you.

HIMSELF *(Out)*. It was a moment of . . . revelation, I suppose is the only word—the wonder of it, of *being*.

WOMAN. What are we going to tell the children?

HIMSELF. Hm? I beg your pardon?

WOMAN. What are we going to tell the children? You can't just grow a third arm without telling the children *some*thing . . . and a lot of other people, too, I should imagine. By the way, which arm is it?

HIMSELF. What do you mean?

WOMAN. Well, is it a right arm or a left arm?

HIMSELF. It's a *middle* arm.

WOMAN. Don't be ridiculous.

HIMSELF. Well . . . which arm does it *look* like?

WOMAN *(Peering)*. That's why I asked. Every time I look at it, it seems to be different. Right now it looks like a *left* arm, but when I was tickling it, before, I could swear it was a *right* arm.

HIMSELF *(Out)*. One of the wonders; truly, one of the wonders. It had, by I knew not what gymnastics, what leverage, the ability to be whichever arm, right or left, it needed or wanted to be. More of that later.

I must describe to you now my state of mind, my view from this particular bridge. I was possessed of a third arm—a growing armlet which, I was told, would reach normal, or arm size, and be content with that. And this was, at the moment, a secret shared only by the doctor, his nurse, my wife . . . and myself, of course. The children had not been told. That it would not—*could* not—remain a secret for long was evident. I had—well, you've seen it—a splendid wife . . . intelligent, level-headed, a no-nonsense, good and good-humored wife; that was a help, but we were not dealing here with your ordinary run-of-the-marriage situation. There was also the vague but nagging sensation that it

457

was not *me* we were concerned with here . . . but it. Does that distinction make any sense to you? Oh! and we must add a sudden complication: my high-paying, permanently secure executive position vanished in a recession retrenchment. And there I was out on the street. And me with a third arm to feed.

WOMAN *(As WIFE; having risen)*. What *are* you going to do—*we*?

HIMSELF. You're going to help me hold it all together until I figure it out.

WOMAN. O.K.

(Afterthought)

But I still think we ought to tell the kids.

HIMSELF *(Out)*. A cousin of mine—a deadbeat, but inventive—put me in touch with a man; a man who, he said, could work miracles.

(The MAN moves forward, as HIMSELF finishes.

To WOMAN, not quite convinced)

This man can work miracles.

WOMAN *(To MAN)*. And I can keep the kids quiet during nap-time. Howdy.

MAN *(Expansive; oily)*. You must be the little lady. Howdy-do to *you*.

WOMAN. Work miracles, hunh?

MAN. Nah, it just seems like it.

HIMSELF *(To the WOMAN)*. I've told him . . . everything.

MAN. He even let me have a look at the little fella.

WOMAN. Cute, isn't it?

HIMSELF *(To them BOTH)*. It scratched my back this morning.

(Out)

It did; I was about to shave, felt an itch, was about to put the razor down, when all at once I noticed I—it!—was scratching away.

WOMAN. Did you say thank you?

HIMSELF *(To WOMAN; mildly impatient)*. You don't say thank you to your *arm!*

WOMAN *(Shrugs)*. I don't *know*, way things are *these* days.

MAN. I've drawn up what I think are some pretty good ideas on how we handle this thing. When this comes out it's going to be one big story, one knock-'em-on-their-ass sensation.

HIMSELF *(Uncertain)*. Yes, I suppose *so;* for a little while.

MAN *(Abrupt laugh)*. For a little *while!?* Are you *kidding!?* Man, you're going to be the hottest thing going!

HIMSELF. I am?

(To the WOMAN)

Act Two

I am?

(Out.

SHE *shrugs)*

MAN. Fucking-A right! There hasn't been a story like this since the cruci-fixion.

HIMSELF. I'm afraid I don't see the connection between the Lord's agony and my having . . .

MAN. I'm talking news value.

HIMSELF. Oh.

(Beat. Out)

Oh?

MAN. Right! Mister, I can make you the most famous man in America.

HIMSELF *(Pause; some wonder)*. You can?

MAN. Shit! I can make you the most famous man in the *world!*

HIMSELF. You're kidding!

MAN. I kid you *not!* And, on top of it, if we play our cards right . . . I can make us . . . *rich!*

(MAN and WOMAN turn, go to their seats)

HIMSELF *(Out)*. I want you to understand that the reach of my ambition —*before* all this started—had been grand, perhaps, but not excessive: I wanted a lovely wife, some decent kids, a fine home, a rewarding and well-paying career, the respect of my community and a painless, sleeping death when I was old enough to want it.

(Shrugs)

All within reason, the American Dream—the Anglo-Saxon, *Protestant* American Dream, at any rate. *And* I was well on my *way* to it, gathering it all together nicely. And then, of course, the shit hit the fan, with me offering neither one, neither shit nor fan, unless you go with the minor-ity says I *willed* my martyrdom—my monsterdom—drew it out of my-self . . . from the pericardial unconscious, I dare say. Believe me! I wanted nothing less than big frog in reasonably big pond, and nothing *more.* I did *not* want what *happened!*

(Almost choking with sudden rage and tears)

And you can be *certain* I *never*—in my wildest dreams, *nightmares!*—I *never* wanted to be standing *here,* where I am today!

(Stops, shoulders shaking)

WOMAN *(As herself)*. Are you all right?

HIMSELF. A minute!

459

MAN *(To the* WOMAN*).* Is he all right? Does he want another gin, do you think?

HIMSELF *(Loud; to them).* I'LL BE ALL RIGHT!

(Gathers himself; out)

But you see, in spite of all I wanted—a splendid life, but with limits—in spite of the really *little* I wanted in return for going through it all . . . it just wasn't to *be* that *way*. I grew a third arm, and my career was destroyed from under me.

What . . . to do!?

My very own Colonel Parker—or so I dubbed him—arranged it all, and I must give him credit . . . he was a *pro*.

MAN *(Seated; side of mouth).* Thanks.

HIMSELF *(To the* MAN*).* You're welcome.

(Out)

My wife and I agreed that we had to do *something*—the doctor was planning a book *plus* I owed it to medical science *plus* the kids now knew and it's against the law to cut out the tongues of the young *plus* a lot of ugly bills were coming due, and I mean a *lot* and I mean *ugly* mortgage, insurance, school, medical bills, car, food, clothes and on and on and on! Plus I still had three arms.

There was nothing for it, the wisdom went, but to hit and hit hard.

(Slams fist into hand as, simultaneously, the MAN *does the same)*

Now, when I say I must give the Colonel credit, I kid you not—as he would say.

(SLIDE: *press conference*)

The press conference he called to unveil my arm was equal to that announcing the second coming or—a less likely event—the democratization of the USSR.

(SLIDE *out*)

When it occurred, it was a lollapalooza! I vetoed the Colonel's suggestion that it—the arm—be first seen waving a tiny American flag; that—at the *time*—struck me as, well . . . crass. HA!

Well, I needn't remind you how it went. Unless you were in a loony bin somewhere you *know*.

(Pleasure in recalling)

Has there *ever* been anything like it? My goodness, I think back to it, the awe—the jaw-dropping, pencil-dropping, *camera*-dropping awe—as I removed my shirt and tie, smiled—shyly, diffidently: truly shy, truly diffident—spread my two visible arms in a kind of combo benediction-greeting, and slowly turned to reveal the eighth wonder of the world. The intake of a thousand breaths; the silence; the *last* silence, and then the tumult! Thank God we had a double line of guards!!

It was unbelievable! The crowds outside my apartment.

(SLIDE: *crowds)*

The riots if I dared go to a restaurant or a movie.

(SLIDE: *riot)*

The ticker-tape parades.

(SLIDE: *ticker-tape parade)*

The medical conventions.

(SLIDE: *photo of famous turn-of-the-century painting of medical demonstration)*

The presentation of royalty.

(SLIDE: *someone being received by Queen Elizabeth II)*

The summons from the President.

(SLIDE: *someone entering the White House)*

The magazine covers.

(SLIDE: HIMSELF'*s face on cover of* Time, Newsweek, People—*1 slide)*

With all of them, I insisted they photograph only my smiling face—the Colonel insisted. There was, as you may have imagined, more than decorum in the Colonel's caution.

MAN *(As* COLONEL). I'll make us rich!!

HIMSELF. What *does* a man do?—what is a man to do who had grown a third arm of considerable agility and attractiveness—given the parameters—who, at the same time, has been thrown into unjustified career ruin and financial instability, and who has become—with barely a tap on his shoulder—the most famous man in the world? The answer is so simple—inevitable—as to state itself: make the most of it; get it while you can, and get it big. Does that sound crass to you? A bit . . . grasping? Well, think about it: we do or we do not do, and if there is either excess or regret, which do we mourn the more—that which we *have* done, or that which we have *not?* Eh?

(SLIDE *out)*

Things were not . . . well . . . *ideal,* however. The kids had been taken out of school and were being tutored privately, at great expense. First it was their schoolmates taunting them—Daddy's a freak; your

461

Daddy's a freak—and then, without much wait, the kidnapping threats began.

WOMAN *(As* WIFE*)*. Jesus Christ!

HIMSELF. . . . which led to the guards—the *extra* guards, the ones on top of mine, the four I had at all hours. And if you think the city was paying for my protection, I laugh at you—har, har, har! It was coming out of *my* pocket . . . well, the Colonel's pocket as part of the tab I was running up. Within six weeks of the great unveiling, I was into the Colonel for $78,400!

WOMAN. Jesus!

HIMSELF. The guards, the lawyers, the two-and-a-half-million-dollar insurance policy on "the arm"—in case of loss!

WOMAN. Christ!

HIMSELF. There was a lot of money to be made. And the Colonel told me *our* split would be fifty-fifty.

WOMAN. Jesus!

HIMSELF *(To the* WOMAN*)*. It was fair!

(Out)

It *was* fair: the Colonel was making a fortune for us, and fifty percent of a lot is more than ninety percent of nothing!

WOMAN *(Still as* WIFE*)*. Christ!

HIMSELF *(To* WOMAN*)*. Hussy! Bitch! Abandoner!

(Out)

Ignore her! She left me . . . finally!

WOMAN *(Shrill)*. Tell them how you'd go to sleep and *it* wouldn't. Tell them how it'd wait until I'd gone to sleep—*you'd* gone to sleep—and it would play with me, stroke me, finger me to orgasm.

HIMSELF. Silence, woman!!

WOMAN. And how I would wrestle with it, and it would slap me!

HIMSELF *(Weary)*. No more.

WOMAN. Tell them how you changed; tell them about your ego; tell them about your temper; tell them about the groupies; tell them about giving me the clap!

HIMSELF. Silence!

WOMAN. . . . and the kids, and how you *became*. No one would blame me!

HIMSELF. Please; no more.

WOMAN. No one could take it.

HIMSELF *(Rage)*. All right! You've done it! I've forgotten you! Leave me alone!

WOMAN *(A pleased snarl)*. *You* haven't forgotten me;
(Harsh laugh)
you'd give your right arm to have me back. I'm going to write that book; really, I *am*.

HIMSELF *(Spitting it out)*. *Write* it! Spill my guts out! You're a little late, sweetheart: who the fuck cares!?
(Out)
Would *you* buy her book? Poor wifelet, stands arm in arm in arm with her man some part of the way, then *takes* off, *takes* the kids, *takes* the alimony . . .

WOMAN *(Cold)*. You're behind, by the way.
(Turns away)

HIMSELF *(Out)*. Ignore her: She couldn't take the blinding light.
(Quieter)
I regret giving her the kids without a fight; I regret everything.
(More assured—laughter in the dark)
And I regret nothing. Je ne regrette rien! as the little lady used to say, to sing. Je ne regrette rien! I mean . . . I had a lot of fun! While it lasted . . . I had a ball! Are any of you celebrated? Really . . . famous? Some of you probably are—one or two—and you know what it's like— what happens *within* the awareness of *self* that comes as revelation, the knowledge that one *is* larger than life, at least larger than others; the fact that one can change whole areas of public perception, help alter the course of history. This is not small potatoes. The money, the sex, the adulation, the perks, all those are gravy on the pot roast; the meat is the sense of self. Let us pray.
(After the pause following "let us pray.")
Do you find me . . . well, what *is* the word? . . . unsympathetic? Not fit for pity? Yours, or anyone's?
(Laughs)
I met someone once said no one ever earned the right—not ever. What about Job, I said. Not even Job, he said: see God. Well, *I* feel bad about *me* now and again; sometimes I just . . . wallow in self-pity, and I think I've earned the right, and anybody doesn't go along, I say fuck 'em!
(Small smile)

Or, is that "unsympathetic" too? Probably.
(Shrugs)
Fuck it. Anyhow, as I said, things were not . . . ideal.
(Pause)
I had a talk with the Colonel.
(MAN *has risen; moves into position.*
To MAN)
What am I going to *do?*

MAN. I don't get you.

HIMSELF. I owe you a fortune; I'm going under fast; I . . .

MAN *(Laughs)*. Oh, that! Well, we're going to sell you, boy!

HIMSELF *(Out)*. And he whipped out a scenario.

MAN. We've worked up some preliminary figures, in case you're interested, and, uh . . .
(HE *fishes out a piece of paper which* HE *shows)*
. . . this looks like what you'll be taking in each week—we'll be taken in.

HIMSELF *(Looks; gasps)*. Jesus Christ!

MAN *(Returning to his seat)*. On we go, boy; gold at the end of the rainbow and silver along the way!

HIMSELF *(Out)*. I won't even tell you the figures he showed me; I am unhappy with envy in myself and I will not be party to it in others. Enough to say it was ransom sufficient to twist the arm of *any* man. And off we went! Well, you watched it. No one has ever ridden higher or loved it more! And the Colonel orchestrated it so beautifully!

MAN *(From his seat)*. Thank you, thank you!

HIMSELF. And I was getting laid a lot. I bring this up—childish or adolescent as it may seem—because it is a matter not everyone comes face to face, or crotch to crotch with. Most people—most of *us*—marry, or carry on long-term relationships of one sort or another, and we cheat now and again, though not as often as either chance or our memory has it; we have reasonably good sex lives: we get by. But with celebrity—with *great* celebrity—the thighs of the world swing open—and I am speaking heterosexually, you understand; our gay brethren have their own images—the thighs of the world swing open, the universal clitoris and the great divide await, *plus* Nabokov's brown rose, *plus* head to turn the head of a martyring saint. And all one has to do is . . . show up. You don't even have to undo your own belt. It all becomes part of a way of life, and has nothing—or little—to do with morality, or fidelity, or . . . anything.

So, I became what he promised, the most famous man in the world. It was a high ride and a good one.

Though, I guess, you can't win them all.

The Colonel was getting rich. Why wasn't I? Answer in thirty words or less.

And then the day came, the day I shall remember above all others to the day of my dying, above even the revelation of the identity of the bump growing from my back, above even my first orgasm.

Do you remember that famous story of the identical midgets in the circus,

(SLIDE: *midgets*)

both stars, both in love with the same midget*esse?* How she was wooed by them both, and married one, and the other brooded and bided his time? Do you remember it? These two midgets wore tails and top hats in their act and carried canes—regular little Fred Astaires. Well, all at once the married of the two became morose and developed a far-away expression in his eyes; his wifelet asked him over and over what was wrong.

(Tiny voice)

"What's wrong? What's wrong?" And finally he told her.

(Tiny voice again)

"I'm growing," he said. Midgets did this sometimes, in middle age—they just started growing: sometimes they grew a foot—not a *third* one, but . . . up. And what it meant was the end of midgethood, the end of employment, the end of marriage, of course, and the end of celebrity. To make it short, the despondent midget killed himself, and his widow married the other one. And at the end of the story it's revealed that the poor little fellow wasn't growing at all, that the other one, the rejected one, was sneaking into the wardrobe every night and sanding just the tiniest bit off the bottom of his rival's cane, just the tiniest bit more each night, enough to persuade the horrified little fellow that he was growing.

(Cheerful)

You don't remember that story? My goodness, *I* do!

(SLIDE *out*)

I mention the midgets only to talk about my shirts. Is that unclear?

Unclear enough? Let me explain. One day, I noticed in a new batch of custom-made shirts a . . . disparity of sleeve, by which I mean that my two normal, or regular, sleeves had been made too small, too short, for there was a fullness, a largeness in the third one. I mentioned it to the Colonel: I mean, a hundred and thirty-seven fifty per shirt, and they couldn't even make the sleeves of an equal length anymore!

This . . . disparity of sleeve produced in me a normal—enough—attack of celebrity paranoia. Of course, the shirt people were enraged, insisted they made shirts by hand, with great care, that all my sleeves were of equal length, and if I persisted in my calumny I would hear from their solicitor. "You have made my right and left sleeves too short," I insisted. "How else can we account for the third sleeve being too long? If you insist that all three sleeves are of equal length, then one of two things is possible, neither of which is likely: either my right and left arms have suddenly begun to grow—ha, ha, ha!—either that or my central or third arm has suddenly begun to . . .

(Pause)

And my world . . . fell apart.

Could it be happening? *Was* my arm, my *new* arm, the cause of . . . everything I now valued . . . going away? Was it returning whence, et cetera? Jesus Christ! I measured it carefully—the arm—locked, double bolted in the bathroom—

(Out)

It was almost a full inch shorter than it had been. Even now I can barely bring myself to think about it, much less talk about it. My arm, my livelihood, my celebrity had diminished—a trifle, to be sure, barely an inch, but, still, diminished. The panic I fell into was . . . well, encompassing. I had to tell the Colonel; there was no choice.

MAN *(As* COLONEL; *up and in position).* Jesus Christ!

HIMSELF *(To the* MAN). It's two weeks now, and it seems to be going at about an inch a week.

MAN. Jesus Christ!

HIMSELF *(To the* MAN). I don't know what to do.

MAN. Jesus Christ!

HIMSELF. There's that medical convention in São Paulo.

MAN. Jesus Christ!

HIMSELF. And the three-hand piano recital in Tokyo? I can't even reach the black *keys* anymore with my third arm! I've tried!

MAN. Jesus Christ!

HIMSELF. What am I going to *do!?*

MAN. Jesus Christ!

HIMSELF *(Out).* Jesus Christ, indeed! What was decided, finally, was *not* to disguise the fact of what was happening, but to make capital of it. The Colonel called an enormous press conference—almost as well attended as the great First—and revealed that the Lord giveth and the Lord taketh away; announced, as well, what was to be, in effect, a farewell tour of the arm. Those who had not seen it: hurryhurryhurry; those who would like to watch it as it lessens, come right on up; last chance! The question was raised as to whether I thought it might re-grow—disappear, and then pop up again, somewhere else: on the top of my head, I suppose. I expressed enthusiasm for the idea, but deep inside I knew better; I knew the jig was up.

The farewell tour,

(SLIDE: *ticker-tape parade)*

at the beginning, fueled by both my world celebrity *and* the new sensation, began splendidly—the crowds, the riots, the usual, but as the attention-getter—the moneymaker, if you will—diminished, so did the audience for it: when it was back to half, so were the crowds; a quarter, a quarter; and when the poor thing was down to a nubbin, waving its little fernlike fingers in a pathetic farewell, I remember once that no more than twenty people showed up, sullen and embarrassed.

And then . . . and then it was gone. My ex-wife sent me a card of condolence.

The Arabs folded their tents and crept off into the night. Shall I describe the falling away of my retinue? There's no need to; you can imagine it. And the Colonel left as well, with not even a farewell, just . . . left. A very wealthy man, he . . . left. Swine.

MAN. Now, now.

HIMSELF. And I! How was *I* left? Well, a meeting with my accountants shed some black light on that: with one thing and another, fees and endorsements out the window, the failed farewell tour, tax disallowances, plus I had been coasting along on anticipated income for quite a while now, when the whole thing was totaled up, I was in debt to the tune of \$2,134,625.22, *and,* the accountants wondered, wouldn't I like to pay *them* right away.

Thank God for the insurance policy on my arm—or loss thereof—I mused out loud. Oh, that, they mused right back, that was taken out in the Colonel's name; that doesn't belong to you; we imagine he's cashed that in already.

(To the MAN *as* COLONEL*)*
Swine!

MAN *(As* COLONEL*; so mild)*. Now, now.

HIMSELF *(Out)*. So, I had been had, had I not. But I was to blame, as well, I suppose: the hog I had been living high off of was of my own devising, was . . . myself. Nor had I carried too many friends along with me to the heights of my celebrity—too rarefied a place for many, and I was startled, when it all came crashing down, by how many people wished me ill, how many had a smug smile at my extremis. I declared bankruptcy, as you doubtless read but may have forgotten; I suffered what is termed a nervous breakdown—Jesus!, who could blame me!?—and for a year and a half I sat, staring off into the middle distance. Remember the middle distance? And I drank a lot, and I cried a lot.
I still drink—oh!? Does he!?—and I still cry. And so, here I am—here we are. And how do you like your blue-eyed boy now, Mr. Death?
(Pause.

Harsh tone; claps hands once)
So! Here we are! How did you like the rendition, boys and girls? Did you enjoy your little trip to voyeur's heaven? That oh-so-sad-sad story? Well, good for you.
(Pause; quiet, growing loathing)
I think I've finished; I've laid the sorry tale out for you; you've paid your money and you've seen what's left of the freak! Go home! GO HOME!!

*(*MAN *and* WOMAN *become apprehensive)*

MAN *(To* WOMAN*)*. Are we done?

HIMSELF. Go home, you mothers!! Haven't I humiliated myself enough for you!?

WOMAN *(Rising; out)*. I think we're done. I would like to thank our . . .

HIMSELF *(Ignoring her)*. You owe me something, you people! You loved me in the good times, and you're fucking well going to love me now!!

WOMAN *(Moving Center)*. I really *do* think we're done.

HIMSELF *(Waving her off)*. Get away from me!
(Out; pleading alternating with hatred)
I'm no different from you; I'm just like everyone you know; you love

Act Two

them: you love *me*. Stop treating me like a freak! I am *not* a freak! I am *you!* I have always *been* you! I am YOU!!! Stop looking at me!! Like that!!

WOMAN *(Off)*. Will you have them lower [close] the curtain?

HIMSELF. No!! No one leaves!! I am *not* a freak! I'm just like you. *(Gets an idea; begins to remove his shirt)* Look; believe me; I am *you;* I have always been *you;* there's no difference between us. *(Shirt off. . . . has he ripped it off? Perhaps)* One head, two ears, two eyes, one nose, one mouth—though it doesn't always seem that way; one chest, two nipples —vestigal remains of the old self-generating days, most probably. I am just like you! You see!? Stop treating me like a freak! I am not a freak! *(He begins to weep)*

WOMAN *(Comes over to him, to comfort)* Yes, yes; of course you are; of course you're not.

HIMSELF *(To the audience)*. Stop looking at me like that!

WOMAN *(As he shudders, weeps)*. Shhhhhhhh! Shhhhhhhh! It'll all be alright. *(She strokes his shoulders, his back)* Shhhhhhh! Shhhhhhhh! *(She notices something on his back)* Oh! Oh, how extraordinary!

HIMSELF. I'm no different from. . . . *(becomes aware of her)* What!? What is it!?

WOMAN *(Moving behind him, looking at his back)*. Well, I. . . . if I didn't know better—although I *do* know better, or should—if I didn't know better I'd say you. . . . had something growing there—on your back. *(To the MAN)* Come; come see.

MAN *(Moving in)*. What? What is it?

HIMSELF *(Disbelief and wonder suffusing his face)*. Something. . . . ? Growing. . . . ? There. . . . ?

WOMAN *(Pointing)*. See?

MAN *(Peering)*. My goodness! Why, *yes!*

HIMSELF *(Eyes more-or-less heavenward)*. It's coming back, you fuckers! *(Fist upward and clenched)* You'll get yours, you mothers! *(To the two behind him; joy and pleading)* It's coming back? You can see it?

MAN. Yes! Look there!

WOMAN. Isn't that extraordinary!

HIMSELF *(Eyes closed tight)*. Just wait, world!

469

WOMAN. Why, its. . . . I think its waving at me, or. . . . yes, look
there; its. . . . its wiggling its little toes!
HIMSELF *(A long beat).* Toes!? *(A longer beat)* TOES!?
(A beat. Blackout)

END